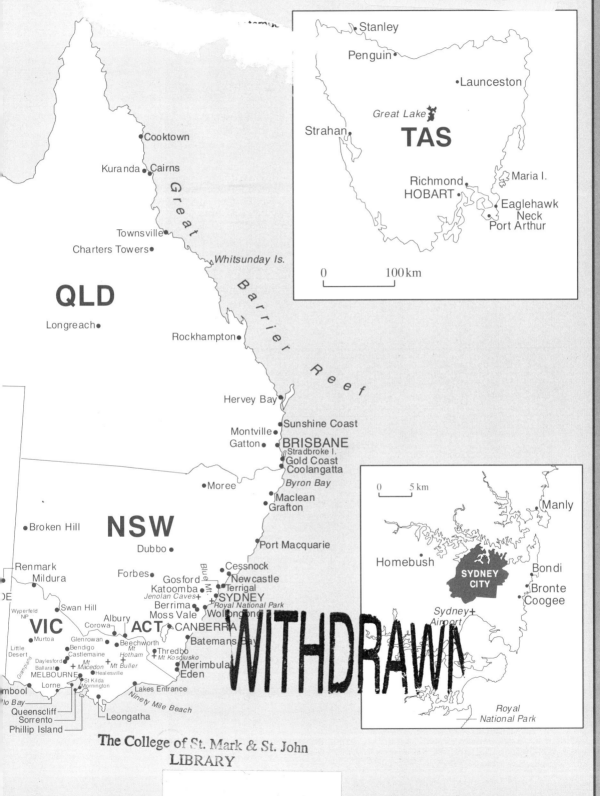

Stanley

Penguin

•Launceston

Great Lake

TAS

Strahan

Richmond
HOBART

Maria I.

Eaglehawk
Neck
Port Arthur

0   100km

Cooktown

Kuranda •Cairns

Townsville

Charters Towers

QLD

Great

Longreach•

Rockhampton•

Whitsunday Is.

Barrier

Reef

Hervey Bay

Sunshine Coast

Montville
Gatton **BRISBANE**
Stradbroke I.
Gold Coast
Coolangatta
Byron Bay

•Moree

Maclean
Grafton

Port Macquarie

•Broken Hill

NSW

Dubbo •

Cessnock

Renmark
Mildura

Forbes•

Gosford
Katoomba
Jenolan Caves
Berrima
Moss Vale

Newcastle
Terrigal
SYDNEY
Royal National Park
Wollongong•

Blue Mts

Swan Hill

Albury
Corowa

ACT•**CANBERRA**

VIC

Murtoa•

Glenrowan

Beechworth

Batemans Bay

Little
Desert

Bendigo
Daylesford Castlemaine
Ballarat

Mt
Hotham
+ *Mt Macedon* +*Mt Buller*

Thredbo
+*Mt Kosciusko*

Merimbula
Eden

MELBOURNE
Lorne

St Kilda
Healesville
Mornington

Lakes Entrance

Ninety Mile Bay

lo Bay

Queenscliff
Sorrento
Phillip Island

Leongatha

Homebush

0   5 km

Manly

**SYDNEY
CITY**

Bondi

Bronte
Coogee

Sydney+
Airport

*Royal
National Park*

WITHDRAWN

The Miegunyah Press
at
Melbourne University Press

The General Series
of the Miegunyah Volumes
was made possible by the
Miegunyah Fund
established by bequests
under the wills of
Sir Russell and Lady Grimwade

'Miegunyah' was the home of
Mab and Russell Grimwade
from 1911 to 1955

Holiday
Business

The image of Trans-Australia Airlines for the following twenty years, the archetypal 1950s air hostess combined good looks with attentiveness and efficiency.

*H*oliday *B*usiness

Tourism in Australia since 1870

JIM DAVIDSON AND PETER SPEARRITT

The Miegunyah Press

MELBOURNE UNIVERSITY PRESS
PO Box 278, Carlton South, Victoria 3053, Australia
info@mup.unimelb.edu.au
www.mup.com.au

First published 2000

Designed and typeset by Lauren Statham, Alice Graphics
Typeset in 12.5 point Perpetua
Printed in Australia by Australian Print Group

National Library of Australia Cataloguing-in-Publication entry

Davidson, Jim, 1942– .

Holiday business: tourism in Australia since 1870.

Bibliography.
Includes index.
ISBN 0 522 84884 2.

1. Tourism—Australia. 2. Tourism—Australia—History. 3. Australia—
Description and travel. I. Spearritt, Peter, 1949– . II. Title.

338.479194

Contents

Illustrations

Illustrations whose sources are not given here have been drawn from the collections of the authors.

Colour plates

ix

Black and white illustrations

Preface

Holiday Business reflects a continuing conversation between the authors about past and present Australia, and the imprint of travel and tourism on the landscape. We define the tourist industry as that which has arisen in response to the convergence of people on recognised routes and resorts; this focus has been our prime purpose. Nevertheless, tourism history is also a variety of social history, so we have been at pains to point out how various developments were enmeshed with other social assumptions and practices, with radical changes in transport and technology, and with shifts in taste.

In the course of our research we have visited every state and territory, but as there are hundreds of tourist destinations in Australia, all with their own particular history, we attempt in this book to draw attention to the broad trends and meanings in tourism, taking examples from a limited number of sites. Of necessity, some significant locations have been left out or barely mentioned; but then the process of excavating all the main elements involved has itself taken considerable time. It is no surprise to us that a national history of tourism, such as this one, exists almost nowhere else in the world.

Detailed studies have been made of some of our most important tourism sites, including Tasmania, the Blue Mountains and the Gold Coast. Others—including all the capital cities—await further research on the role tourism has played in their development. One of our aims, then, has been to produce a map of the subject, to provide a context for such research.

A Large Grant from the Australian Research Council made possible the early research, together with supplementary assistance from Victoria University of Technology and Monash University's Metropolis and Region project. Research assistance has been provided by Anne Burke in Sydney, Jenny Gregory in Perth, Tom Weisselberg in London, Christof Pforr in Darwin, and Peter Robinson, Carol Hinschen and John Young in Melbourne.

Friends and colleagues in every state gave further help, putting up with inquiries large and small—from the name of an abandoned local guest-house to the impact of being bypassed by a freeway. Jan Field and John Arnold of the National Centre for Australian Studies assisted with the book from start to finish. In addition, we would particularly like to thank Brian King, Tim Rowse, Humphrey McQueen, Edmund Swinglehurst, Miles Lewis, Tom Griffiths, Libby Robin, Toly Sawenko, Nigel Lewis, Jeff Jarvis and Ian Manning. Librarians at the Mitchell, La Trobe, Mortlock, Battye, Oxley and Allport libraries have been most helpful, as were those at Thomas Cook's in London and the National Maritime Museum at Greenwich.

Finally, we would like to record our thanks to various people who extended hospitality during the course of our research: the Benedictine Community, New Norcia; staff at Sovereign Hill; Clyde and Norma Spearritt, Brisbane; Mark Barnard, Fitzroy; Anne Edwards and John Mottram, Adelaide; Adrian and Audrey Young, Canberra; Clem and Heather Macintyre, Adelaide; Don and Jean Spearritt, Sydney and Mollymook; Mary and Stephen Foster, Canberra; and Rod and Maria Thomson, Hobart.

Jim Davidson
Peter Spearritt

Introduction: Tourism, Postmodernism and Australia

THE GROWTH OF TOURISM and Australia's development have proceeded simultaneously. The word 'tourist', with a hesitant hyphen between the two syllables, came into use at the very time that the British were establishing themselves in this country, but it is only recently that tourism has come to occupy a central place in the national consciousness.

Partly this reflects a worldwide trend. When people throughout the world took some 595 million trips abroad in 1996, that was an increase of 5.5 per cent on the previous year, and all of 77 per cent more than ten years earlier. The World Tourism Organization, which compiled these figures, estimates that by 2010 the total number of trips made will be 937 million. It may then be the world's biggest industry.[1]

Early tourism and the rise of Cook's

The point is often made that tourism of any kind began relatively recently. Although the Romans turned the Bay of Naples into a resort area, this was to remain unmatched until the nineteenth-century development of the Riviera. Equally telling is the fact that the ancients' Seven Wonders of the World were essentially figurative; the list did not acquire canonical status until the Renaissance.

Even so, much human activity recycles itself under different labels: the current academic preoccupation with theory echoes the debates of medieval schoolmen. So it is with tourism. *The Canterbury Tales* reminds us that there was a strong secular element in medieval pilgrimage, and it has been remarked that, with their attendant fairs, relic-hunting, illicit souveniring, sexual escapades and graffiti-writing, pilgrimages could be host to many of the less endearing attributes of modern tourism. There was holyday business long before there was a hospitality industry.[2]

We commonly speak of a 'tourist mecca', and the very word 'holi-days' smothers in that compression its sacred origins. An interesting transition is afforded by Mark Twain's *The Innocents Abroad* (subtitled *The New Pilgrims' Progress*), his best-selling work in his lifetime. In 1867 Twain joined what was advertised as 'The Grand Holy Land Pleasure Excur-sion', a luxurious liner full of Americans headed for Europe and Palestine. They reached present-day Israel just before the first tours or-ganised by Thomas Cook's, bent on visiting exotic places familiar from the Bible. 'None of us had ever been anywhere before', wrote Twain. 'We all hailed from the interior; travel was a wild novelty to us.'[3]

A new word had become necessary for those tour-ists around 1800 to denote the relatively new phenomenon of proclaimed travel for pleasure, all the more conspicuous because the thrust of it overturned many entrenched assumptions. Roland Barthes has noted of mountain scenery how nowadays 'quite stupidly, the gracelessness of a landscape, its lack of spaciousness or human appeal', together with 'its verticality, so contrary to the bliss of travel . . . accounts for its interest'. But this was not always so. Medieval people regarded the mountains as places of dread; although Luzern in Switzerland was situated among them, a town ordinance forbade the climbing of nearby Pilatus, and it was not broken—and then only by a courageous preacher—until the 1530s. Similarly a seventeenth-century traveller, in the course of journeying around England, happened upon a region 'like a solitary wilderness'. It was the Lake District, where he found 'nothing but hideous hanging Hills, and great Pooles'.[4]

Many of the features of modern tourism were already in place in the eighteenth century, as Ian Ousby has shown. Those elegant gentlemen who now went to the Lake District specially armed with a Claude glass, so that they could focus on a feature and tint it to taste, were metaphorically anticipating the depredations on the landscape by thousands of sightseer successors. Whereas, a century before, maps of England showed a sequence of villages linked by thin roads—a cluster of capillaries—now strip maps appeared, boldly certain of the route and confidently designating landmarks. The first guidebooks appeared, along with the first stately homes to be opened to the public—so long as one wrote ahead to request admittance. For this was still tourism for the aristocracy and the upper middle class: the opening up of country seats reflected new political realities.

The traditional Grand Tour of the Continent still took place, but whereas once it had been restricted to young noblemen being 'finished', now it was emulated by wealthy middle-class pleasure-seekers. As early as 1738 there were comments on the 'epidemical' British 'fondness for gadding beyond the seas', but this was still so novel that the word 'hotel' entered the language from French a generation later. The first 'trippers', so designated as early as 1813, were often so keen to reach coastal resorts that they would walk. Feudal man had been tied to the land; now, with an increasing sense of liberty, mobility was prized. 'The working class are moving about on the surface of their own country', noted a factory inspector in 1865, 'spending the wealth they have acquired in "seeing the world" as the upper class did in 1800, as the middle class did in 1850'.[5]

Instrumental in much of this had been the firm of Thomas Cook & Son. The original Cook was a Baptist zealot who campaigned against drink and tobacco; the first excursion he organised was in 1841, when he arranged for a special train to run from Leicester to Loughborough for a temperance meeting. Immediately he saw the possibilities: 'One cheer more', he urged the crowd, 'for Teetotalism and Railwayism'. Hitherto mainly a printer of tracts, Cook had found his mission: tours would become 'agencies for the advancement of Human Progress', helping to wean the workman away from the bottle. Cook believed that places of interest 'should not be excluded from the gaze of the common people'; to argue otherwise was 'exclusive nonsense'. At a time when Chartism indicated massive social unrest, he pointed to travel as enabling 'the broad distinctions of classes [to be] removed without violence or objectionable means'. Frequently Cook waxed lyrical, particularly once he founded his own newspaper, *Cook's Excursionist*, to coincide with the Great Exhibition of 1851.

> God's earth with all its fulness and beauty, is for the people; and railways and steamboats are the result of the common light of science, and are for the people also . . . The best of men, and the noblest minds, rejoice to see the people follow in their foretrod routes of pleasure.

Such high-mindedness, even when combined with exceptional skills of organisation, would not in itself have guaranteed success. Cook was carried along by the railway; as has been pointed out, the massive capital outlay required as the iron horse pushed further and further afield necessitated greater custom to keep the network running. It is no accident that Cook's first excursion took place the year after the introduction of Penny Postage; common to both was the principle of inverting an expensive and exclusive facility to make it cheap, accessible, and ultimately more profitable. A larger market was becoming available as legislation followed the lead given by the better employers, who had already seen that workers needed relief from the drudgery of factory employment. By the 1870s the Bank Holiday had been introduced, while bank clerks now enjoyed a fortnight's paid holiday a year. Someone would have to guide these people over the points—quite literally if they wished to undertake a journey of any complexity.

Cook expanded his operation steadily. By 1851 he was in a position to take 165 000 people to the Crystal Palace; a little later came the first circular tours of the Continent and, in 1862, what was described as a 'package tour' to Paris. Cook declared, 'I now see no reason why a hundred may not travel together as easily as a dozen', likening such a party in Switzerland to the way 'the first Napoleon crossed the Alps with his grand army'.

Thomas Cook had 'gone in for numbers', but his son John, who became an equal partner in 1871, was determined to move the operation upmarket. Egypt had been reached by Cook's in 1869, the year of the opening of the Suez Canal; John was determined that the growth of British power there would be matched by the hegemony of Cook's in the tourist trade. Before long Cook's were carrying the mails, running a fleet of steamers on the Nile, and carrying the expedition to relieve Gordon at Khartoum. Egypt became the source of the company's most flourishing and regular business; in the process the firm itself became imperialised. (Eventually there would be a Department of Indian Princes, specially charged to handle the travelling arrangements of Indian dignitaries and their entourages.) Increasingly Cook's prided itself on the prestige of its clients: members of European royal families, including the Kaiser, were escorted to the Near East. While humbler folk were still catered for, a French edition of the *Excursionist* spoke of the firm's 'voyage from vulgarity'. At the high noon of Empire, Brighton could now be disparaged even at home as being 'much frequented during the summer by trippers', the very class of people who had enabled the firm to become established in the first place.[6]

The tourist as postmodernist

Eric J. Leed, in *The Mind of the Traveler*, argues that travel is the neglected dynamic of Western civilisation. It helped, through the refinement of observation, to sustain the scientific revolution; and, apart from the colonies established in the wake of exploratory and military expeditions, gave northern Europe in particular a new sense of centrality. But, says Leed, classic travel is over now. No longer is it even basically male venturing; one of Thomas Cook's achievements was that he made it possible for unattached women to travel. Generations of journeys have spanned the world, creating the postmodern global culture. 'Travel as tourism', he writes, 'has become like the activity of a prisoner pacing a cell much crossed and grooved by other equally mobile and "free"captives. What was once the agent of our liberty has become a means for the revelation of our containment'. Travel he sees as no longer affording distinction: 'It is a way of achieving and realising a norm'. This, Leed argues, is 'the common identity we all share', that of a stranger.[7]

Today's frontiers are elsewhere, even internal. Much of the humour of Woody Allen's Jewish mother in *New York Stories*, turning up at his office with a friend to openly comment on his workmates and their private lives, rests on the ubiquity of tourist behaviour, and the fact that —so far—it has rarely ventured into this holy of holies.

Leed's conclusions seem less exaggerated when the scale and growth of mass tourism are considered. Even in Australia, where distance and isolation have delayed our getting caught up in the trend, the figure for inbound tourists has risen from 100 000 in 1964 to 2.2 million in 1990, 4.1 million in 1996, and a projected five million for the Olympic year 2000. Australians, as Meaghan Morris has pointed out, are changing from being tourists to being *toured*. The implications of this are still to be fully worked through. But with tourism now earning six times as much money for the country as does wool, Australia no longer rides on the sheep's back but on the tourist dollar.[8]

Since tourism is fast becoming the largest sector of world trade, it is a matter that involves governments more and more. It has been suggested that, with the onset of the world economic crisis in the 1980s and 1990s—causing many traditional ways of life to collapse with the onset of globalisation—the large industrial countries have found it necessary to adopt tourist promotion almost as a model for development, even as an economic lifeline. Hitherto this had been thought of only in the context of the Third World.[9]

Moreover, leisure and the arts took an increasingly higher profile as the twentieth century moved on. In the 1930s the British government discovered that, having founded the BBC, it was soon subsidising Covent Garden and the Prom Concerts in order to fill the airwaves. The onset of an age of privatisation has added a new complexity to the situation, but it has not stopped the trend, since everybody wants a share of holiday business. Apart from economic motivation, governments have taken to using tourism as a way of providing a *de facto* ministry of popular culture. In addition to offering bread and circuses, exemplified by governmental wooing of the Grand Prix to Melbourne,

Tourism and the economy. Albany was Western Australia's main port until Fremantle was developed in the late 1890s. It was a thriving town with a bustling main street. By the late 1920s big ships no longer called, and kids could walk down the main street with scarcely a backward glance.

tourism has also been seen as a way of sending messages, of backing up new policies with tangible signs. Under the Cain government, the campaign to restore the name Garriwerd to Victoria's Grampians acquired functional reality once the two names appeared together in promotional literature. Similarly, the successor Kennett government's preoccupation with arranging events became a metaphor for how it saw itself and Victoria—in the words of its slogan, 'On the move!'.

Some theorists have seen tourism as being peculiarly illustrative of the postmodern condition. When Dean MacCannell returned to his 1976 work *The Tourist* in a 1989 preface, he remarked on the way his subject was 'an early postmodern figure, alienated but seeking fulfilment in his own alienation'. Baudrillard, on tour in America, went further, commenting on this 'soft, resort-style civilization', irresistibly evoking the end of the world. Certainly Fredric Jameson's description of postmodern responses as often precluding the unique and the personal, thereby effectively ending some traditional modes of feeling—to be replaced by a set of free-floating *intensities*—seems ready-made as a description of contemporary tourism, even before he caps it by speaking of the dominant presence of a kind of euphoria.[10]

Tourism combined conspicuous patterns of consumption with a self-reflexive quality—in which the state of being a tourist often became predominant—relatively early. Comfort, in the end, is inimical to curiosity, perhaps inversely proportional to it; and comfort has been emphasised in tourism since its increasing democratisation in the late nineteenth century. It has served to deny the fact of mobility, allaying attendant anxieties, in the way that muzak is meant to in a lift. At the same time, organised tours to various sites overwhelmed by signification have tended to ritualise the whole process. In contemporary Australia, even lookout points are often signposted as camera stops. All responses to new locales become mediated; tourists in organised groups are free, it seems, to interact only with one another.

Some have therefore spoken of tourists as proceeding in a kind of hypnosis, a semi-automatic state akin to the undemanding chain of responses induced by driving on freeways. 'Little old ladies', scarcely knowing what country they were in, have been described by one Fijian as travelling about the world 'like registered parcels'. Often tourists go to places that have become so thoroughly adapted to their needs that they can now only be regarded as pseudo-places. Sometimes it is less the locale than an amenity that is the attraction: sun, sea and sand are greater imperatives than the Seychelles, Sri Lanka or Surfers Paradise. The place itself is not the object of the journey; returning home is what matters, after an acceptable flirtation with the idea of adventure or, increasingly, a restorative indulgent holiday that will enable the tourist to cope better with the stresses of contemporary life.

Increasingly it must be acknowledged that whereas these attitudes could have been disparaged in the 1970s, it is the nature of postmodern culture to involve skimming, sampling, and acknowledging complexity by staring it in the face for a second, before moving on. Tourism has always been predicated on consumption; the difference now is that the whole culture is also consumption-based. Hence, instead of the multiplicity of journeys and information offered by the Baedeker guides, there are now some that emphasise shopping above all else. The tourist now is not a member of the public—the very word, with its sense of inclusivity and parallel notion of shared standards, today sounds increasingly quaint—but a privileged postmodern consumer. She or he feels that it is not important to perceive sites so much as simply to recognise them. At Westminster Abbey, a constant wash of tourists pours in and out, rarely noticing even the grave of Churchill at their feet. The building holds sufficient meaning in its fame. For most, it is no longer a *site* of past events and continuing religious observance; it has become a *sight*, something to be taken in with a few glances.[11]

Australian Po-Mo

Two concerns of postmodern theorists apply increasingly to tourism in Australia. One is site sacrilisation, the recognition of an appropriate site and its packaging for touristic consumption. MacCannell lists the stages of the process. First, the site is marked off from similar objects as worthy of preservation. National parks provide an example: the landscape features contained therein are privileged, compared with similar ones just beyond the somewhat arbitrary boundaries. Next comes the framing and elevation phase, when the chosen object is displayed or featured, as in the ruins at Port Arthur being set off by manicured English-style lawns. With most tourists similarly framed by the amenities that guides and tour operators provide, MacCannell might have added, mediation may come to confront mediation. If this occurs on a sufficiently large scale, then a third phase can occur, of enshrinement.

The Melbourne Shrine, in fact, provides a good example: a vast building whose basic function is to shelter and dramatise, for the populace in general, a representational Stone of Remembrance to honour the fallen. (There Anzac Day, rather than tour guides, provides the human mediation.) But MacCannell, writing with American tourists in Europe largely in mind, cites Sainte-Chapelle, a splendid Parisian church built to house a sacred relic and which itself has become a tourist attraction. An Australian equivalent of this kind of thing might be the new $4 million Eureka Stockade Centre at Ballarat, which not only features an enormous Eureka flag, but also has a fragment of the original in a glass case on display inside.

Fourthly in MacCannell's model comes the site enhancement brought about by mechanical reproduction, via such things as prints, postcards and replicas: a child given a Sydney Harbour Bridge pencil sharpener might, if the object is admired by his peers, one day want to see the real thing. As a final stage of site sacrilisation MacCannell points to social reproduction, when groups, cities and regions name themselves after famous attractions. Here the Eureka flag and the Eureka League again point to a symbolic site, itself sacrilised as a sight till recently only by a single-columned monument.[12]

Sight sacrilisation in Australia is likely to become conspicuous over the next decade or two. This is partly because tourism, having been overwhelmingly domestic throughout our history, has really been a hidden industry. International visitors even now comprise only one-tenth of Australian tourist traffic, but they account for almost one-third of the income. In the eyes of the industry, a lot of ground has to be made up. So up go the signposts, signifying the sight, marking the marker, even if it is only an obscure cairn saying that Major Mitchell passed this way.

The landscape must also be filled. In recent years there have gone up, among other things, a Big Pineapple, a Big Cow, a giant Koala, and even a Giant Earthworm. These are not generally museums, but punctuation marks in empty tracts; not so much pagan idols as icons for a post-

Tourist lookouts began primitively. The ladder against the dead tree was sufficiently normal in 1910 for this Lakes Entrance example to appear on a printed postcard. By the 1930s the Arthurs Seat Lookout (also in Victoria) had evolved into an art deco edifice.

modern culture, specialising in selling souvenirs of themselves. They are too preposterous to be taken seriously, and in their artificiality almost send up the idea of a site. The sight alone is all they offer.

These *monstres sacrés* littering the landscape are a peculiar variant of the second postmodern concern, the simulacrum. We are meant to recognise them as archetypal, as having elaborated the essential characteristics of the subject even as it caricatures them. In America, as Umberto Eco demonstrated, replication is an altogether more serious matter. There it is seen as an expression of the original's potency, and often as an improvement. As he journeyed between Los Angeles and San Francisco, Eco encountered seven wax versions of the Last Supper, at least ten Davids, plus several Pietas; usually a cheap print of the original was placed nearby. Its function, he concluded, was not to remind viewers that there was a distant masterpiece that one day they ought to see, but rather to state implicitly, 'We are giving you the reproduction so you will no longer feel any need for the original'.

When Jean Baudrillard went to California shortly afterwards, he was struck by the raw energy of such ventures into hyperreality. So-called American banality arose directly from the monotony of wide-open spaces and 'a radical absence of culture'. California might be 'the world-centre of the inauthentic', he decided, but this is what gave it its originality and power. Pointing to the enormous variety of such simulacra, John Urry notes that when they are put together with other elements drawn from all over the globe at world fairs or the larger shopping malls, the result is a form of 'global miniaturisation'.[13]

Ideas that a simulacrum is, as the OED defines it, the image of something, a shadowy likeness, a mere pretence or even a deceptive substitute, no longer suffice in the age of postmodernism and cultural crossover. The definition is rooted in cultural certainties that are long gone. Indeed the erosion of cultural hierarchies license simulacra as never before, while—more specifically in tourism—sheer pressure of numbers often necessitates them. Atmospheric pollution has wreaked havoc with the Acropolis; human breath was sufficient to damage the prehistoric cave paintings at Lascaux, to the point where an exact replica of the site was carved out beside the original in order to protect it.

Recently, certain undesirable qualities Eco and Baudrillard discerned in America have become evident in tourist sites here. As discussed in Chapter 9, the label 'historic' no longer indicates a sometime importance of function; it has become separated from process, and now simply means old—usually with the sheen of restoration. In this we have taken on the New World alienation from history that Baudrillard talks about. 'Having no primitive accumulation of time', he says of America, 'it lives in a perpetual present'.[14] The result is commodification; history becomes an exotic, and what cannot be commodified falls away.

Australian distinctiveness

Apart from its overwhelmingly domestic nature, there are a number of features of tourism in Australia that render its history unusual. For one thing, until the recent interest in Aboriginal culture, it was not, as most writing on tourism assumes, a matter of encountering the Other so much as variations on the self. Tourism has always been a kind of appropriation, and nowhere more so than in a seemingly empty continent. Journeying near and far was a way of making good one's claim, of giving one's emigrant existence an imaginative dimension. A new home in a strange land is never appreciated so much as when one returns to it after venturing further afield.

The Australian elite, of course, remained fixated on European travel: that story is beyond the scope of this book. In this it was in no sense unusual. But since both Cape Town and New York were less than two weeks sailing time from Europe—whereas Sydney and Melbourne were always more than four—the disjunction there was less striking. Here, at least until World War II, one of the most telling divides was between those who had made the trip 'Home', as many of them still called it, and those who had not (Richard White has coined the instructive phrase 'the travelling classes').[15] Another consequence was that, despite the swank hotels that arose in the capital cities and beyond, the predominant tone of Australian tourism was that it was neighbourly, practical (for many the last frontier) and democratic.

Again it differed, even from America, in the sheer abundance of available space. Initially peripheral settlements such as Manly in New South Wales or Sandringham in Victoria doubled as resorts, while in a number of cities trams would take families from the working-class suburbs to nearby beaches, where amusements proliferated on the foreshore. Beyond the urban perimeter there was camping—in Melbourne's case from Brighton to Mentone, and beyond to Carrum by the 1900s; today it survives at Rosebud. Further afield there was no shortage of suitable places. It was not until the increased population pressure and urgent environmentalism of the 1970s that camping and picnicking became delimited like everything else.

A further property of space in Australia has been to dramatise shifts in touristic fashion. These have been partly determined by broader cultural assumptions, often universal in Western culture at the time. One of these was the taste for mountain, lake and riverine scenery which,

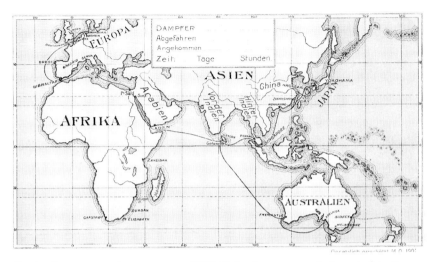

For this German steamship company in 1910, 'Sidney' was very much the end of the line.

when coupled with an anxiety to flee the heat of the mainland summer, propelled Edwardian tourists to Tasmania in large numbers. Later a somewhat more attenuated anglophilia fastened on Western Australian wildflowers, which could—at least in the mind's eye—be romantically picked as if in an English country garden. It was the Transcontinental Railway that made the west accessible; transport revolutions generally have allied themselves with the latest fashion in opening up new areas. The car and the aeroplane enabled Queensland to rise to prominence, with the dominance of the beach culture in the 1950s; then later the Centre, with the discovery of Aboriginality, and later still Kakadu, with the rise of environmentalism. In time some of these will dwindle in touristic importance, just as Tasmania has done and some older Queensland resort towns are doing now.

FOR ALL THESE REASONS, while *Holiday Business* is a study in social history, it sets out to consider tourism as the industry that has arisen in response to the convergence of people on recognised routes and resorts. Valene Smith, the editor of a useful collection of anthropological studies of the subject, defines the tourist as 'a temporary leisured person who voluntarily visits a place away from home for the purpose of experiencing a change'.[16] This definition is not as serviceable as it seems, not least because of convention traffic, which deliberately blurs the distinction between leisure and business. It also tends to omit day trippers, historically of greater importance than they are today.

The contemporary tourist industry lumps all overnight travellers together in its reckonings, while increasingly engaging in niche marketing and product differentiation. In the chapters approaching our own time we intend to do much the same. More generally we shall note the dynamic of mobility and response on the part of the tourist, and development on the part of the industry, a triad that can repeat itself indefinitely until a place loses drawing power. Ours is now what Lévi-Strauss calls 'a proliferating and overexcited civilisation'.[17] Australia has learnt to recognise that tourism is at the heart of it.

Origins

INTERNATIONAL TOURISM TO Australia has a very definite baseline. In 1871 Thomas Cook conceived the idea of a conducted round-the-world tour. The Suez Canal had recently opened, and the time seemed propitious for expanding his operations to take in the Australasian colonies. To his surprise, he found that he had not a single genuine taker. But 'as soon as he remodelled the programme by leaving out Australasia', *Cook's Excursionist* recalled ten years later, 'applications were received, and the first party soon made up'. Similarly, the first American trans-Pacific service, initiated in 1875, had to be discontinued ten years later when the US government cancelled its mail contract. There were not enough passengers to sustain the route.

Why was there so little interest? Cook's was the first projected round-the-world tour, and it would have been aimed at a fairly exclusive market: Jules Verne's *Around the World in Eighty Days*, which appeared two years later, began and ended in a London club. Only the leisured could have afforded the time it took to travel to the Antipodes, some seven weeks, and Australia and New Zealand were simply not regarded as exotic enough. English interest in the Empire was, for the moment, at a low ebb, and those upper-class people who could travel would have been largely incurious about colonial society and its achievements. When Anthony Trollope set out for the Antipodes precisely at this time, it was to write a comprehensive account he in part conceived as an emigrant's guide. Working-class improvement was the narrative in Australia,

Not in Cairo, not in Calcutta, but in Sydney—Petty's, the city's first quality hotel, as it appeared in 1900

and it did not appeal to everyone. Besides, convictism was only now being sloughed off. Western Australia had received its last consignment of convicts in 1868, and memories of Van Diemen's Land were still fresh in Tasmanian minds: a hotel at Oatlands, an important administrative centre in convict days, felt it necessary to list among its amenities 'civil servants'.[1]

Tourism in Australia had scarcely begun. The explorers still moving through remote parts of the country as the first agents of Western civilisation were often cowed by its enormous distances and seeming emptiness. Like tourists everywhere, they sought reassurance, and found it by inscribing the biography of their expeditions on adjacent landmarks— Mt Misery, Cape Catastrophe—as if sending postcards to posterity, proclaiming their capacity to rise above all setbacks. In moments of homesickness, Australian features were made to register their attachment to localities elsewhere, as when Captain John Hayes named the Derwent after a sheet of water in the Lake District, and the large mountain nearby Skiddaw, after the Cumbrian peak overlooking the English

Derwent. In so strange a land it was not the exotic that was prized—for here it was often wan, and dun-coloured—so much as echoes of the familiar, particularly as they often came with land that might be suitable for settlement and cultivation.[2]

The next figure in the landscape, the traveller, had a more even-handed view. The stakes for him were not so high. Driven by a belief that the world of necessity must be opened up—Anthony Trollope likened the Isthmus of Panama to a divinely laid-out leg of lamb awaiting the carving knife of the Canal—he was drawn to the frontiers, to unusual localities. Etymologically the word 'traveller' is connected with 'travail', and Victorian travellers did not mind this in the least: hardship was proof of adventurousness. Moreover it was all good copy for their books. Numerous travel accounts were written and published, and many of them dwell lovingly on all the arrangements, improvisations and difficulties of travel.

The tourist, however, expected ease of access, regular timetables, and accommodation with a premium on comfort: all facilities should be in place, ideally spiced with a touch of adventure. The last-mentioned was easily supplied in Australia in 1870, since up-country hostelries were generally basic and Cobb & Co. coaches still provided the main means of overland transport. Railways were advancing up the mountains from Sydney, but the southern line had only recently reached Goulburn; the rail link with Melbourne would not be completed till 1881.

In 1856 Bradshaw's, whose famous guide to British rail travel was described by *Punch* as 'England's greatest work of fiction', began issuing a Victorian edition, soon matched by one for Sydney, which included all forms of public transport available down to coaches, cabs and omnibuses. Melbourne, explained Bradshaw's in their preface, 'has been *without a guide* for new arrivals, visitors from the diggings, adjacent colonies &c', a need that they alone supplied in tabular form for quite some time.[3]

A guide of sorts had appeared in Sydney almost twenty years before, when Maclehose published his *Picture of Sydney; and Strangers' Guide in*

New South Wales in 1839. Right from the heading of its first chapter, it was directed to immigrants; only a fraction of the book took the reader beyond Sydney. Another *Stranger's Guide to Sydney* appeared in 1858, doubling its size for a second edition in 1861. It appeared to be directed mainly at people 'who have but a short time to spend in town', presumably from up-country, and it arranged the sights of the city in walks. Again there was no expectation of tourists. Sydney was a tight society, and 'stranger' was then the right word for a newcomer as yet unaccustomed to a place's amenities and mores. This usage of the word persisted until at least 1880, when a Victorian guide addressed itself to 'The stranger or visitor to Melbourne'.

But towards 1870, even as the Suez Canal was being dug, 'our shores are frequently visited', ran the preface to the first Sydney guide for a generation, 'by what we truly term "travellers",—people of substantial means, who, in search of health or pleasure, "take a trip to Australia", as our forefathers used to "take a run over the Continent"'. Leigh's *Handbook to Sydney and Suburbs* was, in fact, dedicated to the most prominent of them all—Prince Alfred, the Duke of Edinburgh—who, in stopping a would-be assassin's bullet at Clontarf, was to bring some unwanted publicity to Sydney picnicking. Leigh's saw itself as supplying a new need, providing a general guide as well as 'a companion to the business-man'. The quickening of interest Leigh's perceived was felt elsewhere. In 1868 appeared Thomas's *Guide for Excursionists from Melbourne*, 'the first attempt at publishing, in this shape, some account of what may be seen in and about the colony'. Three years later came *Walch's Tasmanian Guide Book*.[4]

Implicit in these early guides was a new sense of pride in colonial communities: one boasted of Sydney having 'grown up to proportions of greatness within the space of little more than a life-time', shipping from 'nearly every nation of the world' being present in its 'magnificent free port'. Leigh's saw itself advising the traveller so that on leaving 'he may carry with him the impression that New South Wales has, beyond her fine harbour and her salubrious climate, some substantial proofs of civilisation, and even of refinement'. Often, partly to validate the subject material, descriptive accounts were peppered with literary quotations, and in one case included a reference to an aria in Weber's *Oberon*. These guidebooks were a display, not only of learning in an age when people regularly committed verse to heart, but also of what the colony had to offer. *Walch's Tasmanian Guide Book* in particular reads as part gazetteer, part Domesday Book, a reckoning of the appropriation of a large antipodean island three generations after settlement.[5]

Most were more mindful of what the colonies lacked. Burton's *Visitors' Guide to Sydney* conceded that 'there are no ivy-mantled towers or other old ruins with their deeply interesting historical associations', but pointed out that the scenery around any other city in the world was no match for Sydney's. Many, however, could not make the adjustment: one writer in Thomas's *Guide for Excursionists*, while believing that 'as we have voluntarily left the good things of the old world behind us, we must make the best we can . . . of the new', could not help feeling ecstatic when, somewhere south of Melbourne, he came across what could have passed for an English lane. He was bereft when he could not find it again. Equally tellingly the anonymous compiler of *Walch's Tasmanian Guide Book* (Louisa Ann Meredith), commented that while some circulars sent out seeking information had been returned with full, usable comments regarding landmarks, others had come back from the same district stating 'Don't know', 'Can't tell', or 'Not any', 'No' or 'None'.

Some people appear to have been sceptical that one could enjoy oneself in Australia at all. 'We may at once dismiss romance', said a writer in Thomas's *Guide for Excursionists*, 'and say you can'. True, the greatest pastimes and amusements were outdoor ones. But whereas in England hunting and shooting were the prerogative of the rich, in Australia any man could participate; while there might be no genuine big game, there were birds aplenty. Thomas's *Guide* carried an account of hunting on the Mornington Peninsula as an example of what one could do. Five men had set out with a wagon, two hacks, five blankets, five guns and ammunition, a fishing rod, four saddles and bridles, cooking utensils and a small tent. It was a regular expedition; even so, two of the party became separated and could have been lost. This kind of pleasure excursion seemed very much like pioneering. Simple sightseeing was not much better. A few years earlier the visiting Englishman B. A. Heywood had caught a train from Melbourne to Brighton. The place, though marked out as a town on the map, was much smaller than he imagined. 'At that period in its existence,' he wrote, 'it presented no attraction to the solitary tourist; and therefore, after a short walk on the beach, where pieces of native sponge lay strewed about, I returned by rail to town'. Pride in colonial achievement perhaps encouraged description—whether verbal or written—and the writer to enumerate, rather than to identify and focus on particular sites.[6]

These earliest guides had been conceived partly as collaborationist ventures. Thomas's went further than the others in that it contained pieces from some thirty contributors. It also included blank sheets of paper at the end, to be torn out and sent back with appropriate comments. Australian guidebooks were still acquiring form, and substance; even the industry had to be educated about them. Leigh's in their first (and only) edition had been unable to attract hotel advertisements.

It may well be that the enormous success of Trollope's *Australia and New Zealand* (1873), both in England and the colonies (where the various sections were republished in cheap editions),[7] served to validate descriptive accounts of the colonies and helped create a demand for further information. Unlike its predecessors, the *Visitors' Guide to Sydney* of 1872 survived and was steadily reprinted. It was given a fillip by the 1879 Sydney Exhibition, which saw other successful guides appear as well. By 1889 the *Visitors' Guide* was in its seventh edition; Trollope's descriptive accounts were still listed three times in the contents.

Caves

Trollope had certainly 'done' Australia thoroughly, and often at some discomfort. Never was this more so than when, in the company of the Governor of Tasmania, he was taken to see the Chudleigh Caves (now Mole Creek). The caves at Cheddar in Somerset, he declared, were

Burrangalong Cavern, c. 1843 (above). *The emphasis here is on cave as grotto—still plausible as the mythological entry point to the underworld. By 1900 the geological revolution had brought about a whole new conception of time: as in this postcard* (below), *such an appreciation had become an implicit part of the tourist gaze.*

prettier. 'But the caves at Cheddar are nothing to the Chudleigh caves in bigness, blackness, water, dirt, and the enforced necessity of crawling, creeping, wading, and knocking one's head about at every turn.' The celebrated author, whose figure was as ample as his prose, almost got stuck in a crevice. On regaining daylight, Trollope was told by the guide that even he would not re-enter the caves until another governor might want to see them.

Why all this fuss and discomfort, to visit a site that was scarcely prepared? Partly it was that caves were a notable feature in what was perceived to be a rather undifferentiated landscape, something at last to show the visitor. There were also a number of broad cultural reasons. The eighteenth century had romanticised the grotto, domesticating it, and this impulse still lingered. A fountain erected in front of the Melbourne Exhibition Buildings in 1880 was described as 'charmingly romantic, being formed of rustic rockwork to resemble grottos—the rock stained to look like moss and stalactites'. Even caves were perceived partly as grottos, in order to domesticate them. Conrad Martens painted Wombeyan in a way that recalls the cavernous Piranesi, but his depiction of Burrangalong Cavern attempts, by placing groups of people in the foreground, to domesticate it, to make it seem unthreatening. A further distant figure stands at the mouth of a classic grotto-shaped opening, its diminutive size pointing up the large scale of the aperture, before it broadens out to form the vast, dark chamber in the background. Here Martens, painting in the early 1840s, expressed awe before the sublime, a major element in the romantic response to landscape.

At a more popular level people commonly spoke of 'nature's handiwork', and caves could be counted upon to provide fine examples. In addition to their often intimidating scale, the very intricacy of their formations appealed to a sensibility drawn to bric-a-brac, damask lace and cast iron. 'The stalagmites and stalactites are wrought into shapes of exquisite beauty', ran an account of Jenolan, 'and possess great brilliancy of lustre . . . Some of the halls, or apartments, seem to be filled with the most delicate looking sprays, all reflecting back the light and each other's brilliancies with wondrous splendour, the caves sparkling as if bejewelled with thousands of sapphires and rubies'. Rider Haggard merely heightened popular expectation when, in the best-selling *King Solomon's Mines* (1885), he placed the sought-after treasure in some caves.

Trollope had been of the bluff mid-Victorian generation, too distant from the grotto but not yet placed to confidently share another stand-point for viewing caves—that of the evolutionist or the geologist. By the end of the century the 'geological transformations and the slow processes of nature', so evident in caves, carried much of the burden of proof that the world could not have been created (as Archbishop Ussher had demonstrated by adding up the ages of all the people mentioned in Genesis) in 4004 BC.[8]

In New South Wales a major cluster of caves had been found, so it was said, while a bushranger was being pursued in the Bathurst district. By the 1850s visitors were riding in on horseback from Bathurst, Oberon or Tarana, some having specially ventured along the Great Western Road and staying at inns at Hartley or Bowenfels. Having reached the Fish River caves, people generally camped under a rock at the base of a grand natural arch. By 1866 the government was moved to proclaim the area a reserve; shortly afterwards Jeremiah Wilson was appointed warden, at a salary of £25 a year. A road in to the site was planned, and alarm was expressed at the degree of vandalism that had taken place.

In 1872 the Southern Line reached Tarana. 'To visit the Caves *comfort-ably*,' advised the first *New South Wales Railway Guide* in 1879, 'the best way to proceed is for a number of friends to form themselves into a party'. Such a party would have to provide its own blankets and camping equipment, and be mindful of provisions, either taking them in or arranging to have them supplied by the guide. It was advisable to write to him in advance; he would then meet the train with horse and buggy, and later provide lanterns as he saw the excursionists through the caves.

Government involvement in Jenolan (as the Caves were renamed in 1884) was tardy. In 1879 £450 was voted by parliament for the preser-vation and improvement of the Caves, now augmented by recent dis-coveries; the long-planned road was also built. A 'rough house' was to be erected on the initative of the warden, who would be assisted to the extent of being charged a nominal rent and being provided with corrugated iron. This desultory attitude resulted in bad timing, for the Caves were closed for these works just as some overseas visitors arrived in Sydney for the International Exhibition. Although £2500 was subsequently found to construct a bridle path from Katoomba, the government refused to take over the accommodation house. Complaints were constantly made about its inadequacy and, although two-storey extensions were added, by the 1890s outside interests were clamouring for permission to construct a £10 000 hotel on the site. The government, having promulgated regulations banning liquor from the Caves, looked upon the proposal sourly.

Matters came to a head when a fire destroyed much of the accommodation house in 1895. The warden, Wilson, requested that the Department of Mines (which then administered the site) 'resume and compensate me for all buildings and improvements'. If they would rebuild, he would furnish the buildings. 'I . . . have been keeper of these caves for 28 years,' he added, 'and have erected all the buildings . . . at my own expense'. The authorities now decided to act, and a new limestone Caves House was designed by the Government Architect and leased out to a new proprietor in 1898. The complex was developed, running to a photographic kiosk and a provisional school. The regulation of entry to the Caves became more sophisticated, and a standard guide to them, Trickett's, made its first appearance. The public duly responded, there being a noticeable increase in visitors from 1901.[9]

THE TRUE MEASURE of the primacy of caves as tourist sites is afforded by the case of Western Australia. This colony, finding itself between the desert and the deep blue sea, believed the caves of the south-west to be its only notable tourist attraction. Thus it was that the first governmental agency for tourism in Western Australia was the Caves Board, established in 1900. A high-profile body, the Board included the proprietor of the *West Australian*, Sir John Hackett, the mayor of Busselton and the commissioner of the Public Service Board among its members. It spent

The hope of Western Australian tourism, c. 1907—the plain but elegant Margaret River Caves House, government-built.

some £35 000 on improvements in the decade of its existence. Foremost among these was Caves House—an airy establishment at Yellingup, where electric light was also installed in the caves. From 1909 Yanchep, north of Perth, also came under the control of the Board.

Not everyone was happy about the scale of operations. Though glad to see the caves protected from further vandalism, the government whittled down the surrounding reserves. The Caves Board secretary, Edgar Robinson, toured the eastern states in 1905 in the hope of drawing '10 000 visitors to the caves this year', but the actual numbers attracted were nothing like that, despite extensive publicity. Most of the visitors remained Western Australian, and numbers were not high: the Margaret River caves drew only 191 people in 1909. The relatively high expenditure of the Caves Board therefore came under attack. Norbert Keenan, the mayor of Kalgoorlie, said it was an 'extravagance' to light caves 'to which only tourists went'. Robinson responded by pointing to Jenolan, saying that the NSW cave resorts demonstrated that tourism had the potential to bring much revenue to the state. Each incoming tourist would spend £10; and, before his jaunt east, Robinson estimated that there would be a thousand of them a year. But, given the fact that not even these more modest expectations were fulfilled, parliamentarians attacked the Board. 'Caves were not accessible to the poorer classes', said one. Another described them as 'A beauty spot for the pampered few', kept open 'for a few fat families in the country'. At a time when roadbuilding had been halted and wages reduced, the Caves roads did not carry 'a single bag of wheat, but allowed friends of the Minister and others with plenty of money to go there for a pleasant holiday'.[10] In 1909 the Board's funding was cut; the members resigned en masse. They were not replaced. The Board was abolished in the course of a general rearrangement a year later.

The Blue Mountains

Mountain scenery had not always been highly esteemed; it was the English Lake poets who popularised it at the beginning of the nineteenth century. Notions of the sublime, with its jarring hint of terror, had by the 1880s given way to the idea of nature as a succession of vistas —camera-ready art—its performance and function almost secondary to the pleasing effect it might produce. The *Picturesque Atlas of Australasia*,

A great attraction in Victorian times was the 'mystic sea' of cloud that rolls into the Jamieson Valley in the Blue Mountains.

a centennial work issued in parts for popular consumption, presented the Blue Mountains this way:

> he who would really know the mountains . . . must let the majestic colouring and clothing of the sunset sink into his being. He must watch while Nature weaves the robes of imperial purple and royal gold; while down in the gorges the pale grey mists and the deep blue shadows are prepared; while every salient point, every unshadowed ridge is flooded with fiery light; while the bare crags gleam and glow as if in process of transmutation, and the gnarled and stunted trees of the summit stand out in spectral light.

It is a set for *Götterdämmerung*; Wagner without the music.

In contrast to all this grandeur, it was the temperate nature of the climate that drew people to the mountains. It was, after all, a time when Melbourne's weather could be described by a sophisticated traveller as 'the finest climate in the world for healthy men', and applauded for its invigorating effect. The climate of Katoomba was similarly praised. 'The heat during the waking hours is scarcely felt, so bracing is the air, and one feels fitted for any exertion under a sun, which, if experienced in lower levels, would produce a lassitude and fatigue.'[11]

Wherever the British had gone, they had usually abandoned the plains in hot weather for some adjacent hill station—most notably in India, where for many years the entire government would move up for the season from Calcutta to Simla in the Himalayas. The hill station syndrome was to some degree evident in Australia, when wealthy professionals, politicians and businessmen built salubrious residences for themselves in elevated localities adjacent to the cities. Governors' summer retreats were also built in the Adelaide Hills, at Sutton Forest near Moss Vale, NSW, and most notably at Mt Macedon in Victoria, where David Syme's existing house was taken over and annexed to an impressive new brick-and-timber chalet, Government Cottage. A number of large houses set in superb exotic gardens had already appeared on the southern slope of the mountain, located so that they would catch the evening breeze

The Governor of Victoria, Sir Henry Loch, set the seal on Mt Macedon as a hill station when he built Government Cottage there in the 1880s. It later became a guest-house.

sweeping in off the Bay. There had been a hotel at Mt Macedon since the 1860s, the first guest-house appearing a decade later; by the turn of the century these had increased in number, substantially modifying the exclusivity of the place. By then Kuranda, in the hills behind Cairns, Queensland, was exercising a similar role—without the intervening gentility. Advertising the settlement as 'the health resort of North Queensland', the expanding Hotel Kuranda, located strategically near the impressive Barron Falls, nevertheless offered patrons facilities for 'sketching, shooting and fishing'.[12]

THE CASE OF THE Blue Mountains, and of Katoomba in particular, is instructive as providing the clearest example of the transformation from hilly retreat to popular resort. The Great Western Railway, opened in stages until in 1868 it had reached Mt Victoria, was the driving force in this, an incidental consequence of servicing Bathurst and the west. Initially, the engineering wonder of the Great Zig Zag, as the line coiled up the slope near Lithgow, was itself the great sight of the region, and was commemorated as such by a visiting Italian when he wrote his account of a world tour. The natural scenery could still seem a little too unmediated for comfort—'wild and grand in the extreme', as one guidebook put it. Psychologically, the railway line was the lifeline. Sidings were not always fixed, and even when they were they could bear such unromantic names as The Crushers—identifying a place's purpose as the point where crushed stone was loaded for gravel and ballast.[13]

This first name for Katoomba (The Crushers) indicated its purely utilitarian function; a subsidiary railway serviced a shale and coal mine. In 1880 the place consisted of the platform, a gatehouse where the road crossed the main line, and a weatherboard pub. Four years later Katoomba was being noted as a 'township of some importance', with two hotels. Land that had sold for £1 an acre in 1880 was, nine years later, fetching anything up to £20 a foot in the town centre. By then Katoomba had four churches, a School of Arts and a newspaper, and had been declared a municipality. Tourism had well and truly arrived.

Initially urged to go and see the mine, visitors had become so conspicuous that the offshoot line was turned into a scenic railway.

It had been noted that tourist accommodation was already quite diversified: boarding-houses existed for 'those who take their champagne, to those who hire humble lodgings and take their own provisions'. But the grandest hostelry of all stood on a knoll in the centre of the town. Built in 1882 as the Great Western Hotel, three years later it was extended and renamed the Carrington, after the popular governor of the day, a patron; Katoombans believed he might even build a house in the town. As it happened, the Governor showed the traditional preference for visiting Jenolan via Mt Victoria, but in other respects the Carrington had stolen a march on its up-country rival, the Imperial Hotel. At the beginning some seventy to eighty people could be accommodated there, and after the extensions of the mid-1880s it ran to 119 bedrooms and seven suites. In addition to the regulation ladies' drawing-room and gentlemen's smoking and reading room, a music room displayed what was described as 'one of the finest grand pianos in the colonies'. A sense of privilege was affirmed by the view from the roof, which extended to the Harbour and the distant city of Sydney.[14]

Women were, of course, prominent among tourists, residents and guest-house proprietors, and they brought a different perspective to new

16

Illustrated postcards began to appear at the time of federation, originally slightly smaller than they later became, and with space for messages on the front. Meanwhile the train remained the fastest form of transport. People dressed up even for a short journey into central Sydney.

This set of stamps (enlarged) was issued by Tasmania in 1899, one of the first pictorial issues to appear anywhere in the world. They were based on photographs by J. W. Beattie, a tireless campaigner for Tasmanian tourism.

landscapes from that of men. In addition to being more observant of the interior of hostelries—although many became quite adept at camping—lady travellers were more inclined to sketch and to paint in water-colour. They were attracted by waterfalls, and usually had a keener eye for flora than their male counterparts. Louise Atkinson, writing in the *Sydney Morning Herald* in 1860, was one of the first to wax lyrical about the Blue Mountains fern gullies.[15]

Meanwhile the railways—the largest government department of the time—extended its activities by producing handbooks for tourists. A comparison between the first edition of the *Railway Guide* (1879) and the edition of 1884 indicates an increasing popularisation: illustrations of private residences had been replaced by pictures of hotels and natural scenery, while Baedeker-style appendixes on the flora and the geology of the Blue Mountains were deleted in 1886. By then the railways had been selling special excursion tickets for some time, at twopence a mile first class, or one penny second; amounting to 5s 6d at weekends, the latter was less than half what the traveller would have paid in 1878. To cope with the increasing traffic, the railways improved carriages (complete with lavatories in second class for the first time) and established a chain of refreshment rooms. An unintended consequence of the new amenities—which extended to better seating and footwarmers—was a massive transfer of passengers from first class to second. The depression of the 1890s had made people more careful with their money.

Although country passenger numbers slightly dropped in the early 1890s, by 1905—at 35 158 150—they were almost twice what they had been in 1895. In the Blue Mountains there was now a *Guide Map of the Sights*; demand for the *Railway Guide* was such that it could be sold for a shilling instead of 2s 6d. Local progress associations—rather than government—prepared tracks, lookouts and shelter sheds, which politicians were then perfectly happy to open. Of particular interest to visitors was Orphan Rock: Victorian sentimentality over foundlings was projected on to the isolated outcrop, which unwittingly served as a metaphor for the colonists themselves, separated from England. The

Three Sisters, that icon of later popular tourism which drew on Aboriginal legend, emerged as a sight considerably later.[16]

Exhibitions and other festivals

While the Blue Mountains were, by the end of the century, the leading tourist district in Australia, there were other places that could momentarily eclipse them.

The activities at Glenelg, South Australia, on 28 December each year (which still continue) were shaped and magnified by the dearth of holidays in the nineteenth century. In addition to being the place where the settlers landed and the colony was proclaimed, Glenelg functioned for fifty years as South Australia's main port. The 380-metre jetty proved ideal for promenading. Linked by rail with Adelaide in 1873, Glenelg capitalised on its accessibility to the city by building swimming baths shortly afterwards.

Proclamation Day soon became the one day of the year, and councillors successfully urged residents to organise activities to entertain the visitors after the formal commemoration. Thousands and thousands of 'happy, well-dressed, well-conducted people descend upon Glenelg', a newspaper reported in 1874, 'giving evidence of the material prosperity of the colony'. When, two years later, the now traditional public holiday was brought forward to consolidate working days, there was a sense of outrage. People stayed away from their jobs in droves. The trains were packed, and even larger crowds than usual were reported to be watching the ketch and boat races.

By 1883 the Glenelg railway was carrying over one million passengers a year. A few years later the town boasted eight hotels, plus lodging-houses; there was also a thriving trade in souvenirs for day trippers. A sporting carnival was developed around the Sheffield Handicap, a professional footrace. Forty thousand people—a quarter of the then population of Adelaide—are said to have been present when the first race was run in 1887.

What drew them as much as anything was the vast fun fair that had sprung up on the foreshore. Here were tents and wagons, for 28 De-

The crowds gather at Glenelg for South Australia's annual Proclamation Day festivities. The location of the picnic was the first step towards going into the water, only tentatively achieved by 1900.

cember still had enough sense of being a foundation day—as well as a picnic one—to be a favourite for family reunions. In addition to the improvised family marquees of quilts and bedsheets, providing necessary protection from the sun, there were others housing food and drink stalls (some proclaiming temperance), shooting galleries, Aunt Sallies and other sideshows. Around the pier there were further entertainments, with boat races and swimming and diving contests. Later, bands might play. One evening in 1896 there were three of them, with the Adelaide Glee Club producing from a nearby steamer the highly desirable effect of music wafting across the water on a velvet night.[17]

By the time Bendigo in Victoria held its first Easter Fair in 1871, new rail links could be relied upon to bring the crowds. The following year a particular drawcard was the first ladies cricket match to be held in the colonies, an affair of ankle-length skirts and scarlet or blue garibaldi jackets; but right from the beginning there was a Chinese presence. Members of the 850-strong community first held a race 'in full Mongolian costume', each participant handicapped by a length of bamboo balancing two baskets. There were occasional bands, and also theatrical performances, but as this ethnic component became more pronounced, the Chinese came to occupy a 'traditional' place in the annual march with what was virtually a second procession at the end of the main one.

In 1892 they stole the show with a dragon specially imported from China; so much of an icon for the local Chinese community did Loong become that a special ceremony was devised, unknown elsewhere, of Awakening the Dragon—not least with the object of making money for local charities. Forty men were required to activate the beast, but by 1949 there were not sufficient Chinese for the task: several Australians had to stand in. Even so, by 1970 there was enough interest to install a successor dragon, Sun Loong, and in an increasingly multicultural Australia his future is assured.[18]

THERE WERE OTHER public occasions besides annual festivities. Most notable of these were the exhibitions—particularly Sydney in 1879–80, Melbourne in 1880–81, and again in 1888–89. All were in the style pioneered by the Great Exhibition held in London in 1851—paeans to progress housed in vast cathedral-like spaces, hymns to industry, an implicit celebration of European hegemony in the world. Machinery and manufactured goods were laid out for the appraising eye, rather as new towns were—and goods in that more recent phenomenon, the department store. Visitors were needed to complete the process; otherwise exhibits were simply a collection of objects. And they came: 1.1 million to Sydney in 1879, 1.3 million to Melbourne in 1880, and two million to Melbourne in 1888.

Public men expatiated on the way that workers, simply by moving from one display court to the next, could learn from the relative proficiency of overseas technology; in some cases factory hands were taken along by their employers. But it was the sideshows and, in Melbourne 1888, the extensive art displays and ambitious concert programme, that were the most popular attraction. International fairs have been seen as the first amusement parks. With their element of the exotic supplied by foreign displays, they also provided an ersatz sense of travel for the masses. Moreover, by highlighting novelty and providing competing products as well as attractions, all in a context of hype, they accelerated the growth of advertising. The sober typography of Melbourne papers was punctuated with engraved illustrations of various wares once the exhibitions came along.[19]

Even though Melbourne 1880 had more exhibits than Sydney, and was housed in a larger building, the gathering momentum of the exhibition movement took people by surprise. The buildings to be constructed in the Carlton Gardens were lopped by a third in the late planning stage, and it was only after the exhibition opened that it was decided to allow visitors to go up by hydraulic lift to promenade around the dome. The railways were slow to advertise concessional fares, slower in fact than Cobb & Co., which offered excursion coach-and-rail fares from Wilcannia. However Thomas Cook's sent out an agent from London to make arrangements for incoming tourists; they felt safer building up custom focused on an exhibition, a tactic they had employed successfully several times before. Meanwhile fears were expressed that hotel accommodation would be inadequate; there seems to have been no special hotel-building. One Fitzroy hotelier did advertise, however, that at his establishment 'English, French, German and Gaelic were spoken'. Special guidebooks appeared, and the pull of the exhibition was so great that in Adelaide it was cited as the reason for a 10 per cent dip in the local traffic to Glenelg.[20]

Melbourne was better prepared for the Centennial Exhibition of 1888. A cable tram now ran up Nicholson Street, and even local boarding-houses built extra wings in anticipation of increased patronage. Thomas Cook's now expanded their activities to set up a branch office, which they hoped would be ready in time to cope with an expanding local traffic. Meanwhile the Exhibition Buildings were enlarged by annexes, so that the complex now covered 14 hectares, as against the original 9; it was twice the size of Sydney 1879. Sydney's centennial celebrations, of necessity yoked to 26 January, had been caught in the lees of those for Queen Victoria's Jubilee; the Melbourne exhibition, conceded the *Daily Telegraph*, was 'essentially national and popular. It is truly a celebration by the people and for the people'. 'They are going in dozens, our sisters and cousins', began a verse in another Sydney paper. While there were

marble staircase and columns, took its cue from the recently opened Paris Opera; that foyer had facilitated display as never before. It was planned to extend the Federal so that it had more than 500 rooms, but before this eventuated the bubble burst.

At the other end of Melbourne, almost opposite Parliament House, the Grand Hotel had opened its doors in 1883, catering for visiting families and some of those just off the weekly steamers. Its modern features included two bathrooms on each floor, an electric bell in each room, and 'speaking tubes'—an early intercom system. At a time when good restaurants were scarce, the palatial dining room would have been a particularly notable feature. In 1886 the building became the Grand Coffee Palace: soon it doubled in size, to assume the profile which as the Windsor the building still has today. This too was done in expectation of visitors for the Centennial Exhibition. Now gas and electric light made their appearance, though not yet sewerage. At the opening a buoyant James Munro, one of the two main investors, is said to have burnt the place's liquor licence.

It was all show: the alliance between temperance and speculation, encapsulated in the coffee palace (for Munro was also behind the Federal) proved to be an insidious one. Munro crashed, and with him many people who had counted more on his respectability than on sufficient security. The establishment now became the Grand Hotel again, proud of offering 'all the luxurious surroundings of . . . a large [i.e. aristocratic] mansion'. This grandeur was sustained by lavish fittings and maintained by a staff of 100 servants. Today the Windsor—as it became in 1923—is the last of Australia's big nineteenth-century hotels. Unbidden, the travel writer James Morris (as she then was), described it as 'on the whole the most comfortable [hotel] I know'.[22]

Quality travel

Many of the clientele of the grand hotels would, as soon as the Depression began to lift in the mid-1890s, avail themselves of pleasure cruises—particularly when visiting Europe. On board ship they could mix with people of a similar social caste, forging friendships when they went ashore together. But how could this be done enjoyably in Australia? W. C. Ballard was pondering this problem, and the broader one of how to spend Easter without resorting to 'hackneyed old haunts', when a friend burst in and said he could show him how to 'have the combined pleasures of a sea trip, exquisite scenery, mountain climbs and places with never-dying associations connected with them, all within the compass of your means and leave'. The Union steamer *Manopouri* was off on a week-long cruise to Hobart via the old penal settlements.

Significantly, when Ballard turned up at Queen's Wharf in Melbourne, he found he knew quite a few of the passengers already; a company official deftly made further introductions. The party of 150 were soon 'on as familiar terms as would be a family gathering'. Bonding would be further achieved by the private printing of Ballard's account of the cruise, and by the activities of the shipboard photographer. When the party landed at Maria Island, the inhabitants turned out to see them and were duly photographed. But rather than provide a guide from what they thought of as their number, they delegated the only Chinese resident to show the visitors round. Since he was inclined to amble along, people struck out for themselves, taking in the 'ruinous' prisons and the more recent cement works.

Later that day they reached Port Arthur. At that stage the church alone was in ruins. It had been gutted by fire only a dozen years before but already, with 'its Gothic design and clinging ivy', the building conveyed a sense of antiquity. In the Penitentiary they found a guide who had been a convict. He explained, somewhat disconcertingly in the second person, that 'These little squares are to enable *you* to call the attention of the sentry on duty, and if *you* do so without sufficient cause *you* are taken to the yard in the morning and get a "dozen" (100 lashes) for trifling away the officer's valuable time'. Their sense of themselves was soon restored by a recital from the City of Hobart band, which had come to Port Arthur specially to entertain the passengers. However, they did not carry all before them. Moving on to the Model Prison, they found that nothing could induce the owner (a retired clergyman and MP) to allow them to look even briefly inside. 'It is a great pity',

The manner of genteel tourists on the Continent has been brought by these passengers on an 1893 cruise to Maria Island, Tasmania. Note how, for a privately printed account, 'the inhabitants' have been grouped on one side of an image and the tourists on the other. Maria Island's attractions already included convict ruins such as the old treadmill (top right).

grumbled Ballard, 'that the Government did not see its way to retain this very interesting relic of the penal system, for from the very nature of its history'—particularly now that people were familiar with Marcus Clarke's *His Natural Life*—'every visitor is anxious to see it, and if carefully looked after, it could have been made a permanent source of revenue'.[23]

WHAT IS STRIKING about Ballard's cruise is that it could almost have been conducted as what it substituted for: an upper-class cruise on the Aegean. On-shore tourist facilities were minimal. There was not yet the expectation of large numbers, in Tasmania or elsewhere. Beauty spots near big cities might draw the crowds, but even this would be largely on a daily basis. In 1912 labourers were paid seven shillings a day; this

The church, Port Arthur. The first building at the old penal settlement to be destroyed by fire, its resemblance to English ruins had conferred iconic status on it by 1900.

would have bought them one night's boarding-house accommodation, with a shilling over to cover meals and incidental expenses. Most visitors would have still been day trippers. For second class passengers, weekend railway excursion fares to Katoomba, introduced early in the 1880s, were less than a weekday single fare. Even so, this still would have taken the greater part of that labourer's daily wage.[24]

The age of mass tourism had clearly not yet come. Large numbers could be drawn to the big exhibitions, but then these were in one sense an intensification of urban life, involving minimal travel for many of the patrons, who clearly got into the habit of using them while they lasted as an additional amenity. Moreover, in the resorts there was some apprehension about the possibility of the 'working masses' being able to spend a weekend holiday there at minimum cost. More monied tourists, it was argued, might flee. The *Blue Mountains Echo*, editorialising on the subject, pointed out that the mountains, one of 'Nature's gifts', should be accessible to everyone, and damned the 'priggishness' of those who sought to sustain exclusivity.

The prospect of a tidal wave of the proletariat was more revealing of class prejudice than anything else. Holidays were still few and far between. One of the reasons the Glenelg celebrations were so popular was the happy fortuity of South Australia's anniversary falling in the middle of the festive season; people could mass together then in a way quite impossible at other times. In Sydney, workers in the 1870s received, in addition to Christmas Day and Good Friday—still regarded as being sacred and in a class of their own—New Year's Day, Anniversary Day (26 January), Easter Monday, the Queen's Birthday and Boxing Day. Individual trades had their picnic days, as some still do. ('A peculiarly Australian custom', asserts the *Australian Encyclopaedia*.) In Melbourne, more unions joined the Labour Day procession as they succeeded in gaining the eight-hour day. Only some salaried workers had won the right to paid annual leave when the twentieth century began. It was not until 1940 that workers generally became entitled to a week's paid holiday.[25]

Australia was still too far away in 1900 to expect much international traffic: Baedeker guides existed in English for America and Canada, but not for Australia or New Zealand. Meanwhile domestic tourism would not really get under way until leave conditions were much improved.

Messing About in Boats

WHILE AUSTRALIA HAD BEEN federated in 1901, most people still thought of it in Edwardian times as a British Dominion. The Royal Navy, which deliberately aimed at being twice the size of its nearest rival, was the guarantor of both Australia's defence and the Imperial connection. While King Edward VII himself rarely went near the water, except to the odd regatta, both a brother and his son and heir had naval careers—and had visited Australia in their ships. The British Empire was acknowledged to be a maritime one, and ships of all kinds were essential for communication and for maintaining its sea-lanes. In Australia ocean liners were complemented by coastal steamers, and these in turn by ferries. And often where there was no seacoast—and even where there was—people turned to rivers for regattas and a display of manly prowess on the water.

Henley and other regattas

The nineteenth century saw the steady growth of rowing as a sport. The first competitions between Oxford and Cambridge took place in the 1820s, and in 1839 a regatta was founded at Henley-on-Thames, the first to be sited on a river. Gradually racing eights took the lead from other boats; with the invention of sliding seats rowing became more dynamic, and the synchronised movement more spectacular. The sport quickly developed a following, at least among the elite, and by the end of the century there were complaints that 'its popularity may be its undoing, for the regatta has become one vast picnic'.

Australians took to rowing with avidity: a regatta was held in Melbourne in 1841, when the settlement was six years old, while it was the proud boast of the Victorian Rowing Association that it was the oldest such organisation in the world. New South Wales was not far behind, but it was in sculling (one oar for each hand) rather than racing eights that the state made its mark, producing a number of world champions at the turn of the century. Some even professed to discern a distinctive Australian style of rowing, characterised by short and quicker strokes.

The connections with English rowing are more striking now. The Fairbairn family of Victoria produced a famous Cambridge coach in the sport, and his brother—who had been a notable oarsman himself—was one of the three founders of Henley-on-the-Yarra in 1904. By the time of the third regatta in 1905, the *Argus* could assert that Henley was 'a water carnival to rank in aquatics as a fixture like the Melbourne Cup in racing, the final match of an English cricketing tour, or the Austral Wheel race in cycling'. The English Henley was very much the model, as it was for a number of regattas that sprang up around the world at this time: Shanghai ran its at a place soon called Henli. The Melbourne one was deliberately imitative, even to the names of the races and the facsimile trophies.

Nevertheless there were a number of additional factors working for its success. The recent straightening and broadening of the Yarra provided a suitable course for racing adjacent to the city (unlike Henley on the Parramatta River in New South Wales). At the same time, Government House provided a backdrop to a fashionable spectacle in what was then Australia's capital. Flags and pennants flapped in the breeze: Melbourne, as became a Dominion capital in a naval Empire, presented itself as shipshape.

Eight or ten houseboats stood by the shore, while people also stood on moored ferries and the bridges, or hired rowboats and decorated them; others sat on grassy banks. While the organised races took pride of place—there was much rhetoric about team spirit and 'self-sacrifice',

The original Henley, on the Thames (left)
Melbourne's maritime pageant, as it was in 1910 (below)
The Alice Springs parody, Henley-on-Todd: the essential dry river bed, the crews shooting along on other liquids (bottom).

and nearly 1400 men from Victorian rowing clubs would volunteer in World War I—they soon became merely the focus of various social activities. Girls were seen parading their new spring dresses in what was sometimes called 'Henley weather'; at night there would be fireworks displays, guests in evening dress, and bands playing.

Much as the Melbourne Cup still does—and by the same expedient of demarcated areas—Henley combined social cachet with being a genuinely popular festival. It is said that 300 000 attended in 1925. In 1933 there was the first Miss Henley competition; the following Henley saw the Duke of Gloucester make a royal progress on the water.

After World War II Henley declined sharply. The new Swan Street bridge bisected the traditional course, and while the opening day of the new Moomba Festival in 1955 was focused on a Henley, the day had become leached of meaning. Few people messed about in boats now. Car ownership had increased, and with it mobility and access to the beach.[1]

Nevertheless Henley had been the pinnacle of a boating culture. The smallest country towns had their rowing clubs, and bigger ones would run to a regatta, centred on the local boating club. At Warrnambool Proudfoot's Boathouse was described in 1894 as 'the most complete establishment of its kind in the colonies'. Built in three stages, it included a dock as well as an attached residence, and offered tourists not only boats by the hour, but free bait, a variety of fishing rods and other gear made on site, and mackintoshes in the event of wet weather. Proudfoot's functioned as a riverine entertainment centre.[2]

Ferries and steamers

A variety of pleasure craft were also available to the public. Ferry networks existed not only in Sydney, but across the Swan estuary at Perth, while in Queensland they connected the resorts on Moreton Bay. These were basically passenger services, but there were also frequent cruises for excursionists. Melbourne ran a ferry across to the industrial suburbs on the other side of Hobson's Bay, and even more notably sustained a network of small craft cruising up the Yarra and the Maribyrnong.

I HAVE JUST ARRIVED AT LAUNCESTON

I HAVE JUST ARRIVED AT SYDNEY

Gendered fantasies of arrival, Edwardian-style

At a time of frequent mail deliveries, few phones, and a new capacity to print photographic material (often in colour), postcard-collecting swept the world in the early 1900s. These two cards show how generalised images were earthed to particular localities—in one of these cases with tinsel.

There had been pleasure gardens along the Yarra before, but the opening of the Hawthorn Tea Gardens in 1898—further upstream than its pre-decessors—gave pleasure craft a clear destination. Above Dight's Falls there was for a time a second, smaller service that similarly aimed at a Fairfield tea-house and boathouse, Rudder Grange. The lesser Maribyrnong River took its first steamer in 1896 and, once a tramline reached it ten years later, a similar network—complete with tea garden—sprang up in this less fashion-able area. Although it might be said that the 1930s were the heyday of Mel-bourne's river ferries, by then they were essentially elaborating the pattern established in Edwardian times. An attempt to develop a regular passenger service to South Yarra was a failure; increasingly the ferries were marginalised, until after World War II they functioned largely as dance boats and were generally thought to be unsavoury.[3]

In addition to the river ferries there were the Bay steamers. 'One can go to Queenscliff by rail', wrote the well-known columnist The Vagabond, 'but very few people do so. The land journey, via Geelong, is more than double the distance of that by water, the expense is four times as great and the trip not half so pleasant'. Although Port Phillip Bay is rarely thought of in terms

In Edwardian times ferries were used for mass touristic transportation.

of its local steamers now, the *Hygeia*, specially built for the traffic, was said to be the fastest excursion ship in the world at the time, while the later *Weerona* was claimed to be the largest. Two of these steamers took some 150 000 passengers to Sorrento in just three years.

Steamers had been servicing the Bay since the 1850s, but the first to establish a regular first-class service to Queenscliff and Sorrento was the *Williams* in 1872. This paddlesteamer was specially refitted for the task, and became popular because of its promenade deck—complete with space for dancing—and its comfortable saloon. Soon there appeared on the scene the *Golden Crown*, which gave rise to fractious rivalry. Owned by a company in which the entrepreneur George Coppin had an interest, the *Golden Crown* was touted in the newspapers as 'having destroyed an illiberal monopoly', since it would take passengers of 'all classes' at reduced fares to Queenscliff and Sorrento—particularly to 'the most picturesque and convenient' Sorrento. The response was quick. The owners of the *Williams* advertised it as 'the excursionists' steamer par excellence', sneered at their rival's self-interested attempts to advance Sorrento, then brought down the return fare even further to five shillings. By 1914, on Saturdays and Tuesdays, it would be halved again.

Although regular services down the Bay ran all through the year, the excursion steamers were laid up during the winter, then drydocked around Melbourne Cup time in readiness for a season extending to Easter. People boarded them for a change of scene, for diversion, and for 'wholesome air or *lung food*', as one contemporary guidebook put it. Particularly popular were the trade picnics: often many more tickets were sold than the ship's licensed capacity would allow, which sometimes led to angry scenes as fathers, having allowed their family to go on board first, found themselves stranded on the dockside.

The most popular Bay steamer was the *Ozone*, first put on the run in 1886. Four years later she was joined by the *Hygeia*, a larger ship with elegant lines facilitating her considerable speed of more than 20 knots. A promenade deck ran almost her entire length, while novel facilities extended to a barber shop. In 1910, at the height of the excursion traffic, Huddart Parker added to their Bay fleet the *Weerona*, which was capable of carrying 1900 passengers. Even though Sorrento could be reached in two hours, she was fitted out with cabins in addition to the usual luxurious appointments, together with the novelty of an air-conditioned saloon.

There were eight excursion vessels on Port Phillip in 1910, seven in 1920, three in 1930, and only the *Weerona* and one other in 1940. Both went during World War II. Any postwar revival was crippled by the spread of car ownership.[4]

Day tripping: Queenscliff and Sorrento

Queenscliff had been the first resort to emerge: three steamers converged on it one day in 1855, letting loose a thousand people. A hotel had just opened its doors, and by 1861 there were five of them. High on a bluff just inside the Heads, the place was conspicuous for its commanding views and equable climate; it also possessed, in addition to its fishermen and pilot station, a military presence. Redcoats and an army band added to its pretensions, enunciated in the lists published in the local paper of gentlefolk staying at its large hotels. Adman's Grand, the most impressive, even called its largest space Assembly Rooms, in the old English style. Nevertheless guests would from time to time have to be warned of snakes lurking about.

Admans of the Grand also had interests in Bay steamers; George Baillieu found it expedient to rename his new hotel after the smart new paddlesteamer, the *Ozone*. So important was the Bay trade to the town that only one of its hotels, the Royal, was sited on the road in; the rest were placed close to the town's three piers.

Queenscliff was a place where people came to stay. In summer men would remain in town, and come down for a night or two at weekends on the 'Husbands' Boat'. There was hunting, and fishing, and a free public library with 2000 books in it, but no 'sights' in particular. Nevertheless, it gradually became democratised by sheer pressure of numbers.

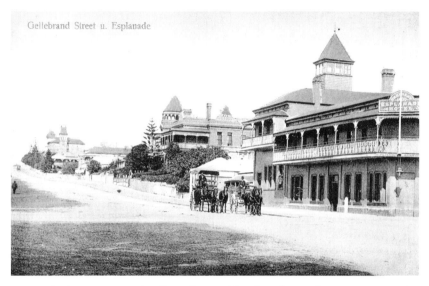

Gellebrand Street u. Esplanade

To meet the Bay steamer trade effectively, grand hotels and guest-houses sprang up close to the pier at Queenscliff (German-printed postcard, c. 1910).

While excursionists from steamers might not stay long, there was also the railway, which would bring day trippers—often in large groups—from Melbourne, Ballarat and beyond.

By Edwardian times Queenscliff had an air of static splendour. None of its half-dozen hotels had been built since the crash of the 1890s, and possibly only one of the half-dozen guest-houses. It was to quietly subside in importance until resurrected in the 1980s.[5]

Across the Heads lay Point Nepean and Sorrento, remembered for having been the location of the first abortive white settlement in Victoria. By the 1860s both limeburners and retired public figures had discovered the place, sheltered from the southerly winds, while George Coppin, the famous theatrical entrepreneur, moved from dreaming of a holiday home there to advancing it as a full-fledged resort. It was he who publicised the name Sorrento for the locality, and who ferried down a group of businessmen to assess its potential as 'the nucleus of a large and important city'.

Unlike that of Queenscliff, the development of Sorrento was, if scarcely systematic, then certainly the continued elaboration of one man's scheme. Coppin invested in steamers to take people there, floating one company in 1874, and then the more famous Bay Excursion Company Limited, which had the *Ozone* built and launched. Another Coppin company built the Continental Hotel, with its marble staircase and concert hall available for balls. Such is the desire of tourists to have fashionable surroundings that twelve years after the Continental had been built, another £1000 was added to the initial cost of £12 000 to have it refurbished. Guests and others might swim in the baths—another Coppin venture like the Sorrento Tramway Company, which took people to the Back Beach. Here was the Ocean Amphitheatre, where a trust created by Coppin had cleared the tea-tree, laid out walks and built rotundas. Overall—despite the normal activities of a land developer—Coppin seems to have lost money in these ventures, but he had the satisfaction of having virtually created the town, and the foresight to get much of the Back Beach declared a reserve. That also kept out any competition.

Sorrento was geared to the steamer traffic. In 1892 its population was a mere 246 people, doubling in summer. The arrival of one steamer would treble that again, and there could be as many as three or four at the jetty at one time. Porters would turn up with the names of the hotels or guest-houses emblazoned on their caps, and wagonettes to hand; meals would be held back till the passengers arrived. The majority, down for the day, would catch the steam tram (in off-peak times pulled by horses) to the Back Beach; 60 000 were said to have done so in a record season. And so things proceeded until World War I, when the educator Alexander Leeper found it 'an awfully cockneyfied place'. In addition to its two hotels, Sorrento had eleven guest- and boarding-houses in 1915, but only five in 1920.[6]

Networking by water

Beyond Port Phillip Heads, there were other ferry networks operating on Westernport Bay and radiating from the Gippsland Lakes. A line of steamers serviced Victorian west coast ports, in much the same way as a passenger service catered for Geelong. But beyond these local services spread a whole network. People could sail on coastal steamers from Melbourne to Queensland's Great Barrier Reef, or (as many did) to Western Australia. Ships sailed from one Tasmanian port or another for the mainland almost every day. From Adelaide, one could travel by the Adelaide Steamship Company not only to the South Australian gulf ports, but as far west as Wyndham in Western Australia and as far north as Cooktown, Queensland. A train journey to Murray Bridge might also be made to connect with the paddlesteamers patrolling the Murray–Darling basin.

From 1901 passenger accommodation on Australian coastal shipping doubled, to reach its zenith of just over 17 000 berths in 1914, when twenty-seven ships (excluding Tasmanian services) provided some 350 interstate departures. 'Travel in the colonies', declared Cook's as late as 1910, 'is still done largely by steamer'.

There were a number of reasons why this seemed to be so. First, the railway networks were not yet complete; it could still be time-consuming to travel even along the coast. Thus, in 1905, the Illawarra & South Coast Steam Navigation Company ran a service to Eden four times a week, and seven years later the Western Australian government founded a State Shipping Service to connect the small townships of its long coastline. Elsewhere, though, intra-state services were already beginning to do battle with the improved communications that followed closer settlement. Second, the interstate Australian steamers increasingly offered a comfort and stability comparable with that of ocean liners, and by 1912 a number of them were similar in size to ships on the England–Australia run. Third, the coastal steamers had not only sometimes undercut the local fares of the international shipping companies but, with an early appreciation of the principles of niche marketing, had come to offer a wide variety of facilities and fares on the same vessel. In 1914, for example, a ship on the Melbourne–Fremantle run, the *Dimboola*, offered fares at £11 return saloon class, and only £4 return for third class passengers.[7]

Tasmania: prime tourist destination

Bass Strait was notorious for its rough crossings: one publicist delicately alluded to seasickness as *mal de mer* to reassure his readers that in summer it was usually quite calm. By Edwardian times ships had become faster—the *Loongana* did the crossing to Launceston in fifteen and a half hours. A later rail extension to the docks meant that passengers could transfer to the train immediately, and be in Hobart within six hours. Fares had dropped too, so that for middle-class people such as public servants, who from 1902 enjoyed three weeks annual leave, Tasmania was a desirable destination. In 1900, tourist numbers at 10 000 had dropped to almost half of what they were in 1890; by 1905 they were 20 000, to be doubled by 1912. With some justice Tasmanians thought of their island as holding the 'premier position' in Australia as a 'pleasure resort', so in this discussion of Edwardian tourism it is worth a digression.[8]

From as far away as India, Tasmania sought to be known as the 'sanitorium' of Australia—even though Hobart had had a substantial number of typhoid deaths in the 1890s. Testimonials from medicos appeared in early guidebooks, while the image of the 'Premier Health Resort of the Australian Colonies' was boosted by the recovery experienced there by an ailing governor of Queensland. In fact, a lot of the talk of its healthy climate masked a nostalgia for things English, for England was still 'Home' for the Edwardians. Although the photographer J. W. Beattie was initiating a response to the island's own wild beauties and its tortured history, even the Port Arthur church could be seen as 'Australia's Glastonbury' by those intent on seeking climatic asylum from the excesses of the mainland summer.[9]

The Hobart Regatta was the peak of the season, and had traditionally been held on the anniversary of the discovery of the island. It had now come to honour both Abel Tasman and its founder, Sir John Franklin—two famous navigators—and was a kind of national celebration. Encoded in the display was again a hint of martial readiness, and indeed Tasmanians would be chosen to row the boats at Gallipoli. For a time in

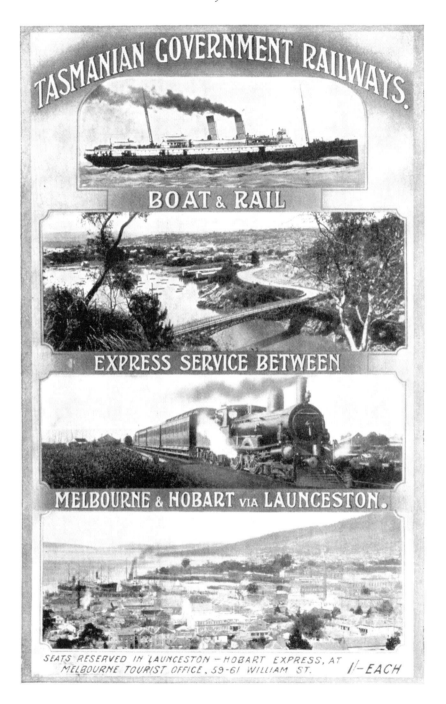

the Edwardian period the regatta was actually held on Australia Day. The Governor-General usually came down from Melbourne, while a naval squadron always contrived to be in port. Social climbers appeared too, hoping to effect an entry into circles that might be closed elsewhere.[10]

A more local sense of community was also evident in the first organised responses to tourist traffic. Launceston, eager to detain visitors who might otherwise speedily move on to Hobart, formed an Improvement Association in 1889 and began to develop Cataract Gorge as a resort. A similar organisation appeared shortly afterwards in Hobart, but failed; it was only after the Premier, Henry Dobson, took alarm at the fall-off in tourists as a consequence of the Depression that he initiated the Tasmanian Tourist Association in 1893. Dobson was to remain its president until 1914, effectively forming a coalition with J. W. Beattie, a tireless publicist for Tasmania. In 1896 Beattie became government photographer; in 1899 his images of the island's natural beauties went forth on a series of pictorial stamps, the second such set in the world.

In a context of limited government assistance, such improvisation and practicality typified the approach of the TTA. Although some government officials were permanent members of its committee, they were there to bring expertise to what was seen to be essentially a civic task, that of making Tasmania more attractive to tourists. So band concerts were organised, as well as tracks cut and shelters and benches constructed for tourist use; there was also much signposting. From its Tourist Bureau, the TTA organised drives and excursions inland, and publicised places such as Lake Hartz, deep in the wilderness; for the less adventurous it would book cruises on adjacent waterways. Its most ambitious venture, a carnival in 1910, included everything from the usual nautical activities to boomerang-throwing, woodchopping, literary competitions, and what was billed as Australia's first historical pageant. The carnival was a failure: a coal strike restricted shipping.[11]

The development of Mt Wellington demonstrates how the Edwardian taste for shady fern glades and clean mountain air was catered for by locals who saw tourism partly as an opportunity to show some civic pride. For some time young men had built huts on the slopes, making

All their own work: male sylvan idyll, Mt Wellington

them as sophisticated as native materials (sometimes augmented by linoleum) would allow. People went to see them, and to enjoy the facilities constructed by TTA working bees; they might also attend the organisation's annual strawberry feast at Fern Tree Bower. In all this there had been no direct help from the government or the city council, but tourist numbers on the mountain quadrupled in the five years to 1907. A large hotel went up at the Springs the following year.[12]

One of the frontiers of Edwardian tourism was Tasmania's north-west coast. As the great forests were cut down and the tide of settlement moved inland—with two places being named after Bass Strait steamers —the first guidebook appeared, laying out the landscape for the tourist's delectation. Infusing this was a sense of achievement: no hamlet was too small for inclusion. Besides, colonial traditions were such that you could get a cup of tea almost anywhere, even if at a nominated house, where you might have to pay for it.

After the turn of the century, publicists would describe the coast as the 'Switzerland' or 'the Riviera' of Australia, appropriations on which they had no monopoly. Behind these rotating clichés lay the fact that the

The hotel at Penguin, on the north-west coast, Tasmania. This publicity card helped to draw people like Tom Roberts to the district's scenic and sporting amenities. Note how the hotel has doubled in size in little more than a generation.

new local progress associations had little to offer beyond a confidence in the local scenery and their own good life. The listed attractions of Penguin, a popular place where the artist Tom Roberts spent his honeymoon, ran to fishing, shooting and boating (together with sea-fishing), all things the locals might indulge in themselves. Nevertheless they were right for the time: the extension of the railway and steamer services direct to Melbourne brought a marked increase in visitors.[13]

'THE TOURIST', stated a guidebook around 1905, 'does not consider his visit to Tasmania complete unless he "does" Port Arthur'. Officially the place was Carnarvon, and had been so since 1877, in an attempt to expunge its convict associations. Moreover the Tasmanian government had not only sold off as many of the ruins as it could, but had originally in 1889 made demolition a condition of sale, until persuaded otherwise by a petition signed by 100 locals and some Hobart notables. These people were aware of the commercial value of the site, for there had in fact been parties of tourists to the area even during the convict period. Some were day trippers by steamer, but one of the sights for those who stayed overnight was to view the criminal physiognomy of the sleeping prisoners.

By the early 1900s there was a real ambiguity in Tasmanian attitudes. Tourist curiosity in the place was encouraged by J. W. Beattie who, in addition to his photographs and postcards, compiled the first popular account of Port Arthur. He also opened a convict-era museum in Hobart, a great attraction for tourists from visiting ocean liners. J. Walch & Sons, too, republished popular books from the convict days. But guide-books were much more equivocal, even if they were not so heavily in denial mode regarding the convict past as their Victorian predecessors had been. A flyer for a steamer devoted as much space to the peninsula's impressive natural features as it did to the ivy-clad church and other ruins; mention was made of Marcus Clarke's *[For the Term of] His Natural Life*, the most popular Australian novel of the day. This was an encoded way of referring to the convict past and moving on. Sometimes guide-books simply referred to the splendid oaks and elms, and left it at that. One visitor in 1918—possibly the first to declare Port Arthur 'Australia's only *bona fide* ruin'—managed to convince herself that it almost seemed like an old monastery. Others seized on the 'romantic' quality of the Isle of the Dead, the settlement's cemetery, sometimes venturing the name in bad French, *Isle des Morts*. One 1912 guidebook contained a long poem full of pathos about the island, but could not bring itself to identify any of the nearby ruins.

On the ground, though, a 'horror tradition' was firmly in place. Guides elaborated their stories; others scarcely had to. One charged a shilling to remove his shirt, so that people could see the scars from floggings. A Tasmanian distaste for the place was thereby sustained; as late as the 1950s there were people who wanted to see the ruins bull-dozed. Even in Edwardian times mainland interest in Port Arthur may have exceeded Tasmanian, as is still the case. But recognising its poten-tial for the local economy, in 1914 the state government began a pro-gramme of resuming control of the site.[14]

IN EDWARDIAN TIMES Tasmania also traded as 'the Angler's paradise'. A popular tourist spot was the Salmon Ponds near New Norfolk: here English trout and salmon were, in 1864, successfuly hatched in Australia for the first time, and disseminated throughout the region. There was some doubt at first as to whether the salmon—then the main concern —had taken to their new environment. The trout were found by English anglers at first to be leaden and unsporting, fish with no fight in them, since they were used to being fed in hatcheries. They were also declared to be muddy to the taste.

But from the time that Governor Hamilton landed his 28-pound trout in the 1880s—a record unbroken for seventy years—anglers would track many a wild stream in the hope of finding fresh pools of giant trout. As early as 1870 some fishermen had taken a billycan of tiddlers up to the Great Lake, where they thrived; by 1905 the average size of the catch was 9 pounds. Shortly afterwards, with an eye to the main railway line, the government built a chalet at Interlaken, well to the east; but, though it was commended as a sanitorium, there was no prospect of its attracting fishermen. Those who came that way spurned the three-pounders of Lake Sorell and Lake Crescent, and headed straight for the Great Lake, even though its main accommodation house slept only ten. From Deloraine mainlanders would go there, first by coach and then by packhorse, with guide. Even before World War I broke out, the combined exertions of local municipalities, tourist associations, the Northern Tasmanian Fisheries Association (the first in Australia), and a new power in the land—the state Automobile Club— had prevailed upon the government to replace the track with a road.

After the war the focus shifted, to the southern outlet of the Great Lake. Here a new dam in 1916, and the much larger one of 1922, had had an unanticipated effect. Water now poured into the Shannon, attracting the Snowflake Caddis moth. This would breed only in fast-flowing water, of which there was now lots, and around the end of November something like a white cloud would be seen to hover over the river as the moths hatched and took wing. This brought the trout, which would rise out of the water to catch them. That in turn brought the anglers—challenged by the need for skilful casting, all the more so as the moths would get in their eyes, ears and clothing. The rewards were great: fish were measured by beer bottles—some scoring a length of two and a half. Indeed, in 1937 it was declared that any fish less than 15 inches long would have to be returned. Some fishermen came from Britain, but the Shannon Rise never attracted great numbers, for the race between Miena Dam and the lagoon was only about two-thirds of a mile long. By 1964 it was all over: the Hydro-Electric Commission had diverted all the outflow from the Great Lake to the north. As one Tasmanian official put it, 'What the Hydro giveth, the Hydro taketh away'.[15]

P & O and ocean liners

The sea that separated Tasmania from the rest of the country also connected Australia with the rest of the world. Until the completion of the Overland telegraph in 1872, even the speediest news to reach the colonies from Europe was slowed down for at least part of the journey by having to come by ship. Even when this was no longer so, the two most famous companies operating the run were in 1888 compelled by the British Post Office to arrange their timetables so that between them they offered a weekly sailing to Australia.

Apart from P & O and the Orient Line, there were a number of companies in the Edwardian era offering Australian services. There was the White Star Line, a pioneer in one class travel; the Aberdeen Line and Shaw Savill Albion, both of which sailed round the Cape; and the Union Line, which sailed to Canada and offered speedy connections to England in an 'All-red route' (the colour of the British Empire then on maps of the world), thus avoiding the intense heat of the Red Sea. Other shipping lines connected Australia with New Zealand, the Pacific islands, the United States, China and Japan.

In addition, there were two foreign lines offering Europeans monthly sailings to and from Australia. The first of these was Messageries Maritimes, a French company that in 1881 first visited Australian ports as it

130. MELBOURNE — Princes Bridge (sur le Yarra)

A French postcard of Melbourne, published by Messageries Maritimes. If cards were posted on board ship, French stamps could be used.

serviced New Caledonia and other French colonies. Although there were much larger ships on the run, its five steamers were admired—not least for the cuisine offered, which extended to table wines and cognac supplied gratis to first class, with free claret for second and third. The second foreign company was German, Norddeutscher Lloyd, which began sailing to Australia in 1885. Although its ships appeared no more frequently than the French, they made a much greater impact: NDL, which operated a trans-Atlantic service, simply transferred some of its large ships from that run when it was summer in the southern hemisphere and winter in the northern. By having few ships specifically tied to the Australia service, the company was able to deploy its whole fleet to maximum effect—and to make a point about German power as well. Its largest ship, the *Grosser Kurfürst*, by far the largest seen to that time in Australian waters, was put on the run to cater for the coronation trade in 1911. Many people loyally making the journey 'Home' must have wondered what these large German ships might portend. But for the moment they could enjoy the comforts made possible by the ships' massive superstructures, and experience what was in effect a floating Continental hotel. NDL sailings were popular, and for a time boosted interstate travel by sea.[16]

The name most people associated with international shipping lines, however, was the Peninsular and Oriental Steam Navigation Company, P & O, the first of the major companies to sail to Australia and increasingly the most dominant until the end of the steamship era.

In 1834 P & O began sailing to Spain and Portugal, the Iberian being the Peninsula of its title; the house flag still incorporates the colours of the Spanish and Portuguese merchant flags of the time. Extending its services first to India (which at the time necessitated negotiating the Suez by an overland route), the company soon extended its operations to China. It was from Singapore that P & O first entered Australian waters, having won in 1852 the mail contract to colonies growing vigorously after the discovery of gold.

Mail contracts were to remain a significant element in the company's operations. An important source of revenue—worth £2 million in payouts for 1905 and 1906—at times they were the tail that wagged the P & O dog. The 1888 contract not only imposed a rationalised alternation with Orient Line services, but paid at a rate per pound of letters carried, 'leaving the Contractor all the *certainty* of an enormous expenditure, and all the *uncertainty* of what the postal revenue might prove to be'. P & O increased receipts by taking small cargoes of luxury goods as well as passengers, but a basic tension remained: the greater speed increasingly demanded by mail contracts not only cost more to effect in coal consumption, but sometimes ran the risk of adding to passenger discomfort. Nevertheless the times became faster and faster, even as payments for the service lessened. A number of smaller lines carrying mail collapsed, but P & O survived because it was more broadly based. Moreover the company was able to guarantee a reliability of service given its capacity to replace any ailing vessel relatively easily.[17]

The P & O fleet was vast: some 63 ships in 1906. Even in 1946, having sustained the depredations of two world wars, the company was still the largest shipping organisation in the world. By that stage Britain had lost its easy dominance of global shipping, which had been highest in 1890 when its early industrialisation facilitated a considerable lead in the construction of iron-clad steamships. So great was the margin through-out the Edwardian period that the British percentage of world shipping still stood at 41.1 at the outbreak of war in 1914.

These were Imperial ships, patrolling the primary axis of a maritime empire. Nearly all the ports they visited were under British rule, and some of the steamers contained gun platforms built to naval specifi-cations—with a special subsidy—so that they could be turned into troop carriers or armed merchant cruisers at short notice. At the height of Empire-consciousness they had borne such grand names as *Britannia* or *Oceana*, a name made popular by the title of the best-selling account of a tour to Australia and other settlement colonies by J. A. Froude in 1886. And while the Australian service was recognised long before the end of the nineteenth century as P & O's premier route, it was the Indian antecedents of the company that helped to preserve these liners as floating bits of the British Empire almost to the end. The crisp white uniforms of the ship's officers suggested discipline and an affinity with the navy, while the Goanese waiters and the lascars in their smart blue tunics and red turbans replicated on board the racial hierarchy of India. (The once common expression 'head sherang', Hindustani for bosun or head man, probably came to Australia with P & O.) Moreover P & O sought to maintain its standards by carrying no third class passengers, at least on the main line.[18]

By the beginning of the new century passengers were carried to Aus-tralia relatively swiftly. Whereas in 1873 the journey took forty-eight days, and could be taken by P & O only once a month, by 1898 the com-pany's ships set out once a fortnight and, to satisfy the mail contract, had to reach Melbourne in thirty-one days and six hours—only four or five days longer than the same trip took in the 1960s.

Passenger numbers rose too. Surviving records are patchy, but it is known that the Orient Line took some 9000 passengers to Colombo and Australia in 1900, and some 22 000 in 1912. While some of these would not have reached Australia at all, and others would have been

Australians returning home, the drift is made even clearer by the steady growth in the size and passenger-carrying capacity of the ships.

It was in this period that the P & O fleet used regularly on the Australia run had greater homogeneity than at any other time. Between 1903 and 1912 the company commissioned ten new liners for the Australian service. These, while varying in size, bore a considerable resemblance to each other and were referred to as the 'M' class: the names chosen for these ships all began with that letter. They grew progressively larger. The first, the *Moldavia*, had been 9500 tons; the *Maloja*, one of the last, was 12 431 tons. By the time the *Medina* came back on the run, having been specially chartered to take King George V and Queen Mary to India for the Delhi Durbar, P & O decided that since the Australian run now had nine new steamers—enough to sustain the service—one could even be taken away and profitably used elsewhere.

Such a fleet was necessary as competition was keen on the Australian route. In 1913 Messageries Maritimes advertised some higher return

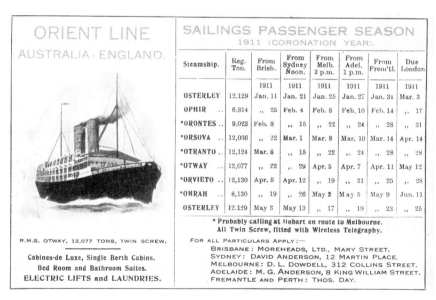

ORIENT LINE
AUSTRALIA - ENGLAND.

R.M.S. OTWAY, 12,077 TONS, TWIN SCREW.

Cabines-de Luxe, Single Berth Cabins.
Bed Room and Bathroom Suites.
ELECTRIC LIFTS and LAUNDRIES.

SAILINGS PASSENGER SEASON
1911 (CORONATION YEAR).

Steamship.	Reg. Ton.	From Brisb.	From Sydney Noon.	From Melb. 3 p.m.	From Adel. 1 p.m.	From Frem'tl.	Due London
		1911	1911	1911	1911	1911	1911
OSTERLEY	12,129	Jan. 11	Jan. 21	Jan. 25	Jan. 27	Jan. 31	Mar. 3
OPHIR ..	6,814	,, 25	Feb. 4	Feb. 8	Feb. 10	Feb. 14	,, 17
*ORONTES ..	9,023	Feb. 8	,, 15	,, 22	,, 24	,, 28	,, 31
*ORSOVA ..	12,036	,, 22	Mar. 1	Mar. 8	Mar. 10	Mar. 14	Apr. 14
*OTRANTO ..	12,124	Mar. 8	,, 15	,, 22	,, 24	,, 28	,, 28
*OTWAY ..	12,077	,, 22	,. 29	Apr. 5	Apr. 7	Apr. 11	May 12
*ORVIETO ..	12,130	Apr. 5	Apr. 12	,, 19	,, 21	,, 25	,. 28
*OMRAH ..	8,130	,, 19	,, 26	May 3	May 5	May 9	Jun. 11
OSTERLEY	12,129	May 3	May 13	,, 17	,, 19	,, 23	,, 25

* Probably calling at Hobart en route to Melbourne.
All Twin Screw, fitted with Wireless Telegraphy.

FOR ALL PARTICULARS APPLY:—
BRISBANE : MOREHEADS, LTD., MARY STREET.
SYDNEY : DAVID ANDERSON, 12 MARTIN PLACE.
MELBOURNE : D. L. DOWDELL, 312 COLLINS STREET.
ADELAIDE : M. G. ANDERSON, 8 KING WILLIAM STREET.
FREMANTLE AND PERTH : THOS. DAY.

This Orient Line publicity postcard indicates the frequency of sailings on the Britain–Australia run. This was in effect doubled by the running of a P & O vessel each alternate week.

fares than P & O, but Norddeutscher Lloyd charged exactly the same first class fare, £71. The Orient Line charged a little less—but then its passengers had to share the ship with those in third class, who paid less than half these fares. Profits, while solid, were therefore not inclined to rise: facilities had to be updated to meet passenger expectations, while the Post Office's demands for increased speed boosted coaling costs. In 1888 P & O posted profits of £159 262; in 1901 (after three better years) £184 015.[19]

The great fear, kept at bay by discipline, constant emergency drill by the crew, and the occasional sounding of emergency bells to summon passengers to assembly points to participate in emergency drill themselves, was that there might be some disaster at sea. In 1905 an Orient Line steamer, the *Orizaba*, ran aground near Rottnest Island, Western Australia; a major disaster was averted. Quite otherwise was the case of the Blue Anchor steamer *Waratah*, which in 1909 simply disappeared without trace off the South African coast, on its second return run to England from Australia. It seems that the *Waratah*, which had something of the reputation of a 'hoodoo ship', may have been top-heavy; at any rate she took all hands, some 200 people.

A shipping disaster of this magnitude was so contrary to the image of speed and stately comfort that the Blue Anchor Line simply could not sustain it. People took their bookings elsewhere, with the result that the company was soon sold to P & O. The line to Australia via the Cape was still serviced, indeed with five new ships, but it was now known as the P & O Branch Line—so that it would not be confused with the main line via India. And it was very different. Here P & O was happy to provide a service for emigrants and, in an inversion of its main-line ships policy, have third class only. Taking out settlers would be the main purpose of the outward voyage; holds filled with cargo would sustain the return.[20]

Until World War II one of the great divisions in Australian society was between people who had made the trip 'Home' and those who had not. This of course would have applied even more sharply in reverse, although in Britain other more brutal determinants of class would have been evident first. Suffice it to say that in 1913 even the very cheapest return fare by Orient Line, which might have procured you a bunk in an overheated cabin near the ship's engines, would at £32 have been twenty or thirty times a labourer's weekly wage in London.

Hence although a correspondent for the *Illustrated London News* could write in 1895 that 'A voyage to Australia nowadays is so ordinary an occurrence' that copy could no longer be made of the commonplace, the experience had become routinised only for members of a limited class. These the P & O *Pocket Book* series addressed directly, singling out 'the tired statesman', 'the overworked professional man' or a bishop engaging in a tug-of-war for particular mention. Businessmen were also named, but prestige generally still lay elsewhere. Commercial imperatives were perceived as being of such secondary importance that effective isolation on board ship, away from 'daily letters and telegrams', was paraded as a virtue. Present too was the notion of the ocean voyage as a cure. It was suggested that not every middle-aged man was up to mountaineering, or grouse-shooting, or salmon-fishing. 'Indeed', the 1888 *Pocket Book* advised, 'the attempt to recruit an exhausted nervous system by violent muscular exercise . . . too often leads to an attack of acute disease'. For such people, the 'rest' offered by an ocean voyage could be most beneficial.

The Pocket Books also provided a thumbnail sketch of Australia for the more regular tourist. What is striking about the account by Hume Nesbit, reprinted in the 1900 edition as though the country had changed little since its first printing in 1888, is how anglocentric a view it was. Adelaide and Tasmania receive particular mention, as replications of the mother country, while part of the countryside around Albany, 'an ideal colonial township', is likened to 'the plains of Surrey'. Order, and familiarity: at the height of Empire British travellers wanted their view of the world confirmed, not simply to pass unchallenged as most tourists do. But by the time of the 1908 edition of the *Pocket Book,* Australia had become federated and some acknowledgement of difference was necessary. So Beatrice Grimshaw, an Irishwoman who became an enthusiast for Australasia and ended up living in New Guinea, was on hand to explain that whereas whites in tropical colonies became 'hopelessly listless and indolent', the Australian-born were 'as energetic as one might wish'. P & O passengers were told that, in Adelaide as elsewhere, they would notice 'tall, thin, wiry men, sharp-eyed and keen of look, yet curiously leisurely of demeanour'. American space and freedom thrived under a Mediterranean climate, 'the strong British infusion colouring the whole'. This was, Grimshaw stated, 'a nation in the making'.

In the meantime, from one port to the next, the P & O vessel functioned as a temporary home for the passenger—or a bolthole, if the Indian and Red Sea ports proved overwhelming. By the 1880s P & O and Orient Line ships were described as 'floating hotels', and there were journalists who were prepared to say that, given their comfort and convenience, this was almost an understatement. When the *Oceana* was launched in 1888, the largest ships were symbols of technological progress, and facilities had to match. So this ship contained patent spring beds and folding lavatories, superior ventilation and marble baths, as well as the still novel electric light and refrigeration. Conditions were constantly being improved. In 1927 the chairman of P & O, Lord

The bands played (even if over loudspeakers) and the paper umbilical cords tautened, then snapped, as people left Australia for the great adventure overseas. Streamers were more popular here than anywhere else.

Inchcape, attributed the company's small profit margins to the demands for greater luxury. He pointed out that the cost of staying in a luxury hotel was more than two-thirds of that for the maximum first class fare to Sydney for the same period. Even so, as late as 1952 the company recognised that 'passengers pay their fare with the expectation of being more (not less) comfortable and better (not worse) looked after than they are in their own homes. It is the Company's aim to see that these expectations are fulfilled'. Meanwhile the stewards actually serving passengers would drily refer to unreasonable complaints as 'Titti-fa-la'.

Cocooned in conditions of relative luxury, shipboard life nonetheless had its own rituals and observances. At mealtimes, often in splendidly panelled dining rooms, people sat at a designated table unless invited to dine with the captain. The two classes were kept separate: rigidly at the end of the steamship era, more implicitly in days of clearer social gradation, interaction then perhaps extending to a first class 'at home' offered to second class passengers or, on the Orient Line, athletics competitions between the (fitter) second and third classes.

The public framework was sustained by the ethos of a ruling race, and intended to dampen down or contain public excess or private indulgence. It was recognised that, in the words of an Orient Line souvenir, 'Many life partnerships have resulted from the meeting on board during the first day of the voyage'. The illustration was dominated by the image of a middle-aged man promenading with a young woman —an alliance apparently endorsed—while at the deckrails a young man was giving a girl the glad eye; she remained turned away from his gaze. What is striking now is that even shipboard games, of which there were many, were all formalised by sets of rules, so that in deck quoits the small rings of rope were thrown, four at a time, at a numbered board from twelve paces if you were male, eleven if female, the game being played in singles or doubles.

People were, of course, free to follow whichever amusements they wished. Ships had lounges, a library, a music room and a smoking room. The last, with its upholstered furniture, papers and cigars, functioned as the shipboard gentlemen's club. The ship's newspaper informed passen-

gers of card tournaments, dances and balls, including those in fancy
dress, with many costumes ingeniously devised on the voyage (and some
specially brought on board). Later, the arrival of swimming pools gave a
fillip to the old ceremony of Crossing the Line, when King Neptune
dunked those crossing the equator for the first time.[21]

Since 1887 P & O's main competitor had been the Orient Line,
which alternated its fortnightly sailings to Australia so that between
them—for the benefit of the mails—they maintained a weekly service.
In the 1890s the Orient kept nine ships on the Australian run. One of its
ships, the *Ophir*, was used for the royal tour of 1901, and another new
one a year later, the *Orontes*, was larger than any P & O vessel for a considerable time. The standing of the line was high, but financially it was
shaky. In 1894 the company did not declare a dividend, and a later
merger with the Royal Mail Company also proved unsatisfactory. When
the Orient Line re-emerged in its own right in 1909, it began to rebuild
its fleet. Five large new ships appeared in as many months, with another
two following in the next few years. With P & O continuing to launch
new ships in its M Class, the liners on the England–Australia run were
more modern than they had ever been, before or since.

The Orient Line was popular with Australians, for it was less self-
consciously British than P & O. Specialising in taking third class—and in
that way avoiding too direct competition with P & O—the Orient was
also obliged, by the Merchant Shipping Act, to have its emigrant ships
manned by all-white crews, again unlike P & O. (This also made it more
susceptible to stowaways, some of whom had friends in the crew.) Nor
did the Orient Line call in to India: its route ran straight from the Red
Sea to Fremantle, via Colombo. Australians felt it was their line, and
were glad that it wasn't so insistent on dressing for dinner.

Nevertheless the Orient Line was concerned to develop a tourist
traffic to Australia, and in 1928 a brochure identified four main kinds of
British traveller. The first two consisted of businessmen who wished to
expand their operations, and people intent on settling there—including
fathers who wished to explore possibilities for their sons. Both of these
categories would need some special assistance, but the third, 'the

Empire Tourist', would be 'content with a general survey of the various phases of Australian life'. Finally came 'the sun seeker and his family, who travel to avoid unpleasant climatic conditions in their own country'. These pleasure-seekers, the nearest of the four categories to the modern tourist, would 'according to their age and tastes . . . require amusement', and a variety of activities from golf and surfbathing to dances and up-country life were commended, along with 'motor touring through interesting country but of not too strenuous a nature'.[22]

The inter-war period saw considerable changes in the operations of both companies. Each had suffered greatly during World War I, six of P & O's M-class ships having been sunk; the Orient Line similarly lost four vessels. But the Orient's financial difficulties facilitated some timely rationalisation, once P & O acquired a controlling share in the company in 1919. When the *Orama* was launched in 1924, it carried first and third class passengers only, more clearly avoiding direct competition with P & O's first and second. Meanwhile P & O had, the year before, launched its first ships over 20 000 tons, the third *Mooltan* and the second *Maloja*; each was notable for its spacious and airy cabins, for the ships had been designed to provide portholes for all of them. Another welcome change was a 'veranda' right across the bridge, complete with glass screens that could be folded back in good weather—necessary because air-conditioning remained primitive. Nevertheless these ships were modern in that they ran on fuel oil instead of the traditional coal.

In 1928 P & O included a third class section on one of its ships for the first time, and in 1936 two such ships were refitted entirely as 'tourist class'. The stage was set for the type of travel that survived till the end of regular sailings. There were the British £10 migrants, the balance of their fare paid by the Australian government, coming out one way, and sometimes returning after the statutory two years required in Australia to avoid refunding passage money, effectively turning themselves into tourists. And, going the other way, were Australians more obviously embarking on a working holiday in England—though some of these did not come back. It was the culture that sustained Barry McKenzie,

*As the mass passenger traffic fell away by
the early 1970s, P & O began to trade on
romance at sea.*

among others—and in the original comic strip of the mid-1960s he
arrived in England by sea.[23]

But when the subsequent film was released in 1972, Bazza arrived in
England at Heathrow: the jumbo jet killed off P & O regular sailings
very quickly. Initially people had persuaded themselves that air travel
might actually assist the shipping lines, since people would probably

prefer to sail one way and fly the other, halving the time and having a sea holiday. Sir William Currie, at the launch of the *Canberra* in 1960, actually went so far as to say, 'I really believe passenger ships will . . . become convalescent homes for the weary air travellers.' But this was fanciful. The *Canberra*, launched by Dame Pattie Menzies, at 45 733 tons was the largest P & O liner ever, but it was also the last to be built for the run. Whereas in 1965 it was still cheaper for a family to sail to Europe than to fly, by 1967 P & O found it could no longer compete on fares alone. The *Canberra* would soon be a dinosaur, useful only for cruises and for ferrying troops in 1982 to the Falklands, the last Imperial war.

Although P & O had taken full control of the Orient Line in 1960, so that the joint enterprise was styled P & O – Orient Lines, the merger came too late to bring any real benefit. Talk of the company endeavouring 'to keep British shipping supreme', declared as the *Canberra* stood in the slipway, was quickly forgotten. Rising costs and intensified competition from the airlines resulted in greater diversification, so that by 1973 passenger liners accounted for only 5 per cent of the group's assets, and six liners were disposed of in three years. Today a few P & O ships still sail in Australian waters, but on cruises only.[24]

3

The Rise and Fall of the Tourist Bureau

THE IMAGE OF TOURIST bureaus as massive government organisations still lingers, despite the privatisations of recent years. But the first great initiative in their establishment was a commercial venture, and came from abroad.

Cook's discover Australia

Although there had been no British takers in 1871 for their projected world tour via the Australasian colonies—perhaps the first time Thomas Cook's had not anticipated travel trends correctly—the firm tried to tap this new market and connect it with their worldwide enterprise. These early attempts were not successful: one agent neglected the interests of Cook's while feathering his own nest. Meanwhile John Cook had become aware that 'every year the number of well to do and wealthy Australians desirous of travelling increases considerably'. So instead of being primarily concerned with taking people *to* Australia, as it had been from 1880, Cook's sought to gain as large a market share as it could of the tourist traffic away from it.

In 1887 Frank Cook was sent to Australia to ascertain whether it would be worthwhile for the firm to establish its own offices with its own personnel—in Melbourne, and perhaps also in Sydney. The omens were good: contact had been made with the Victorian Chief Railway

Commissioner, who had introduced some excursion travel 'so as to pave the way for us going into the matter generally'. John Cook proposed that terms be sought similar to those that Cook's had obtained in India: namely a 10 per cent reduction on tickets for the public, and a further 10 per cent commission for the firm. Should such terms be granted, then (in addition to its international operations) Cook's would be 'quite prepared to work up a system' of local excursion travel. The growing trickle of overseas tourists could be included in this too.[1]

By the end of 1887 Cook's had opened an office in Melbourne; soon there were sub-branches at the Federal Coffee Palace and the Grand Hotel. In Sydney, the operator of The Tourist Bureau, an office in Bridge Street that provided various services to travellers, joined up with Cook's. Melbourne was the base of operations but, as Cook's advised their agent, 'owing to the jealousy between [NSW] and Victoria', Melbourne '*must never* be mentioned as the Chief Office for Australasia'. By 1892 Cook's also maintained offices in Adelaide and Brisbane—Hobart would open the following year—together with agencies in another eight or ten towns. Cook's became the agent for all the government railway systems, the Silverton Tramway Company, and the few notable private railway companies as well. It also represented shipping companies, including Murray River steamers, while it held the sole agency for the Gippsland Lakes Steam Navigation Company.

From 1889 news of these enterprises was carried in *Cook's Australasian Traveller's Gazette and Tourist Advertiser*, a monthly which, even as the firm laid out its wares in this part of the world, proudly proclaimed on its cover the importance of the firm's Egyptian operations: 'Sole Contractors to the Egyptian Government for the Conveyance of Mails and Government Officials between Lower and Upper Egypt . . .' Articles on Egypt, aimed at enticing Australians to such conveyance, were frequent; by the late 1890s so too were pieces on Tasmania and New Zealand, the 'oversea colonies'. Copy was frequently repeated, often with little change, for the journal was essentially an advertising medium rather than a newspaper.[2]

Cook's could offer the tourist a very great deal. Uniformed figures would greet arrivals from overseas at the wharf, while Australian domestic travellers were able to utilise the facilities that had been developed to maintain a worldwide system: individual travellers could buy a set of tickets tailored to their needs. Since Cook's had been able to secure the kind of arrangement with the railways and steamship companies that they sought, they could assure the public that they charged the tourist no commission: that came 'from the carrying companies whose agents we are'. The proud boast was that 'We alone are in a position to book for combined steamer, rail and coach tickets'. When it came to accommodation, graded lists of recommended hotels appeared at the back of *Cook's Australasian Traveller's Gazette*, while a more detailed guide came with the hotel coupons the traveller could purchase, obviating the need to carry large sums of money and guaranteeing the price. 'In addition to this', stated Cook's, 'by means of our chain of officers and interpreters . . . we are enabled to offer our patrons a means of obtaining such detailed information . . . that no other organisation can possibly afford'. As the 1890s went on, and times became harder, appeals to the public to do the right thing and buy tickets from the source that provided general information became increasingly shrill.[3]

Cook's would assist people leaving a depressed Victoria for South Africa, or take prospective miners to the Western Australian goldfields. But it was with rail excursions, Thomas Cook's original concept in the 1840s, that the firm made its most striking contribution. Excursion trains were run to the Melbourne Exhibition of 1888, and special trains at special fares became a feature of the company's operations. Overseas tourists would find that they could move about south-eastern Australia at little additional cost, while for locals the boast was that fares were reduced to approximate steamer rates: excursion rates from Broken Hill to Melbourne were dropped by as much as 40 per cent. The 'Inter-colonial excursions' organised by Cook's, encouraging people 'to extend their holiday trips across the borders of their respective colonies', may have been one factor helping to create a climate conducive to federation.[4]

Package tours were also important, whether to places like Jenolan, involving rail and coach in various combinations, or to Mildura, which also necessitated a Murray River steamer, or to Mt Bischoff tin mine in Tasmania, which from Sydney involved steamer to Hobart, government railway, private railway, then steamer to Melbourne and rail again to return to Sydney.[5]

Indeed the company's operation in Tasmania both shaped, and was propelled by, the growing demand for holidays there. Port Arthur was not mentioned in *Cook's Australasian Traveller's Gazette* until 1893; three years later Cook's were priding themselves on having 'opened up' the overland route, and offered a series of package tours to the site. Among other things, tours to the Lakes basically for fishermen were on offer by 1900, since Cook's were aware of interest as far afield as India and England. Private accommodation in the countryside could also be arranged. From the mid-1890s, guidebooks and pamphlets laid out what was on offer.

Cook's was moving as fast as it could, but the firm was determined to make haste slowly. Accommodation had to be of a certain standard before it could be recommended, that is to say used by the firm; where it did not exist in an area, that place would not be visited. In Tasmania, then, Cook's urged the upgrading of hotels and the provision of accommodation, however basic, in wild places. 'Tasmania', declared *Cook's Australasian Traveller's Gazette*, 'is the Lotos-land of Australia . . . Its inhabitants have hardly realised yet what a valuable asset they possess in their lovely climate and varied scenery'. But some progress had been made, for which some credit had to be given 'to a purely local organisation—the Tasmanian Tourist Association'.[6]

Tasmanian initiatives

The Premier of Tasmania, Henry Dobson, initiated the Tasmanian Tourist Association (TTA) at a public meeting held in 1893. Arousing and shaping local interest by yoking it with Cook's was very much his conception: when Cook's was established in Hobart and working hand in glove with the railways, Dobson saw that its agent would make an ideal honorary secretary of the new organisation, and indeed shortly afterwards he was organising tours and writing the necessary pamphlets.

There was, at the time, no tourism ministry anywhere in the world: New Zealand would establish the first in 1901. Tasmanian businessmen were becoming aware of the possibilities of what one writer already termed 'the tourist industry', and in an age when voluntarism (or self-help) was fashionable (as in a grosser form it has become again), Dobson merely saw the government's role as providing a stiffener for other people's enthusiasm. The Premier and the Government Statistician may have sat on the large committee, together with other government officials, the mayor of Hobart and two aldermen, but they saw their obligations as strictly limited. A TTA display room and information centre was soon set up in the museum, but a promised pound-for-pound subsidy broke down in practice—and under the governments of less enthusiastic premiers.[7]

When the government, under TTA pressure, decided to build an accommodation house at Lake St Clair, parliament voted for the measure only when assured that the Association would pay the rent. Similarly, the TTA initially had to pay the interest on the cost of building a hut at Lake Hartz. Beattie the photographer railed that it was 'a monstrous thing' for a group of enthusiasts to have to 'put their hands in their pockets to further the interests of practically the whole colony', but although the government later took over these accommodation houses and built more, it was most reluctant to be drawn further into tourism ventures.

The TTA believed (thanks to Beattie's photographs) that romantic scenery was what Tasmania had to offer, but it was of course often located in inaccessible places. These needed hotels or, if truly wild, hostelries. Private enterprise could not really be expected to build them when additional infrastructure was often needed, the tourist season was still short, and the local population too small to sustain them, at least initially. It would take years to establish such businesses, but their development was clearly in the interests of the state as a whole. So was effective publicity, but here too the government pleaded a shortage of money. It was only when the government was made aware of the scale of New

Zealand's investment in tourism—some £20 000 a year in 1904—that it increased total annual tourist subsidies in Tasmania to £500.[8]

The TTA then upgraded its relationship with Cook's, operating from the same prominently sited building in 1907. Less interested in historical sites—there was still ambivalence about Port Arthur—the Association aimed 'to preserve and improve places of national beauty and interest'. Beattie's photographs were dispatched abroad, and in one year had provided the basis for some 200 lantern-slide lectures in Britain. The TTA, in addition to providing tours, rest rooms, and booking facilities through Cook's, also came to put out a daily newspaper through the season, which claimed a circulation of 50 000.[9]

By 1914 the TTA was in trouble. There was a bookkeeping crisis and, because of misappropriated funds, a government inquiry. Not the least of the organisation's problems was increasing criticism: the task set by tourism had become too big for what was essentially an association powered by civic pride. Indeed, it was precisely because of this that similar organisations elsewhere in Tasmania refused to accord it any special status. At the same time, while the TTA did promote the state abroad intermittently, it lacked the resources to represent it permanently elsewhere in Australia—at a time when New Zealand and Queensland had set up offices in other capitals. There were also complaints of favouritism, of businessmen members swinging contracts to serve their own interests. Some hotels claimed that they were passed over, as did a notable firm supplying charabancs.[10]

Also unhappy were the railways, which under an energetic new commissioner began to explore new possibilities. A guidebook to Tasmania was published, the most comprehensive to date. Soon its compiler, E. T. Emmett, was sent across to open an information office in Melbourne, in association with the Victorian Railways. Bookings were not taken at first, but there was a change of policy in response to the surprising demand, and then gratifying takings.[11]

So it was that Tasmania, bypassed by other states that had established their government tourist bureaus, decided now that it should do the same. There was a recognition of the immense economic potential of

The civically minded Tasmanian Tourist Association headquarters, run in tandem with Cook's, Hobart, just before World War I (top)
The office of the Tasmanian Government Tourist Bureau for most of the years of its existence (centre)
Almost back to the beginning: the Tasmanian Tourist and Information Centre, 1997 (bottom)

tourism, and a belief that the 'tourist business' should not 'drift into private hands', since it was 'unquestionably a national one'. A tourism department, it was hoped, would centralise the whole operation: it would represent the state on the mainland, supervise country tourist associations, work to improve roads and accommodation, take bookings (perhaps regulating the demand for particular accommodation), and also provide information about the state in the form of lectures, pamphlets and advertising. In the beginning advertising consumed half the budget.

Set up in large offices—the largest then in Australia—the Tourist Bureau emerged at much the same time as the Hydro-Electric Commission: it has rightly been pointed out that these two institutions were to shape twentieth-century Tasmania. But in the case of tourism, shortage of resources would again crimp the vision. For a long time the Tasmanian Government Tourist Bureau remained a division of the railways; its clerks could be seconded elsewhere in the offseason. In 1923–28, following a Royal Commission into the Tasmanian Government Railways, the tourist department was drastically downsized. But by 1934 it had been fully restored, for the first time as an autonomous body, with the experienced Emmett as director.[12]

The mobilisation of NSW

In May 1905 the Premier of New South Wales, J. H. Carruthers, called a conference of government officials. A frequent visitor to Tasmania, Carruthers had been struck by the way the island state had been able to create a tourist profile for itself—not least when he became aware that two teachers at the Sydney Technical College had given lectures based on Beattie's slides. 'Advertising', he called it, aware as he was that there were no such sets available for New South Wales. Worse, a great many people in Sydney scarcely travelled beyond the Blue Mountains. They showed little inclination to seek information about the local countryside, while every year a large number set off for holidays in

New Zealand, Tasmania and other places. 'They seem to learn', said Carruthers, 'before they leave these shores, much about the places to which they are going, . . . by reason of the organised effort to encourage a tourist traffic put forward by the Government and Tourist organisations in those States'. The NSW Railways had done useful work in distributing books, pamphlets and pictures, but clearly very much more was needed.

Carruthers announced the establishment of an Intelligence Department, designed to gather up all relevant news about NSW and publicise the state as much as possible. It would be a centralising agency attached to the Premier's Office, and the heads of existing departments would be *ex officio* members, to facilitate the gathering of statistics and information. One of its sub-departments would be the existing railway tourist bureau, while a major concern would be to upgrade the effectiveness of New South Wales House in London, where it seems that only the Agent-General had first-hand experience of Australia.[13]

By 1907—after the Secretary had been sent to Hobart to study the operations of the TTA—the Intelligence Department was fully functioning with a staff of seven. In line with Carruthers' belief that 'it is an advertising age', and his desire to emulate business practice, smart, centrally located premises were found in Challis House, a building then under construction in Martin Place. Here the Tourist sub-department was ensconced behind a large display window, with a railway booking office located on the floor below. Publicity was stepped up, along Tasmanian lines, but extending to 'paragraphs, articles and paid advertisements' in the press, even including motion pictures for dispatch abroad. Particular pride was taken in the low cost to the taxpayer (thanks to advertising) of publications such as the *Guide for Immigrants and Settlers*. But it was noted that when it came to more specifically tourist publications, 'the modern tendency is for the public to expect this kind of assistance . . . free, and the sales of such publications do not reach considerable proportions'.

Tourism, in fact, ran a poor third to immigration and the gathering and dissemination of information among the Intelligence Department's activities. Settlers and immigrants (differentiated presumably because the first-named went on the land), and particularly investors with large capital, were more likely to engage the Department's interest, and were the focus of its publicity abroad. Indeed the Tourist Bureau sub-department was seen as popularising the state's beauty spots 'with the people of New South Wales, our neighbours in the other States, and with travellers from abroad'. By comparison it was almost a domestic operation, still perceived primarily as a way of encouraging people to visit the resorts of their own state before venturing beyond it.[14]

To overcome inertia and to reverse the existing flow to other states, the Tourist Bureau embarked on a vigorous programme to make NSW more attractive to the tourist. Country pubs in scenic districts received suggestions, followed up by visits from the local constabulary, as to how they should lift their game. Again noting the example of Tasmania, country tourist associations were formed at the Tourist Bureau's direct prompting. Meanwhile the Sydney office answered correspondence, arranged itineraries and, beginning with a trip to the Northern Rivers at Easter, 1906, organised a series of tours conducted by a guide— 'personally-conducted tours'. These were claimed—with the amnesia that characterises the industry, and that in this case overlooked Cook's —to be the first of their kind in Australia. As far as the Bureau was concerned, the aim of these tours was not so much to make a profit (which they did) 'as to advertise the tourist resorts involved, and induce a general flow of tourist traffic within the State'. In this, too, it was successful: guided tours to Moss Vale and then on to Nowra via Kangaroo Valley, for example, encouraged coach proprietors to follow up with a regular service at weekends. By 1910 it was proudly pointed out that since the Bureau's establishment, the railways had almost doubled ordinary services as well as tourist trains to recognised tourist destinations.[15]

The Tourist Bureau also created a resort at Mt Kosciuszko. With the emergence of snow sports just after the turn of the century, there was a new interest in the region, and the first of the Bureau's personally conducted tours there was announced in 1906. A particular enthusiast was the Tourist Officer, C. D. Paterson, who was not only a key figure in organising the early lifesaving movement on the beaches, but himself became an expert skier and held a tobogganing championship for five years. A road up to the summit was put in, since it was expected that fashionable snow sports, supplemented by trout-fishing, golfing and riding, would make this 'pre-eminently the holiday and health resort of Australia' all the year round. A weatherboard bungalow built by the Bureau on the Thredbo was soon followed by the Hotel Kosciuszko. Opened in 1909 by the Governor, the hotel soon drew the Governor-General and his party, as well as an increasing number of guests from all over Australia and New Zealand and from England, America and India. By 1914 the building had been enlarged, acquiring a ballroom. There were occasional grumbles that this was a resort for the toffs, but it was advertised in trams and defended in parliament on the basis of its moderate tariff.[16]

Tourism and immigration

Linked by the common theme of mobility, and requiring the same kind of outreach, tourism and immigration seemed best promoted together. At a time when the mother country was concerned about falling birthrates and a decline in the virility of the race, NSW was also concerned about a possible fall-off in population. The cessation of state-aided emigration some twenty years earlier had, by the earliest years of federation, resulted in new arrivals from Britain often falling well short of a thousand per year. State-aided schemes would now be set in place, for, as Carruthers explained, 'so long as we are a colonising Government, belonging to a colonising power, our prime purpose is to get this rich virgin territory of ours occupied by population'. Crucial to this strategy would be to 'get the tide of population streaming out of our city [Sydney] on to the land'. Tourism then was both caught up in this programme and furthered by it. The Intelligence Department, of which the Tourist Bureau was part, represented a mobilisation of the state and its resources; in 1906 it drew in the Government Statistician. His office was to be separated again a few years later as the Bureau of Statistics, while the rump Intelligence Department was now known as the Immigration and Tourist Bureau. This linkage was to remain until immigration faded away for a time, overtaken by the Great War.[17]

The link had persisted because, in the federation period, many of the everyday assumptions about tourism and immigration were similar. In Tasmania, more advanced in tourism than NSW, the priorities of the senior state had been reversed and the Immigration League had amalgamated with the TTA. A 1913 Tasmanian government advertisement cited tourist attractions and immigration advantages interchangeably, listing produce and other amenities while also proclaiming the island 'Australia's Summer Playground'. The prevailing developmentalist ethos also meant that the work of people subduing the land—whether immigrants or townsfolk who had relocated themselves—could become sights too. Local exhibitions in the new potato-growing districts of Tasmania's north-west coast in the 1890s required special trains. Moreover there was a common belief—perhaps a back-formation from 'trade follows the flag'—that 'the settler follows the tourist'. Certainly it was claimed that one of the measures of success of the NSW Northern Rivers guided tour of 1906 was its 'stimulating a desire for settlement on the land among those who took part'. Similarly, at the opening of the new premises of the Tasmanian Tourist Bureau in 1915, E. T. Emmett claimed that it was 'no uncommon thing' for members of a family from abroad who first came as tourists to return a few years later as permanent residents. But these seem to have been statements of hope as much as useful observations.[18]

The interest in Australia of British residents in India, or of Americans, tended to be exaggerated because they were so conspicuous, particularly at a time when personal enthusiasms and networks figured more directly than they do now in the attempts of government agencies to influence people. The distribution of a certain amount of tourist literature by people visiting overseas could always be counted upon, since it was believed to be rather patriotic; Tasmanians living on the mainland sometimes approached the government, offering to do the same. Similarly there existed a specially entitled pamphlet telling people how they could nominate a friend for an assisted passage to New South Wales. At the local level—and still relatively common till at least the 1950s—was the 'Back to' movement, where a town would hold a carnival and put itself on display, hoping to draw not only former residents or the relatives of townsfolk, but perhaps build on that to attract tourists and so give the place and its commercial life a real boost.[19]

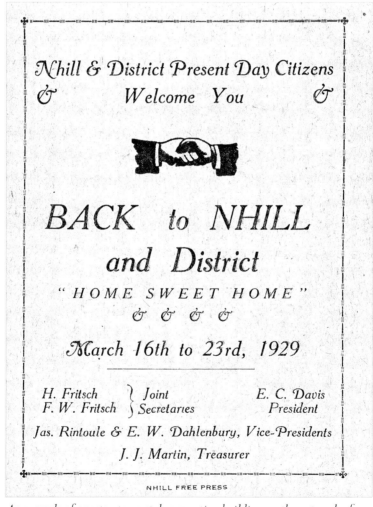

An example of country-town-style promotion building on the outreach of local networks

State tourist bureaus

In most cases the railways had assumed a generative role in the estab-lishment of tourist bureaus. This was true of NSW, but strikingly the case in Victoria where, technically at least, the Tourist Bureau remained an agency of the Victorian Railways until 1959. The Tasmanians, who tried to link their bureau with the unprofitable railways, were first in-duced to take the venture seriously after the success of their Melbourne publicity office. Meanwhile the Victorians, the possessors of a much more extensive railway network, soberly advised that their Bureau 'does not perform the functions of a general intelligence office concerning matters outside railway business'. This more restrictive attitude explains why the Victorian Tourist Bureau did not follow its NSW counterpart in building a hotel like the Kosciuszko. In 1909 the Public Works Depart-ment built the Mt Buffalo Chalet, but the Railways did not take over its administration till sixteen years later.[20]

The other influence, coming in strongly in the federation period, was the NSW model of the Intelligence Department, copied in name and structure in Queensland and in South Australia—although the latter state had tellingly begun with a separate Tourist Bureau (1908–10) under the direction of the former secretary to the Railway Commissioners. The NSW precedent also smoothed the path for Victoria to set up an interdepartmental Tourist Committee in 1911 to work upon Railways intransigence.

The developmentalist impulse underlying much of this activity can be seen most clearly in Western Australia. Although a Caves Board was established in 1900, and a State Hotels Department in 1902, Tourism was not thought of in a general sense until 1910, and then only as one element in a department modelled on (though not named after) the NSW Intelligence Department. In 1912, though, Tourism virtually dis-appeared, being merged into State Hotels, and did not re-emerge till 1921. Tourist infrastructure was then provided, but there was little overall sense of an industry. The government's preoccupation was with immigration and the state's development: 'one of the most stimulating

73

The guest-house culture on wheels: a sing-song around the piano on the Transcontinental Railway in the late 1940s

able to buy special stamps of low value which, once accumulated, allowed them to pay for their holiday on layby: 25 000 participated in 1930. The Railways also took over Mt Buffalo and, since it was made to pay, supplemented it with other snow resorts; organised weekly talks on two radio stations, pushing out information; and produced publicity material extolling places such as 'Belgrave the Beautiful', or 'Delightful Daylesford'. Meanwhile the Tourists' Resorts Committee increased public consciousness by putting up calico notices informing the visitor that where they drove was a 'Proclaimed Tourist Road', or a beauty spot a 'Proclaimed Tourist Resort'.[24]

Enter ANTA

In 1927 T. E. Moorhouse from the Development and Migration Commission and Charles H. Holmes, chairman of the Betterment and Publicity Board of the Victorian Railways, prepared a confidential report for the federal government on developing the 'tourist business of the Commonwealth' and stimulating greater travel among Australians.

Moorhouse and Holmes noted that Australia was a long way behind other countries in attracting tourists, pointing out that only 20 000 a year visited our shores.

They found that

> there is no authority in the travel business today to speak for Australia, to exploit travel in the tourist markets of the world, and in a big way to encourage Australians to see more of their own land. True, there are Tourist Bureaux in each State, but they have little voice outside their own States, and none in the world beyond our shores.[25]

Moorhouse and Holmes pointed out that 'travel is a commodity that requires selling', not least in a 'young country' like Australia little known to the large mass of people overseas. Australia's remoteness from the great centres of population in the English-speaking world demanded 'greater zest in salesmanship'. They identified Australia as 'the Cinderella' of the world's tourist business and argued that an 'Australian Travel Bureau' be established to co-ordinate state efforts, and bring together the interests of the state railways, the shipping companies, motoring organisations, tourist agents, hotel proprietors, retailers and the state tourist bureaus.

They proposed both an overseas and an Australian strategy. For the overseas market this included the circulation abroad of 'propaganda' for the 'English Speaking world' and certain Continental countries, the appointment of Australian tourist officers in London and New York, the creation of 'group travel', including reciprocal farmers' tours, and the development of tours for industrial leaders under the auspices of the Empire Marketing Board. They also recommended the preparation of a pamphlet entitled 'What the Tourist Means to You' to point out the value of the tourist to Australia and to urge the provision of better hotel and guest-house accommodation. What is remarkable about the Moorhouse and Holmes formulations is that they have been repeated, with only modest changes in concepts and nomenclature, every decade since first enunciated.

To boost domestic tourism Moorhouse and Holmes wanted other states to follow the Victorian example of the Natural Development Resources Train. (This venture had become so well known that people spoke of the 'Reso' train and the 'Reso Tour'.) Engineering and agricultural experts accompanied the train to 'enlighten the travellers regarding any phase of Australian life and production', as the *New York Times* explained. Foreigners could also see the 'mustering of kangaroos' and the flora and fauna of the land.

In supporting their request for an annual commonwealth government budget of £20 000 per annum for five years, Moorhouse and Holmes calculated that an increase of 100 000 overseas tourists per annum (assuming an average stay of twenty-one days and expenditure of 40s per day) would mean an additional £21 000 000 spent in Australia. Their optimistic target: selling one trip to Australia for every two thousand people in the English-speaking world. While more than two-thirds of that world lay within the British Empire, it was unclear how the Americans would be successfully wooed. By 1938 the Australian National Travel Association was asking its Australian readers to point out to their English-speaking relatives overseas that 'the voyage to Australia and back is the cheapest long-distance cruise in the world!'.[26]

Holmes went on tour to promote his idea of a national tourist association. In February 1928 he addressed the Associated Chambers of Commerce at their annual conference in Hobart, telling them that 'the world is passing Australia by because we do not get together in co-ordinated effort and energetically and systematically sell the idea of visiting our country'. He pointed out to his audience that 'we have a huge slice of the world and but a handful of people, there being only two people to the square mile throughout the Commonwealth, while within a few days' sail of our shores is Java, with a population of something like 35 000 000'.

Holmes' proposals received considerable press publicity, and were noted with interest by state governments. In September 1928 the NSW Colonial Secretary was asked what he thought of the idea of federal authorities publicising the tourist resorts of the nation:

> Will the Minister take steps to ensure that proper publicity is given in the Commonwealth publications to the tourist resorts of NSW? In all previous publications by the Commonwealth Government very little has been said regarding the attractions of the tourist resorts in this State . . .[27]

This jockeying between states for attention and what today is called 'market share' has been a constant feature of government intervention in tourism. In the late nineteenth century the colonies were already aware of the importance of promoting themselves as destinations for travellers and holidaymakers, as well as for potential migrants. With the growth of Australian cities, each state saw its capital as a worthy attraction in itself. The rivalry between Sydney and Melbourne was exacerbated by Sydney's population overtaking that of the southern city in the late 1890s, while Melbourne temporarily housed the new federal parliament. Its grand colonial parliament building was much more suitable for the national seat of government than the decayed NSW parliament, which still exuded its origins as a rum hospital. These rivalries spilled over into tourist promotion.

When the Australian National Travel Association opened its doors in 1929, no one thought it odd that its headquarters would be in Melbourne because its leading lights were Melburnians and all the major federal government departments remained in Melbourne, despite the opening of a new (provisional) parliament house in Canberra. Nonetheless all state governments, particularly the ever-suspicious NSW government, decided to retain their own tourist bureaus. The state bureaus lived in a more politically pressured climate than ANTA: it had a broad charter for promoting Australia first, whereas the state bureaus had to satisfy every electorate that purported to have tourist attractions.

The board of ANTA represented the full spectrum of interests in national travel promotion. The Sydney-based retailer Charles Lloyd Jones represented general business interests, while the Victorian Railway Commissioner, H. W. Clapp, represented the Australian railways, a consortium of the state bodies. Overseas shipping interests, hotel interests and the federal government all provided finance and board members.

ANTA set up its office in Melbourne's Flinders Street Railway Building, near where Holmes had his publicity headquarters. With promotion and propaganda at the heart of its operation, ANTA immediately started commissioning journalists and poster artists to promote Australia. These included noted graphic artists who had already worked for the Victorian

Railways, Percy Trompf and James Northfield. One of ANTA's first posters, Trompf's 'Still Building Australia', showed the Sydney Harbour Bridge moving towards completion. By the early 1930s ANTA had commissioned posters for every Australian state, emphasising prime tourist sites and regions, including the Great Barrier Reef. As the northern railway finally reached Cairns in 1926, even the reef could be marketed as a rail destination as well as being accessible by coastal steamer.[28]

Charles Holmes, one of the directors of ANTA, undertook a 19 000 kilometre tour around Australia in 1932. Accompanied by a photographer he travelled by rail from Melbourne to Perth; flew, with four stops, from Perth to Broome; took a boat from Broome to Darwin; journeyed thence by rail, car and aeroplane to Mt Isa; and returned to Melbourne by train. Holmes went on to write *We Find Australia*, which immediately became a bestseller in Britain and Australia. He wrote of the country as an 'outpost of empire', a 'continent where the people speak but one language', where 'immense tracts of primeval forest' had been 'conquered'. Writing of Aborigines as a 'stone-age people', a 'vanishing race', he visited missions where he found 'some of them are as white as you and I, but inside, somewhere, they are black'. On being taught English they would know 'how accursed they are'. As the most popular travelogue of the 1930s, *We Find Australia* portrayed the country as a strange mix of open spaces and civilisation, of tourist adventure and stone age culture.[29]

One of ANTA's first acts was to establish the monthly magazine *Walkabout* in November 1934. Building on the success of the American *National Geographic* magazine, but with a rather larger format, *Walkabout* aimed to enable 'Australians and the people of other lands' to 'learn more of the vast Australian continent and the colourful islands below the equator in the Pacific'.

The deliberately Australian choice of the title *Walkabout* reflected both national and international concerns.

> The title has an 'age-old' background and signifies a racial characteristic of the Australian aboriginal who is always on the move. And so, month by month, through the medium of pen and picture, this journal will take you on a great 'walkabout' through a new and fascinating world . . .

Walkabout sought both pictorial and text material. Liberal payment was offered to people submitting good photographs and articles about outback Australia and Australian 'by-ways', New Zealand and the South Sea Islands. *Walkabout* prided itself on its Southern Pacific focus. Like the *National Geographic* it had considerable success in attracting advertisements from government tourist bureaus, shipping lines, brewers, car manufacturers, classy hotels and individual tourist sites, from Mildura to the Jenolan Caves.

for the year, an increase of 28 per cent on the figures for 1935. Country passengers at 800 948 had risen less sharply, since presumably some of them simply adjusted the timing of their visits to Adelaide; even so, there was a 21 per cent increase here too. Of those who came by car, the Registrar of Motor Vehicles reported that there were at least four times as many interstate visitors in December 1936 as in the same month the year before. One estimate put total visitors to the capital, from country and interstate, at 200 000, with £1 million being spent on hotel and boarding-house accommodation. International visitors, however, were conspicuously absent from Ryan's final report.

Nevertheless there were hopeful signs that tourism would continue at a higher level than before the centenary. Two films commissioned from Frank Hurley, at a price Ryan considered exorbitant, proved to be so much in demand that the prints wore out. By 1940, helped along by an economic recovery, tourism in South Australia had expanded considerably. The Tourist Bureau inquiry staff had grown to seven, while a second representative had been appointed in Melbourne.[32]

Learning from the promotional successes and failures of the Victorian (1934–35) and South Australian centenaries, ANTA became much more aggressive and ambitious in its marketing of the Sydney sesquicentenary celebrations in 1938. Posters from both Australian and British artists

Still the hub of the NSW transport system: Central Station, Sydney, 1930

were commissioned and an extensive advertising campaign undertaken in the British press, pointing out to Britons that their pound would be worth twenty-five shillings in Australia. Although unable to attract a member of the British royal family, as Melbourne had done, the Celebrations Council planned and staged a re-enactment of Governor Phillip's landing at Farm Cove, including costumed actors and 'a troupe of aborigines'. Sydney also hosted the British Empire Games, bringing athletes and supporters from every Dominion and from most colonies. To capture the domestic market, advertisements with the heading 'All roads lead to Sydney' graphically reminded interstate residents that they could visit the 'mecca' of the 'nation's pride' by ship, train, car or aeroplane.[33]

State bureaus, state attractions

At the beginning of 1930 Miss M. A. Evans of Mt Gambier wrote to the NSW Government Tourist Bureau about her forthcoming trip to Sydney and other possibilities for travel within New South Wales.[34] Like thousands of other inquirers she was sent a list of hotels and accommodation houses and 'literature descriptive of the various places of interest in and around Sydney', along with details of organised tours. Like other state tourist bureaus, and the Cook's network, the NSW bureau conducted a one-stop shop.[35] They offered to book accommodation in the city, Darlinghurst, Cremorne, Neutral Bay and North Sydney, all accessible by tram and in the case of the latter three by ferry as well. Accommodation options varied from bed and breakfast to full board at 'residential chambers' and guest-houses.

The motor tours offered to Miss Evans were provided by Day's Motor Tourist Service Ltd in conjunction with the Bureau. All the tours were to government-owned natural sites, including national parks, beaches, the Blue Mountains, along with the guest-houses at Wombeyan Caves and Jenolan Caves. The only major privately owned installation to be featured in the brochure was the Coogee Beach Pier, erected in 1928.

Throughout the inter-war years tourist bureaus remained so closely integrated with government-owned transport systems—especially the railways and the emerging highways, with government-owned accommodation such as the cave houses, and government-owned national parks and other recreational facilities, such as beaches—that it seemed perfectly natural for the state governments to continue to own booking and promotional organisations. In July 1928 the NSW Government Tourist Bureau and tourist resorts were gazetted as 'an industrial undertaking', along with state brick works, metal quarries, pipe works, the Murrumbidgee Irrigation Area and the Metropolitan Meat Board. The government of the day, a non-Labor coalition, saw all these enterprises as legitimate state activities with a commercial purpose. In 1934–35 the NSW bureau collected £112 000 in sales but, as its working expenses amounted to £125 000, it lost £13 000 that year.

The concerns that state governments voiced on the establishment of ANTA continued to figure in their approach to tourism in the 1950s and 1960s. In every state, government worried about the quality and quantity of tourist facilities, especially accommodation, the availability of transport, and boosting the particular attractions of their own states. Victoria concentrated on its alpine regions, while Queensland pushed the Great Barrier Reef. South Australia sang the praises of Adelaide, while the Western Australians marketed their wildflower season. Tasmania promoted its temperate climate and its picturesque historic buildings, including Port Arthur. New South Wales continued to advertise the attractions of Sydney while other destinations, whether beach or alpine, received rather less promotion.

Like other states Victoria bemoaned the 'lack of sufficient first class accommodation', especially in the metropolitan area, where an agricultural show, a race meeting or 'even a large conference' would see the city booked out. The State Development Committee in its 1951 report on tourist facilities in Victoria pointed to the difficulty of accommodating 'sizeable tourist parties from overseas'. In tackling this issue the committee visited other states and noted the success of the Tasmanian Tourist Bureau, including its interstate branches, in booking accommodation in private homes. The South Australian Government Tourist Bureau offered the same service, while the Western Australian bureau did likewise, offering homes 'in good-class suburbs'. The Committee noted that the United Licensed Victuallers' Association and the Victorian Railway Commissioners had contemplated such a scheme for the 1934–35 celebrations, but as 'visitor numbers fell far short of the original estimate' it had not been implemented. Nonetheless, not least because of the impending royal visit, the committee recommended that Victoria adopt a system of booking guests into private homes, as well as instituting a survey of guest-houses and a scheme for the grading of guest-houses and hotels, along the lines of schemes to be found in the USA, Europe and New Zealand.

By 1951 the Victorian Government Tourist Bureau, which continued to operate under the authority of the Railway Commissioners, had branches in every state capital and in Victoria's main provincial cities—Geelong, Ballarat and Bendigo, along with one branch in Mildura, to cater for the Murray trade. The interstate branches were established

A young woman receives professional advice at the local Tourist Bureau, Mt Gambier, in 1959.

between 1935 and 1938. The Perth branch, while managed by a senior Victorian tourist officer, represented four states, the 'Eastern States Government Tourist Bureau', with NSW, Queensland and South Australia also footing the bill. All the Victorian branch offices were closed during the war, but by 1951 they had, with the exception of Perth, been reopened.

With its impressive headquarters in Collins Street, the Victorian Bureau served as both an information centre and a booking service for transport and accommodation. The Bureau was proud of its hotel and guest-house guide, *Where to Go in Victoria*, claiming it to be the 'most comprehensive' holiday guide issued by any state in Australia. It offered a telephone inquiry service of thirty-five inward lines, logging 740 000 calls in 1949–50. The Bureau catered for overseas travellers and sporting organisations as well as the usual array of individual and group demands.[36]

When a large passenger vessel arrived at Melbourne the Bureau would supply an experienced officer to join it, courtesy of the Customs launch, before it berthed. The officer arranged shore excursions and distributed the weekly diary of Melbourne events. The Bureau also targeted regional and seasonal activities, including the winter snow season, offering a booking service and weather condition reports made available to the press and the ABC.

While the Victorian Bureau was indirectly involved in publicising particular resorts, publicity as such remained the responsibility of the Railways Department's Public Relations and Betterment Board. This Board, charged with awakening the interest and the co-operation of local residents in the development of potential tourist attractions, was supposed to encourage tourist areas to form their own associations and to amalgamate into regional bodies, with the aim of eliminating parochialism.

From ANTA to the ATC

When ANTA commissioned two New York consultancy firms to report on Australia's travel and tourist industry in 1964, it was conscious of a worldwide recognition of the growing economic importance of tourism. By 1964 ANTA had expanded to a board membership of thirty-one, approximately half of them representing the commonwealth and state governments and the remainder representing travel organisations. ANTA's budget had grown from £17 300 in 1930 to £417 000 in 1963–64, of which 70 per cent was provided by the commonwealth government, 20 per cent by the travel industry, and the remaining 10 per cent by the state governments. While it was not unusual for a national tourist association to be funded by both central government and industry sources, the deep involvement of state and territory organisations in international tourism was, the consultants pointed out, 'unique'.

The mid-1960s mark a high point in the sales, image and booking influence of the state and territory bureaus. Despite the gradual growth in the number of international tourists, the domestic market still constituted over 95 per cent of visitor nights. Most of the work of the state bureaus continued to be booking accommodation and transport for home state and interstate travellers. The power of these bureaus impressed itself on the New York consultants, who pointed out that, while most of the bureaus had their origins as railway inquiry and ticket offices, with accelerating travel growth

> the travel bureaux have taken on additional capacities and expanded services, varying from state to state, but all of them act as regular travel offices selling travel of all kinds not only to and within their state but elsewhere in Australia and the world. The people of Australia have come to expect and depend upon the services of the state- and territory-operated travel bureaux to the extent that they are now regarded as a public service facility.

While the New York consultants thought that the bureaus played an important role in providing promotion and travel within Australia, they questioned their effectiveness in overseas promotion; they also noted the fact that, as government enterprises, they came within the overall public service structure and so were often subjected to the transfer of staff from other departments 'totally inexperienced in travel activities'.

The consultants therefore called for the bureaus to get semi-government instrumentality or commission status. The consultants also concluded that the states should exert their efforts in promoting and servicing travel within Australia but that it would be 'undesirable, costly and ineffective' for each state to maintain overseas offices and fragment what should be a concerted promotion effort.[37]

The consultancy team therefore proposed the creation of a new Australian travel authority to provide national co-ordination of attractions and facilities, an intensified overseas promotions programme, a redefinition of the role of the commonwealth and state governments, and sufficient funds to achieve these objectives. ANTA's general manager, Basil Atkinson, ran a lobbying campaign to have the recommendation implemented. John McEwen, Minister for Trade and Industry, agreed to the establishment of a statutory authority occupying the middle ground between government and the private sector.

The Australian Tourist Commission (ATC), created in May 1967, was established for 'the encouragement of visitors to Australia, and travel within Australia, by people from other countries'. It had an explicit educational and promotional function and could hire staff in other countries to this end. It was not given any role in the planning or development of destinations, attractions or facilities, although that had been earmarked by the New York consultants as a core area of its activities.[38] All issues of internal tourism infrastructure remained with the state governments, including accommodation and transport (rail and road) and the development of facilities. The only infrastructure areas controlled by the Commonwealth were those that it had had previously, including the regulation of interstate and international travel by ship and aeroplane, its government-owned airlines, TAA and Qantas, and a handful of interstate railway lines, most notably the Transcontinental.

The ATC emerged as a glorified promotional bureau with a large advertising budget. In this role it could build on the image-making success of ANTA, in its posters, magazines and brochures, and in the establishment of international offices. The ATC concentrated most of its efforts on the international market. Its rise as an organisation coincided with the coming of the wide-bodied jet and the Boeing 747, so it is fond of claiming that it presided over the spectacular increase in overseas tourism to Australia, from 220 000 in 1967 to five million in 1997.

The railways

The railways established by the colonial governments were the backbone of Australia's internal transport system, but in terms of facilitating interstate travel the colonies and then the states had to confront one major impediment to travel and trade—an extraordinary variety of railway gauges. New South Wales chose standard gauge (4 feet $8\frac{1}{2}$ inches), Victoria a wider gauge (5 feet 3 inches), which was also adopted in part by South Australia, while Queensland, Tasmania, Western Australia and some South Australian lines used a narrow gauge (3 feet 6 inches). The history of passenger rail in Australia is inextricably linked with the question of creating standard gauge links between the capital cities and determining how much of the cost would be met by the Commonwealth and the respective state governments.

The railways were big businesses. They not only had trains, railway lines and passengers, but in modern parlance they had thousands of point-of-sale promotional opportunities in the railway stations that dotted city, suburban and country landscapes. In the 1930s the NSW Government Railways employed 40 000 people; in 1954, 15 per cent of the workforce in Rockhampton worked for the railways. Each state's railway department had impressive central city stations. These premises, along with railway stations throughout the land, offered not only promotional but also ticketing services. Posters advertising special events, from horse races to agricultural shows, could be put up at a moment's notice by the vast railway staff. Even the railway carriages themselves were promotional vehicles, with their photographic insets of typical Australian scenes.

The early 1900s, a time of growing state government interest in the organisation and financing of tourist attractions and facilities, was also a time of very rapid growth in both railway patronage and railway infrastructure. Most states embarked on ambitious extensions to their networks to service both freight and passenger needs. The railway systems grew from 6557 kilometres in 1881 to 20 241 in 1901 and 38 491 in 1921, peaking at 43 771 kilometres in 1942. By the early 1900s all the mainland capital cities, except Perth, were linked by rail.

The construction of a railway linking Perth to the eastern states was one of the inducements held out to Western Australia to enter the Australian federation. The commonwealth parliament finally authorised work on the route in 1911, and track-laying began in 1913. The line, from Port Augusta in South Australia to Kalgoorlie in Western Australia, opened for traffic in October 1917, its most remarkable feature being the longest section of straight railway line in the world, 478 kilometres. The following year the commonwealth government took over the operation of the Northern Territory's railways, and in 1921 a Royal Commission investigated the cost of converting major rail routes to standard gauge. This proved so prohibitive that little was done.

In June 1924 the commonwealth government opened a railway station in Canberra (linked to the NSW system via Queanbeyan) to service the new federal capital. A standard gauge line from Perth to Kalgoorlie did not open until 1968. With the completion of the standard gauge from Port Pirie to Broken Hill in 1969 it became possible, for the first time, to traverse Australia without a break of gauge. In March 1970 the Indian Pacific passenger service began, taking 65 hours to travel the 3961 kilometres between Sydney and Perth. Dubbed one of the world's great train journeys, it opened in the jet era. For about half the price, and a twelfth of the time, the aeroplane had replaced the train as the means of mass long-distance transportation. The Indian Pacific remains a major tourist attraction, but only a small proportion of Australian and overseas travellers can afford either the time or the expense of the experience.[39]

In the late 1950s and early 1960s the state bureaus were at the height of their power, a time when their respective governments still owned the major source of internal transportation, the railways. State bureau booking services expanded and changed in direction to meet both demand and supply, adapting to motels as well as hotels, while transport booking services took on buses, car hire and air travel. With the rapid fall of railway patronage in the 1960s, primarily because of the spectacular growth of car ownership and usage, the state bureaus found themselves increasingly competing for business with the motoring organisations, especially the NSW-based National Roads and Motorists Organisation (NRMA) and the Royal Automobile Club of Victoria (RACV), both of which began issuing Australia-wide accommodation guides in the late 1950s. These guides effectively supplanted the accommodation directories published by the state bureaus.[40]

The fate of the bureaus

Because the charter of the Australian Tourist Commission did not extend to on-the-ground tourist infrastructure, the state bureaus increasingly took on this role, and often had a say in other areas of state tourist activity such as national parks and the creation of real and purpose-built heritage sites, including The Rocks, the Fremantle redevelopment, Old Sydney Town and Sovereign Hill. In these new roles some of the bureaus became commissions or departments of tourist activities in their own right. Their nomenclature changed with ministerial reorganisations, bureaucratic ambitions, and changing perceptions of the importance of the tourist dollar.

In looking for new areas of endeavour, the state bodies, especially those of Queensland and Tasmania, not only expanded their Australian marketing and booking programmes but became major players in package tourism. By 1993 the Western Australian Tourism Commission, ever conscious that an Australian Tourist Commission headquartered in Sydney could not be relied upon to promote the West, boasted eleven international offices in Europe, North America and Asia. In Victoria, the state with the most virulent privatisation programme, the RACV actually won a contract in the early 1990s to supply the booking and information services formerly offered by the bureau, and a new government body, Tourism Victoria, took on a statistical, planning and strategic advice role. As in all other states this body was charged with maximising its own state's share of interstate and overseas tourists by an elaborate series of advertising campaigns, special events (including the Grand Prix, filched from Adelaide) and the specific targeting of certain lifestyle and ethnic groups.

All the state instrumentalities, bolstered by visitor surveys from the Bureau of Tourism Research (jointly funded by the states and the commonwealth government), have specific national and ethnic markets in their sights, especially the Japanese, Korean, Chinese and, to a lesser extent, American and European. Emerging markets, such as those of Indonesia and India, are closely monitored, and the definition of relevant tourist infrastructure has gone well beyond the accommodation and travel sectors to include cultural and educational activities, such as festivals and tourism study programmes. The Asian currency crisis of 1997–98 was closely monitored by every state tourism organisation.

Over the past century the role of the state tourist bureaus has altered irrevocably. They usually began as state agencies and all developed close links with one or more government departments, such as the railways. Indeed some bureaus were the creature of just one government department. They developed for promotional purposes to encourage both migrants and travellers. By the 1920s they had all become major booking offices for both accommodation and transport. They continued in this role for the next five decades, but their market share was eroded by both technological and commercial developments. The rapid growth of privately owned travel agencies from the 1950s seriously undermined their role. By the early 1970s many suburban shopping strips and all shopping malls offered at least one travel agent. The state bureaus also found themselves in competition with the motoring organisations, which came to dominate the accommodation guide market.

With the rapid increase in households and businesses with telephone connections from the 1950s onwards, the state bureaus had to offer both over-the-counter and telephone bookings. By the mid-1990s almost one-third of all airline bookings were made directly between the client and the airline, the transaction being confirmed by credit card.

Hobart as Hollywood: Tasmania trading as the birthplace of Errol Flynn (newspaper advertisement, February 1992)

Electronic ticketing, introduced in the late 1990s, made the traditional paper ticket a mere reminder of an earlier age of travel.

The state tourist bureaus ran out of steam, just like *Walkabout*. By the early 1970s *Walkabout* had become a cheaply produced glossy magazine, its stories more likely to come from public relations blurbs than travel journalists in the field. Its last issue, in July 1974, featured Lord Snowdon's dreary photographs of Hill End, and a feature on iron man Hancock, the 'richest man in the West'. *Walkabout* had lost the spirit of exploration and adventure that had sustained it from 1934 to the 1960s. In the 1980s a new generation of travel magazines, including ones with such indulgent titles as *Gourmet Traveller*, captured the imagination of middle-class households.

Most of the state tourist bureaus still continue in one guise or another, but often their services have been contracted out. They are no longer the one-stop-shop—the veritable hall of state promotion—the role they confidently played from the early to the mid-twentieth century. State governments, on the other hand, are just as interested in tourism as they have ever been, if not more so. But their attentions and their investments go well beyond promotion and booking to the attraction of grand events (the Olympic Games, a Grand Prix) and tourist-oriented infrastructure projects (docklands redevelopments, casinos). The bureaus no longer command a central place in the landscape of tourism promotion. Only one, the Queensland Tourist Bureau, remains in its original 1936 Anzac Square headquarters. Where they still exist, the bureaus now compete with convention marketing organisations, capital city promotional bodies and state government departments, more concerned with image, new and refurbished tourist precincts and market share than with their traditional role of state promotion and the provision of advice and booking facilities for the people.

Rooms at the Inn

MUCH OF AUSTRALIAN LIFE has traditionally been centred on hotels. Even so, the significance of the role taken by the public house in the early days of settlement remains considerably underestimated. Wayside inns were often the first structures to go up in the wake of the explorers. Sited on the top of a hill, or beside a generous bend in a river—where animals might drink and also be relatively easily corralled—these early hostelries often defined a natural stopping place. Towns therefore often followed. In the Blue Mountains Lawson, Wentworth Falls, Katoomba and Black-heath all grew up around inns. Elsewhere were towns like Swan Hill, which sprang up around a pub and a punt, or Wangaratta, which to these facilities added an early store. Even where this did not occur, as in the case of Frankston, Victoria, the furphy spread that the place was named after an early inn run by a Frank Stone. A standard evolutionary pattern as well as the name served to endorse its veracity.[1]

No less important was the variety of functions these early pubs performed. Often hotels were the largest buildings in a town for a considerable time, and so played host to all sorts of public gatherings. Dances, theatricals and court sessions were held there, even church services. Thirty years after Sydney was founded, it was a pub that was chosen as the site for the meeting at which the Bank of New South Wales was founded. Further out, publicans often stood at the centre of their district, acting as constables, pound-keepers or postmasters. Across the counter, the gathering of the clientele meant that the bar also functioned as a primitive labour exchange, raided by squatters intent on hiring men.

The need for shelter on country routes led to a number of improvisations. For people travelling to the Victorian goldfields, Caroline Chisholm provided basic accommodation sometimes referred to as dak bungalows, after their Indian precedent. Elsewhere bush inns grew up at spots that bullockies would reach after a day's travel with their wagons and teams; on the 70 kilometres of road between Dubbo and Gilgandra in NSW, there were nine wayside inns by the 1890s. Little trace of them remains today; they were wooden structures, slabs and shingles, offering few comforts apart from a clean bed and a warm fire—with perhaps some local 'firewater' or rum from an illegal still. Such inns or hotels—the terms seem to have been interchangeable—were supplemented by shanties that sold the grog alone.[2]

With the coming of regular coach services, and with them the possibility of real travellers if not tourists, conditions steadily improved. By 1830 all major settlements were linked by coach runs, and by 1850 these had thickened to form a network across the settled parts of the country. In 1887 Cobb & Co. advertised ninety-eight separate routes in Victoria and NSW alone. More substantial hostelries sprang up in response to this timetabled traffic. Many were simple, single-storeyed structures, essentially a series of rooms entered from the veranda. Coach travellers stayed at some, but simply ate their meals at others—paying twice the normal price. Meanwhile in country towns, often the junction of a number of routes, substantial two-storey hotels appeared from the 1850s, often running to thirty or forty bedrooms.[3]

The first impact of the railways, which began to spread out in the 1870s and 1880s, was in the way they streamlined travel. In 1857 it took two and a half days to reach Beechworth from Melbourne by coach; in 1875, even before the branch line had been opened, the journey by rail as far as Wangaratta reduced travelling time to little more than half a day. The rest of the trip was still done by horse and carriage: coach travel had become relegated to a secondary position. Cobb & Co. now ran feeder routes, the last of them surviving in Queensland until 1924. While the

Whatever happened to the Grand Pacific? Lorne's lavishly appointed Grand Pacific Hotel, dating from 1878, was a fashionable resort from the moment it opened. By 1930, however, it was regarded as outmoded. Thus the tower, clipped in the middle image (a postcard), had by the 1950s been removed, and the cast-iron balconies largely replaced by fibro.

firm's livery and letting stables were maintained at many hotels, others went out of their way to identify with the new mode of travel. A rash of Railway Hotels appeared, usually handy to the nearest station; in the case of Oakleigh in Melbourne there was the Junction Hotel, a forlorn reminder of the short-lived Outer Circle railway.

The ease of rail encouraged the wealthy to travel. Initially fares were high, even higher than the matching journey by steamer. The coming of the train also encouraged higher expectations of accommodation, for easier travel made people less inclined to be adaptable. Up-to-the-minute facilities therefore had to beckon even from distant places: the Grand Pacific Hotel at Lorne, generally reached by rail followed by a jolting coach-ride over the Otways, was one of the first hotels to summon the servants by electrical means. The surprising result, though, was that people often flocked to such establishments in a way that had not been generally anticipated. Much scepticism was expressed by locals about the new Euroa Hotel, which they believed would be a white elephant. In 1892 it was reported to have become one of the most profitable in the district.[4]

Around the turn of the century the monitoring of conditions in hotels was most effectively done by commercial travellers who, because their business was facilitated by the more intricate railway system in Victoria, arose there as a force earlier than elsewhere. Conscious of the need to appear a gentleman ('Ambassadors of Commerce', they styled themselves), a traveller might be glimpsed in a railway carriage sitting in a top hat surrounded by cane baskets containing his wares. Dealing basically with retailers, he would arrive in a town with his goods and spread them out in a special room provided by the hotel. There storekeepers would come to inspect them and place orders.

Hotels soon learned to provide these Sample Rooms, and to call themselves the Commercial; Percy Grainger, staying at the Commercial in Leongatha, wondered at the 'floods of local cream' brought to the table by 'flirtless unconversational women waitresses'. Grainger was probably staying there because the Commercial Travellers' Association (CTA) provided an endorsement that was often taken as a cue by other travellers, and which therefore could be used by the association to bargain for improved conditions. Even this technique, however, was not always successful. The Victorian CTA journal, the *Traveller*, was in 1892 so outraged by the continuing poor sanitary conditions in so many hotels—clean, comfortable establishments but with lavatories distinctly malodorous—that it raised the matter editorially, at the risk of affronting decency.[5]

Traditionally public houses and inns had been separate establishments in England, but they were merging at about the time Australia was settled by Europeans. Here licensing regulations quickly completed the process. But it was the dramatic change in drinking habits, combined with easier travel, that led to a phenomenal growth in the number of hotels. In the ten years to 1880, they almost doubled in NSW to just under four hundred. A marked swing to beer-drinking then occurred—nationally, more than seven times was being consumed per capita in 1885 than in 1877—following the rapid spread of refrigeration. This had a number of consequences. Being slower than spirit-drinking, and inviting a long bar, beer-swilling required more space and therefore more money. Increasingly the breweries came to control hotels, often using an initial minority holding to squeeze out proprietors. This in turn encouraged unionisation among employees.[6]

Australia's first female union secretary was Cecilia Shelley, of the Western Australian Barmen and Barmaids Union. Generally, however, women had to face a barrage of discrimination. While in New South Wales they were never less than 25 per cent of licensees—if often in fringe areas—in other states there was an increasing campaign, orchestrated by the Woman's Christian Temperance Union, to strictly control their involvement in pubs altogether. Barmaids, who were both relatively well paid and more independent than factory workers or domestics, were increasingly regulated. In 1916 Victoria considered reserving such employment for girls of plain appearance (who would, it was presumed, be placed in no moral danger). Definition proved too difficult. Meanwhile South Australia aimed at abolishing them altogether. Similar restrictions were applied to licensees with varying severity across the bunk, but no mattresses; he did not provide meals, but they could buy food over at the store and cook it on the perfectly good fireplace. By the 1950s such hotels could be mildly tyrannical, especially at mealtimes—ruling, if they had any pretensions, that a man wear a jacket and tie in the dining room on even the hottest of days, or else insisting that the guests turn up for meals on the dot if they were to be fed at all. More recently the English newspaperman Michael Davie recalls how, after having spent a hot night on the veranda in one such place, the guests sat at a single long table for breakfast. 'We waited and waited. Finally, a hatch was flung up and a slattern poked her head through. "Hands up for porridge!" she cried.'[10]

Until the 1960s, conditions often remained primitive. The Melbourne journalist Keith Dunstan recalls beds made of iron, linoleum on the floor, wardrobes lined with newspaper, and lights so dim (never more than 40 watts) that it was impossible to read by them. Bathrooms and lavatories were always down the corridor, or even outside. Most had neither heating nor cooling, and even Hobart's relatively glamorous Wrest Point Hotel did not provide radiators in its rooms when it opened. Hotel proprietors therefore had no need to be surprised by the sudden popularity of the motel.[11]

Desperately they tried to compete. Their car parks, which rarely consisted of more than a few ramshackle garages, were gradually refurbished. But, especially in the suburbs and the country towns, hotels found it both difficult and expensive to provide private facilities in structures—whether built in the 1880s or the 1930s—whose layout assumed shared bathing and toilet facilities. In the 1950s and 1960s the cost of cannibalising bedrooms to make way for motel-like private facilities was simply too great. Those hotels that did try to meet the challenge, like Greenacres at Apollo Bay in Victoria, opened adjoining motel wings, with private facilities and car parking within viewing distance of the room. These often forlorn little motel wings are still to be seen attached to hundreds of hotel/motels around Australia, especially on highway routes and in country towns that have ceased to prosper. Only the most successful have been able to rebuild, masking their modest origins.[12]

Guest-houses: domestic comfort

In the 1880s a new kind of establishment was emerging. Guest-houses were dedicated to temperance, and liquor was not taken even with meals. Country pubs had offended people not only by the amount of drinking that went on, but its nature: a barman might be entrusted with a shearer's entire pay, so that he could set about going on a binge. Guest-houses, though, were often tucked away from the main roads, and prided themselves on their domesticity and solid decency, pitched between the squalor of the downmarket country pub on one hand and the flashness of a grand hotel on the other. Clustered in recognised tourist haunts in the mountains or by the sea, they were places (unlike most hotels) where a whole family might stay for a week, ten days, or even longer. Before World War I their homeliness could extend to the building—often a pre-existing dwelling that required little capital and minimal adaptation before opening its doors to the public.

By 1950 many guest-houses were ramshackle structures, 'weatherboard swastikas' as Barry Humphries calls them.[13] Even where the core

Carinya guest-house, Lorne. Croquet, one of the organised activities habitually dominated by stiff-backed ladies

Elsiemere guest-house at Tuggerah Lakes, north of Sydney. This publicity postcard shows the variety of activities available in an Edwardian guest-house. In 1908 it slept fifteen people, and charged 5s to 6s a day.

Friday, to work upon the arrangements for the following nine days. These included five picnics (all to nearby waterfalls), games and card tournaments, and tennis, bowls, golf and croquet competitions; athletic sports, which included novelty races and a tug-of-war in which married men were pitted against bachelors; and a Plain and Fancy Dress Ball. The last-mentioned was restricted to guests at Erskine House; there would be prizes for the best costumes.

In the inter-war period, a holiday in a guest-house was the kind that most Australians had in mind. Indeed there were some who would pronounce, from a deckchair on the veranda, 'I always say you should see your own country first'. It was just as well, since any alternative was usually beyond them. Tariffs of guest-houses, particularly away from the sea, were reasonable: £2 10s 0d a week was common. While Erskine House charged just over twice that, nearby Kalimna, which had some pretensions to smartness, charged £4 4s 0d as its maximal Christmas tariff—in 1930 two shillings less than the weekly basic wage. Single women in particular went to such places in the hope of finding 'a nice friendly lot of people', some of whom might remain friends for years. Carinya, also at Lorne, uniquely managed to persuade the manufacturers of Rose postcards to place, under the caption identifying the guesthouse, the words 'A NEW HAPPINESS. A NEW OUTLOOK ON LIFE. A NEW CIRCLE OF FRIENDS'. The assumption of community, albeit a temporary one, would often be ratified in group photographs taken of the guests, sometimes with the proprietress seated in the front row like a slightly exasperated headmistress. Even at Carinya, the first accommodation house in Lorne not to insist that young women have a chaperon to accompany them, young men loitering with intent were shown to their rooms by the proprietor's daughter.[14]

The decline evident in 1950 had become marked a decade later. Guest-house stock was ageing, and standards of comfort had shot well past the facilities traditionally provided. Even Edwardian visitors would complain of the cold in mountain guest-houses, away from that log fire; and by the time of the long boom the draughty corridors, and the shared

By the 1960s most guest-houses had become run-down. They were poorly heated, plagued by mosquitoes, and often subject to makeshift renovations. By the time they were demolished or burnt down few regretted their passing.

bedrooms and bathroom facilities, had become outmoded. Guest-houses at the beach, with their fibro additions, louvre windows, and an inability to keep out mosquitoes, were slipping further and further down the accommodation listings. A new generation was rising with the spread of car ownership, and greater mobility began the segmentation of social life along consumerist patterns that has continued unabated ever since. Motels quickly took over; guest-houses disappeared, many in fires that some said were deliberately lit. The decline in numbers was dramatic. In Katoomba in 1930 there were sixty-six guest-houses; in 1990 just six.

Luxury hotels

In the 1920s Australia's grand hotels published hotel annuals, and in the case of Sydney's Wentworth Hotel, a quarterly magazine. One of the city's most expensive hotels, with an inclusive tariff starting at twenty shillings per day, the Wentworth promoted itself as 'Australia's Hotel de Luxe', being the only hotel in Australia 'steam heated in winter and air cooled in summer'.

> Every bedroom has a telephone, also hot and cold running water. Many suites with private bathrooms. Close to stores, banks, theatres and railway terminal, but away from noise and traffic roar. Magnificent lounge always bright and cheerful with freshly cut flowers.

During the summer the Wentworth advertised its Palm Court Cafe as 'Sydney's coolest spot', offering three-course 'Business Men's Luncheons' and an hour's dominoes, 'sheltered from the heat of the day'. The Cafe also catered for bridge parties, charity dances and weddings. The *Wentworth Magazine* promoted day trips around Sydney, photographically celebrated the emerging arch of the Sydney Harbour Bridge, and even included an article on Aborigines, noting that 'there is increasing interest shown in the lives and the ways of these people whom the whites have displaced by their civilizing influence, and by the steady force of ruthless evolution which has apparently decreed the extinction of this race'. The Wentworth prided itself on being a civilised address at which thinking people, of sufficient means, could stay or foregather. During the Great Depression the hotel acknowledged 'difficult times through which we are passing' with 'drastic reductions in tariff', but with continuing high standards in service and cuisine.[15]

The Depression proved more shortlived in the hotel business than in almost any other area of commerce. Despite reduced, sometimes almost nonexistent incomes, working-class men continued to drink beer and those members of the middle class who found themselves somewhat insulated from the crisis, especially doctors and lawyers, continued to travel. Flush with cash at a time when building costs were low, the breweries embarked on the largest single series of facelifts ever seen across Australia. Hotels from Albury to Ararat, from Ashfield to Cottesloe, their 1880s facades complete with ageing cast-iron balconies, now acquired smart new entrances and suspended steel awnings, while inside the bars were reshaped and retiled. Other hotels were demolished, and new art deco establishments, with their striking verticals and strong horizontal brickwork, appeared in many suburbs and the more prosperous country towns.

Art deco extensions to already large hotels appeared in major tourist spots and in the cities. The Hotel Manly, built in the 1920s, added a ten-storey tower block in 1934. High up on the new facade stood a statue of Governor Phillip gazing forth on the harbour for which he had held such high hopes. Splendid views were offered from all rooms in the new extension, which also included a lavish ballroom. Wood panelling gave the suites a plush feel; adventurous guests could retrieve their own laundry from the Hills Hoists on the roof, which could also be used for sunbathing.[16]

One of the largest private hotels in Australia, the Canberra, opened in Brisbane in 1929; its 350 rooms were insufficient to meet demand, and in 1934 another three floors were added. Its guest list grew steadily, even during the Depression, from 55 545 in 1930 to 71 028 in 1932 to 80 911 in 1934. The Canberra proclaimed its fireproof status, with walls, floors, ceilings, staircases and most furnishings built of fireproof materials. The hotel explained to prospective customers that 'because of

In many Australian towns some hotels are the second or third on the same site. This example, from Lakes Entrance, Victoria, shows the Central Hotel before and after it was rebuilt in the 1930s.

no fire risk, *The Canberra* carries no fire insurance'. Such touching faith in fire prevention had some justification in fact. Most of Australia's major urban fires in the twentieth century have been in woolstores, theatres, department stores, chemical storage facilities and industrial plants. Fifteen people died in a fire at the Savoy Residential Hotel in Kings Cross, NSW, in 1975, but no major Australian hotel was destroyed by

SOUTH AUSTRALIAN

1836 CENTENARY CELEBRATIONS 1936

OFFICIAL
SOUVENIR
PROGRAMME

SPECIAL
CARNIVAL
PERIOD

DECEMBER 18th - 31st 1936.

Price 6d.

An example of publicity from a state Tourist Bureau and Intelligence Department, aimed more at the immigrant, in fact, than the tourist. Note the extent of South Australia: the Northern Territory was not transferred to the Commonwealth till 1911.

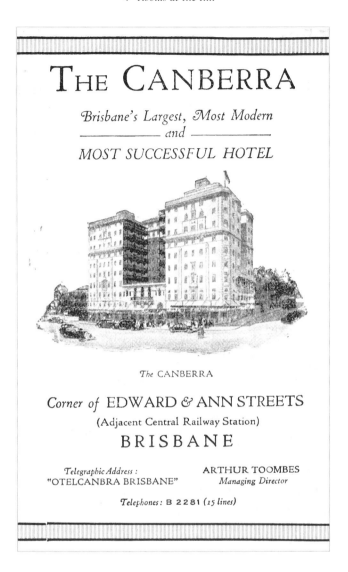

The CANBERRA

Brisbane's Largest, Most Modern
——————— *and* ———————
MOST SUCCESSFUL HOTEL

The CANBERRA

Corner of EDWARD & ANN STREETS
(Adjacent Central Railway Station)
BRISBANE

Telegraphic Address :   **ARTHUR TOOMBES**
"OTELCANBRA BRISBANE"   *Managing Director*

Telephones: B 2281 *(15 lines)*

fire in the twentieth century. Nonetheless, after a catastrophic hotel fire in the USA, today's hotel proprietors are less sanguine about the risks than the Canberra's management in 1934.

Melbourne's Hotel Australia, rebuilt on the same Collins Street site in 1938 and 1939, rose to the maximum 132 feet allowed by the building regulations. With an arcade of forty-two shops, and ready access to the Australia Theatre (an air-conditioned cinema), the Tatler

News Theatrette, the Silver Grill and two public bars, the hotel could legitimately proclaim itself 'Melbourne's social meeting place'. A banquet hall and dance floor accommodated over 500 guests, and there were nine floors of bedrooms; the hotel could cater for any function. To assist tourists with travel arrangements, the hotel's arcade included an entrance to the Victorian Government Tourist Bureau's magnificent new booking hall, which claimed to offer 'the most comprehensive travel service in Australia'.[17]

To foreign visitors the most distinctive aspect of the Australian hotel trade was what was known locally as 'the six o'clock swill'. Victorians voted in 1955 to retain six o'clock closing. The Melbourne Olympics put such arrangements under the world spotlight. One journalist wrote that nowhere in the rest of the world was there 'anything as revolting and disgusting' as this 'daily demonstration of piggery'. Life for the bar-men and barmaids in this smoke-filled environment proved very un-pleasant. Barmaids at the time were paid less than barmen and subjected to regular sexual advances, though most were skilled at dealing with their drunken male clientele. Women were restricted to the Ladies Lounge, where the drinks cost more but the atmosphere was more relaxed.

New South Wales had abandoned six o'clock closing in 1955, and at the same time allowed RSL and sporting clubs to serve liquor. There patrons could drink until 10 p.m. The following year sporting and RSL clubs were allowed to introduce poker machines. By 1962 there were 1285 clubs in NSW with hundreds of thousands of members.[18] Some of the largest clubs were built in the NSW Murray River towns of Albury, Moama and Corowa. Victorians flocked to these glamorous clubs, which offered luxurious dining rooms and gambling opportunities unavailable in their home state other than in illegal premises. The hotel, motel and caravan park trade blossomed on both sides of the Murray. Victorians were finally allowed to drink until 10 p.m in 1966, ten years after the Olympics. It would be another two decades before they would be allowed to gamble on machines in their own state. In the meantime the NSW border clubs made a killing, bussing up professional and pensioner groups from Melbourne and rural Victoria to play the poker machines.

The five-star hotel room

International tourists who arrived in Australia during the 1960s and 1970s found, with few exceptions, a range of increasingly decayed city hotels and a modest range of new ones that did not keep pace with demolitions. In Melbourne the Australia, the Windsor and the Victoria, and in Sydney the Australia and the Metropole (the city's largest with 350 rooms but only one suite) lingered on. They were all run-down, and none of them were able to provide something as basic as a telephone connection to all rooms. At the Metropole guests could hire a TV, radio, radiator or refrigerator, and a room was set aside for television viewing. In 1966 the public bar opened from 10 a.m. to 10 p.m., following the maximum twelve-hour licence granted to bars. While the public bar opened from Monday to Saturday, the hotel's other bars were open only from Monday to Friday. To enter the dining room or the lounge gentlemen were required to wear a coat and tie or cravat. If you arrived at the hotel after 8 p.m. on a Sunday night, as many country travellers did, you had to rely on room service for a light meal or liquor.[19]

Melbourne's Southern Cross Hotel (opened 1962), on the site of the old Eastern Market, had zigzag lines, blue panelling, an ice-cream parlour and a ten pin bowling alley.[20] Visiting Americans could feel right at home. Sydney's answer, developed by Qantas, took the name Wentworth, the veteran hotel demolished to make way for a Qantas skyscraper. At Chifley Square the new Wentworth (1966), with 452 rooms to the Southern Cross's 418, claimed the largest air-conditioning plant in the southern hemisphere. All of Sydney's grand pre-war hotels were demolished in the 1960s, including the Metropole in Bent Street, the Arcadia, Adams and the Sydney in Pitt Street, Ushers and the Australia in Castlereagh Street, and the Grand Central in Clarence Street. All gave way to office blocks. Between them they had well over 1750 rooms. The consequence was that not until the five-star hotel boom of the 1980s did Sydney's room count surpass the peak of the early 1960s. The demand for more spacious rooms and suites meant that the new hotels fitted fewer guests per square metre than their older counterparts had.

Melbourne's Majestic Hotel in St Kilda remained a private hotel, code of the day for no liquor. Like the big Sydney hotels it could accommodate 350 people, in rooms or suites, although only the latter had central heating. Even as late as 1960 it advertised itself as offering hot and cold running water to all rooms, but telephones were not provided. Melbourne's Chevron Hotel, on the corner of Commercial Road and St Kilda Road, not only provided telephones in all rooms, but a heated swimming pool as well. Proclaiming itself to be within easy tram reach of both the city and St Kilda Beach, it advertised extensively to the interstate market, with its forty lock-up garages, and convention and reception facilities. Melbourne's middle class promptly adopted it as a venue for family and business functions.[21]

Building on the success of the Melbourne Chevron its owner, Stanley Korman, launched Chevron Queensland Limited and Chevron Sydney Limited, to which the public could subscribe by buying shares at five shillings each. Chevron Queensland undertook to build a luxury hotel on the Gold Coast, with only Lennons Broadbeach and the Surfers Paradise Hotel (Korman bought and refurbished the latter) as competition. The Chevron Queensland opened with a 'skyline beer garden' and shops

The Melbourne entrepreneur Stanley Korman goes modern for Surfers Paradise. This cabaret and the car park were built before the Chevron's main accommodation block.

in 1957, adding an accommodation block for two hundred guests the following year. Korman's lavish prospectus for the Sydney Chevron superimposed the proposed hotel, eventually planned to house an astonishing 1200 guests, on the Sydney skyline, and emphasised its proximity to the new Overseas Terminal at Circular Quay, about to open. Acknowledging the coming supremacy of air travel, the prospectus also pictured a jet flying overhead: 'CHEVRON Australia's sun-drenched Sydney . . . only hours from World Capitals by Jet-age Aircraft. The building now being erected is an hotel of the most modern design with each bedroom having its own bathroom'.[22]

But only the first section of this hotel was ever built. Korman's companies ran into trouble in the credit squeeze of 1960–61, and he fled Australia in 1967. A gaping hole awaited the forty-storey tower block that never happened.

Arriving at Tullamarine or Kingsford Smith in 1970, international guests had the choice of a private airport bus or a taxi of uncertain age to take them to their hotel. If they were unlucky enough to arrive on a Sunday their hotel was almost the only place where they would be able to find a meal, let alone a drink. International tourists, especially the Americans and the Japanese, were not much taken with the quality of Australian accommodation. American troops on rest and recreation leave from Vietnam in the 1960s and 1970s put up with the scraggy Kings Cross hotels not just because their attention was focused on activities other than sleeping but because this was the largest concentration of hotels the metropolis had to offer, most of the downtown hotels having fallen to Whelan the Wrecker. Middle-aged American and Japanese tourists and Japanese honeymooners wanted luxurious accommodation, not least to rest up from what was probably the longest flight they had ever taken in their lives. Most of the Kings Cross hotels were dives, and even newer establishments like the circular Gazebo soon lost their gloss. The Chevron became very run-down and spent its last few years boarded up.

Australian, American, Singaporean and Japanese investors were quick to appreciate the new opportunity. In the 1980s Sydney and Melbourne experienced a spectacular growth in new luxury hotels, aimed primarily at the international tourist and interstate business market. One of the first to open was the Regent Hotel, overlooking Circular Quay. Work began on the site in 1979 and the hotel was opened by NSW Premier Neville Wran in January 1983. It took the developers of the Regent ten years to persuade the Sydney Cove Redevelopment Authority, successfully targeted by green bans in the 1970s, to give them permission to build the hotel on land owned by the Authority. The full-colour commemorative book crowed about the result:

> All redevelopment and construction had been halted by the Green Bans. And for the moment it appeared as if all progress had also been defeated. But despite the exodus of family business, some people clung to the belief that this was the chosen spot for the first truly international hotel of Sydney. This is where the Regent of Sydney could pay homage to the true value of the Rocks. This is where nostalgia and progress could cohabit to the benefit of all concerned.[23]

Every room boasted a harbour view, and the foyer, formal and informal dining spaces were spacious and spectacular. The Regent soon established itself as the place to meet and be seen, replacing tired and cramped competitors such as the Hilton and the Menzies.

Melbourne, with fewer international visitors to cater for, was slower to invest in grand new hotels, but the Rialto on Collins Street nicely blended nineteenth-century architecture with twentieth-century facilities, as did the Hotel Intercontinental in Sydney, which appropriated the Colonial Treasury building for its elegant public spaces. Melbourne was the only Australian city to boast a few grand hotels remaining from the Victorian and Edwardian eras. Of these, by far the most imposing, the Windsor, was taken over by the Oberoi group in the 1980s. Overlooking Parliament House at the top of Spring Street, the Windsor is Australia's sole surviving grand metropolitan hotel.

Sydney became the focus of the five-star hotel boom, which reached its height in the bicentennial year, 1988, when seven five-star hotels were under construction, adding another 2400 rooms to the eight existing establishments. Melbourne also boasted eight five-star hotels, but was only adding another two. Perth, with seven, reflecting the mineral and investment boom of the previous two decades, had no further plans on the books. Two-thirds of the guests in these hotels were Australians and New Zealanders, with the North American market (12 per cent) and the Japanese market (10 per cent) making up most of the remainder. People in five-star hotels were much more likely to be attending a conference or on a business trip than visitors in cheaper accommodation.[24] A goodly proportion of the guests, whether international or domestic, were able to tax-deduct their food, drink and accommodation costs.

In 1998, 73 000 people (full-time equivalent) worked in licensed hotels providing accommodation; 31 000 worked in guest-houses and motels; and another 8000 were employed in the serviced apartment industry. The number of staff per bed varied enormously, according to the type and grade of accommodation. In Australia's 55 five-star hotels there were seven staff members for every bed, while in the 1778 three-star hotels and motels there were one and a half staff per bed. Such figures may be reassuring for guests who ponder why the five-star tariff tends to be three to four times the three-star tariff. The figures also indicate that while some parts of the tourism industry, including restaurants, cafes and high-quality accommodation, are very labour-intensive, other sectors of the industry, such as caravan parks, with one staff member for every twenty-eight sites, are not. Of the 112 000 (full-time equivalent) people working in the Australian accommodation industry in 1998, over 100 000 worked in hotels, motels and guest-houses. Our larger five-star hotels are now on a par with big manufacturing plants as major employers, often having over 500 workers on site.[25]

Bed and breakfasts

As the guest-houses burnt down, were demolished, were converted into luxury inner city flats or simply fell apart, their place in catering for family and other group holidays was promptly taken by a new form of accommodation, the bed and breakfast establishment, which provided primarily for singles and couples without attendant children, and the holiday flat, which has become a dominant feature of tourist accommodation not only in resort areas but in the cities as well.

Bed and breakfast establishments had long been part of the holiday-maker's fare in Britain, which is where most Australians first encountered them. Here, listings for bed and breakfast establishments did not become a common feature of national accommodation guides until the early 1990s. Even in Tasmania, with a surfeit of suitable properties for B&B establishments, the motoring organisations took a long time to pick up the new trend, celebrated in a series of separate books by enterprising authors who could see that the B&B and farm stay movement was a growing phenomenon. Janette and James Thomas explained in the 1994 edition of their *Australian Bed and Breakfast Book* that 'the 400 hosts listed are homeowners who want to share their love of the country with travellers'. The listings were written by the hosts, so that the authors could claim that 'ours is not simply an accommodation guide but an introduction to a uniquely Australian experience'.[26]

The most spectacular growth of B&B establishments has taken place in both old and new wine regions, including the Barossa Valley in South Australia, the Hunter Valley in NSW, the Yarra Valley and the Mornington Peninsula in Victoria, and Margaret River in Western Australia. Pokolbin, a tiny settlement outside Cessnock, did not rate a mention in accommodation guides until the 1980s. When Max Lake planted vines there in the early 1960s he created the first new vineyard in the Hunter Valley in the twentieth century. The success of Lakes Folly, famous for its cabernet sauvignon, was followed by that of scores of other vineyards, both big and small, in both the traditional wine-growing areas and in the Upper Hunter.

In the 1960s and 1970s, the only accommodation to be had in the area were two licensed hotels and one motel in Cessnock, a hard-nosed, depressed mining town. By 1989 there were five motels, two establishments offering self-contained apartments, two guest-houses, including the lavish Peppers, and two sets of cottages. Ten years later there were ten motels, a five-star Cypress Lakes Resort, six sets of cottages, nine guest-houses, one lodge, two bed and breakfast establishments and two groups of self-contained apartments.

Accommodation guides underestimate the B&Bs because the smaller operations do not always bother to seek a listing. Pokolbin has gone from being a rural backwater of vineyards and farms to offering a veritable plethora of restaurants, accommodation outlets and vineyards, from the earliest (McWilliams, Tyrells, Tullochs), to the relatively long-established (Lakes Folly, Rothburys) to the upstart boutique. Even Cessnock has benefited, with motels, guest-houses and its own B&B establishments.[27] Tourism simply didn't figure in the Rev. Alan Walker's 1945 account of Cessnock, *Coaltown,* which revealed that the town had among the highest proportion of 'illegitimate births' in Australia.

From holiday flat to holiday apartment

Modest holiday flats, rarely of more than two storeys, were to be found at most of the more popular resorts. Their facilities, especially the fibro blocks, were not often any better than those of the guest-houses, except that you could usually do your own cooking. But in the 1960s more substantial brick holiday flats were built at many coastal resorts, and in the 1970s and 1980s high-rise luxury apartments, often purchased by naive southerners, spread like a rash along sections of the Queensland and northern NSW coasts. In the 1980s and 1990s Australia saw a surge in the building of hotels and holiday flats reminiscent of the frenzied motel-building of the late 1950s and 1960s, when any self-respecting suburb or country town wanted to be in the motel stakes.

The four- and five-star hotel boom in the capital cities and other major urban coastal resorts, including Cairns, the Gold Coast, Terrigal, Lorne, Glenelg and Scarborough (Western Australia), was soon overtaken by an investor-led boom in both walk-up (four storeys and under) and high-rise (five and above, requiring at least one lift) holiday apartments. Over 80 per cent of high-rise apartment blocks built in the 1980s and 1990s are located on the NSW and Queensland coasts, with fewer than a hundred blocks to be found in the coastal resorts of

Victoria, South Australia and Western Australia.[28] Most of the development on the NSW south coast, including Merimbula (a Victorian colony) and Batemans Bay (the coastal outgrowth of the ACT) is low-rise. The high-rise starts in earnest at Terrigal, east of Gosford, and continues to disfigure the coastline at regular intervals: Nelsons Bay, Port Macquarie, Coffs Harbour, the Gold Coast, the Sunshine Coast, Hervey Bay and Cairns. Some of the ugliest, most oppressive and most environmentally unfriendly blocks ever built in Australia are to be found along this coastline. Only a handful of the older fishing communities, blessed by being some distance from the highway, including Harrington (via Taree) and Yamba (via Maclean) have retained modest structures and avoided the depredations of developers.

Other communities, most notably that of Byron Bay, have managed to keep both high-rise developers and fast-food chains, including McDonald's, at bay. This has only been possible by the unlikely alliance of well-heeled local business people and environmentalists electing a local council without the usual number of real estate agents. Most coastal councils have pursued development at almost any cost, bridging inland lakes, creating fake canals, and completely disregarding damage to

Purpose-built beach resorts like Surfers Paradise offered a wide range of accommodation. Here are some 1950s-style serviced apartments.

the water table, sand-dunes and beach vegetation. The Victorian coastal town of Torquay finally succumbed to McDonald's in 1999, some years after Paris and Venice had opened their golden arches.

Holiday flats along our coastline are nothing new. Small-scale developers built single-storey fibro units and two-storey fibro blocks of flats in every major holiday destination in Australia, and in many minor ones as well. These flats, alongside camping grounds and the occasional hotel, were usually the main form of accommodation in almost every coastal resort that developed from the 1920s. Coastal resorts of the Victorian and Edwardian eras, including those dotted around Moreton Bay and Port Phillip Bay, already had a substantial accommodation base in the form of guest-houses, as did many of the Sydney beaches. They too saw their quota of fibro flats, but the real fibro capitals were places like Narooma, The Entrance and Foster/Tuncurry in NSW, and Surfers Paradise, Caloundra, Mooloolaba, Noosa, Hervey Bay and Magnetic Island, off Townsville. These were all popular fishing and surfing spots, where fibro cinemas and fibro surf livesaving clubs gave the built landscape a slightly decayed air within just a few years of construction.[29] Many of these settlements did not get town water until the 1950s or 1960s, so rainwater tanks were a standard feature.

Most of the fibro flats were demolished between the late 1950s and the 1980s, depending on the popularity of the resort and the keenness of developers. Occasional pockets survive, sometimes within a block or two of the beach, especially where local councils have allowed high-rise building immediately overlooking the beachfront, effectively obliterating the outlook of their immediate neighbours.

The flats of the 1930s were usually advertised by name and by proprietor—usually, as with guest-houses, female. Cottesloe, Perth's leading beach resort, offered revamped art deco hotels, flats, apartments and even rooms with use of a kitchen. Western Australia's widest choice of accommodation was to be found at Rottnest Island, 18 kilometres northwest of Fremantle and accessible by 'excursion steamer' throughout the tourist season. The Board of Control, appointed by the government in 1917, was charged with creating a permanent reserve for the people's use. In the inter-war years the Board provided a commodious hostel, furnished cottages, bungalows, flats and campsites. All were sewered, the water supply was secure, and the island had electric light, telephone and bank facilities. While intending holidaymakers were told a lot about the facilities, there was no mention of the island's past as the site at various times of an Aboriginal prison, a penal settlement, a prisoner-of-war camp and a boys reformatory. Prison buildings were adapted to holiday use, while canvas and timber structures, along with new timber bungalows, were built for families.[30] But only an unobservant visitor could fail to notice the regimented feel of some of the buildings and of parts of the island itself. Since the 1970s Rottnest's past has featured explicitly in tourist promotions.

The high-rise holiday apartment boom has seen ever more luxurious units, with spa baths, designer kitchens, pools and gyms. These now feature regularly in the work of crime novelists, including Peter Corris, whose private eye Cliff Hardy is a connoisseur of harbour and beach views. By 1997 holiday apartment blocks provided more beds than the nation's hotels. To fight this trend, some new hotels termed themselves all-suite hotels, often with kitchen facilities. Holiday apartments are the preferred form of accommodation for longer stays—three nights to one or more weeks. Motels have found it difficult to adapt to a more discerning and more demanding market. They are still popular as overnight destinations for people travelling on, but are less and less used otherwise.

Run-down apartment blocks and ageing hotels and motels have provided the core of a new type of accommodation, the backpacker hostel, which by 1997 provided 32 000 beds around Australia, almost half of them in Queensland. Cairns' Captain Cook Motel, complete with a three-storey-high model of the Captain, fell on hard times in the 1990s and turned to the bunk-style accommodation of the backpacker hostel.

'Inns' can still be found in many parts of Australia, especially on the old highway routes. The telltale form of the 1840s and 1850s inn, with its veranda and low-slung roof, is a reminder of the horsedrawn era when thirsty travellers rested up for the night. Most of them were supplanted by hotels and guest-houses, and then by the motel and the short-stay apartment block. Just as some destinations manage to renew themselves, so too do forms of accommodation. Convenience, price and expectations of luxury all contribute to the provision of and demand for the different types. The great variety in accommodation, covering over 250 000 rooms countrywide, can be seen from the following table.

Table 1   Tourist accommodation, beds by sector (000s)

	Caravan park sites[a]	Motels & guest-houses	Hostels	Licensed hotels	Holiday flats
1981	197	182		64	
1985	210	223		90	
1989	281	286		136	136
1993	288	303	25	175	154
1997	287	323	33	203	193

[a] About one-third of all caravan park sites are occupied by permanents.

Source: ABS, *Tourist Accommodation Australia*, cat. no. 8635.0, December quarter.

Beside the Seaside

PEOPLE BEGAN TO GO to the beach in droves only in relatively recent times. In the eighteenth century the Mediterranean coast was usually avoided during the course of the Grand Tour to Italy. Instead of the warm water, people were conscious of hot sands, a pestilential coastline, lurking immorality and a sun that might painfully weather you to the hue of the working classes.

A heightened interest in the seaside has quite an unexpected provenance: it originated in therapeutic courses of treatment engaged in by the upper classes. With the shift in sensibility that occurred in the mid-eighteenth century, people began to feel some attraction to the sea because of its untamed nature: in itself this might act as a corrective to the perceived evils of urban civilisation. But the cures quickly became more specific. Doctors believed that immersion in water had a tightening or loosening effect upon the tissues, according to the temperature. 'To bathe in the sea is to have not only a cold bathe', declared one, 'but a medicinal cold bathe'. Others added massages with freshly collected seaweed. For those who went into the water—swimming was usually not included in the cures—there were bathing machines, as well appointed as a bathroom.

A social life sprang up around these activities. On the beach itself there was no sunbathing—mainly walking and conversation, although also horseriding and, for a time, some organised races. But in the resorts that first grew up in Britain—such as Weymouth, Scarborough and Brighton—elaborate social patterns were soon articulated.[1]

This can be seen most clearly in the case of Brighton. In the middle of the eighteenth century the fishing village of Brightelmstone had been declining when fashionable society began to resort there, attracted by its sea breezes and relative shelter from northerly winds. Once the Prince Regent decided to grace it with a Royal Pavilion, the place functioned almost as a second capital. By 1833 it was remarked that the line of splendid buildings banked up along the seafront had no equivalent outside St Petersburg. Its social rituals, taken over from spa towns, reflected its social importance: a master of ceremonies made introductions, settled matters of precedence, arranged for the names of new arrivals to be published, and so forth.

Once the railway bridged the 80 kilometres from London, as it did in 1841, this exclusive order was doomed. In the first six months of 1844, Brighton trains carried 360 000 people—seven or eight times the town's population. By 1890 day trippers were so numerous that for a short time they were actively discouraged. Foremost among the attractions luring them were an aquarium (the first) and the West Pier, which extended for 340 metres. The band playing there each morning and evening was soon augmented by a theatre, and then a concert hall, to entertain the promenading crowds. By the 1890s an even more extravagant second pier, with cafes, a ballroom and shops, complemented the first.[2]

Brighton therefore was the resort uppermost in Australian minds right down to World War I. This can be seen by looking at the map: there are Brightons in every state except Western Australia. Indeed Sydney could be said to have two, since in addition to Brighton-le-Sands there is Manly, which well into the twentieth century would sometimes be promoted as 'the Brighton of Australia'. The link remains in the North Steyne and South Steyne, which circumscribe Manly Beach; promenaders in the English Brighton would walk 'along the Steyne'.

Promenading, with its opportunity for agreeable exercise combined with social display, had often taken place in England, usually after

The importance of Brighton. All over Australia, beyond the half-dozen localities named directly after the primal English resort, there were a number of hotels drawing on the memory of its glamour.

church, when people could show themselves off in their Sunday best. In Brighton, and about the same time in Nice—where one of the main streets is still called Promenade des Anglais—the custom migrated to the seaside. Nineteenth-century Australians were only too happy to follow suit. If malaria was—quite literally—bad air, then that available at the seashore was decidedly fresh and bracing: ozone-bearing breezes contained oxygen in a particularly pure form. Indeed ozone became a buzz word for the late Victorians, much as aerobics has become today; the paddlesteamer *Ozone* regularly took Melburnians across the Bay to the Ozone Hotel at Queenscliff.

The vogue for piers was, quite literally, an extension of that for the promenade, effectively rerouted to become a highway to ozone. The piers were a seeming triumph over nature, carried on the back of the vastly improved Victorian metallurgy; from the beginning they were much more democratic. Above all they offered opportunities for amusement,

ST. KILDA from Pier

St Kilda, in the days of its elegance. The Duke and Duchess of York, world tourists, entered Melbourne from the pier to open the first federal parliament in 1901. The suburb was already beginning to double as a popular seaside resort.

Gert Sellheim, an Estonian immigrant, perceived Australia's lifesavers through a modernist mindset in his 1931 poster.

Amusement strips sprang up at the seaside because the crowds were large, mixed and idle. Often they began with relatively simple entertainments, such as this one at Bondi, c. 1900.

for social mixing, and possibilities for adventure. It is no accident that risqué postcard humour was invariably located at the seaside.

Australia, being a pioneering country—and exultingly democratic—went in for functional jetties rather than piers. The only grace note on a jetty at Cottesloe was its widening halfway along to encompass a bandstand. At Manly there had been plans to build a grandiose Palace Pier in the manner of Brighton (as the name indicated), but these came to nought. One that was built, however, was the Ocean Pier at Coogee, complete with neo-oriental pepper pot towers that paid homage to the Royal Pavilion. Constructed in 1928, amid optimistic statements about its supplying a much-needed facility in 'SYDNEY, THE CITY OF PLEASURE', the pier was soon declared unsafe by the local council, which in 1934 supervised its demolition. Another long pier, that at Glenelg in South Australia, also had a chequered history; in its early days it serviced shipping, and was destroyed after a heavy storm in 1948. It was not replaced for a long time, and then only in truncated form.[3]

Nevertheless it was the sea that was the major drawcard. In 1881 St Kilda boasted no fewer than five bathing establishments, and it was possible to buy rail tickets that not only included admission to Hegarty's Railway Baths (as they were eagerly styled) but to most of the others; extras such as towel and costume hire could also be paid for in this way. Advertising hype had quite early put the baths in people's consciousness. In 1865 hundreds of posters posed a cryptic question: 'Where Is Sam?'. The answer turned out to be at Hegarty's Baths, where he was the new proprietor.[4]

Sunbaking and its consequences

When in the 1840s a rich landowner built Strathbarton near the Tasmanian township of Hamilton, the facade of this Georgian house looked in the direction of a romantic glen. It also faced south; it was not till eighty years later that subsequent owners effectively turned the house round by building a double-storeyed veranda on the north side, to catch the sun. This was no isolated fancy; sunbaking had become popular in Germany since the turn of the century, and in 1923 a number of Riviera hotels—hitherto always frequented by those seeking to escape the northern European winter—decided for the first time to remain open during the summer.[5]

St Kilda, then, got caught up in this massive shift towards the sun and the sea. Attempts to keep it decorous extended, as late as 1931, to its having a Battle of the Flowers, just like Nice. Earlier there had been extensive land reclamation, with gardens and embankments put in place, complete with palms, just like Cannes. But there were still many residents who, if they had an image of any other place at all, would have thought of respectable Bournemouth. Moreover, that site of pleasure the pier doubled as Melbourne's ceremonial entrance: while the city was the national capital, royalty and governors would land here, then sweep along Fitzroy Street and St Kilda Road and so to Government House. The issues suddenly presented by the upsurge in bathing—as swimming was constantly referred to even as late as the 1950s—therefore involved

132

St Kilda in a contest between countervailing images more sharply than anywhere else.

In NSW, the position of Manly was relatively uncomplicated. By contrast, the large seminary there scarcely dented the place's ambience as a resort; indeed, since there was no rail or tram link, the only way most people could reach it from Sydney was by ferry. So when in 1902 the crusading editor of a local paper, William Gocher, became bent on publicising his personal defiance of the prohibition on daytime bathing there, resistance was slight. The following year the Council rescinded the relevant bylaw, contenting itself with the regulation of costumes and conduct. With a surf beach that could now be readily enjoyed, Manly leapt ahead. Five years after all-day bathing had been legalised, Manly's population had increased by 50 per cent, while house rents and rates had doubled, with property values rising even more spectacularly.[6]

Given this extraordinary change in Manly's fortunes, it needs to be explained why swimming in Australia took so long to emerge. Initially the attitude of government was unequivocal: an 1833 ordinance in NSW was confirmed and extended in 1838, forbidding all bathing between 6 a.m. and 8 p.m., not only in built-up areas but also in waters adjacent to bridges and roads. But there was simply not a great deal of interest, as those who attempted to found a gentlemen's bathing club in Hobart in 1847 soon found. Standards of propriety were still British, and it was only when people began to take to the wilder, un-English surf beaches that these were increasingly perceived as irrelevant and restrictive, although often not by local residents. In the words of St Kilda's historian, the move to the beaches entailed 'a social revolt . . . a bathing revolution by the new generation'.[7]

Three separate issues soon emerged, the hours and location of bathing being the first. Apart from the fact that initially costumes were scarce, and there were no changing facilities, the new craze for bathing did contain an anarchic element in its rude democracy. 'Plain primitive manhood and womanhood', said the *Lone Hand*, 'are the only tests the surfbather applies to distinguish one from another'. So while Tom Roberts was painting *The Sunny South*, with its idealised male nude bathing, a

of serious swimming. On the whole, though, regulations were simply ignored as fashions became bolder: attempts to impose standards sometimes produced laughable results. Concerned about the way costumes tended to feature the male anatomy, councillors insisted that men wear briefs over their costumes—and later, since that did not always result in a becoming modesty—that trunks should have a 'modesty skirt'. At St Kilda it was only a sudden unavailability of neck-to-knee costumes that led to the council abandoning them in 1938; the churches were still actively lobbying to maintain suitable standards of decency. Even at Manly there were attempts to put the clock back, but after World War II the battle shifted to women. Bondi had only just made the 'modern costume' legal in 1951, when shortly afterwards inspectors were escorting the first bikini-clad woman off the beach. She was lent a jacket to preserve her modesty.[8]

Towards lifesaving

Much of this story represents white Australia's belated adaptation to a new environment. Captain Cook had approvingly noted Aboriginal body-surfers, and it was a Pacific islander, Tommy Tanna, who first showed white youths how to 'shoot' the waves at Manly in the 1880s. Soon the more adventurous of them were searching for 'boomers' much further out. Again, even though Hawaiian-style surfboards had already reached Australia, it took the visit of the champion swimmer Duke Kahanamoku in 1915 to show people how to use them properly. Journalists of the 1960s who likened the ways of surfies to a Polynesian lifestyle wrote truer than they knew.[9]

But there was a cost from the very beginning. By 1902, seventeen deaths from drowning had occurred at Manly alone. Early attempts at rescue were basic, extending to a lifebuoy and rope hanging on a pole put up on three of Sydney's beaches. The first to have a lifeboat, operated by a local fishing family, was Manly. The government was approached for funding and, when the request was turned down, it was decided to raise money by holding a surf bathing and lifesaving display. This was the very first, in 1903; by 1908 the prototype of later lifesaving carnivals had been held, while the 1913 carnival drew 30 000 people.

The Royal Lifesaving Society had been present in Australia since 1894, but its methods had been imported from England and were more applicable to still waters and closed spaces than to the surf, which required different techniques. And so at Bondi, arising from a committee designed to defend the local vicar—who had broken the swimming laws —there grew a Bondi Surf Bathers Lifesaving Club. Only a matter of definition would determine whether this one or a rival at Bronte (formed three years earlier, but not constituted as a club until later) was the first such organisation in the world. Whichever, there were enough of them in Sydney in 1907 to form an association. Australia's emerging beach culture had found its focus.[10]

The growing popularity of the beach forced local councils to adjudicate not only on questions of the timing, the dress and the gender of surfbathers, but also on what facilities might be made available to cater for this new activity. When the mayor of Waverley in NSW suggested, in 1905, that the council might provide dressing accommodation for

The car became an accessory to the beach. For many, such as people visiting Bondi, it functioned as a bathing box on wheels.

surfbathers, several aldermen complained that there was no revenue to be gained, indeed that encouraging surfbathing would 'depreciate the value of the municipal baths'.[11] However, beachside property-owners and small businesspeople had no hesitation in encouraging the council to build such facilities. Changing sheds and toilet blocks gradually appeared at popular beaches around the continent. Some were simply plonked in the landscape, while others, especially from the late 1920s, were architect-designed.

The lifesaving club formed at Bondi in 1906 had included politicians, doctors and commissioned officers among its members. The club developed a new rescue device, a surf reel, first displayed at Bondi later that year. It soon replaced the cumbersome circular lifebuoys that easily became entangled in lifelines.

Although all the earliest developments in ocean surfing, as distinct from bathing in bays or in municipal baths, were in Sydney, Queensland also took the sport seriously. The first lifesaving reel on a Queensland beach was installed at Greenmount, near Coolangatta, in 1909. Six years earlier a commanding guest-house had opened there, the same year that the railway was extended from Nerang to Coolangatta. The first lifesaving club in Queensland was formed at Coolangatta in 1911, a joint club with the NSW border town of Tweed Heads.[12]

The first full-scale surf lifesaving carnival appears to have been held at Manly in January 1908. It included rescue demonstrations, surf races and a re-enactment of Captain Cook's landing in Australia. Flags to bathe between were introduced at Bondi just before the outbreak of the Great War, and in 1918 a surf carnival at Cronulla, restricted to returned soldiers and competitors under twenty-one, was held to celebrate the peace. In the 1920s surf lifesaving clubs sprouted anywhere in Australia where groups of people gathered to surf. The image of the bronzed lifesaver began to appear in popular magazines, a telling image in a society that had lost 60 000 men in the war. The clubs had a quasi-military approach to training, with emphasis on levels of ability confirmed by the awarding of a bronze medallion. Given the masculine composition of the clubs, this award was not available to women until after 1980. The

Surf Bathing Association of NSW changed its name to the Surf Life Saving Association of NSW in 1920, and in 1922, with the entry of clubs from Queensland, to the Surf Life Saving Association of Australia. By the mid-1930s Australian surf clubs had over 8500 volunteer members.[13]

Elaborate surf carnivals became a regular feature of Australian beach life. In 1923 Jean Curlewis, Ethel Turner's daughter, wrote a children's book, *Beach Beyond*, in which she captured the military rhythm and colour of the carnival:

> The cobalt sea and tan-gold sand made a brilliant background as the teams came swinging along the beach, rank on rank of lithe, well-knit, brown-skinned men marching in perfect rhythm. Each team was preceded by its banner. Eight paces behind him a squad of four carried the trim reel. All wore the distinctive colours of their club . . .

On the first weekend in January 1938, the start of the sesquicentennial celebrations in Sydney, 36 000 crowded the beach at Bondi, with almost as many at Manly and Maroubra. In heavy seas that Sunday, lifesavers rescued over a hundred swimmers. A month later 200 surfers were swept out from Bondi; all but four were saved. Surfing had become the most popular participatory sport in Australia, its guardians the volunteer lifesavers. So important was the beach and the lifesaver to the Australian image that the NSW Government Tourist Bureau and the Australian National Travel Association asked the Surf Life Saving Association of Australia to organise a mammoth surf carnival at Bondi for 19 February as a major event for both the sesquicentenary and the British Empire Games, which had attracted many overseas tourists to Sydney.[14]

Bondi and Manly dominated the championships throughout the interwar years. Its carnivals suspended during the war, Queensland did not host a championship until 1947, when the Southport Club had that honour. Western Australia had to wait until the championships came to Scarborough in 1951, while South Australia did not play host until Moana in 1961. Melbourne hosted an Australian and International Carnival (including New Zealand, South Africa, Ceylon, Great Britain,

The NSW Minister for Local Government, Mr Spooner, attempted to ban men from wearing topless costumes on Sydney beaches in 1937.

Hawaii and the USA) during the Olympic Games. Stormy conditions had removed most of the sand from the beach at Torquay just before the events, so bulldozers and road graders were called in. Over 50 000 Australian and international visitors, including the now ageing Duke Kahanamoku, braved the wind and rain to see this sport demonstrated at the Olympics for the first time.[15]

By the 1930s urban Australians and country folk on their holidays had been frequenting the big resorts, including Manly and St Kilda, for many decades. In Sydney most of the northern and southern beaches were well served by tram, as they were in Melbourne, where the rail system extended the reach of the tramlines to service more distant Bay beaches as far afield as Williamstown and Mornington. Trams or trains also serviced the beaches of Brisbane, Adelaide and Perth. Access to beaches beyond the capital cities depended more on the road system than on the railways because the latter rarely broached the coast. Sydney's southern line stopped at Bomaderry, just short of the Shoalhaven River at Nowra. For much of its route it travelled inland, save for the coal-mining towns north of Wollongong, and the seaside villages of Kiama and Gerringong. The north coast railway did not near the coast except at Newcastle (via Merewether), Nambucca Heads and Byron Bay, before heading inland. The Brisbane–Cairns railway, finally completed in 1924, reached the coast only at Bundaberg, thereafter calling at major ports.

The Gold Coast

In December 1925 a group of local male surfers met at Jim Cavill's just-opened Surfers Paradise Hotel in the township of Elston, and the Surfers Paradise Surf Life Saving Club was formed the following year. Operating out of a council shelter, it did not get official recognition from the Royal Life Saving Society of Queensland until 1928. Its first fibro club house, built during the Depression in 1931 with voluntary labour, used materials bought with donations from the Southport and Nerang councils. The club rarely boasted more than six members, cater-ing for the locals and adventurers from Brisbane who, if they came by road, had to spend almost a day getting there. By 1932 the last two vehicular ferries on the Brisbane to South Coast road were replaced by bridges over the Coomera and Logan rivers, and suddenly this coastline became just a few hours drive from the state capital. By then the name Surfers Paradise had caught on, although the local councils did not gazette the name change until a couple of years later. Surfers Paradise became synonymous with the development in Australia of a new kind of beach culture, so that 'the seaside' became 'the beach.' The Southport town council ceased its opposition to modern one-piece swimming cos-tumes for men and women in 1933, but a bylaw prevented men from rolling down their tops on the beach until 1937.

The club house, and its wooden watch tower, burnt down in July 1936. Seventeen days later Jim Cavill's hotel, a half-timbered structure in the English style, suffered the same fate. Encouraged by Harold Clapp of the Victorian Railways, Cavill built a new hotel, with an eye to the growing southern market, which had rail access via the Lismore to Mur-willumbah spur line, with a bus link to Coolangatta and beyond. The new Surfers Paradise Hotel offered private suites with bathrooms, a private zoo with performing seals, along with its mainstay in the off-season, the local bar trade.[16] The holiday houses that gradually invaded the surrounding beaches were much more modest. Brisbane real estate companies subdivided 'scrub and dunes into building allotments' with localities named after famous American coastal settings, including Palm Beach, Miami and Los Angeles. In 1934 the writer Frank Dalby Davison's caravan party encountered 'two-roomed shanties of iron and clap-boards', which brought to mind 'fowl-houses on stilts'.[17]

Popular with American troops during World War II, Surfers Paradise and its neighbouring beachside settlements grew slowly in the early postwar years. Camping grounds, often with makeshift facilities, spilled over the foreshore onto the beach in busy periods. Even some working-class families could afford to buy foreshore land in the subdivision frenzy of the early 1950s, but building shortages meant that many dwellings started as small fibro garages that a single person or a couple would live in while building their holiday house. All of these structures were built on sandy soil, often remnant sand dunes.

Conscious of the enthusiasm of American servicemen for the Surfers Paradise strip, the board of Lennons Hotel in Brisbane, one of the city's finest establishments, secured land at Broadbeach, two miles south of Surfers Paradise, and built Lennons Broadbeach, a five-storey hotel accommodating 300 guests. Aerial photographs of the time show the hotel, built on land mined for mineral sands, in a small strip of sandy desert, with an immediate hinterland of mangroves. A couple of years later these mangroves were transformed into the Miami Keys Estate canal development, where waterways were carved out of 'scrubland' and con-nected to Little Tallebudgera Creek.

Lennons opened in December 1955 as the only high-rise building on the coast. The early brochures advertising it were misleading, as they implied that it was set in a tropical wonderland. Locals at the time re-ferred to it as being out in the desert. Too far from Surfers Paradise, it had low occupancy rates and Lennons gave it up in 1961 to Federal Hotels, which abandoned Lennons' attempts at beachside luxury (staff traded in their formal black regalia for Hawaiian shirts) and placed coloured masonite panels over the veranda railings to jazz it up for a more moderately priced youth market.

After changing hands a few more times, Lennons was finally demolished in the 1980s and replaced with a huge shopping centre, opposite Jupiters Casino. By this time the coast was developed to a point where the site value belatedly approximated the $4 million that the Lennons company had invested in the first place.

Much more successful was Stanley Korman's Chevron Hotel, built in the centre of Surfers Paradise in the late 1950s. Korman, a Polish-born textile manufacturer from Melbourne, controlled Melbourne's Chevron Hotel and aimed to create a national chain, also building the Chevron at Kings Cross in Sydney. A key part of the new complex was the Skyline Cabaret which, along with other cabaret venues, attracted major local and international stars, including Billy Thorpe and the Aztecs, Max Merritt and the Meteors and the Bee Gees.[18] The handful of modest resort towns in NSW and Victoria had neither the venues nor the concentration of holidaymakers to attract big name acts.

Despite intensive activity along the strip and its immediate hinterland, the real focus of what came to be called the Gold Coast was the beach. By 1954 *Penrod's Guide to the South Coast* could claim that in a little more than half a century the coast had 'been transformed from the wild bush land, the home of the kangaroo and the blackfellow to the Playground of the Pacific', attracting holidaymakers from Australia and overseas. The only reminders of former Aboriginal occupation were to be found in place names, including Tugun (breaking wave), Tallebudgera (watering place), Coomera (plenty fern) and Currumbin (quick sand). The *Courier Mail* told its readers that the area had become a playground for the rich and for tired business executives and that the term 'gold coast' was 'not just a figure of speech'.[19]

As the Gold Coast grew in sophistication and reputation in the latter half of the 1950s and the early 1960s, early devotees of the area, if they didn't like the racy pace of development, turned their attention to other beaches up and down the coast. A combination of cheaper air travel and rising car ownership meant that even southerners could travel a little further up the coast to the beaches of Caloundra, Mooloolaba, Maroochydore and further north to Noosa. Compared with the Gold Coast, these 'near north coast' settlements were unspoiled, with foreshore and riverside camping grounds, one- and two-storey motels, fibro holiday flats and, in the early 1960s, not a single high-rise.

There started a bitter battle over naming and branding rights for sections of the Australian coastline. In 1956 the welcome hoarding at the entrance to Surfers Paradise, near the El Dorado Motel, was subtitled 'The Sunshine Coast of Australia'. Within a couple of years real estate agents on the near north coast (Caloundra to Noosa) started referring to their beaches as the Sunshine Coast. In October 1958 the 'Town of the South Coast' belatedly changed its name to 'Town of the Gold Coast', proclaiming itself the 'City of the Gold Coast' the following year. Less than two years later the Nambour Chamber of Commerce, which in true country town style had largely ignored the beaches within its municipal reach, regretfully agreed to a request from the Sunshine Coast branch of the Real Estate Institute of Queensland to change the name of the area covering Caloundra to Noosa from 'near north coast' to 'Sunshine Coast'. The name took off, its authority sealed by postcards, brochures and real estate advertisments.[20]

Surfers Paradise and the Gold Coast took Australia by storm. At last we had a coastal strip and beachside architecture to match the French Riviera, Miami, and Waikiki Beach at Honolulu. Such comparisons were regularly drawn in the promotional literature. La Ronde, a circular cafe on 'The Walk' in Surfers Paradise, advertised freshy ground espresso, cappuccino and vienna coffee, amid a setting of staghorns, elkhorns and umbrella ferns. It was open daily from 11 a.m. to 11 p.m., and its bar stools and umbrellas were the height of sophistication.[21]

The decayed beach resort towns of Victoria and NSW had nothing like it. In Lakes Entrance and Terrigal patrons had to beg for real coffee; espresso was unknown. While Queensland's coastal regions were fight-

HOLIDAY and TRAVEL

MARCH 1949
Vol. 2. No. 3.

ONE SHILLING
Registered at the G.P.O., Sydney. for
transmission by post as a periodical.

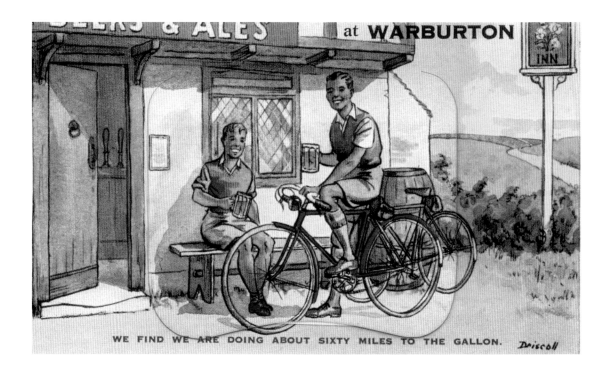

WE FIND WE ARE DOING ABOUT SIXTY MILES TO THE GALLON. *Driscoll*

The persistence of stereotypes. The top postcard, c. 1930, represents the Australian countryside, and rambling there, as though it were England. The other card, in the seaside humour vein, works hard to transform a misty mountain landscape into a beach scene, c. 1950.

"Mist"-erious doings at KATOOMBA. Tourists frolicking in the morning mist in the Jamieson Valley. The bare and rugged beauty of the "Three Sisters" is an inspiring spectacle.

ing it out for image, nomenclature and what today would be called market share, NSW and Victoria were left way behind. New South Wales had only one new coastal hotel, the Florida, at Terrigal Beach just north of Gosford. The remnant beachside hotels of the 1920s and 1930s, like the Hotel Cecil at Cronulla and the Hotel Manly overlooking the ferry terminal, did not even offer balconies. They were run-down and no match for the glamorous facilities, let alone the striking beachside images, coming from Queensland. Sydney still controlled the Surf Life Saving Association, but Queensland seized the iconographical potential of the beach, and has dominated Australian beach imagery ever since.[22]

Victoria lagged even further behind than New South Wales. The Publicity and Tourist Services section of the Victorian Railways persisted, throughout the 1940s and 1950s, with its brochures *The Seaside Calls* and *Seaside Calling*. The latter brochure brazenly featured a woman in a two-piece, but the emphasis was clearly on family life at the beach, not least because most of the beaches near Melbourne offered swimming in secluded bays, not surf.

> The beach is unmatched for family picnic groups. Shade-trees, fringing the beaches, are settings for happy al-fresco meals. For the kiddies there are all the joys of paddling and tumbling in safe, shallow waters, with the inevitable spade and bucket to keep them amused and contented on the nearby sand.[23]

For the Queensland Tourist Bureau Victoria was easy pickings. Sunny Surfers Paradise offered a carefree atmosphere, brief swimsuits, a choice of beachside accommodation from self-catering apartments to a great array of hotels and motels, together with caravan parks and some residual guest-houses, usually owned by trade unions or the RSL. Nothing in Victoria matched it, and Victorians flocked to the Gold Coast in even greater numbers than the New South Welsh, especially in winter. The competition was so intense that the Victorian Government Tourist Bureau had no choice but to ape the sun, sand, surfboard and bikini propaganda of their northern rivals, scrapping their Seaside Calling campaigns and going instead with the extraordinarily cumbersome *The*

Golden Thousand: Victoria's Beaches. Even so, the prose and imagery of the Victorian Bureau was no match for the racy style of the Queensland boosters: 'Along Victoria's 1000 miles of golden and azure coastline are scores of delightful holiday resorts . . . From Mallacoota in the east to Portland in the west are many beaches with excellent shark-free surf'.[24] The Bureau made no mention of Queensland, apart from the back-hander about sharks—frequently seen off Queensland beaches in the 1950s and 1960s before professional netting made them shark-free too.

By the late 1990s the Gold Coast, with over 8000 hotel and motel rooms, and 8500 apartments, was indisputably Australia's greatest beach resort. It offered every standard of accommodation, from luxury suites with superb waterfront and hinterland views to decaying 1960s motels and walk-up blocks of flats, where the accommodation was modest and the rents cheap. With its canal developments, casino, boutiques, shopping malls, marinas, and the nation's first private university, it had gone from coastal resort to become the seventh-largest city in Australia. But fewer and fewer Australians regarded it as the acme of beach culture and sophistication. It continued to offer sun, sand and sex, as it had always done, but more and more of the sex was to be found in the legalised brothels and escort agencies that catered for every taste and every age. The marketing ploy of wholesome, attractively built meter maids of the 1960s had been replaced with an aggressively commercial air, where shops and restaurants and accommodation providers vied with each other for market share, a far cry from the handful of hotels and kiosks of the 1930s. The difference was money; now there was lots of it, although it didn't circulate to all the people on the coast. The opening of Jupiters Casino in 1985 revealed highrollers, gawkers, problem gamblers and old-age pensioners, all willing to part with their money in the hope of making more. With an economy based on retailing, real estate, building and service industries, the Coast is particularly subject to economic downturns. The booms and busts of the 1980s and 1990s often left half-completed apartment towers forlornly casting incomplete shadows over the beach.[25] Late at night, once the traffic noise has died down, the dominant sound is of rooftop airconditioning plants.

Souvenir
Programme
Price 2/-

1964 AUSTRALIAN
NATIONAL and
INTER-CLUB SURF
CHAMPIONSHIP
CARNIVALS

COLLAROY BEACH, NEW SOUTH WALES
SATURDAY, 28th, and SUNDAY, 29th MARCH, 1964

As an important fixture on the holiday calendar, surf carnivals could require an eighty-page booklet such as this one.

Much of the rest of Australia saw the Gold Coast as a model of beach-front excess, to be avoided at all costs. While the Sunshine Coast and Cairns, and even Wollongong, had succumbed to the lure of the high-rise beach apartments in the 1970s and 1980s, many other beachside communities resisted the pressure to develop. The best documented and the most newsworthy was the battle over Byron Bay, in northern NSW, where a combination of celebrity developers, superannuated landowners, devotees of the counter culture and municipal authorities battled it out over the nature and extent of development. Even in Melbourne's St Kilda, where there had been remarkably little high-rise development, locals feared that sections of Port Phillip Bay would be turned into another Gold Coast. Their first taste of such a development was Beacon Cove, which opened opposite Station Pier in 1997.[26]

Beach culture

The late 1950s and the early 1960s saw the emergence of a well-articulated and well-publicised beach culture in Australia. Hollow wooden surfboards came to Australia via Hawaii some decades before, but it was not until the Olympic Games in 1956, when a group of Californian surfers visited Australia, with their new 'Malibu' boards made of light plywood and fibreglass, that the surfboard craze began. The earlier boards were long and heavy, hard to manoeuvre in the surf and difficult to transport. The new boards caught the imagination of younger surfers, even though the Surf Life Saving Clubs did not approve, regarding the boards as a challenge to their well-proven reel rescue. Small surfboard manufacturing operations were set up in Sydney at Brookvale, near Manly, and surf movies proliferated. Bernard 'Midget' Farrelly, a talented 17-year-old surfer, travelled with a group of other surfers on the *Oriana* to Hawaii in 1961. The following year Farrelly won the 10th international surfing championship, putting Australia on the international surfing map. He became a hero for high school students, a symbol of 'a new generation of surfers who were more interested in surfing than surf clubs.

Patrol duty and training for the bronze medallion began to conflict with chasing waves (and girls) and doing the stomp'.[27]

Surf culture loomed large in the imagination of most teenage Australians. US bands, including the Beach Boys, topped the pop charts, while local singers, including Little Pattie with her 1963 hit, 'My blonde headed stompy wompie real gone surfer boy', captured the carefree mood of a society where full employment created a safe backdrop for school leavers to peroxide their hair, drop out for a while and cruise the beaches. Odd jobs were easy to come by, so surfies and their chicks had little difficulty in surviving on and near the beach. Women were rarely seen on boards. Indeed the girlfriends of dedicated boardriders were often referred to as 'surf widows', admiring their lad's skill and physique from a vantage point on the beach or from the vehicle.[28]

The surf clubs, controlled by men in their thirties, forties and fifties, were not keen on the surfing craze. They persuaded local municipal councils to make boardriders pay a fee, and for the first time the Australian beach was divided up: between bodysurfers and recreational swimmers in areas demarcated by the traditional yellow and red flags, and the boardriders, whose boards could be confiscated if they strayed into the marked area. Surfriders formed their own association, spawned beachside surfboard and clothing shops to cater for their needs, and closely followed developments in California. Surf contests, which emphasised individual ability rather than regimented group efforts, developed into a kind of international surfing tourism, especially between Australia and the west coast of the USA. The culture became so pervasive that the ballet dancer Robert Helpmann sent it up in his record 'Surfer Doll', with accompanying TV clip. The era was well captured in the epic surf movie, *The Endless Summer*.[29]

The surfies of the 1960s could sleep on the beach, in beaten-up old vans or find cheap rental accommodation in the fibro holiday houses and run-down blocks of flats located in virtually every beachside town. In a full-employment economy that continued to see the beach as a place for holidays and relaxation, rather than as a commodity to be sold to interstate and overseas tourists, the primitive accommodation and eating facilities at most Australian beaches were accepted as part of holiday culture. Batemans Bay, on the NSW south coast, and Mooloolaba, north of Brisbane, were predominantly fibro settlements, with sprawling camping grounds, modest cinemas, decayed guest-houses, a handful of milk bars and general stores, and a pub. Church groups often ran Sunday schools and children's activities in large tents on the beach. Such holiday sites, like many other former fishing villages, have been transformed with medium- and high-rise buildings, taverns, classy restaurants and surf lifesaving clubs financed not by volunteer labour but by poker machine revenue.

While many urban Australians could get to their local beaches by public transport, the rise of mass car ownership saw the car, for both families and surfies, as not only the means of transport but also as providing the best way of surviving a day at the beach. Canvas beach umbrellas, deck chairs, transistor radios and 'eskys' (portable ice boxes) were transported, along with cold chicken, and chops, sausages and steak that could be cooked on a makeshift driftwood fire. Some beaches ran to milk bars, with pies and ice-creams, along with a fish and chip shop, but the more isolated beaches required families and surfies alike to provide their own food. While surfboards were predominantly the preserve of teenage and older males, tyre tubes and other flotation devices were popular. Rubber surfaplanes could be rented at popular surf beaches around the continent.[30]

At beaches beyond the reach of the capital cities the welfare of surfers depended entirely on the training, membership and facilities or lack of them in the surf lifesaving clubs. In the more isolated areas the clubs had neither electricity nor a telephone. Life safety provisions were often primitive. Television and bank sponsorship of surf rescue helicopters did not become common until the 1980s, when lavish 'ironman' competitions made plain the distinction between professional and voluntary surfing activity.[31] Australia's first paid 'lifeguards', the American term, as distinct from volunteer lifesavers, appeared at the Gold Coast in the 1980s.

From the late 1960s local councils took beach conservation much more seriously. A series of spectacular beach erosion incidents in NSW

Beauty contests were once a common feature of beach life. This one was staged by the Mooloolaba Surf Life Saving Club in 1962.

and Queensland—where beaches were washed away and high-rise blocks of flats built too close to the coastline were in danger of collapsing—made councils, the conservation movement and even property developers much more aware of the need for conservation. Replanting programmes in protective fenced enclosures spread rapidly along the more popular beaches in every state. In NSW and Queensland scores of beaches that had been mined for rutile and zircon were allegedly returned to their original state.[32]

The Australian beaches, regularly proclaimed as the cleanest, the safest and the best in the world, lost both innocence and a degree of centrality through four main factors: rising concern about skin cancer, the establishment of legal nude beaches, the rapid spread of in-ground private pools, and the aggressive marketing of Pacific and Asian beach resorts, from Vanuatu to Bali. The 'slip, slap, slop' anti-cancer campaigns, from the mid-1980s, made many young people suspicious of the merits of dedicated sunbaking, at precisely the same time that their parents and grandparents were having skin cancers removed at an ever-increasing rate.

But the penchant of many young and even middle-aged Australians for the beach and the sun surfaced again with a strident campaign to legalise topless bathing on suburban beaches and to establish nude beaches. Australia had had nudist clubs for many decades, but the idea of turning a public beach into a nude beach was a big step. Nonetheless the newly elected Wran Labor government decided to take it in NSW in 1976 when it pronounced Reef Beach, in Mosman, a legal nude beach. Beach inspectors, employed by local councils all around the continent, were gradually phased out, or took over lifesaving duties from volunteer club members. Kenneth Slessor's 1930s poem of praise to 'backless Betty from Bondi' finally bore fruit. Indeed on some beaches—like Sydney's fashionable Balmoral—one could see Betty's front as well. And at nearby Reef Beach both Bruce and Betty could be seen in all their natural glory. Religious groups and some local residents protested, and for a while some parents attempted to keep teenage children of either sex away from such beaches. They did not succeed. One of the cornerstones of wowserism in twentieth-century Australia was finally laid to rest.[33]

At the same time more and more middle-class households, especially in Brisbane and Sydney, were installing in-ground pools despite their proximity to excellent bay and surfing beaches. In the major urban areas this was partly to do with concern about pollution, but it also suggested a more privatised approach to water recreation. It is difficult to control the company you keep on the beach, but in your own backyard pool you select the company. The pollution factor loomed particularly large in Sydney, where the ocean outfall sewers at Bondi, Manly and Maroubra disgorged sewage 'Bondi cigars'—to the discomfort of the locals and the amazement of interstate and international tourists.

The rise of Pacific and Asian beach resorts, especially island resorts, posed a different kind of challenge to the Australian beach. Combined airfare and accommodation packages meant that these resorts were often no more expensive than those of North Queensland. Moreover these resorts offered duty-free shopping, a more vibrant local culture and cuisine—at least that is what the advertisements said—and a more memorable beach experience.

The beach may be one of the few tourist sites in Australia that cannot be completely colonised by tourists, either domestic or international. Visitors and local residents using tourist precincts now dominate many sites in Australia, from Darling Harbour and The Rocks (Sydney) to Southgate (Melbourne) and to all the big casino and hotel complexes in every state. The tourist impact on nineteenth-century metropolitan seaside resorts, from St Kilda to Glenelg, is obvious, as it is on the middle to late twentieth-century developments in Cairns, Surfers Paradise, Coffs Harbour and Lakes Entrance. But there is a continuing sense in which the beach in Australia remains a special site. The novelist Robert Drewe explains this in terms of emotional experience and generational memory.

> Many, if not most, Australians have their first sexual experience on the coast and as a consequence see the beach in a sensual and nostalgic light. Thereafter, the beach is not only a regular summer pleasure and balm, but an *idée fixe* which fulfils an almost ceremonial need at each critical physical and emotional stage: as lovers, as honeymooners, as parents, and, after travelling north to the particular piece of coastline befitting their class and superannuation (and offering the most lenient death duties), the elderly retired.[34]

The Australian beach remains one of our few free-of-charge tourist landscapes. Many national parks demand an entrance fee, golf courses require either membership or a fee, skiing establishments levy all manner of charges, and most resorts restrict their grounds to paying guests. Not so the beach. Whether it is Surfers Paradise or the isolated Ninety Mile Beach in Gippsland, the beach in Australia is free: from the south, with its 1-metre tides, to Broome, with its 10-metre tide. Over 95 per cent of the Australian coastline is in public ownership. Only a handful of islands and some pre-1910 subdivisions in NSW are in private ownership, along with perhaps 150 marinas developed around Australia since the 1960s. A society in which the beach is free is an unusual society. Australians, as Keith Dunstan pointed out in *Walkabout* in 1963, take this for granted. But Americans, Italians, Malaysians, indeed tourists from almost anywhere else on the globe, do not.[35]

mark on mapmakers and guide publishers, all of whom owed their early accounts of road routes and conditions to the work of the cycling clubs. The advent of lightweight mountain bikes since the 1980s has seen a modest resurgence in cycle tourism, especially among backpackers.[2]

The coming of the car

The motor car revolutionised travel and holiday-making in Australia. Families could travel wherever the roads were well enough graded to allow passage, and they could take the necessary equipment in their own vehicle. Car ownership grew rapidly in Australia in the inter-war years, from next to nothing in 1920 to one in five families having access to a car by 1938. Nonetheless cars were still the preserve of the middle class and a small proportion of the better-off working class, especially trades-men who acquired a car or truck for work purposes.

The early travellers definitely regarded themselves as pioneers. A Brisbane couple, Mr and Mrs Jack Dorney, undertook what they called *The First Motor Honeymoon Around Australia* in 1926 and 1927. Having an eye for sponsorship they drove an Overland Whippet, used Plume fuel and Mobil Oil and rode on Barnet Glass Tyres for their 16 900-kilometre trip. The Northern Territory and northern Western Australia proved the most difficult part of the journey, but they nonetheless enjoyed 'the free, open life of the outback'. At Daly Waters they encountered a 'wild tribe', 'uncivilised and living practically as their ancestors did'. Near Emungalen (now the site of the town of Katherine),

> The travelling was very difficult and slow. Sometimes we would be driving among grass which might hide a rock or tree stump, and to hit it would mean, perhaps, the end of our car and our trip . . . There were so many rivers and creeks to be crossed and, although we always tried to find the best place to cross, the banks were so precipitous that I did not think it was possible for any car in the world to climb them.[3]

They finally managed the ninety creek crossings between Darwin and Katherine, a little over 320 kilometres of very difficult country. At the

WEBSTER, ROMETCH & DUNCAN LTD., ROYAL MAIL MOTOR COACHES TO FERN TREE,
HUONVILLE, FRANKLIN, SHIPWRIGHT'S POINT AND GEEVESTON.
OFFICE: 78 MURRAY STREET, NEXT DOOR TO HOTEL ARCADIA, HOBART TAS.
TELEPHONE 714.

Some coaching firms were quick to take up the challenge presented by motor transport.
This Hobart company had made the transition successfully by the 1920s.

end of their epic journey a great crowd awaited the motoring honey-mooners at the Brisbane GPO in March 1927.

The 1936 edition of the *Herald Road Guide* told motorists that they could drive from Sydney to Brisbane via the Pacific Highway in three days; but, on account of the many curves and the beauty of the scenery, the *Guide* recommended that five days be allocated. Drivers and passengers enjoyed a bitumen road to Peats Ridge, where they encountered their first obstacle, the Hawkesbury River, and the first of many vehicular ferries. 'Tourists' were counselled to spend a little time in Newcastle, with its giant steel works open to the public. Just north of Newcastle another vehicular ferry appeared at Hexham where, as at Peats Ridge, long delays were common during holiday periods. At Stroud, 240 kilometres north of Sydney, the bitumen ran out and the going got tough. Weary travellers, whether camping or seeking hotel accommodation, usually headed for Taree, a pretty country town on the banks of the Manning River; or Port Macquarie, which offered a hotel on the water's edge and a church built by convicts 'about 112 years ago'.[4] Frank Dalby Davison, in his 1935 book *Blue Coast Caravan*, reported that 'no more than a small town had developed' from Governor Macquarie's grand plans, made after his 1821 visit. 'The streets dwindle rapidly once the little shopping centre is left.'

Further north, the Hastings River offered a free vehicular ferry. Davison, driving with friends from Sydney to Cairns, described crossing the 500 metres of the Hastings on a ferry that drew itself 'from bank to bank by means of a wire cable that is fastened to a heavy post on each shore, and is picked up from the bed of the river by the craft as it progresses'. The Davison party enjoyed the opportunity to 'get out of the car, to watch the bird life of the rivers, and to hear the plop of the mullet as they leapt'. At the Macleay River, leading in to Kempsey, a rickety timber truss bridge, opened in 1900, offered passage to the motorist. North of Kempsey, Nambucca Heads and Coffs Harbour provided spectacular coastal scenery. Like the railway line, the Pacific Highway then headed inland to Grafton, as it still does. At Grafton both rail and road travellers had the pleasure, from 1932, of crossing the Clarence River

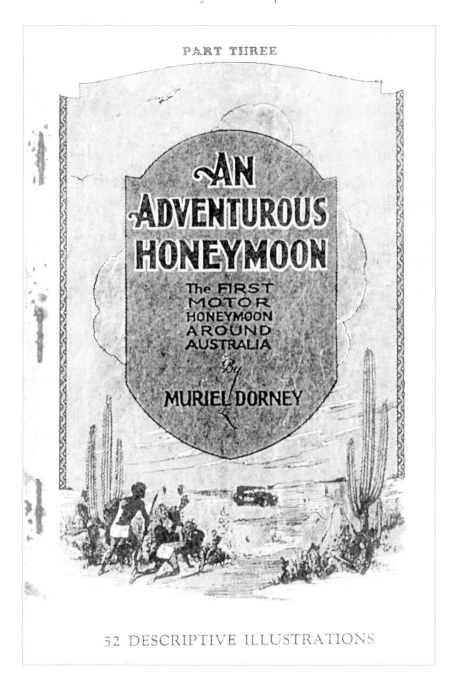

The vehicular steam ferry at Batemans Bay, on the Princes Highway, was not replaced by a bridge until the 1950s.

on Australia's only double-decker bridge, with rail on the lower deck and vehicular traffic on the upper. Grafton, the 'City of Trees', with its jacarandas and poinsettias, offered respite from the dusty road. Davison found it a delightful contrast to most of the towns along the Pacific Highway, to which his party had 'to draw down the blinds of the aesthetic soul'. In Grafton they found that

> Plate-glass shop windows faced each other across the street under a canopy of green boughs. In the centre of the road and by each footpath were great trees and tall palms . . . The street was a busy one; cars and horse-drawn vehicles were numerous on the roadway . . . We were struck by the number of bicycles used in Grafton; by girls and matrons as well as by men and boys. Absence of hills was apparently the condition that encouraged their use. Anyone having an errand in the town or its outskirts seemed to have a cycle for the purpose.

While their car was being repaired the Davison party saw a ship 'passing the end of the street'. To see two masts and a funnel 'glide silently past'

160

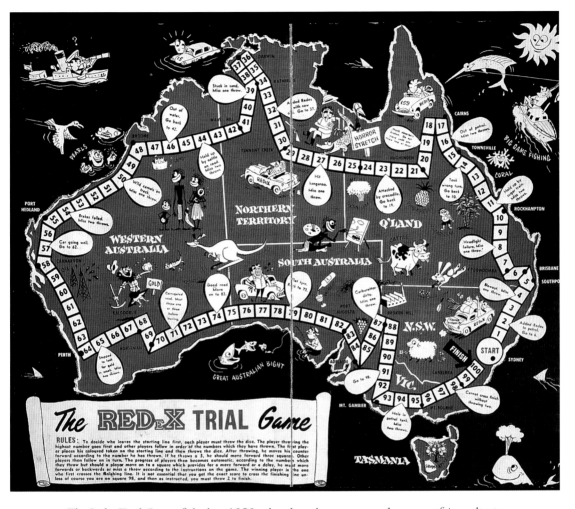

The Redex Trial Game of the late 1950s played on the romance and vastness of Australia, its horror stretches, its flora and fauna; it also lightly satirised the indigenous inhabitants.

Elaborate re-enactments were pioneered in Australia by Old Sydney Town. Here, escaped convicts (paid actors) ambush often unwilling tourists. They are later satisfactorily brought to justice (inset).

reminded them that although they were many miles inland they were on a navigable river.

On leaving Grafton the Pacific Highway soon degenerated into a narrow road, 'sometimes resembling a country lane'. Wooden one-lane bridges were alarmingly frequent on much of the rest of the highway. The rich country of the Clarence River, with its tall palms and sugar cane, pineapples and bananas and elevated timber houses, signalled to the southerner that tropical Australia was at hand.[5]

At Ewingsdale one could leave the highway and visit Byron Bay and its lighthouse at Cape Byron, the most easterly point of Australia. Home of the Norco Milk Co-op and an abattoir, by 1954 it also boasted a 'new industrial company' mining minerals from beach sands. Tourist facilities were modest, with a hotel and guest-house catering for visitors by rail or sea.

Just south of Mullumbimby the 'highway' climbed through the range in curves and steep grades, meeting the coast again at Brunswick Heads, which from 1938 offered a smart new hotel to accommodate the growing number of holidaymakers in their own cars. Heading inland to Murwillumbah, travellers encountered cane fields and more rich dairying country. This was the terminus of the north coast railway, and car travellers could thumb their noses at railway brethren who, if they needed to get to Brisbane, had to take a bus from Murwillumbah to Coolangatta railway station.

The *Blue Coast Caravan* party were unimpressed by their entry into Queensland, passing through an open gateway in a wire fence. They couldn't see how the gatekeeper or the fence would keep Queensland cattle ticks out of NSW. Once they crossed the 'boundary fence', users of the *Herald Road Guide* were told that at Coolangatta they would encounter 'one of the most beautiful towns on the coast.' Davison and his friends thought it 'a wide and wind-ridden town'. Coolangatta offered four large hotels and eight guest-houses, two of which, Greenmount and the Beach House, accommodated over 100 guests. Motoring parties on their way to Brisbane left the coast at Southport and headed inland 'through miles of bush country', before reaching the capital.

States often had border gates, such as this one on the NSW–Queensland border at Wallangarra—sometimes to check the spread of fruit fly and ticks, at other times for appearance's sake.

The Pacific Highway was not really worthy of the name until the late 1960s, when it was finally completely sealed and all one-lane bridges eliminated. Before that, drivers looking to get to Queensland quickly hived off at Hexham, near Newcastle, and took the New England Highway, via Tenterfield and Warwick to Brisbane. A flatter route, less subject to flooding, it enabled the 50 miles an hour that drivers of the day thought a highway should allow.[6]

Roads for the tourists

The state of the roads has been a major topic of conversation ever since Europeans came to Australia. Most European settlers, even some of the Irish, had left highly urbanised settings, where roads were taken for granted, to come to a continent without any. It took the early settlers some time to recognise that the Aborigines did in fact have tracks.

The great bulk of Australia's nineteenth-century road system was built for moving goods, beasts and people. But in the last two decades of the century some tourist routes were opened, usually little more than tracks catering for horse riders and hardy horse-drawn vehicles. Routes

Broadbent's, publishers of maps and guides, released this booklet in 1927.

were opened up to natural attractions, like the Jenolan Caves and the coast at Lorne. Often such tracks were also used for timber-getting, and in many instances this was the initial reason for their construction.

With the coming of the car, motorists needed maps. Australia's first major tourist map publisher, George Robert Broadbent, developed his interest in maps as a cycle-racing enthusiast. At one time he held most Victorian and Australian records. A foundation member of the League of Victorian Wheelmen and the Good Roads Movement, he issued, in 1896, a road map of Victoria, prepared after sixteen years of riding and touring in all parts of the colony. It classified roads as 'good', 'fair' or 'ridden with difficulty', and became the basis of a continuous publishing programme by Broadbent's Official Road Guides Co. A force behind the creation of the Country Roads Board in 1913, he became manager the following year of the Royal Automobile Club of Victoria's new touring department and was an active member of the Trust appointed to create the Great Ocean Road from Torquay to Peterborough via Lorne.[7]

The guest-house town of Lorne could only be reached by an inland route. In 1908 the *Geelong Advertiser* pointed out that a coastal route

would open up some 'fine seascape'. As the road was beyond the resources of the state government's Country Roads Board, a public meeting
held in Colac in March 1918 raised £7000 towards it. The state Premier
attended the opening ceremony for the construction of the first part of
the road—from Lorne to Cape Patton—in September 1919. It took
him ten and a half hours to travel from Melbourne, via timber lorry,
with the last part of the journey on foot. The first section of the road
opened in March 1922 and by December the Trust had decided to levy a
toll, which continued for fourteen years. With the assistance of relief
workers the whole road finally opened in November 1932, and the Trust
handed the road over to the state government in 1936. The road has
been much improved since then, especially with the addition of passing
lanes, though a small section remained unsealed until the mid-1980s.[8]

By the 1930s Broadbent's company could claim to serve 'many thousands of tourists and holiday-makers' with its 'numerous up-to-the-
minute Road Maps and Guides'. In 1939, their forty-fourth year of issue,
Broadbent's guides were the official road guides of the Victorian Government Tourist Bureau and of the RACV. They had the mapping business
sewn up in their home state. One of Broadbent's sons, R. A. Broadbent,
succeeded his father as tourist manager of the RACV.

In NSW Kenneth Craigie dominated map-making, but in the 1930s
his mapping empire came under challenge from Cecil Albert Gregory.
Like Broadbent's, Gregory's path to mapping success came via a motoring organisation. Born in Bathurst in 1894, Gregory started work as a
cub reporter on the local paper in 1911. In the early 1920s he moved to
Sydney, where he worked on the *Daily Telegraph*, writing tourist supplements for which he sold much of the advertising himself. Hired by
the newly formed National Roads and Motorists Association as publicity
director and manager of the touring department, he gained the right to
publish maps and guidebooks on behalf of the NRMA, keeping profits
from the advertising he sold. He masterminded the NRMA's *Road Before
You* series, strip maps showing precisely what motorists would encounter
on any particular route. He sold this idea to the Robinson mapping
company but soon formed his own publishing imprint, Gregory's. His

Scamander Hotel, Scamander River, East Coast, Tasmania
Under Vice Regal Patronage. Visitors to this Hotel for Season
Sept. 1910, to May 31st 1911, caught 11246 Black Bream, total
weight over five tons
                                J. G. Walker, Proprietor.

The Scamander Hotel, on the east coast of Tasmania, proved popular with motorists both before and after World War I. By the mid-1920s it had to add another storey to accommodate visitors.

firm drew new maps for Sydney and suburbs and outpaced Robinsons's as the major street directory publisher.

By the early 1950s he had thirty-five guidebooks, street directories, booklets and maps in print, including his most famous guide, *One Hundred*

Miles Around Sydney. Gregory's also published specific guides to the Princes, Hume, Pacific and New England highways. In 1951 Gregory cheekily published a *Guide to Victoria*, a reference for motorists, tourists, holidaymakers and home-seekers, but he was unable to break into a market dominated by Broadbent's and the *Herald Road Guide*. Mapping, like railway gauges, was a state matter.

Until the 1980s, with the coming of national guides published by Readers Digest, Penguin and the petroleum companies, most state and regional guides in Australia were published from their state of origin. Gregory's dominated the market in NSW, Broadbent's in Victoria, while in Queensland the Penrod Guide Book Co. published *150 Miles Around Brisbane* and guides to the north and south coast. With the ever-increasing growth in motor car ownership and use, two highways stood out as Australia's most frequented: the Hume, the principal freight link between Melbourne and Sydney, and the Pacific, between Sydney and Brisbane, predominantly a holidaymakers' route.

The Pacific Highway remains one of the most popular tourist routes in Australia. Unlike the Hume and other inland highways it does not carry a great deal of interstate freight because much of the road is still slow going, especially in the mountainous stretches around Buladelah and Mullumbimby. To the modern traveller the route still offers picturesque country towns, from the larger centres of Taree and Grafton to the smaller settlements of Ulmarra and Maclean on the Clarence, two little port towns that have known better days. The highway runs through some major coastal resorts, including Coffs Harbour and Nambucca Heads, and leads to many others, notably Port Macquarie and Byron Bay. The former has become a pile of high-rise apartments, primarily servicing the Sydney market, the latter a low-rise tribute to the environmental lobby and astute investors from Sydney and Brisbane, who to date have managed to keep McDonald's out of town.

As the Pacific Highway links Australia's largest city, Sydney, with its third-largest city, Brisbane, it draws traffic from both the south and the north. A journey that took from three to five days in 1936 can now be done comfortably in one and a half days, or one long day (twelve hours

Railways met the demand for travel from Melbourne to Sydney by the more picturesque coastal route, going so far as to supply cars to take passengers from Orbost to Bomaderry.

driving time) with few stops. A series of horrific car and bus accidents in the 1980s, including one near Grafton in October 1989 that killed twenty people, and another near Kempsey in December 1989 when two tourist buses collided, killing thirty-five people, drew attention to the inadequacy of a two-lane road purporting to be a major tourist highway. The state and federal governments shared the cost of upgrading the road.

Redex trials and the lure of the road

Motoring in the 1950s might have been a sedate affair in the cities, where cars were still more likely to be used for a Sunday drive than for the journey to work, but on a continental scale motoring remained an adventure. In 1953 the oil company Redex proposed to the Australian Sporting Car Club a nation-wide reliability test. The first trial attracted 192 starters and covered 10 500 kilometres, from Sydney to Brisbane, to Townsville, Darwin, Adelaide, Melbourne and back to Sydney. The following year the route was extended to take in Western Australia. The promoters saw the 'vast Australian Continent' as providing a testing ground for the world's motor car manufacturers, pointing out that 'good motor cars' were 'vital to the future of Australia' because it was impossible to provide good roads everywhere. The trial attracted all the major makes of cars, along with high-profile teams and famous sponsors. The *Australian Women's Weekly* fielded an all-woman team in a Humber Snipe in 1954, switching to a Holden in 1955.

Making a circuit around the continent, the drivers found every imaginable driving condition. At that time only the adventurous or the foolhardy would contemplate driving to Perth, let alone the far north-west, where boulder-strewn roads brought many a suspension unstuck. School children and teachers would leave the classroom to cheer on competitors. Many cars did not make it. In 1954 the Arthur Murray Dancing School team had to withdraw at Katherine. Wrecked suspensions, cracked cylinder heads, broken steering columns and ruined clutches dogged drivers along the way. Followed on radio, in the newspapers and magazines, and from 1956 on television, the Redex Trial captured the imagination of the nation, in much the same way as aviators had done forty years before. Except that this time it could be the bloke next door in the race. Individuals as well as companies entered cars, including Austins, Citroens, Fords, Hillmans, MGs, Vauxhalls and Volkswagens. The promoters said that the entrants were 'people who still have that pioneer spirit and like overcoming difficulties'.[9]

The adventure of driving on Australia's roads was compounded by the difficulty of buying petrol, especially at holiday times, when motorists

168

were most in need. In the 1950s and 1960s petrol was virtually unprocurable on Good Friday and Anzac Day, and garages in NSW were also closed on Christmas Day. On Sundays, Victorian garages opened only from 10 a.m. to 12 noon. Intending motorists would normally write to one of the state motoring organisations or one of the publishers of road guides to obtain guidebooks and roneoed sheets that gave up-to-date advice on accommodation and the opening hours of garages. Without such information motorists could easily become stranded, frequently at the mercy of the automobile club emergency staff who grumpily attended vehicles that had run out of fuel. As these problems were not viewed as emergencies, motorists and their passengers were often stranded for hours, sometimes days. It was a common sight in Australia to see 'Dad' hitching a ride into town to get a 5-gallon can of petrol. Failing that, motorists often asked farmers for assistance from the 44-gallon drums of fuel held on most rural properties. Some farmers did very well out of this; a stranded motorist is not in a good bargaining position.

Garages proliferated throughout the suburbs and in rural Australia. Every country town worthy of the name had a garage or a least a petrol pump, often on the kerbside in front of the general store. Fuel consumption was poor, tanks small, and motorists had to refuel at frequent intervals. At smaller tourist resorts all one's requisites, including petrol and kerosene (for lighting and heating) often came from the one establishment. Petrol stations sprouted on all the major highways and many secondary roads. Key towns became known as refuelling stops. On the Hume Highway Euroa, Benalla, Wangaratta, Albury, Holbrook, Tarcutta, Gundagai, Yass, Goulburn and Mittagong were major refuelling and repair stops. With relatively unreliable cars, many purchased second-hand, and bad road conditions (some of the Hume was still dirt in the 1950s), breakdowns were common. It was not till the 1980s that the number of petrol stations in Australia peaked at 12 000 (it has halved since then).

Better roads, interstate freeways, more reliable cars and better fuel consumption have led to fewer refuelling stops. By the early 1990s rural Australia was littered with abandoned garages, some of which had also offered camping sites and even on-site vans. The big car and truck refuelling towns, including Yass and Wangaratta—now bypassed—had dozens of garages that went out of business in the late 1980s and early 1990s. Residents and local businesspeople welcomed the decrease in traffic through what was usually their main shopping street, but feared for their local economy. Towns with populations of more than 2000 have survived, but smaller settlements, like Longwood and Mangalore in Victoria, and Jugiong and Gunning in NSW, have fallen on hard times. Unless the old highway settlements have a particular claim to historical notoriety (Ned Kelly at Glenrowan) or can be reinvented as a heritage site (Chiltern and Berrima) or as gateway sites to goldfield towns or vineyards (Springhurst), then they are doomed to the same fate as much of country-town Australia: terminal decline.[10]

With the exception of a handful of tourist toll roads in the inter-war years and the metropolitan tollways of the 1990s, all of Australia's highways and freeways have been built with state and federal government funds. They have been seen as part of the nation's military, trade and tourist infrastructure. Ever since they were founded, the state automobile associations have lobbied for more money for roads. Before World War II they concentrated their attention on state governments, and after the war they also lobbied the federal government. In 1954 their peak body, the Australian Road Federation, claimed that part of the defence budget should be used for roads: 'In an age of military mobility, a vast road system throughout the continent was imperative to defence'.[11] Australia had already benefited from American road-building prowess during the war, including the Bell's Line of Road through Kurrajong, which provided another route from Sydney to Lithgow should the road via Katoomba be bombed by the Japanese.

With ever-improving roads, and the increasing proportion of divided roads on most of the major highways, some motorists wanted to escape the bitumen and go bush. Four-wheel-drive vehicles became popular in the 1980s and, as more and more manufacturers entered the market, cheaper to buy. They even had a concessional rate of sales tax, supposedly to cater for their use as farm vehicles. Most 4WD vehicles in Australia are garaged in the large cities, however. In the 1990s they were nick-

*Bus companies serviced many of the routes that rail did not. This Pioneer Tours group,
c. 1952, was photographed at Nowra.*

named 'Toorak Tractors' and Prime Minister Howard described them as
affordable for many families, even though a new one cost well above the
annual average male wage. Guidebooks on exploring Australia by four-
wheel-drive proliferated, some so large and heavy that you needed a
four-wheel-drive vehicle to accommodate them.[12] The maps and directions in these guidebooks are remarkably like road guides of the 1920s and
1930s, where, in the absence of graded or sealed roads, local landmarks
—from rivers and creeks to gates, abandoned fridges and property
names—become the principal geographic identifiers. The four-wheel-drive
guides offer Australians the romance of the Redex adventures of the 1950s.
Most of the Australian continent will never be covered by sealed roads,
so the adventure of uncharted travel—for both Australians and overseas
tourists—may remain one of Australia's special travel attractions.

Under canvas

Until the late 1950s most Australians who went on camping holidays
were free to choose their own site on the roadside, near the beach, or in

the bush, as formal camping grounds were rare, except on the major highways or in coastal towns that had developed as holiday places. Farmers were normally happy to oblige, so long as permission was requested and people left a site fairly much as they found it. Books on camping, which emerged in the late nineteenth century, continued well into the twentieth, preoccupied with choice of site and suggestions on what to take.

The state motoring clubs, which grew out of the earlier cycling clubs, soon realised that many of their members were campers or potential campers. The RACV produced its first camping guide in 1934 and distributed it free to members. Because of the extraordinary demand for copies, a second expanded edition was produced the following year. It contained explicit advice about 'sanitation' (cover deposits with dry earth or ashes), snake bite (tourniquet or doctor), rubbish (burn or bury it) and food (keep it cool). The guide advised prospective campers to take a corkscrew, tin opener, clothes-pegs, a mirror, matches, petrol lighter and even a shoe cleaning outfit. Hardened campers would have considered the advice patronising, but novices no doubt found it useful.

The RACV guides concentrated on Victoria, along with explicit advice about campsites on the Hume and Princes Highways for travellers to Sydney or interim destinations. The 1934 guide listed seventeen camping areas on or adjacent to the Princes Highway in Victoria and sixteen in NSW. By the time of the second edition, just a year later, another three sites had been added in Victoria—Buchan, Mallacoota and Mackenzie River—while forty-three had been added to the NSW component. Most of the NSW additions were sites already in existence, and some of the lesser-known ones may have been brought to the RACV's attention by knowledgeable members. They included isolated lakeside sites such as Durras Lake and Lake Conjola, and hinterland spots including Kangaroo Valley and the spectacular coastal escarpment north of Wollongong, Stanwell Tops.

In December 1936 a writer for the RACV magazine *Radiator* told readers that

> A suitable site is essential. Choose level ground in an elevated position, covered with short grass. Shelter, such as hedges, is desirable, but don't build against tall trees, as they may attract lightning. Old looking trees

may also be a danger. Cattle, sheep and horses should be excluded from a camping site.[13]

Most family-sized tents in Australia were substantial canvas structures with heavy wooden centrepieces and uprights. Tent manufacturers were to be found throughout Australia, and tentmakers proudly stencilled their name and address on the canvas. These substantial tents were used by whole families for an extended holiday season. Retired grandparents often ruled the roost, while sons and daughters and nieces and nephews would come and go as holidays from school and work allowed. Such encampments of family and friends, often with a boat, can still be found but are less and less common. In the last three decades many campsites have been surrounded by motel and self-catering apartment accommodation, so that while some members of the family may still set up a tent or a caravan, others may stay nearby in apartments boasting various degrees of luxury. They meet on the beach, at barbecues, or in the restaurants and cafes that now infest every resort except isolated fishing villages.

By the late 1960s lightweight tents, usually manufactured in Canada or the USA, started to come on to the Australian market. They made their greatest weight-saving in the poles, usually of aluminium or fibreglass, and in nylon rather than canvas fabrics. By the 1970s most of these tents also boasted mesh screens to keep out flies and mosquitoes, the latter being ubiquitous at most coastal settings, especially those with a lake or stagnant water nearby. These tents were compact and could easily fit into a car boot.

Australia's travel writers and travel journalists have always had an ambivalent attitude towards the provision of facilities for campers and holidaymakers looking for comfort. Dale Collins, a Victorian-born journalist who returned after twenty-five years of living in England, was commissioned by the Melbourne *Sun News-Pictorial* to write an account of the state's attractions for potential travellers. Collins praised Wilsons Promontory, 100 000 acres of unspoiled bushland 125 miles from Melbourne. He acknowledged that there were 'sturdy types who revel in life under canvas, cooking on open fireplaces and being plagued by flies and mosquitoes', but that he was not one of them. He'd prefer to sit down for a meal, with screened windows, an open fireplace and a decent bunk, so he was very taken with the 'little cream, green roofed cottages' that the state government had erected. He admired the 'model holiday homes' and he hoped for similar settlements in 'many more of our beauty spots'.[14]

Local councils in coastal holiday areas created camping grounds of various levels of formality. Some had on-site superintendents during the summer months, while others were rarely visited by municipal officials and therefore could be very cheap to stay in. Camping grounds, usually abutting the beach, developed on Victoria's Mornington Peninsula, on Sydney's northern beaches and, in Queensland, at Coolangatta and Surfers Paradise, on Moreton Bay, and on what is now known as the Sunshine Coast, including Caloundra and Mooloolaba. Most of these areas were served by rail or tram, sometimes with a short bus trip for the final section. All were within a few hours of a capital city.

By the late 1930s there were twenty camping grounds between Mt Martha and Portsea, with the largest at Rosebud. Holidaymakers visiting 'Victoria's Peninsula Paradise' had a whole world of facilities to entice them, particularly attractive to parents wishing to offload children on rainy days. The Arthurs Seat lookout and camera obscura, mini-golf and boat hire, cinemas, kiosks, aquariums and cafes were all there. During the 1950s the facilities were much improved, to the extent that members of the Peninsula Parks Caravan Association could claim that 'facilities as good as at home are provided', including TV and electric washing machines—not to mention seven golf courses, ten bowling clubs and an abundance of tennis clubs.[15]

Melbourne had more camping grounds within easy reach of the metropolis than any other capital city, a situation made possible by the shape and size of Port Phillip Bay. From the 1960s the Peninsula camping grounds were engulfed by metropolitan expansion, so that the survivors now have suburban rather than bushland settings. Camping grounds about half a day away from the capital cities retained their original surroundings for a decade or so longer. Prospective campers visiting Mooloolaba or Alexandra Headlands in the 1930s were either dropped by car (often shared between two or more household groups), or caught

In the early days of camping, some people were as anxious to protect their vehicle as they were to secure their own comfort.

the train from Brisbane to Nambour and a bus to the beach. The Maroochydore Shire Council set aside most of its coastline for campers, and camp superintendents were on the council payroll. The council allowed fish and chip shops, hamburger shops, milk bars and cinemas near the camping grounds and within easy reach of the beach. Their premises were mostly modest fibro establishments, and at some grounds open-air picture theatres flourished. Wooden or fibro surf clubs housed the lifesavers who had custody of the beach.[16]

Camping grounds established at surfing beaches were often seen as more glamorous than bayside, riverside or lakeside establishments. Most of the holidaymakers who frequented the Mornington Peninsula, the Brisbane Water, north of Sydney, or Moreton Bay, were in family groups. Dad would concentrate on fishing while Mum was obliged to find a range of activities to occupy the kids. Camping grounds that boasted a good surf, like those at Coolangatta and Mooloolaba, also attracted families with offspring in their late teens and early twenties.

At both the bayside and surfside camping grounds families would book the same site year in year out. The family car was invariably parked next door to the tent or caravan. The peak times were Easter, the long weekends and school holidays. The facilities were modest. In the 1930s councils paid for the erection of toilet, shower and sometimes laundry blocks. These could be very intrusive structures. Isolated areas had tank rather than town water, often in short supply. Many coastal settlements did not get a mains water supply until the 1950s or 1960s, and large sections of the Australian coastline are still without it. All the townships on Tasman Peninsula, including Eaglehawk Neck and Port Arthur, were still reliant on tank water in the 1990s, and this continued to be true of most small coastal settlements around Australia into the year 2000.

The caravan: a home away from home

The car freed holidaymakers from having to book train seats or boat cabins. With a tent in the boot or a caravan hitched to the car you could set off without a specific destination in mind, or even any certainty as to where you would stay each night. As A. D. Mackenzie put it, in the RACV's *Radiator* in 1936,

> What a different feeling! Carefree, no schedule to adhere to, no time-tables to watch, and an absence of the orthodox routine of the holiday guest house . . . When the motorist becomes familiar with all that the caravan has to offer in the form of an ideal, restful, cheap and health-giving holiday, I can visualise our magnificent highways teeming with this class of transport.

Mackenzie told readers about life in a 15-foot caravan, on an 800-mile journey around Victoria. He pointed out that on such a trip, unlike a shipboard journey, there was no need to replenish one's wife's wardrobe. His Crusader caravan contained all the comfort and convenience of 'a modern suburban flat', including a kerosene stove, an icebox, metal sinks with water storage, and sleeping accommodation for four. As in much other promotional literature of the time, the virtues of the caravan were almost an end in themselves, the experience of life on the road so liberating that destinations could seem secondary.[17]

By 1937 intending caravan-users had their own magazine, the *Caravan-eer and Air Traveller*. Its third issue commented that the holiday season of 1937/38 would see a record number of caravans in Victoria. Readers were told that there were two factors behind the demand for caravans, tents and camping equipment: the ban imposed by many guest-houses on children because of the outbreak of 'infantile paralysis' (poliomyelitis) in some parts of the state, and the limited supply of 'furnished houses at seaside and mountain resorts'. The writer admitted that caravans were 'somewhat costly luxuries to buy', but pointed out that they 'can be hired at rates well within the range of most motorists'.

The *Caravaneer* put a case for the caravan not unlike the argument put today by independent travellers and backpackers: 'If holidays are sup-posed to give rest to those who have toiled in office or factory for the preceding twelve months, then such could hardly be expected from the course laid down at recognised resorts'. Caravans were cheaper than staying in hotels or guest-houses and, unlike such establishments, they provided a 'home away from home'.

In its early years the main proponents of the caravan were manufac-turers rather than proprietors of caravan parks, because there were none. In 1938 Port Fairy became one of the first tourist resorts in Aus-tralia to erect a 'comfort station for the use of tourists'. The facilities were to be provided at 'Caravan Park', a new reserve to be established on the Moyne River. 'Caravan Park' was to have an imposing entrance gate with an electric sign. A Ports and Harbours official told the local progress association that the park would be a revenue-producer, and that its facilities would enhance Port Fairy's development as a seaside tourist resort.[18]

Caravan parks based on American models began to develop in Aus-tralia in the 1950s. But they developed slowly. In 1956 the motoring writer Keith Winser pointed out that while there were over 1500 camping grounds in Australia 'not more than several dozen of the parks' com-bined all the amenities to be found in most of the 9000 trailer parks in the USA. He noted, with antipodean envy, that a typical US caravan park

The idea that Australians would embrace driving from the highway to the driveway does seem a little farcical, given the state of Australia's highways in the 1950s. Nonetheless, motels quickly appeared. By March 1960 there were 272 in Australia, their location an important guide to the demands of car travellers for both accommodation and modernity. In the space of four years this major new form of accommodation had planted itself on the landscape. Victoria had five motels in Melbourne and another forty in country centres, while NSW had thirteen in Sydney and 128 in the country, mostly in recognised tourist locations (eleven at Port Macquarie) and along the highways. South Australia with eleven, Western Australia with three and Tasmania with nine were not embracing the motel with much enthusiasm, nor were the Australian Capital Territory or the Northern Territory, with two each. Queensland soon emerged as the motel capital of Australia, with the Gold Coast claiming thirty-six of that state's fifty-nine motels.[21]

With the rapid growth of car ownership in the 1950s, each state's motoring organisation began to take an interest in the accommodation booking business. More and more families were taking to the road, so that hotels were no longer the preserve of commercial travellers, or families attending specific functions, such as a wedding or a 'back to' week. Guest-houses, like hotels, faced a new challenge from motor hotels, as the first motels were called. When the first *RACV Accommodation Guide* came out in 1959 it did not rank hotels or guest-houses (nor did the Victorian Railways *Where to Go in Victoria*). Rather, it warned that 'the standard of accommodation establishments listed in this Guide vary [*sic*] a great deal'. It indicated, like most accommodation guides of the time, the facilities available—including rooms with a private bath and the availability of hot and cold water—and it also noted whether an establishment was sewered or not. By the time of the second RACV guide, produced a year later, the Club felt obliged to add a 'Motel Supplement', which divided this new form of accommodation into two classes, with two stars for those with self-contained units and car parking, and one star for those offering somewhat less.

Motels spread rapidly from the mid-1950s. They ranged from modest highway establishments such as the Fairway at Kempsey—with its water tanks and petrol bowser—to the ritzy Beachcomber at Surfers Paradise.

The West End Motel in Ballina, NSW, possibly the first structure in Australia to call itself a 'motel', consisted of four 'self-contained' units with cooking and bathing facilities, but it did not have toilets within each unit. The first motels in Australia to have their own bathrooms opened in Orange, Wagga Wagga and Surfers Paradise (the El Dorado) in 1955. The Surfers Paradise Motel followed a year later, and by 1957 had been joined by the Ocean Court and Sea Breeze motels. Accommodation Australia Pty Ltd, formed in March 1955, was the first public company established to build motels. It brought out an American motel expert, who told the company that motoring organisations in America were advising 'prospective tourists against motoring holidays in Australia because of the lack of accommodation and service'. The new company opened its first motel in Canberra in May 1956, having applied to councils for planning approval on a number of highway sites between Brisbane, Sydney and Melbourne. Motel Canberra, two miles to the north of the city at the junction of the main road leading to Sydney and Melbourne, offered 23 double and 23 single suites in six wings connected by covered walkways. By the time it opened the company had already started on another motel at Albury.[22]

Victoria's first motel opened in the Melbourne suburb of Oakleigh in 1956. It advertised under the slogan 'YOUR CAR IN YOUR BEDROOM', pointing out that you could park your car within 6 feet of your bedroom door. The Oakleigh Motel claimed to be 'equal to America's best' with forty-three bed-sitting-rooms including family rooms with interconnecting doors. It offered air-conditioning, en suite facilities and the telephone to most rooms. Such facilities were virtually unheard of in Australia's hotels, except in the swankiest city establishments.

The dining rooms attached to the new motels in suburban and country town Australia often offered the best cuisine around. Local residents might not have occasion to stay at the motel but they would certainly dine there. In the Melbourne suburb of Hawthorn the California Motel, 'close to all state and interstate highways', advertised its Golden Gate restaurant as famous for its 'superb cuisine'. The Jacaranda Motel at Grafton offered à la carte dining in its restaurant or in guests' rooms.[23]

The Mark Anthony Motel at Buderim, Queensland, was the first licensed establishment to open on this tranquil mountain because the local bourgeoisie resisted a hotel until the late 1980s.

Motels spread along every highway in Australia, and were dotted along all the major coastal routes. By the early 1960s no self-respecting resort or tourist destination was without a motel. From Bundaberg to Eaglehawk Neck, from Albany to Parkes, motels flourished. By 1964 the only major destinations not to have motels were some of the larger country towns away from major tourist routes, including Broken Hill and Mt Isa, where licensed hotels still ruled the accommodation market. A few of the traditional guest-house capitals, most notably Marysville in Victoria, resisted the new form of accommodation, but most, including Queenscliff and Katoomba, eventually succumbed.

The design of the motels—at least in retrospect—left a lot to be desired. While they had glamorous American-style advertising hoardings, often with neon signs, all were single-storey. They had more in common with modern petrol stations than traditional hotels. They were usually built around an internal courtyard so that guests could wake up and see their motor vehicle through the plate-glass window. Publicity emphasised the ease of loading and unloading the luggage from your boot. To see the view from most of these motels you had to climb onto the toilet pedestal and look out the dunny window to the ocean, bushland or countryside beyond. Very few of the early motels took advantage of their often superb locations, preferring to direct their biggest windows to their primary target—the car and its occupants.[24]

One of the few early motels to break away from car park architecture was the Black Dolphin at Merimbula, designed by the Melbourne architect Robin Boyd and opened for Christmas 1960. Developed in 'the true Australian style', its native trees and lawns blended 'naturally' into the coastal landscape. Its floor-to-ceiling windows faced the environment, not the parked cars of its guests. Boyd saw the motel as 'an architectural tranquilliser by the Pacific Ocean, about halfway between Sydney and Melbourne'. The motel won the Sulman medal for architecture but still struggled to make its way in the offseason months. Reg Ansett bought it in 1965 to add to his chain of motels. As Merimbula had opened an air-strip just down the road from the Black Dolphin, it catered for air as well as car travellers.[25]

Motels proved particularly economical for family travel because they often followed the American practice of charging per room, rather than per head, as hotels and guest-houses were still inclined to do. And unlike most European and British accommodation houses the Australian motel always provided, at the very minimum, a toaster and an electric jug, so that weary travellers could at least make themselves toast or boil an egg. The motels were marketed, along American lines, by mutual chains, usually representing individual proprietors. The MFA, Flag and later groups, such as Budget and Best Western, ran their own rating and booking systems and developed traveller loyalty schemes.

WITH 95 PER CENT of the population living in just one-thirtieth of its land mass, the car and the road take on particular meanings in Australia. Beyond the thirty airports that are home to regular aeroplane services, the car is literally the only way to explore the continent, from mountains and isolated beaches to rainforest or desert. From motor honeymoons to the Redex trials to the fad of the four-wheel-drive, Australians have taken to the car with alacrity, having one of the world's highest rates of car ownership and car usage. Over four out of five Australian households now have a car, and two out of five households have two or more. While some inner-city residents have abandoned the notion of car ownership, they can still rent vehicles from the hundreds of car rental outlets to be found at airports and major rail terminals, and in the city centres and suburban hubs. Only the poor, the aged, and the small percentage of adults who do not drive are without the spectacular mobility provided by the car.

The continent's wide-open spaces have proved particularly appealing to tourists from western Europe. Certain national groups, especially the Germans, regularly set off in rental cars to tackle the Great Ocean Road, the Pacific Highway, and the Bruce Highway north of Brisbane. For American and Canadian tourists the novelty of the open road is not so

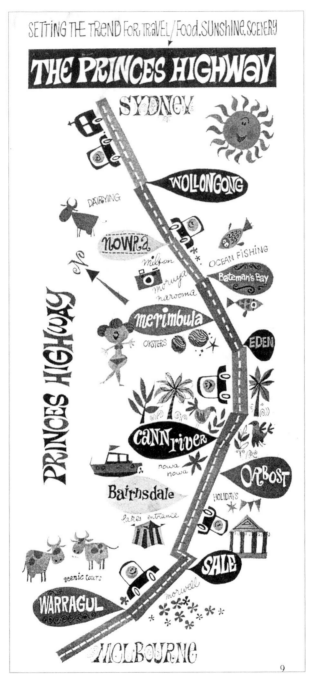

By the early 1960s one motel chain offered ten motels between Melbourne and Sydney via the Princes Highway.

great. The major bus companies have had to respond to changing tourist demands. From the 1920s to the 1980s they concentrated on point-to-point travel, apart from organised tours of particular places. By the 1990s bus companies were offering passes that emphasised zigzag travel, where you got on and off as you pleased.

The car revolutionised travel and tourism in Australia, providing levels of mobility never before contemplated. It catered for planned and unplanned journeys of any length and in any season. Car travellers, depending on their inclinations and income, could be as formal or informal as they liked. Luxury hotels and later motels catered for those who desired classy lodgings. Camping grounds and caravans provided relatively cheap accommodation over long holiday periods. While it is no longer common to camp on the side of the road, car travellers in more isolated spots still camp where they choose. In the cities and in built-up resort areas the car provides mobility between destinations, but on arrival it has to be parked somewhere. There are very few resorts left that have not installed parking meters, so the car can be a burden as well as a boon.[26]

Despite its large cities and a rail network to cater for agricultural and mineral exports, most of the continent is inaccessible by any form of transport other than the motor vehicle. This is true not only of the outback, but for most of the coastline as well. The car has enabled tiny fishing villages to turn into major holiday destinations, and for huge tracts of bushland to be readily accessible to bushwalkers. The car is served by a network of highways, roads and unmade tracks. The consequences of mobility for Australian tourism are there for all to see.

7

The Rediscovery of the Centre and Aboriginal Tourism

ALTHOUGH A SUBSTANTIAL telegraph station was constructed there in 1871, Alice Springs was slow to grow. In 1933, even after a short spell as capital of the territory of Central Australia, the town had a white population amounting to only 526. Conditions were rough and ready. The few tourists staying at the only pub, the Stuart Arms, might find themselves housed in a wooden annexe; the management provided no mosquito nets and, as the rooms were stuffy, people 'lay outside and tried to forget the mosquitoes till a half-caste girl brought a cup of tea at dawn'. On making their way to the bathroom under the pepper trees, they had to step over old boots and trousers discarded by previous travellers. Paid-off drovers were still capable of taking pot shots at the bottles lined up behind the bar. When, in 1932, the three-year-old railway brought to the pub the Territory's first barmaid, she soon found it expedient to keep a waddy on hand to subdue the rowdier customers.

Three years into World War II, the population had doubled; shortly afterwards some 8000 troops were stationed in Alice Springs, with many more passing through on their way to the Top End. As Frank Clune wrote at the time, 'It needed a war to make tens of thousands of Australians realise that Centralia is one of the strangest and loveliest regions in the world . . . The war has put the Red Heart on the map'. The rise in interest gathered force in the late 1950s and 1960s, by which stage a tourist boom had developed, centred on Alice Springs. Old-timers expecting to find a hotel bed saved for them when they made a visit to 'the Alice' now found them 'occupied by pale-faced people in city clothes and collar and tie'. Alice Springs suddenly seemed to be the trendiest location to visit in the whole country.[1]

Why did these people come? Some were former members of the armed forces returning to old haunts, or exploring an area that had intrigued them as they hurriedly passed through. But there was also the broader reason that in the Centre, with its vast distances, real sense of challenge and occasional dangers, city people could experience the pioneering conditions that had been the primal Australian experience, together with the comradeship or mateship that went with it. Moreover, new images of the Centre were now being produced. Work by Albert Namatjira had reached Melbourne as early as 1938, and his European-style watercolours blanketed this strange land with a seeming familiarity, making it more accessible. Soon tourists turned up to watch the painter at work, sometimes pushing him about in order to take their photographs.

Then, in 1955, Charles Chauvel produced the film *Jedda*, which combined a sense of the otherness of Aboriginal ways with splendid scenery, presenting the Territory as a truly exotic place; the tour operator Len Tuit immediately christened one of his operations 'Jedda tours'. No less important were the film and book, *A Town Like Alice*. In Neville Shute's novel (1950), the Alice is the 'bonzer place' referred to by the hero, Joe Harman, and connected with the great national drama of Australians as prisoners of war of the Japanese. When the English heroine eventually reaches Alice Springs, she is surprised to find 'a faint air of an English suburb' about the place, and immediately envisages the possibility of a happy life for herself there, 'with two or three children, perhaps'. As Alan Moorehead wrote, the Alice 'is not so much a town as a pleasant idea, having a special flavour of its own (and the gender of the idea is feminine)'. It had become the ideal white Australian community, a bridgehead of suburban amenity, uncomplicated in its social relations and set in wide-open spaces. Thus even though the story was about building another town *like* Alice, the 1956 film had its world premiere in the increasingly well-known original.[2]

Jacket design by Allan Jordan for Frank Clune's The Red Heart *(Hawthorn Press, Melbourne, 1944)*

Albert Namatjira superimposed on four leading tourist sites. The iconisation came too early for some: 'Excuse the dreadful postcard', the sender wrote from Tennant Creek in May 1959.

Before the war there had been a tour operator, Bert Bond, taking people from the Alice to Palm Valley and Altunga, using seven-passenger Studebakers supplemented by a Dodge truck carrying supplies. In 1946 Len Tuit, then a mail contractor, had the idea of combining his run from Alice Springs to Darwin with a passenger service. Buying out Bond, Tuit went from strength to strength, reconditioning second-hand vehicles as he extended his network over rough roads, servicing local needs as well as tourists. By 1957 his operations, which now included a motel in Alice Springs, employed sixty-four people, including mechanics, drivers, cooks, typists and housemaids.[3]

Tourists came to the Centre by a variety of means. The Ghan arrived twice a week during the season, which ran from May to September; in 1947 it was noted that, of the 250 recent arrivals on one train, 70 per cent were tourists. The major airlines showed increasing interest too. In 1947 Trans-Australia Airlines ran the first Adelaide–Darwin service, via Alice Springs, and in 1960 Ansett began a weekly tourist flight from Melbourne. Locals noted that the planes always seemed to be full.

Through its subsidiary Pioneer Tours, Ansett had already increased its operations on the ground, since it had bought out Tuit's Tours a few years before. As Pearl Tuit explained, 'We just didn't have the money to buy the better types of vehicles' now in demand.

Even so, the expansion of the town on the back of tourism, particularly after 1957, did not always proceed smoothly. Visitors were sometimes struck by a residual primitiveness and a 'stubborn local pride', occasionally evident in some resistance to the annual invasion. Some people resented the buses clogging the main street: eventually it would be turned into a mall and much of it abandoned to tourists completely. Later, too, shopkeepers would employ extra staff to keep an eye on visiting school kids inclined to shoplifting. But initially there was a sense that tourists were no respecters of privacy, a feeling that they were disrupters of community. A definition of a tourist at this time was 'someone who arrived with one ten-shilling note and one clean set of underclothing, and didn't change either'.[4]

Indeed many were not big spenders, as continual upgrading of the road meant that an increasing proportion of tourists drove themselves up from Adelaide. By 1980, in addition to the country club under construction, there were a dozen motels, with more being built, and no fewer than seven caravan and tourist parks.

As the town steadily grew in population, from just over 2000 in 1947 to double that by 1960, reaching 11 179 in 1971 and 18 395 in 1981, the importance of the tourism industry was increasingly recognised. Operators saw advantages in a measure of co-operation. An initial tourist organisation had been founded in the 1950s, and in 1961 there began the Central Australian Tours Association, particularly effective in publicity: from 1966 to 1969 tourists visiting Alice Springs increased by 43 per cent, from 26 600 to 38 000.[5]

Publicity at this time for Alice Springs itself is remarkable for the way it stressed the normality of the place. That was the achievement, rather than luxury. The town's character as a bridgehead of suburbia was caught beautifully on the cover of a 1973 pamphlet that showed a number of elderly men, appropriately clad, on the town bowling green, the red

(*Photo. by courtesy of Dep'. of Information.*)

MISS THE WINTER

In the Life, Colour and Sunshine of Central
Australia and the Northern Territory.

A wonderful escape from the daily routine in a
land of arresting pictures.

Full particulars of tours at

THE VICTORIAN GOVERNMENT TOURIST BUREAU

272 Collins Street, Melbourne	28 Martin Place, Sydney
City Hall, Gheringhap Street, Geelong	34 Lydiard Street North, Ballarat
Charing Cross, Bendigo	35 Deakin Avenue, Mildura

Men for all seasons. This advertisement from Walkabout, *June 1947, highlighted the
climatic contrast in red print.*

hills leading to the Heavitree Gap immediately beyond. As late as 1968 women were being advised to bring a 'Tweed skirt, slacks or jodhpurs', among other items; the publicity writer conceded that while alcohol consumption in the Territory was among the highest in the world, readers could rest assured that 'the drinking is always sensible'. The desire to present the Alice as a respectable mainstream community often involved overlooking the blacks: the bowls pamphlet contained not one picture of them, and only three-quarters of a page of text out of twenty-eight. At the same time the attitude towards the terrain, apart from acknowledged beauty spots, remained equivocal: the setting of the golf course was described not altogether convincingly as country that was 'rugged yet interesting'.[6]

'The Rock' as tourist trophy

Frank Clune's wartime book *The Red Heart* was, as the representation of the love symbol on its jacket showed, both an affirmation and an inversion of the popular stereotype. The name 'Dead Heart', originally ascribed to Lake Eyre at the turn of the century, had come to be blanketed over the whole region. It was this wholesale dismissal that Clune was contesting. 'Australia has a hard heart, certainly', he wrote; 'a stony heart, indisputable; a hot heart, too right . . . but a Dead Heart, ah no'.

At the time Clune wrote, very few white people had been to Ayers Rock. Camels were still used to get there, and few even of the defence personnel based at Alice Springs had bothered to make the journey. Rare indeed had been expeditions like that of Vic Foy, a millionaire globetrotter who was a member of the family running the Sydney emporium Mark Foy's. In 1935 he decided to go out and see the country of Lasseter's last ride. A 'bitzer' vehicle was prepared, and another brought from Sydney. A hundred gallons of water and 100 gallons of petrol were measured out, six camels being loaded up with stores. The Rock was reached, and climbed. But when Foy returned to Sydney he aired the common tourist complaint: his snaps hadn't come out. The heat had ruined his film. Nevertheless twelve names from the expedition now lay in a bottle on the summit, accounting for just under half of the twenty-six people who had climbed the Rock between 1931 and 1946. Although the track from Curtin Springs was graded in 1948, the number of visitors to the Rock did not increase immediately. Few knew about it; the site was part of an Aboriginal reserve. 'Most of those who see it now', wrote Arthur Groom a short time afterwards, 'fly out of Alice Springs in one of Eddie Connellan's small planes'. These would circle the monolith once or twice and then return.

In 1950 Len Tuit, having been approached by the anthropologist C. P. Mountford, met a party of masters and boys from Knox Grammar School, Sydney, at the Finke railway siding and took them with their supplies to the Rock. This was Uluru's first guided tour. Although water was a great problem—they had to double back to Curtin Springs, 100 kilometres away, to get more—the venture set Tuit thinking. But others could see little tourist potential in the area: Nugget Coombs is recalled by Tuit's wife as having said, 'You'll never sell a lump of rock'. The Administration resisted suggestions of improving the track, the Resident Engineer at Alice Springs fearing for his grader. Officially, the Director of Native Affairs had 'no great objection' to the excision of the Rock from the Reserve, but he was opposed to the idea of tourism since there was no appropriate body to govern tourist access. In the face of Tuit's persistence, it was agreed that he would be given a lease of up to 10 acres for a camp, so long as he found water beyond a radius of 2 miles from the Rock.

The establishment of the bore in 1957 marks the beginning of regular tourism at Ayers Rock. Peter Severin at Curtin Springs, directly on the track from the Alice, saw only six people passing through in 1956; the following year Tuit brought a dozen a week. School parties were prominent; the Rock became the trendy destination for May and September holidays. In 1957 there had also been a 'Petticoat Safari', a party of thirty-two women aged from nineteen to seventy, none of whom had been to the Centre before. They slept in a phalanx of Arabian-style tents, 'hearing dingoes howling from nearby sandhills after our kerosene lamps were turned down'. The first of them to reach the top of the

Women taken to Ayers Rock by the Australian Women's Weekly *were housed in Arabian-style tents which open at the sides. This resembles turn of the century British military design.*

climb was a former Melbourne conductress—keeping her balance in trams had stood her in good stead. The capacity to be adaptable, to 'rough it', was still essential. The amenities at Tuit's camp were basic: it now ran to hot showers and electric light, but people slept on stretchers in tents. The one permanent building was made of corrugated iron. The tourists knew that they needed to be in good hands: in 1956 two Sydney men died on the road from Alice Springs, ill equipped when their truck got stuck in heavy sand.

A number of developments occurred in rapid succession. Tuit relocated his campsite adjacent to the bore, on the east side of the Rock; this also had the advantage of being a prime viewing point for sunrise on the monolith. By 1959—Ayers Rock and the Olgas having been gazetted a national park the year before—an airstrip was in place. Sandhills on the road were finally eliminated in 1960, when the distance from Alice Springs was also shortened.

Accommodation was extended and upgraded. Mrs Underwood of the Alice Springs Hotel had a Sidney Williams hut transported to the Rock but, just before the removal truck reached its destination, it became stuck in the sand. The hut was taken off to lighten the load. Since this occurred only a few hundred metres short of the intended destination, it scarcely seemed worthwhile to load the truck up again. The hut with its six rooms stayed put—the original Ayers Rock Chalet. By 1960 Ansett-Pioneer had bought out Tuit, and after first doubling and upgrading the accommodation he had provided, they almost immediately set about building permanent accommodation, soon to be known as the Red Sands Motel. In the course of the next decade three more motels went up.

There was a great deal of camaraderie among the staff at the various hostelries: since many returned for two or three seasons, they all knew each other and would attend each other's parties. Tourists would join in too—the alternative was to lie in bed hearing the thump of the house generator as it went on producing power till 2 a.m. The best parties were those put on between coachloads, but these gaps in the traffic soon disappeared. From a mere 100 in 1956 the number of visitors rose to 4000 in 1961, more than doubling to over 10 000 in 1964–65, to double again by 1970–71, when there were more than 30 000.[7]

Bill Harney, initially appointed 'Keeper' of the Rock by the Administration in 1957, the year before the National Park was gazetted, then became Ranger; the seven months he spent at the Rock each year until 1962—since an all-year-round presence was then felt not to be necessary—gave him a poor opinion of tourists. Taking parties around the Rock, Harney became aware of great gaps in his presentations. He wrote away for scientific information from government departments, and was glad of any lore the older Aborigines might pass on. Having gained his own knowledge only with difficulty, Harney resented the way many tourists seemed to think he was 'a crank to be tolerated'. Resistant to any analogies Harney might make between Aboriginal beliefs and the Christian religion, tourists were seen by Harney as having the greatest reluctance to take any Aboriginal religious ideas seriously.

For most whites, Ayers Rock was simply a place. In an article published in 1960, Joyce Batty listed the reasons why some people on her trip to the Rock were already thinking of returning. There was, for those who made the climb, the feeling of standing on top of the world; the awesome serenity of the Rock itself, particularly at sunrise; and the attraction of 'listening to one of Australia's great story-tellers and of comradeship around the huge camp-fires at night, barbecue suppers, dancing and singing to that old instrument of the outback, the accordion'. Similarly, the reporter of the 'Petticoat Safari' had expressed surprise at finding 'a land of unique colour' rather than extensive gibber plains. Both reports read as though they were describing an empty frontier land, where the Australian pioneering spirit could be sampled and savoured, without any reference whatsoever to Aborigines or their sacred sites.

In the late 1940s no visitors were allowed near the Rock, without first putting a convincing case to secure the necessary written permission. In 1953 Len Tuit and Bert Bond were allowed to take only one special party there. But as it became plain that the Aboriginal grip on the area was slackening, this policy was increasingly relaxed. White encroachment on the area had increased through the 1930s, what with the advance of pastoralists, gold prospectors and dingo scalp hunters; a severe drought completed the rupture of traditional land-use patterns. C. P. Mountford noted in 1940 that there were still some Aborigines living a tribal life around the Rock, whereas in 1960 he could find only one man who had passed through all his initiation rites there. However often—or rarely—Aborigines might return to conduct ceremonies, many had dramatically modified their nomadic patterns as they settled on adjacent missions and stations.

The intermittent nature of the Aboriginal presence meant that the growing tourist interest in the area could not be contained indefinitely. As early as 1956 a party of government officials, including the Administrator, went to the Rock to investigate the impact particularly of unauthorised visitors. Wood was being taken from scarce timber, Maggie Springs (Mutitjulu) abused, and rock paintings vandalised. The decision to appoint Harney as Keeper followed shortly afterwards, along with a tightening of the rules to be observed on visits. Harney soon found that, although people were supposed to camp in fixed places, this rule would go by the board if he happened to be called away. Cattle-owners,

But the driving imperative for many remained the climb up the Rock: it was the goal of 78 per cent of the 1971 visitors. (In the fifteen years from 1968, twenty-five people would die while climbing.) It might be necessary, ran one report, to construct a second pathway up the Rock in order to cope with the traffic. Certainly a monorail around the base of the Rock, it was felt, would be less harmful than the ecologically damaging spur roads that then ran right up to it.

At the time that these reports were tabled, there was a rapid acceleration in the number of visitors to the Rock—from 42 705 in 1971–72 to 50 287 the following year. Already some 250 000 were envisaged, for there was a marked growth in interest. 'In some ways', stated the study emanating from the Australian National University, 'Ayers Rock is acquiring a cultural importance for white people just as strong as it had for the original inhabitants'. Certainly it was the place where many took their first tentative step towards trying to understand Aboriginal culture. Even so, there was still much room for developing segments of the tourist market. In 1971 just under half the buses—which themselves accounted for well over half the visitors—consisted of student groups. Cars brought barely a quarter, with Victorians taking a decided lead over New South Wales. International tourists accounted for one-sixth of all visitors, but only 2 per cent of those who came to Australia then made it to the Rock.

In their report to the Minister for the Interior, the consultants Kinnaird Hill, de Rohan and Young outlined four proposals for development of the Rock and its environs—very quickly dismissing a fifth, closure to visitors, on the grounds that it was 'unnecessarily severe' and would deny Aborigines the chance 'to improve their economic independence'. One option was to increase accommodation directly in response to demand, being mindful that as incomes rose (for such was a common assumption at the time) so too would the demand for increased quality in hotels and motels. Other options, designed partly to reduce government outlay, envisaged package tours to the Rock from an Alice Springs accommodation base, or facilities designed for a limit of two nights only. A new, special village, located some distance away from

The standard shot of Ayers Rock Resort suggests a much greater proximity to Uluru than is actually the case. It was deliberately sited well away from the Rock.

the Rock and nearer to the Olgas, was envisaged in all the local building options, and this proposal was acted upon.[9]

In 1974 a Northern Territory government task force determined the site for the new town—Yulara, 'place of the howling dingo', a name specially chosen by the Anangu people, presumably without irony. Fully 17 kilometres from the Rock, it would enable all the touristic improvisations of twenty years to be swept away. The original plan had been for a rather scattered settlement but, as the architect Phillip Cox explained, Yulara became compact, 'responsive to the environment, minimizing spread and at all stages having contact with the desert itself'. Government-financed, the construction of the village was contracted out to a number of builders and achieved relatively painlessly, within budget and in thirty months. It was opened in 1984.

Confident in its contemporary design, proclaimed in bright colours, Yulara provides a surprising intimacy with its covered walks and confined public spaces; the Australianness of its verandas and corrugated iron are imaginatively supplemented by vast sails, an idea appropriated from the Middle East and serving to break up the impact of the sun. From the time it opened the town was capable of accommodating 5200 visitors a day, its facilities ranging from an international-standard Sheraton to the new, relocated camping ground. However, persistent deficits led the Territory government to decide, in 1991, to reduce its interest in Yulara by 40 per cent, for it had been financed by borrowings then amounting to $238 million. The Aboriginal name was traded in—in the greater interests of product identification—for the more businesslike Ayers Rock Resort. But by 1997 the Territory government had decided to sell out completely, for $130 million. Although the government claimed that this was a 'win-win' solution, the ALP opposition estimated that the resort had altogether cost taxpayers more than $500 million.[10]

Uluru: the Aboriginal presence

The concerns first expressed about Ayers Rock in the 1950s had largely been in terms of the despoliation of the environment, or the damaging of Aboriginal cave art; since no Aborigines seemed to be living there permanently, there was little sense of intrusion upon the ceremonial sites of a fragile culture. The road to the Rock cut clean across the women's initiation ground. Tourists were reported as coming 'to learn something of the environment, wildlife and Aboriginal history and mythology', but it was very much in that order. The caves all came to be renamed, bearing such titles as 'Napoleon's Hat' and 'Kangaroo Tail'.

Such thorough-going attitudes at once gave rise to and endorsed the policy of assimilation which, in the words of Tim Rowse, 'was intended to empty the deserts of its nomads, leaving Europeans free to recognise and develop the tourist potential of Ayers Rock and Mt Olga'. Even so, there was more interaction—much of it by the roadside—than Welfare officials would have liked. Official letters were sent to tour operators, pointing out that payments to Aborigines for artefacts or for being allowed to take photographs undermined the work of the Branch, having an 'adverse effect' on the 'principle of work for pay'. A few years earlier Bill Harney had noted the rise in the production of artefacts and their decline in quality, since they were no longer made with the traditional care and accompanying chants. During the 1960s they replaced dingo scalps as the principal source of independent Aboriginal income.

In 1972 planners could speak blithely of Aborigines imparting knowledge of their culture, although it was conceded, in rather constrained prose, that 'It is by no means certain that tourist interest in these matters is not offensive to the Pitjantjatjara [Anangu]'. It was hoped that, if they were employed as guides, Aborigines would 'contribute to an understanding of the dignity and integrity of Aboriginal culture'. All this was but pie in the sky; there was no sign yet of any Aboriginal interest in becoming involved in the tourist industry in this way. A few years later local Aborigines did work with the architects at Yulara in siting walking tracks and some of the buildings, and were involved in its construction, but early hopes of habitual large-scale employment at the resort were doomed to disappointment. The few houses built for Aborigines at Yulara usually remained empty.

The Anangu had, in fact, an agenda of their own—not an explicit programme so much as a high degree of resistance arising from a deep cultural confidence, recently strengthened fortuitously. Docker River, founded in 1968 as a settlement partly designed to draw Aborigines away from Ayers Rock to the west, grew far larger than had been imagined and, thanks to European food and transport, the ceremonies that took place there were the largest the Anangu had ever known. Intended to be an isolated settlement, Docker River had become instead a place for consolidation and regrouping. Aborigines had been replacing camels with second-hand cars for some time, and once money worries receded after they could claim the dole in 1973, return visits to the Rock increased in frequency. There had already been a very public ceremony there in 1972; now, as elsewhere, there was a move back to traditional lands. An Anangu-owned store and service station—financed from Docker River—were opened at the Rock, also in 1972. Two years later a permanent camp was established there.

Ultimate colonialism: a discomfited Aboriginal child in an opened-out pumpkin, placed on a postcard; from Lake Tyers Aboriginal Reserve, Victoria, c. 1920

'Australia's First Perambulator', says this postcard from the mid-1950s. The Jolliffe image prompted the sender to write on the back, 'I don't think Pauline would like one of these'.

To return to the Rock was one thing, to have land rights acknowledged quite another. While Mr Justice Woodward in 1974 had recommended that Aborigines should have the right to determine the degree to which tourists could enter their lands (a principle embodied in land rights legislation), it was not till two years later that the Anangu had an organisation of their own that would enable their views to be put to government. Meanwhile plans for Yulara had gone ahead and, while Anangu had been consulted about the exact location of sacred sites, it seems they were not told of the intended excision of Yulara from the park and its proclamation as a township. This was partly because it was conceived as the solution, particularly by the Territory government: once Yulara was built there would be no reason for the Anangu to continue to live and trade in the park. Opposition to the new explicit Aboriginal presence was shared by both the federal Australian National Parks and Wildlife Service and the Territory Reserves Board: the former body wished to restrict Anangu activity, particularly hunting, while it also placed great importance on the title to the park being vested in its Director. In 1979 the primacy of the idea of a national park induced Mr Justice Toohey to deliver the judgment that the park already constituted alienated crown land. Once again it seemed like a case of environmentalism before Aborigines.

Even so, the tide had begun to turn. In 1980 the Commonwealth built several houses for Anangu near the store, and in 1982 an advisory role was envisaged for them in the park's first Plan of Management. The following year the Hawke government promised 'Handback'—acknowledging Aboriginal ownership of the park and the Rock (now widely becoming known as Uluru)—a decision implemented in 1985. This initiative met with ferocious opposition from the Northern Territory government, which boycotted the ceremony.[11]

In fact the acknowledgement of native title to Uluru was inseparable from leasehold of the park to the Australian National Parks and Wildlife Service, a principle embodied in the relevant commonwealth legislation. Moreover there was nothing to prevent the federal parliament from otherwise unilaterally amending the agreement by further legislation, although Mabo subsequently made this most unlikely. Meanwhile the benefits for the Anangu were very real. The lease guaranteed them 20 per cent of the admission fees to the park for the first five years, plus an additional annual rent of $75 000. (These sums have moved up since.) Moreover, the Anangu were given a majority on the board of management, although a number of provisions ensured ultimate ANPWS authority. In addition, there was an undertaking to employ them wherever possible, if necessary modifying working hours and conditions to accommodate traditional customs. Evidence of these changes had real impact, not least on tourists: nine out of ten of those visiting Uluru the year after Handback were aware that the park was now owned by the Anangu.

In 1979 the Territory government had urged tourism upon Aboriginal communities as a means of attaining economic self-sufficiency. It had also, in 1982, offered land rights over the park, but with various conditions attached. The Anangu, well advised, resisted these blandishments, and began to show how their increased control of the park would be used to filter tourism so as to preserve their communal way of life.

When the Aboriginal village was set up at Yulara, one of the three view-finders on a neighbouring hillock was focused directly at it. But so little had the Anangu any inclination to be objects of curiosity for whites that in the early 1980s up to 50 percent of the population at Mutitjulu, as the camp at Uluru was now known, moved out for the duration of the tourist season. Indeed, one of the first results of Handback was the Anangu decision to close Mutitjulu to tourists, even though this would mean less custom at the store. They also resisted sending their children to the Yulara school, and set up one of their own.

It was not so much that there was great hostility to tourists: three-quarters of Anangu interviewed at the time thought tourism good, though there were far too many visitors. The plain fact was that only one tourist in seven came to the park primarily to make contact with the Anangu; they were a sideshow compared with the Rock, which half the visitors wanted to climb. The Anangu were well aware of these priorities, all the more so because the sacredness of Uluru meant that they would never climb it themselves. The tourists streaming up the path seemed to them like ants—*mingka*—and every bit as remorseless. It was only in summer that the dotted line ceased, since, as one old man put it, 'the tourists are on holidays then'!

The main anxiety concerned the corrosiveness of tourism on Anangu life. Shortly after Handback, less than half of the community wanted tourist work in future. Similarly, while two-thirds thought it good that tourists should learn something of the Anangu way of life, only half as many endorsed the idea of teaching them about the past and the Dreaming —more strictly cultural matters—as supported the idea of bush tucker tours. Interestingly, support for tourist education was lowest among those under twenty-five, partly attributable to their having had less contact themselves, but also perhaps to both a despair about growing tourist numbers and a greater cultural confidence.

One of the first and most positive adaptations to the tourist incursion has been the growth and regularisation of the manufacture and sale of artefacts. An upsurge in production followed the resumption of occupancy of traditional lands, since it extended a limited economy, particularly when adjacent to tourist sites. Maruku Arts and Crafts was founded at Uluru in 1984, specifically to address the problem of marketing. Four years later the organisation was acting on behalf of twenty Western Desert communities, on the assumption that direct sale to tourists was preferable to distribution through outlets in the southern cities. Indeed only 19 per cent of the artefacts then handled by Maruku were manufactured at Mutitjulu; 590 of the producers came from other communities. Maruku has become the largest regional craft centre in Australia. (An increasing international component helped to push sales upwards, to $701 692 in 1996/97.) Steps were taken to ensure quality control of artefacts. It has been noted that, in the work of the Mutitjulu community, a distinct variant of Western Desert art has become instantly recognisable.

The point has been made that, following Handback and the closure of the Mutitjulu community, most dealings between the Anangu and tourists have been indirect. Artefacts are sold for them, by Maruku, rather than through direct dealing; Anangu investments, such as the Malpa Trading Company, have been managed and operated by non-Anangu.

While there has been some regret at the more impersonal scale of things, for it makes tourism harder to comprehend, this has nonetheless harnessed the industry to the point where Anangu can reap benefits without being quite so fearful that their way of life is being imperilled.

Shortly after Handback a survey showed that two-thirds of the Anangu felt that tourists did nothing that should be forbidden. This was perhaps less a lyrical acceptance of growing numbers than a recognition that their own conditions had improved vastly since the mid-1970s: Anangu now had the right to live and hunt in the park, tourists paid for the right to visit, sacred sites had become fenced off, and the taking of photographs—so intrusive in the early days of tourism—had now been virtually eliminated.

Also important was the way Anangu had become more involved in the running of the park. When it came to tourism, initially Aborigines were generally regarded as suited only to working in a service capacity. It was true, too, that the repetitious and boring nature of much work, such as serving in shops, did not appeal to them much, particularly when their communication skills in English were poor. But work in the park has been relatively popular, even if it has gone through a number of cycles since Handback. By 1992, ninety-three members of the Mutit-julu community, which numbered some 150 to 200, had done some work for the ANPWS over the previous twelve months. They included five trainee rangers, who would lead 'bush tucker' walks among other things, together with eight women conducting interpretive walks, which some of them had devised; the vast majority did casual work, though another five men were engaged in burning off. Indeed Aboriginal involvement in land management grew to the point where they were training whites in 'caring for the country', advising naturalists in the late 1990s during a three-year project designed to establish how various habitats functioned. In 1998 one-third of all Park staff were Aboriginal, the first indigenous ranger having graduated five years before.

While there has been greater confidence in the way the Anangu address the park and the tourist presence, vigilance is still necessary to protect Anangu lifestyle and culture. In 1987 a manual was prepared

The Courier-Mail Annual *for 1956 demonstrates how Queensland captured the new imagery of the Australian beach—even to the extent of turning the men almost into Aboriginal figures as they put on a display for the women.*

The interior of the Uluru – Kata Tjuta Cultural Centre. The architect has successfully reconciled the touristic and ceremonial functions of the building.

Aboriginal cultural centres and keeping places have appeared in recent years throughout Australia. This imaginative building designed by Greg Burgess is the Brambuk Cultural Centre in the Grampians, Victoria.

for coach captains, notoriously loose and prejudiced in their spiel to passengers; shortly afterwards Tour Operator Workshops were held, accredited by both ANPWS and the Mutitjulu community. (Nowadays the old problem is likely to surface mainly in interstate buses, whose drivers might make only one or two trips to Uluru a year.) Buses remain important: A. A. T. King's maintain considerably more buses in service at Uluru than they do in Sydney.

The number of visitors to Uluru continued to climb steadily: to more than 338 000 in 1997–98. But the Anangu see the park 'as an Anangu place where they invite visitors, not a tourist place which tolerates Anangu'. There is therefore a need to present indigenous culture forcefully, and in a setting that might also reduce tourist impact. The Melbourne architect Gregory Burgess, who designed the highly successful Brambuk Cultural Centre in Victoria, saw that building become the spearhead of a reasserted Aboriginal presence in the Grampians; but here the task was different. Burgess therefore provided, for the Uluru-Kata Tjuka Cultural Centre, a design that manages to reconcile the desire to display with the need to protect. Opened in 1995, the Centre contains areas where crafts are made, displayed and sold (for Maruku is now located here), together with a ceremonial ground, further space allocated to explaining the joint management of the park, plus a restaurant and other amenities. Instead of people 'swarming through in an obscenely short time, leaving with not much more than a sausage roll, and irritable memories of toilet queues', the idea is that visitors should be encouraged to explore and make discoveries, sometimes with Anangu interaction, but more often without. The striking double snake-like design of the building—a concept developed with the Anangu—assists tourists to move through unobtrusively, so that when a number of coachloads are present, careful scheduling avoids a sense of overcrowding.[12]

Aboriginal tourism ventures

Aboriginal interest in tourism, in the sense of an organised response to this new incursion by whites, could be said to have begun in 1969, when the Iwupataka Progress Association constructed a store and toilet block at Standley Chasm near Alice Springs. The Aborigines Benefits Trust Fund supported a number of such ventures at this time, but only the Ininti store and service station at Ayers Rock were to prove durable. As Jon Altman observed in the 1980s, Aboriginal participation in tourism 'has been sporadic, small-scale, and largely indirect'.

Nevertheless the range of activities on offer to tourists in the late 1990s was building impressively. Whereas a 1991 Northern Territory Tourist Commission publication, *Come Share Our Culture*, listed twenty-two different tours, its 1997 successor—with a sub-title modulated more appropriately to *Come Share Our Country*—listed thirty-one tours and cultural centres, plus art and craft galleries. Even so, there remained instances where Aborigines merely provided colour and movement. One Alice Springs operator was notorious for his paternalism, for ignoring traditional owners while he negotiated with pastoralists, and

Shops selling Aboriginal curios became more common in the 1950s. Aboriginal Enterprises, Belgrave, in the Dandenong Ranges near Melbourne, catered for the Sunday drive market.

for employing Aborigines from distant tribes to put on corroborees or throw boomerangs. Whites provided the commentaries.

More sensitive altogether was Desert Tracks, which in 1987 began organising tours into Anangu country. No more than twenty people went in each party:

> We travel in a 50 km radius [read the 1996 brochure] around the camp in search of bush tucker and large game. Digging for honey ants or Witchety grubs is hard but rewarding work. We learn how to find water in the desert, to gather bush medicines and to see the subtle tracks of animals on the sand dunes. Return to camp to rest and sample these desert delicacies.

Participants were given a booklet at the outset that provided information, including useful Pitjantjatjara words and phrases, and also a photocopy of their permit to enter Aboriginal land. Tourists were guests, participating in the daily rituals of traditional culture, but supplementary food was taken along as it was realised that local resources were in short supply. Camps were located where permanent toilets had been built. A group of six elders provided translators and guides. Even that degree of involvement can cause dislocation in the Aboriginal community, and so from December to February there were no tours at all, since that is the main ceremonial time. Originally set up by Diane James, the venture became wholly owned by Aborigines. James, from then on the manager, saw the tours as having had largely beneficial effects: tribal lore and traditional techniques were reinforced by this controlled tourism, and were also seen to have economic value. As J. J. Kennedy noted in his report on Northern Territory tourism, cultural tourism can engender 'independence and pride' among Aboriginal people.[13]

In the 1960s there would have been little interest in a tour designed to enable white people to share the lifestyle of desert Aborigines. But the rise of environmentalism, and ecotourism, has thrown into relief the skilfulness of Aboriginal land utilisation in difficult habitats, quite apart from the increasing appeal of indigenous cultures in a world increasingly homogenised by globalisation. Interest has grown sharply. In 1985 A. A. T. King's were utterly dismissive of including Ipolera, one of the first ventures in Aboriginal tourism, on their bus itineraries; now they think nothing of taking middle-aged suburban mums and dads on an Arnhem Land safari camp. Aboriginal tourism has established direct links with the wholesale tourist industry, that is to say with people who put the travel menus together. Tiwi and Kakadu Tours were quick off the mark in the early 1990s, concluding a promotional deal with Germany's largest travel agent network. Aboriginal culture is often seen—particularly by Continental Europeans—as the most distinctive thing this country has to offer.

Aboriginal involvement in tourism has always taken a number of forms. There is the work done in national parks, as board members, rangers, guides and manual workers. Cultural tours were initially often begun in collaboration with whites, who provided management and services, but increasingly Aborigines have come to operate such ventures themselves. In 1993 there were thirty-four tours in the Territory focused on Aboriginal culture; these included dance performances, safari

Desert Tracks, 1987: an early venture in Aboriginal cultural tourism

tours and visits to communities. Only six of them were owned and operated by non-Aborigines; fifteen were joint ventures, with thirteen owned and operated by Aborigines. There has also been the artefact industry, which in 1994 was described as sustaining more than 3000 producers across 165 Aboriginal communities; while it requires subsidy, a good deal of this is the natural corollary of the fact that it is largely located in remote areas. In purely economic terms, the artefact industry is of great value in providing employment where often little else is available. (In 1994, fully forty-eight of the sixty-three retail outlets for indigenous art in the Territory were Aboriginal-owned.)

Then there are Aboriginal cultural centres, established with government assistance as meeting and keeping places; in 1994 proposals for a dozen new ones caused the Territory government to be less mindful of their cultural role than afraid that tourist 'demand would be saturated'. Aborigines have also been increasingly acting as investors: two large international hotels were financed by mining royalties at Kakadu, and managed by Four Seasons and Vista for the Aboriginal owners. More recently, there was substantial Aboriginal investment in the Kings Canyon resort.

While large-scale investment is not in itself a guarantee of personal Aboriginal involvement in tourism, a national organisation based in Melbourne, Aboriginal Tourism Australia, was nevertheless set up in the late 1990s; Aborigines were simultaneously approaching the Northern Territory Tourism Commission with proposals of their own. The greater range of Aboriginal tourism activities itself engenders further confidence. A few years ago, the involvement of Bathurst Islanders in the industry was slight. But in 1995, having just bought back a fishing resort, the Tiwi Land Council established an authority to control all tourism ventures on Bathurst and Melville islands. It immediately bought out the Land Council's partner in previous Tiwi tourism ventures, Australian Kakadu Holidays, giving local people 100 per cent control. All tours now utilise Tiwi guides exclusively. Ambivalence may well remain about proposals to build a motel, develop festivals, and expand the football grand final. But if there must be tourism, then local people want to control it.[14]

Aboriginal people generally regard tourism as providing real benefits, if handled appropriately, for their various communities. But thereafter the difficulties begin. 'In most cases', writes Jon Altman, 'it is neither clear to the community nor the funding body whether tourism is intended to provide an economic opportunity for a community, or whether it is an enterprise serving other social and cultural priorities'. Badly conceived research and unrealistic estimates of potential compound the problem.

Moreover Aboriginal communities find themselves situated very differently according to whether traditional owners had leasing arrangements in place before tourism got under way—as in Kakadu, where in the late 1990s they supplied two-thirds of the Board—or whether they were fighting a rearguard action against it as at Uluru, where Yulara had been appropriated, and ownership was conceded only when tied inseparably to leasehold. Again, while the principle of compensation for mining rights has been conceded, tourism has not been viewed as a form of land use that itself might warrant compensation. Indeed it is striking how small are the returns it has brought to Aboriginal people. In 1992 Altman estimated that Aborigines received only 1 or 2 per cent of the total tourist expenditure in the Territory; a few years earlier revenue even from Uluru and Yulara was at a comparable figure.

One of the problems is that Aborigines simply need more enticements, to say nothing of more capital. Money cannot usually be borrowed against traditional land since that is often inalienable freehold. Sometimes, where capital has become available through ventures such as mining, it is arguable that tourist infrastructure is not the most effective way for it to be spent on behalf of the community. Strictly speaking, Gagadju Association returns on their hotels at Kakadu make them a poor investment.[15]

There is also the matter of training. Around 1990, Aboriginal people began to enrol for courses such as that in hospitality offered by the Alice

Springs TAFE, but this was in the traditional service mould rather than as entrepreneurs. They remained untrained in managerial skills, tourist industry expertise and the marketing experience necessary to establish new ventures. In 1985 the Miller Committee on Aboriginal Employment and Training recommended that government agencies extend greater financial support to such proposals; more recent initiatives include an Aboriginal Taskforce Training working group established by the Northern Territory Tourist Commission in 1996. In the past, there was a confusion of 'cultural competencies with industry competencies'; later there was an awareness of the need for 'gradual induction' of Aborigines into tourism and its skills. Specially devised courses were set up at tertiary centres, and began attracting students. Apart from cultural barriers, the main problems are associated with providing on-site training, particularly for people in remote locations.[16]

Cultural tourism will remain the focus of these initiatives for quite some time. With niche marketing becoming more apparent in tourism, it is where demand increasingly lies. Such ventures also have the advantage of leaving traditional lifestyles more or less intact, and can even bolster certain aspects of them—not least by demonstrating to the young that tribal culture has commodity value in addition to its intrinsic worth. Moreover, participation in cultural tourism enables Aborigines to reduce their dependence on welfare without surrendering it completely, a manipulation of the margins that enables them to continue to deal with whites indirectly.

There has come to be a greater recognition—along with awareness of a need for greater research into tourist impact, and the development of broad strategies to deal with it—that Aboriginal communities must develop tourist ventures at an appropriate pace. Otherwise the possibility that they will be poorer as a result of tourism, if all factors are taken into account, is a very real one. At Wallega Lake in NSW, a full two years were allowed in 1990 for training community members to run a cultural centre with cabins for hire clustered nearby; part of the brief was that they liaise frequently with community members, in order to maintain support. Exhaustive though this might seem, it was based on the clear perception that tourism and authentic lifestyles are almost incompatible. As Altman says, 'an appropriately slow rate of development . . . can best be described as tourism realism'.

However, this does mean that tourism is unlikely to be the panacea for problems in Aboriginal economic development. The numbers involved in cultural tourism enterprises are likely to remain low: only 200 a year could go on the original Desert Tracks tour. Moreover, there is the additional problem that competition has severely reduced margins for many ventures, imperilling long-term viability. The more soundly cultural tourism is conceived, the more likely it is to remain small-scale and highly vulnerable, which is why it must be considered in the context of the overall development of the different communities.[17]

Awareness of these limitations has led, in recent years, to a number of consultants stressing that Aboriginal tourism in the Territory has been oversold, emphasised too much in publicity. Certainly this has been the redneck attitude, since such advertising suggests uncomfortable political implications. But even a report from the Pacific Asia Travel Association came to the same conclusion, noting that 'the visitor experience is not altogether satisfactory', since 'the "non-presence" of the Aboriginal culture is disconcerting'. While some tourists ruefully noted the absence of bark paintings in the Centre, and of the didjeridoo (both traditionally produced elsewhere), interest in Aborigines seems, if anything, to rise during the course of a stay. Certainly it is highest among international visitors, who in 1996–97 comprised nearly 52 per cent of those going to Uluru.

Such numbers will inexorably bring more pressure to bear. Aborigines may be able to resist requests for suitcase-sized bark paintings (while deftly taking up European materials for Papunya art), but the progressivist assumptions of Northern Territory developmentalism may prove harder to overcome. As roads are upgraded for tourism, which is seen to generate growth, greater access is given to Aboriginal land. Even when roads are situated entirely on Aboriginal land, there can be pressures.

This can be seen with the Mereenie road, which in 1998 completed a circuit to Kings Canyon—the site of a major new resort—so that, despite its roughness, tour companies occasionally use it. Individuals do too, after applying for a permit, which must be carried at all times while the road is being used. No camping is permitted. Although it is stressed that the route is a transit one only, in practice it is difficult to keep tourists on the road: sacred sites have been desecrated. The Central Land Council has considered such options as abolishing the permit system, leasing the road or handing it over (as the Territory government would like), but the subtext of all this is an extreme reluctance to change the present situation. For the Mereenie road could be the core of a new one, linking the western MacDonnell Ranges with Uluru—one of a series of routes that have been termed the Desert Rose.

This particular concept has faded away, but more and more it looked as though Yulara, so heavily subsidised by the Territory government, was effectively staking out a claim. As tourism grows, other resorts will arise, even if on a smaller scale: space stations of air-conditioned comfort in what can be perceived as a hostile environment. Already Watarrka National Park, adjacent to Frontier Kings Canyon Resort, has seen tourist numbers move up from 53 892 in 1991 to 228 959 in 1997.

Such intrusion would be less alarming were it not that respect for Aboriginal culture has, if anything, declined in recent years. The failure of the name Garriwerd to stick to the Grampians, and of Uluru and Yulara to cover Ayers Rock, is not accidental. The repackaging of the known tourist resort, emphasising its Aboriginal connections, was not successful. More people, rather than fewer, have come to the Rock intent on the climb: one estimate puts the figure as high as 90 per cent. The views at sunset and sunrise, the climb, and paintings made by 'primitive, stone age people' remain the staple. Since the average length of stay is only 1.6 nights at the Ayers Rock Resort, 'the tourist product has had to be carefully crafted for quick and easy consumption' by the rising number of tourists.

Given the importance of tourism as one of the main industries of the Territory, and given too the indifference of the locals to traditional

Aboriginal culture (in a recent survey 68 per cent of *all* NT residents expressed no interest, compared with 45 per cent of interstate visitors, and only 26 per cent of international ones), the possibility of statehood, with greater powers accruing to the Territory government, can only alarm the indigenous people. While that prospect has been delayed for the moment, it is plain that if Aboriginal cultures are not to be overwhelmed, then strategies for survival are going to have to be formulated more carefully than ever.[18]

National Parks, Zoos and the Green Revolution

THERE HAVE BEEN two main elements involved in tourism and the environment—usually mutually reinforcing, but sometimes at variance. First has been the response to natural scenery, romantic at the beginning but now increasingly ecological. And second has been the recuperative view of the countryside, with attention being given to its function as the site for healthy activities to refresh body and mind. This second attribute emerged surprisingly early in Australia, about the time that people first took to the seaside, and well before they could freely respond to the subtle beauties of the landscape.

In 1888 Ludwig Bruck, a medical publisher, issued a *Guide to the Health Resorts of Australia, Tasmania and New Zealand*. It was intended to be of use to invalids, and particularly useful to the medical profession; a previous complaint had been that some British doctors recommended a trip to Australia to their patients without giving any particulars. Bruck's book was mostly set out in tabular form, with doctors, season, and indications as to which conditions would best be ameliorated at the place in question, together with conventional tourist information. The lengthiest entries were to be found among the thirty-six from New Zealand, but the book included over 170 entries for places all over Australia. Beechworth in Victoria was commended as suitable for those suffering from general debility or from chest infections, while Mt Victoria, NSW, in addition to catering for general debility, was recommended for nervous conditions and liver complaints. Victoria's Mt Macedon, another hilly locality, drew a homily in accordance with contemporary nostrums on the importance of a 'pure, cold and rarefied atmosphere' in preventing tuberculosis. The particularity of some of the entries is quite striking: Lorne was commended for 'Pthsisis [tuberculosis], Asthma, Liver Complaints'. One has the impression, on turning the pages, that there is not only a certain amount of boosterism going on, but that Australia is being appraised— not always convincingly—in terms of an old and very broad tradition of natural healing.[1]

Taking the waters

Most conspicuous was hydrotherapy, or the water cure. This had undergone a revival in the nineteenth century, particularly as a treatment for cardiovascular disease. But its origins go back at least as far as the Romans, who established most of the famous spa towns in Europe. There persisted the belief that there was no complaint for which nature had not devised some cure, in the form of a chemical solution; and so waters were taken internally as well as externally. Those of particular spas were credited with particular properties: Evian, it was said, would dramatically ease the discomfort caused by kidney stones. At other places the baths were more notable: one Italian establishment specialised in combining mineral water with volcanic mud. Such places had—and still have—a particular following on the Continent, so that in France thermal healing is taught as a subject in medical schools.[2]

Australia has one important spa centre, Daylesford – Hepburn Springs in Victoria, but in Bruck's compilation it is fully equalled by Drysdale, or Clifton Springs, also in that state. Here mineral water had been found in 1870, and by 1880 over 5000 dozen bottles were being dispatched per year. Compared with imported waters, which had been flattened by the journey, these, said the government analytical chemist, were 'bright, sparkling, and very brisk indeed, like the best champagne'. Early development of the site culminated in 1888 in the Clifton Springs Hotel, a double-storeyed structure capable of accommodating more than sixty people. Spring water was pumped up to the hotel's baths; from its

A formal picnic at Jubilee Lake near Daylesford, Victoria, in about 1920.

cast-iron balcony the visitor had an unusually good view across Corio Bay to the You Yangs. £3500 had been spent on this cliff-top establishment, for it was felt that with the springs being right on the beach the combination of health resort, the seaside and an agreeable distance from Melbourne would together make for a winner. Sea baths were built, and a jetty long enough to accommodate the Bay steamers; but the crash of 1891 swept the company away, and the springs and the hotel came under separate management. In 1923 the hotel was burnt down; by the 1960s the springs had to be closed, owing to pollution from septic tanks on the development nearby. Clifton Springs thus provides an unusually vivid example of a resort snuffed out by suburban development, and today its foreshore is quite forlorn.[3]

The mineral springs at Daylesford and Hepburn were probably known to Aborigines and certainly to early settlers, but their development was slow. Mining covered some springs with debris, and even after they were tidied up it was some time before all the contents were analysed. Nonetheless the potential attraction had been recognised, and a local committee succeeded in getting a small reserve declared at Hepburn in

1865, to prevent contamination. After the railway reached Daylesford in 1880, efforts were made to improve the town: exotic trees were planted, and by the 1920s two lakes had been created. But hopes that Daylesford would become the Baden-Baden of Australia were not to be realised: Australia lacked the leisured class, while the town contained interests that were sometimes at variance with tourism and the springs. These included a noisy, on-site bottling plant. Then in 1890, and again in 1911, the Pavilion Spring at Hepburn was completely drained by nearby mining activity.

Nevertheless other springs continued to draw the crowds, which numbered between 50 000 and 100 000 per year from 1900 to 1930. The bathhouse, which had opened in 1894, continued to expand down to the 1930s, its enticements now including electrical baths. But hydrotherapy became less fashionable just as people were becoming more mobile, and after World War II Daylesford began to decline. Many of its sixty guest-houses closed their doors. However, since the late 1970s there has been some revival, the renovated bathhouse reopening in 1986 as a 'spa complex'.[4]

When bore water at Moree was found to be hot, and also to contain properties beneficial to rheumatics, a primitive bathhouse was built in 1891 and another small resort born.[5] But so strong was the idea of a spa that one could be created where were no springs at all. Such was Medlow Bath in the Blue Mountains, a venture of Mark Foy, a son of the emporium owner. On the site overlooking the Megalong Valley there had already been a fine hotel, the Belgravia; this was now joined up with an art gallery, a casino (for concerts and entertainments, not gambling) additional bedrooms (the complex could accommodate a couple of hundred), and bathhouses. The Hydro Majestic, when it opened in 1904, had such graces as a pair of turbaned Turks serving coffee, and Chinese waiters. But a Swiss was also there to superintend a strict regimen: there was to be no alcohol, no tobacco, and a healthy diet. (A farm in the valley below provided fresh produce by means of a flying fox.) After a mere eighteen months the rules were relaxed: fashion won out over faddism. Remoteness and exclusivity ensured its market share, at least until a serious fire destroyed a large portion of the complex in 1922. Immediately afterwards the hydropathic cures—with their abdomen packs, electrotherapy, and sponging with water as hot as could be borne—were discontinued. The Hydro became a popular family hotel, and in 1938 opened a large replacement wing. In recent years, after a period in the doldrums, it began to emerge as a resort once again.[6]

When rebuilt, the Hydro Majestic Hotel dominated the Blue Mountains escarpment at Medlow Bath, as it still does. It had been noted earlier for its magnificent corridors and picture galleries.

Swan Hill publicity in the mid-1960s featured its Pioneer Village, 'where past & present meet in the sunshine'.

Books offering advice on caravans and touring were to be found in every newsagency.
This one appeared in 1951.

Fern glades and forests

Dismissive remarks about the Australian landscape are legendary. But as George Seddon has shown in relation to the area around Sydney, it could be dismissed—particularly in a time of scant rain—as poor country while, at another juncture, a visitor with an eye less focused on economic appraisal might view the same tract of land as picturesque. It took a long time for Australians to develop a broadly inclusive response: different members of a band that camped near Healesville, Victoria, in 1881 likened the landscape with its fern glades to a gallery of old masters, to a museum, more aesthetically and fashionably to 'a poem as perfect as the *Faerie Queen*' and, in acknowledgement of its 'lonely and silent' character, to Pentridge gaol. The empty bush—as it was perceived —was a place that would bounce back the visitor's preconceptions and preoccupations.

This changed a little in the 1860s, when Adam Lindsay Gordon popularised the wattle, and even more so from the 1890s onward, when the landscapes of the Heidelberg School began to be influential. Wattle and gum and sweeping sunburnt plains would eventually prevail as an image of Australia, but the fern glades and the tall forests were not easily displaced in public estimation. In England there had long been a craze for ferns, and for collecting and pressing them; superior specimens confirmed the attachment here.[7]

By 1881, the year before it was declared a reserve, Ferntree Gully was being described as 'pre-eminently the scenery outing' from Melbourne. Another writer told of the way it combined 'the vivid verdure, the cool freshness, and the shadowy softness of an English woodland scene, with the luxuriant richness and graceful forms of tropical vegetation'. But its appeal had become much more basic. It became a prime picnic site, complete with musicians, photographers and ice-cream vendors. Even before the railway extended to the Gully, people were warned of tracks lined with empty bottles, sardine tins and bits of paper. Excursionists moved on, as tourists will, to the yet unspoilt districts of Healesville and Marysville. Melbourne's two best-known landscape photographers, Nicholas Caire and J. W. Lindt, even collaborated in producing a guidebook to these places. In 1895 Lindt settled at the Black Spur, receiving tourists at The Hermitage, built in the style of a Swiss chalet. He had already sold, in the decade of the Heidelberg School, 25 000 prints of this district alone.[8]

The first 'National Park'

That the National Park south of Sydney ('Royal' since 1954) has no reference to place in its title is an indication of its age. It was second only to Yellowstone in America (1872), and the first such tract to be designated a 'national park' anywhere in the world. While an early descriptive account enthused about Port Hacking as 'another Sydney Harbour, another Broken Bay', and the *Official Guide* spoke of the government 'bequeathing to the people of this Colony a national domain for rest and recreation', the concept of a national park was still so primitive that the term scarcely functioned as a compound noun. The word 'national' had more to do with the fact that a large tract of crown land (otherwise thought to be next to useless) had been set aside for the purpose, and perhaps too with the edgy advance of NSW to self-realisation, evident in the recent naming of the National Gallery—and shortly after in Henry Parkes' madcap scheme to rename the colony 'Australia'.[9]

Everybody, though, knew what a park was. There had been clamourings for more of them in town, whereas what Sir John Robertson instituted in 1879 was a 'Hyde Park in the bush'. So remote was it at first that visitors had to go by boat; but after a rail link was put in, excursionist numbers shot up from 38 000 in 1892 to 170 000 in 1893. They went to camp, walk, play sport, picnic, perhaps hear a band or participate in military manoeuvres—the last-mentioned based at the largest military camps the colony had yet seen. Elsewhere, in faint recollection of the nobleman's park, deer were on display—until they leapt over the fence and ran wild. Meanwhile 'Acres and acres of the best land have been under-scrubbed and thoroughly cleared', boasted the 1893 *Official Guide*, 'and the useless under-scrub has given place to nutritious and

226

Edwardian guest-house, subsequently demolished, at Port Hacking in the Royal National Park, NSW

ornamental grasses'. That this might destroy the habitat of native animals which the park authorities wished to protect from shooters was not even considered: the Australian bush, after all, was generally seen, in Marcus Clarke's words, as 'the strange scribblings of Nature learning how to write'. Thus even as the National Park was extended in size, to cater for the increasing number of visitors, no inconsistency was seen in permitting new timber-getting and grazing ventures.[10]

There was little sense yet of valuing the environment for its own sake. When South Australia followed the NSW lead with its National Park Act of 1891, the 'sole purpose' of the park at Belair was declared to be 'a public national recreational and pleasure ground'. All kinds of tourist amenities were envisaged. So weak was a sense of conservation that grazing, mining and quarrying would also be allowed to take place there. In Western Australia, the 'improvement' of King's Park was prevented only by a shortage of money, while a flora and fauna reserve in the Murray River area was suddenly resumed by the government in 1911 in order to meet timber requirements. There was no need for permanence, since the concept of a reserve was linked to tourist amenity. As late as 1926, a request for the protection of wildflowers in Western Australian national parks was rejected by the Department of Lands and Survey, on the grounds that 'the primary inducement for people to go to the reserves . . . is to gather the wildflowers with the object of adorning their homes and taking part in the wildflower shows'.[11]

The initial national parks in nearly all states—'*The* National Park', as they were often termed—had been made accessible to the masses by rail, but the relief of urban pressures was less apparent in the selection of the later parks. Queensland, in its Act of 1906, set forth a procedure for proclaiming national parks—a world first—and quickly created nine, while Tasmania, in establishing a Scenery Preservation Board in 1915, was the first state to set up an authority to superintend them. But even there the national parks were starved of funds. Throughout the country for some decades, inadequate government grants virtually compelled the selling of grazing or felling or mining rights simply to meet basic costs. The style of management varied enormously: in Victoria there came to be none at all in one case, while in the 1920s only Wilsons Promontory had a single ranger, unpaid by government. Localism was the pattern; not only was there no state-wide system in most of mainland Australia, but there was no liaison between comparable departments in the different states.[12]

Nevertheless governments were susceptible to some pressure from organisations such as the Field Naturalists, which had begun to emerge in the 1880s. Sometimes, too, a powerful man such as Sir James Barrett, secretary of the Victorian National Parks Association, ophthalmologist and later vice-chancellor of the University of Melbourne, could augment the prestige of science with influence exerted through the newspapers and direct political skills. The state government might thus gradually be brought round to firm up a reluctant commitment to create a new park.

Since about one-third of the Victorian Field Naturalists were people with university degrees, their environmental interest was quite at variance with the concerns of day-tripping picnickers to the original

National Park. But—not least as a result of Barrett's influence—nature study was appearing in schools, while a change from hunting and collecting to watchful observation was being commented on. The first close-up photographs of birds appeared in general publications at this time.[13]

When Arthur Mattingley, secretary of the Field Naturalists Club and himself a photographer, went to the Mallee in 1907, he was struck by the beauty of the Wyperfeld area, with its wattle, tea-tree and heaths, and its flocks of emus and black cockatoos. He saw it as 'a national park already made', to be brought to perfection only with a scattering of Western Australian everlastings and orchids. Mattingley's meeting with a sympathetic Minister resulted in projected boundaries for a park being marked out on a map there and then. It was the classic Victorian formula: a tract of remote crown land thought to be almost valueless, with discreet pressure applied from a man of influence; but with the difference that flora and fauna had now been given added value by the rise of nature study.[14]

Enter the bushwalker

There had always been young men 'rambling': it was seen as a good way of keeping sporting teams together in the offseason. Long-distance walking—proceeding by 'Shanks' pony'—was so much a part of the scene that an early guide to Melbourne's tramways gave nearly half its space to 'Rambles from the Routes'. A Melbourne Amateur Walking and Touring Club was founded in 1894, and the Warragamba in Sydney the year after. Gradually their interest in speed walking diminished; exploration of the countryside had become more enticing. 'The path to health is the footpath', proclaimed Sydney's William Mogford Hamlet as he led (male) parties along country roads—just before cars appeared on them—to stay at country inns, have a hearty breakfast, and then return to town. This was a European-style wandering, but a freer, more bohemian Australian style grew up alongside. Here there was envy of the swagman, and in the case of J. Le Gay Brereton, a revelling in being the 'eternal wanderer, free from morality'. Rather than engaging closely with the country, it was playing out a role: Brereton likened his wanderings to traditional (European) student life. By 1914 the NSW Tourist Bureau had published three editions of a walker's guidebook, *With Swag and Billy*.[15]

Nineteen-fourteen also saw the foundation of the Mountain Trails Club, very much at the instigation of Miles Dunphy. Here was a new, wilderness-focused conception of walking: not putting up at places, but aiming at self-sufficiency, firmly based on fitness, having the proper equipment and food rations, plus ingenuity and bushcraft. Dunphy saw it as 'amateur exploring': by 1927 it would bring the word 'bush-walking' into the language. An important element—well ahead of any wilderness precepts then advanced in America—was a deep respect for the bush and its inhabitants. 'You were not the first over the trail', en-joined the certificate of membership; 'leave the pleasant places along the way just as pleasant for those who follow you'. Powering this was a loose nationalism: Dunphy sewed the new Australian flag on the first tent he made, while the purposeful selection of club members—men

A major walking track went through the remote Baw Baw Plateau in Victoria in the early twentieth century. Note the almost military demeanour of the touring party.

were *invited* to join this club, then tested in the field—resulted in what he termed a 'bush brotherhood'.

Women, active in the Field Naturalists, were effectively excluded here, though they were invited to participate in the easier walks so long as they carried their packs. In 1922 they were joining a new club, the Bushlanders, and five years later participated in the founding of another, soon to be styled the Sydney Bushwalkers. Dunphy assisted in this too, recognising the need for an open club.[16]

Whether he liked it or not, Dunphy's activities in part functioned as a thin end of the wedge for tourism. He was horrified when the government cut a path almost 3 metres wide for bushwalkers at Garrawarra: this was a promenade, not a track! The new style of walking was so little understood by the Tourist Bureau that they routinely forwarded inquiries to him. As these increased in volume, Dunphy advanced from preparing his own fine maps to improving official ones, insisting that they be printed at a useable scale for walkers. The Lands Department insisted they must serve 'the public'—that is, motorists—but became co-operative when Dunphy offered to raise subscriptions for the Blue Mountains map; it was to be styled a 'Tourist Map'. The heading 'Special Walking Clubs Issue' nonetheless appeared on the first printing.[17]

While the walker's outfit had tended to move downmarket—one rambler in 1889 took with him eight handkerchiefs, a spare suit of clothes and four collars—the walker's equipment was steadily becoming more sophisticated. A nineteenth-century guidebook (assuming that campers would generally have a horse) concerned itself with leadership and discipline, and then noted that some had 'a contrivance by which, by means of a series of straps, or buttons and loops, they make the rug into a kind of bag, into which they plunge themselves feet foremost'. Sleeping bags were being imported from Germany before World War I, though Dunphy began with a swag that he proceeded to modify. The rucksack was a further innovation; by 1930 there was enough sense of a new market for increasingly identifiable equipment that Paddy Pallin, when he was retrenched, decided to try his hand at setting up a store that would specialise in it.[18]

Pallin had scarcely established himself when a hiking craze swept the land. The popularity of R. H. Croll's *The Open Road in Victoria*—which sold out within three weeks of its appearance in 1928—showed a new receptiveness to the idea that a taste for walking could yoke a rambling reflectiveness to the landscape. Hiking promised a new source of enjoyment despite the encroaching Depression. It was cheap and healthy, and it brought companionship; community singing was the soundtrack. The railways capitalised on it, sometimes offering 'mystery hikes' at concessional prices; one to the Hawkesbury in 1932 involved eleven trains and 80 000 people.

The three bushwalking clubs, whose membership in Sydney amounted to a mere couple of hundred, were appalled by these developments. They were the professionals—these were the amateurs; they the patrollers—these the despoilers. Advertisements for powder puffs and skin creams in the *Hiking Guide* would have only increased their contempt. The Sydney Bushwalkers club abandoned its boasted openness and applied membership tests, of both walking ability and 'sociability'— that is, class. Then just as suddenly as the craze had come from overseas, it vanished.[19]

Dunphy, a master tactician, had used hiking publications to advance a particular cause—the saving of the Blue Gum Forest in the Grose Valley. Having come across the initial felling of a fine stand of timber, bushwalkers negotiated to buy the lease from the current holder. To this end in 1931 they organised a massive appeal, extending to dances and socials. Support from Melbourne in effect made this the first national conservation campaign. The following year Dunphy organised a Federation of Bush Walking Clubs— soon emulated in other states—and a National Parks and Primitive Areas Council drawn from their members. The NPPAC was intent on tracts of country in national parks being declared Primitive Areas, in order to protect them from roads, 'improvements' and tourists. While the council had some success in this, it was more successful in having new national parks created: of the five that appeared in NSW in the 1930s, three were directly due to the campaigns launched by bushwalkers and their allies. Most notable of all, however, was the creation of a park at Kosciuszko. William McKell, the

Premier, was already concerned about the effects of grazing on soil conservation, and knew, as others did not, of plans for a Snowy Mountains Authority.
But it was Dunphy and the bushwalkers who kept up the pressure, even persuading the government that, since the tract was subject to mixed use, it
could not be styled a 'national park'. So the Kosciuszko State Park was created in 1944, the first intentionally permanent national park in NSW. Its
status could be cancelled only by an act of parliament, then unthinkable.[20]

Zoos and sanctuaries

Although scientists named the platypus *Ornithorynchus paradoxus*, it is
less of a paradox on the part of nature than a brilliant set of solutions.
But displaced Britishers could only see things in terms of what they
knew, and hence misapplied the names thrush, wren or robin to species
quite different from the English ones. The perception of Australia as
terra nullius also had an environmental dimension: an immediate desire
to fill it with familiar plants and animals. The early game laws aimed at
preserving *imported* game; and, with exemplary Darwinism, a radical
member of the Victorian parliament argued that if the native animals
were unable to protect themselves, then they were unfit to live in the
country. Though Tasmania began to protect animals in 1860—about
the time its emu became extinct—it was not until 1901 that in NSW
some native birds were given equal protection with imported ones; nor
until 1903 that a Native Animals Protection Act indicated a concern
about conservation. It was certainly necessary: in that same year, one
London dealer alone handled two and a half million possum skins,
500 000 wallaby, and 250 000 from wombats.[21]

Both the Sydney and Melbourne zoos began as Acclimatisation
Gardens, Melbourne's in tandem with the Botanic Gardens. When it
moved to Royal Park, public interest was not great, since only domesti-
cated or local animals were kept there. The venture nearly foundered.
But the Le Souef family (who would later create Taronga Park and Perth
zoos) saw the necessity of bringing in exotic animals and landscaping the
area. The crowds soon came: by the 1880s, as many as 30 000 to 40 000

233

on free days. Zoos were pleasure grounds, but also display centres for the trophies of imperialism. (Taronga Park would sport an Indian-style elephant house.) In Europe, 'primitive' peoples—including Laplanders—sometimes went on display, so for the 1888 Exhibition Le Souef included an Aboriginal camp. But the elephants—good for rides—and the primates—so like us—long continued to attract most attention. Casey the chimp, said the 1930 Taronga Park guidebook, 'is very active, and just loves dancing'. It was not till 1934 that an Australian section was established at Melbourne.[22]

Meanwhile the Hagenbeck zoo near Hamburg had made great advances towards a 'natural' presentation. Some of these influenced another Le Souef at Taronga Park, which opened in 1916: the natural rock was used wherever possible, while ditches or moats replaced the traditional barriers. Soon a bushland setting was being utilised in Queensland at Lone Pine Koala Sanctuary (1927), the first such private venture, and at the Sanctuary at Healesville, Victoria. Here Sir Colin MacKenzie had engaged in zoological research before he moved to Canberra; the idea of still using the site for a related purpose lingered in this tourist district. The Sanctuary began with a few possums, goats and goat cart, lizards, and a few cockatoos; takings from the first public day bought nails for the enclosures. One of the keen supporters—an early activist in establishing the Kruger National Park in South Africa—established a platypusary at his home, and the tide turned. But finance remained fitful, even after the well-known naturalist David Fleay abandoned Melbourne Zoo for Healesville. Following a period of neglect during World War II, a regular government subsidy was made after 1950. Meanwhile attendance shot up: from 16 000 visitors in 1936 to 100 000 in 1956. Five years later the figures had more than doubled—an early sign of an emerging national sentiment—and by 1963 the Sanctuary was being described as Victoria's leading tourist attraction.[23]

Now wildlife parks have become associated with three of the four major zoos, although mainly as display areas for exotic animals. But the zoos themselves have been transformed. Not only is there a greater concern to replicate or at least simulate the animals' habitat, but the old

Taronga Park Zoo moved to a foreshore site in Mosman in 1916, and displayed both local and overseas wildlife. Visitors came by ferry, tram and bus.

interest in research is now complemented by education and conservation programmes. Rare animals have been bred up in numbers and then, like the yellow-faced rock wallaby from Adelaide Zoo, released back into the wild. While sanctuaries would always double as animal hospitals, zoos have reversed their roles to become embassies for the natural world. It is as if national parks have reached out and engulfed them, a move endorsed by an ecologically conscious public. Since 1980, Melbourne's Friends of the Zoo have increased in number from 160 to more than 20 000.[24]

The snow

Skiing emerged in Australia among the gold miners at Kiandra, in the Snowy Mountains. By the 1860s, following the lead of a few Austrians and a Norwegian, they were organising their first 'snow-shoe club' and

Early snow sports at Mt Kosciuszko

'snow-shoe races' (ski club and races), both among the world's first. These remained essentially local pastimes until the turn of the century. Then Charles Kerry began taking parties of snow-tourists to Kiandra. In much the same way that Beattie, Lindt and other photographers had built on their natural enthusiams to advance tourism hand in hand with their professional activities, so now did Kerry. Born in the district, he was the leader of the first successful skiing expedition to the summit of Kosciuszko in 1897, and conducted some of the first classes in skiing held at the hotel when it opened in 1909. Elected president of the Kosciuszko Alpine Club in the same year, Kerry became the visual propagandist for the new sport and the new hotel. In the years that followed, a number of ski clubs regularly used the government-run hotel, but despite the fact that by 1928 there were some school ski clubs grooming a rising clientele, there was a feeling that the initiative might pass to Victoria.[25]

The relative accessibility of Mt Buffalo placed it in the forefront of snow resorts from the very beginning: the first hospice went up in 1891,

The Chalet. Mt. Buffalo (Vict.)

The Mt Buffalo Chalet, just after it opened

although mainly catering for summer guests. Skiers from the Bright Alpine Club were beginning to move beyond, to Mt St Bernard and Mt Feathertop, but this activity was desultory. While it was now a catch-phrase that Australia possessed larger snowfields than Switzerland, the focus of attention in Victoria remained Mt Buffalo, whose spectacular scenery led to its being proclaimed a national park in 1898.

A road opened ten years later by the Premier connected the summit with the railhead; government fantasies ran to a baronial hotel with 100 rooms, very much in the style of the great Canadian railway hotels. In the end a very much smaller wooden chalet was opened in 1910; so much was it a comedown that a leaky roof led to six of the nine tourists staying there in April leaving in exasperation. Conditions gradually improved, and soon the Victorian Railways were offering a package tour for £4 10s 0d that included all fares from Melbourne, a night in Bright, and six days full board. By 1924 the Railways had taken over the management of the Chalet, which thereafter tended to function like a guest-house, to boarding-school rules.

fires, and then gunfire in the course of recent military training. Accommodation there was said to be unusable. Concern about such matters led to the foundation of the Victorian National Parks Association in 1952, and a little later—prompted by the forthcoming Melbourne Olympics—the new Premier, Henry Bolte, saw the need to smarten up the state's 'pre-eminent scenic places'.

Tourism then—even the will-o'-the-wisp of international tourism—was the motivation for addressing the question of conservation. But it was not seriously addressed using that terminology; indeed the word still tended to be used primarily in connection with resources such as soil or water, or individual species. The traditional attitude to national parks, still very much in evidence, seemed to be that (unless they possessed some extraordinary natural wonder) in practice each was a kind of semi-permanent wasteland unless it functioned as a site for recreation. The predominance of domestic tourism in Australia, combined with traditional utilitarianism, served to strengthen this attitude. As late as 1949 the Parks Branch of the NSW Department of Lands stated that it considered the chief function of 'public parks' to be recreational, and linked with the promotion of tourism. Acting on similar assumptions, the previous year the Queensland government had proposed—until dissuaded by protests—to increase the attractions of national parks by building hotels, scenic drives and golf courses. A short while afterwards in Victoria, a committee sat for six years deliberating on the provision of tourist services in the Alpine region: skiers, a recreational group marked by conspicuous consumption, were represented, but the unobtrusive bushwalkers were not. Mt Buffalo's status as a national park was not even mentioned in the report.[28]

Nevertheless it was Victoria that passed a National Parks Act in 1956—the first such specific statute in Australia, soon emulated in other states. Local committees of management were now brought under a single authority, located in the Premier's office. At the same time, since there was still a general idea that such parks were surplus to basic requirements, no attempt was made to establish a professional service to administer them, as already existed in the case of forests. This did not happen in Australia until 1967, when, closely following American pre-cedent, a NSW National Parks Service was established. Similar enact-ments elsewhere followed soon after.

The slowness of conservation to assume primacy can be explained by the fact that most national parks had come into existence well before there was a widespread appreciation of the Australian environment. In 1960, calendars with views of the Cotswolds were still common in middle-class homes; it is not surprising, then, that a writer around that time lamented the lack of the 'compelling grandeur' of craggy mountains and native pine forests. There had always been an interest in Western Australian wildflowers, for sometimes they blanketed the countryside like bluebells in Scotland. But other plants, with a subtler presence, had to wait until the fashion for native gardens accelerated in the early 1970s.[29]

After generations of developmentalism, Australians were by then beginning to recognise that, as the national park movement put it, 'The wilderness we have today is all that we shall ever have'. A 1963 initiative by the Duke of Edinburgh to set up an Australian branch of the World Wildlife Fund was tactfully turned round, given the pressing need for a national conservation body, to help launch the Australian Conservation Foundation, with the Duke's endorsement and under the presidency of Sir Garfield Barwick. Meanwhile people were taking to the bush in greater numbers. In Victoria, visitors to national parks went up from 174 000 in 1961 to 712 000 in 1972. Wyperfeld particularly benefited from the upsurge of interest: in 1972 it attracted almost 16 000 visitors, fifteen times the number in 1958. But not everybody's eye was attuned to such ecologically conceived parks. 'They should tell you that there is nothing there', said a Melburnian who visited Kinchega National Park in New South Wales.[30]

Kinchega was a manifestation of an important shift in the philosophy behind the provision of national parks. As early as the 1880s there had been scientific interest in conservation, but scientific assessment and classification of all of Australia's natural resources, following precedents elsewhere, made little progress till the 1950s. It was then termed gap analysis, the purpose being to ascertain which ecosystems were missing from the existing network of reserves, in order to make good the deficiency. In Victoria, the most enduring legacy of the bitter Little Desert controversy of 1969 had been the establishment of the Land Conservation Council the following year. This body systematically set about examining the purposes to which crown land could be put, and spearheaded a dramatic increase in the number of national parks and other reserves. These quadrupled from 4 per cent of Victoria in 1970 to the point where they now comprise 16 per cent of the state. It had become a question not of scenic landscapes, but of devising a collection of habitats, scientifically desirable in a world of diminishing resources. If the process ran well in advance of tourist interest, then that was of little account.[31]

A number of factors had contributed to a broader change in social attitudes. Increased mobility, and photographs of Earth from space, emphasised its oneness, and the need for wholeness; it was now less a matter of conservation of specific sites than a new concern for the entire environment. Gough Whitlam seized the day in his policy speech for the 1972 election by referring to the vital components of the Australian natural and built environments as the 'National Estate', a concept which those reporting on it described as 'a powerful crystallisation of an emergent but hitherto almost unfocused idea'. But daily it was gaining force, if not definition.

Union-imposed green bans in Sydney dramatised the new perspective; older-style conservationists were horrified by the confrontationist tactics of the new 'greenies', a term that originated here. As Vietnam was winding down, political activism moved across to environmental issues, campaigns against uranium mining making the transition easier. Even after the term 'counter-culture' began to fade from inner-city communal households, posters of the Franklin River remained on their walls. When the developmentalist Tasmanian Premier Robin Gray dismissed the river as 'nothing but a brown ditch, leech-ridden and unattractive to the majority of people', he spectacularly missed the point. As Paddy Pallin could have told him, there were so many people prepared to rough it in the bush that in the 1970s his new Liverpool Street shop expanded to fill three floors. Further branches would follow.[32]

In tropical Australia, appreciation of the natural landscape was slow. Palm Springs, dating from 1923, was the first nature reserve in the Northern Territory; palm tree romanticism and the faint echo of biblical oases singled it out as a possible attraction, forty years before declaration of the next reserve. Regarding national parks as fit use only for wasteland, the Northern Territory administration was loath to create

Victorian romanticism goes tropical: Mt Tambourine, near Brisbane.

243

them. When asked to set aside what would later become the core of Kakadu National Park, it refused at first, saying that the country might be required for buffalo leases. Initially appreciation of this region was largely centred on the extraordinary wildlife (with all species native to the area intact) and the more scenic elements. Even as late as 1991, neither the woodland nor floodland tracts were classified by the park authorities as wilderness, unlike the plateau and escarpment. And while the first section of the park had been proclaimed in 1979, by the time the third was added in 1987 it was still possible for the then federal Minister to describe it as consisting largely of 'clapped out buffalo grass'. The new ideal of striving to preserve a complete river system—subject of course to the constraints of uranium mining—could still be treated lightly.[33]

Kakadu acquired World Heritage listing almost immediately after the park was created, the first Australian property to be so designated. Listed for both its natural and (Aboriginal) cultural heritage, both increasingly modish, it was tagged for tourist attention. Organised tours, though, contributed only 15 per cent of visitors in 1985, suggesting a high proportion of locals or the more adventurous; by 1995 tour groups accounted for half the numbers. In between had come *Crocodile Dundee* —part of which was filmed in the park—so that numbers more than doubled in the four years from 1985 to 1989, reaching 237 537 the following year. Amid fluctuations, that figure has been overtaken only once in recent years.[34]

Ecotourism

New circumstances require a new tourism. Ecotourism is so new a term that it missed the 1989 revision of the Oxford Dictionary. Some, of course, claimed to have always practised it: 'The Victorian National Parks Association', quipped Geoff Durham, 'has been conducting ecotours almost since its formation in 1952. They are called "excursions"'. Encoded in this remark was an exasperation with the trendiness of the term, and the way a number of tourist operators had adopted it with minimal concession to the values it proclaimed. These are that such tourist activity should be primarily focused on nature; have an educative or interpretive component; and be respectful of the environment (on this score, ecotourism's emphasis on 'sustainable' tourism is often regarded as setting benchmarks for the whole industry). In addition there should be a recognition of the integrity of any local culture (especially when indigenous), and a willingness to involve local people in ventures whenever possible.[35]

It was claimed a few years ago that Australians are second only to the Dutch, of citizens from fourteen developed countries, in their awareness of environmental issues. In this spirit the commonwealth government, when it drew up a National Ecotourism Strategy in 1994, was keen that Australia should set 'an international example' in this area, particularly as, worldwide, it is the fastest-growing sector of the tourist industry.[36]

Australia is well placed to profit from this new trend. Not only does it have an extraordinary range of habitats, but it also possesses *space*—a quality so rare in Europe that when the agency Ciaot Day inserted advertisements in an English Sunday magazine, it made the point by having spectacular photographs fold out to four or five panels. Unspoilt scenery is a particular drawcard; surveys have shown that as many as 78 per cent of Japanese visitors were influenced by this attraction in choosing to come here. The recent international success of Aboriginal art also points to a surprising cultural diversity. And Australia, compared with Africa and parts of Asia, is not only friendly but safe. At the same time, compared with Canada—which could commend itself along similar lines—it is warm.[37]

In 1996 there were some 600 ecotourism operators in Australia. While they accounted for only 1 per cent of the total employment and revenue from tourism, they collected 3 per cent of tourism's export earnings. Europeans alone made up 57 per cent of the visitation rate to Kakadu and the two other main 'Top End' national parks in 1994. Moreover, 31 per cent of the inbound tourists seeking nature-based activities that year were on return trips to this country.[38]

Meanwhile domestic visits to national parks have also increased dramatically. In 1994 Victoria's national parks received ten million visitors, although only 10 per cent of these stayed overnight. Similarly, although it was estimated that a quarter of all Australians at that time were planning to take a trip during the year that would involve learning about nature, perhaps only a third of these would satisfy accepted definitions of ecotourism. Nevertheless, television programmes such as Les Hiddins' *Bush Tucker Man*, dealing with edible native plants in northern Australia previously disregarded by whites, together with an astonishing upsurge of indigenous cuisine over the past decade, have helped bring about a marked change in attitude towards arid Australia. No one now would speak of the 'Dead Heart'.[39]

Indeed, there are ecotourism ventures that specialise in taking people to arid regions. One, Australis, takes parties to the Grampians and on to the once-disputed Little Desert: at the latter people become involved in a number of tasks, including bird-banding. A session at the microscope examines the way the root systems of local plants enable them to survive in such harsh conditions. There is an evening lecture, and a travelling library; but ecotourist operators have become aware that there are limits to the degree of instruction people on holiday will willingly receive. Meanwhile, in the Northern Territory, Discovery Tours actually takes people to scientists working on sites in the Tanami, Simpson and Great Sandy deserts. It also contributes financially to such research. But the firm has had difficulty, despite assiduous efforts, in being taken up by the mainstream industry: bookings through travel agents have very largely been on the customer's initiative. Word of mouth, it seems, remains unusually important in drawing clientele to prime ecotourism ventures.[40]

Resorts have sprung up that are also ecotouristic. Adjacent to the national park at Blackheath in the Blue Mountains, Jemby-Rinjah Lodge aims at involving guests directly with the surrounding flora and fauna. Environmentally friendly materials have been used as much as possible, with minimal site disturbance during the various stages of construction since 1985. Low-energy consumption is a feature of the buildings, which are sited on poles above ground, as are later walkways, enabling water and electricity to be supplied without disturbing the soil. Despite bureaucratic opposition, the resort also installed what was then the largest group of self-composting toilets in Australia. A touch of puritanism ensures that guests are not provided with shampoos and conditioners—luxury items—since these are considered to add unnecessarily to the lodge's waste stream.

Fitness is more evident than ecology at Couran Cove, a resort on Stradbroke Island that is the creation of former Olympic gold medallist Ron Clarke. In addition to a gym and sprint track, as well as a swimming pool with demarcated lanes and diving blocks, there are a variety of amenities that include lifestyle counselling, yoga and tai chi sessions. All this is in the context of good environmental practice, extending to smartly designed apartments over the water. As the travel writer Susan Kurosawa says, noting the way that Australia's sprouting wilderness lodges are drawing international commendation, billy and swag and mosquitoes are no longer an essential part of going bush. 'Communing with nature can now be done in style.'[41]

A turn of the tide?

There has been pressure, though less marked in the late 1990s, for the Commonwealth to use its external affairs power to ensure the creation of a national wilderness preservation system—essential, it is argued, if areas with World Heritage listing in particular are to receive effective protection. Reports such as the recent one from England that humans have, since 1970, destroyed one-third of the natural world, only add to the general sense of urgency. But despite powerful conservation arguments, an Australian wilderness system may not come about. There is the reluctance of governments to extend their sphere of operation in a climate of economic rationalism, and the further predilection of Liberal governments to roll policy-making, and particularly land-use controls, back to the states. Moreover the traditional wilderness concept is itself seen increasingly as being culture-bound. In recent years there have been voices, heeded to some extent, urging that the human history of a particular district might itself be a component of the environment (and

Tidy's Pleasure Resort at Nelly Bay, Magnetic Island, in 1915. By the early 1990s Bright Point, the headland overlooking this bay, had been quarried to provide a breakwater and safe harbour. The developer went broke and the area, despite being part of the Great Barrier Reef Marine Park, has remained an ecological disaster.

often of interest to tourists). This argument, used in connection with mountain cattle men, applies with even greater force to Aboriginal communities.[42]

The case of Kakadu is again instructive here. The first management plan foresaw eventual Aboriginal input, although more comfortable with the concept of 'an untamed wilderness'. But unlike Uluru, all of the land in Kakadu Stage One was already Aboriginal; the park itself had come into existence as a result of an agreement between the local people and the national conservation authority. Once the local people held ten of fourteen seats on the park board, as they did from 1989, the vectors would change completely. By 1996, the management plan began with a 'Vision' that proclaimed Kakadu a 'cultural landscape'.[43]

It is increasingly accepted that the Aborigines have, through time, subtly altered the Australian landscape so that it cannot usefully be considered in pristine terms, just as Aboriginal precepts of caring for the country by adroit use of fire have been blended with Western ideas of conservation by park managements. Less easy to accommodate have been such conflicts of interest as the Yarrabah community's desire to log the local forest, just as it was incorporated in the Queensland Wet Tropical Rainforests proposed for World Heritage listing in 1987. Not consulted until quite late in the proceedings, the Yarrabah were placated with promises of government aid and an upgraded sawmill. 'The notion of wilderness and the institution of the National Park', Marcia Langton has written, 'must be radically redefined in response to indigenous demands for ownership and control of land and resources'. If this does not occur, warns Tim Rowse, national parks become 'a contemporary means of colonial expropriation'.[44]

Again, national parks cannot always count on the support of a significant sector of their keenest users (beyond those who tear up delicate habitats in their four-wheel-drives). While a 1994 Newspoll showed that nearly 95 per cent of Australians understood that the most important feature of a 'nature holiday' was to avoid damaging the environment, other polling shows that a considerable portion of ecotourists—and, even more strikingly, potential ecotourists—may be quite developmentalist, despite their capacity for environmental appreciation. Such a contradiction is perhaps to be expected in an age of increasing globalisation, on one hand, and individualism on the other. The sense of the public has become weak; on an individual level, the emphasis has tended to shift towards greater self-fulfilment. Abseiling, bungee jumping, white water rafting . . . There is a growing tendency to treat nature like a trampoline.[45]

Meanwhile there was in the late 1990s a considerable assault on environmentalism from the Kennett government in Victoria. A residual idea that national parks had been 'locked up' and kept away from the people merged with the current ideology that public assets—if they were to remain state-owned—must be made to earn their keep. Having excised land from an alpine national park for resort development, and having downsized expertise within the relevant ministry and deemed the environment a 'low priority' in the 1998 budget, the Victorian government seemed intent on moving towards privatising national parks wherever possible. Symbolically, the Land Conservation Council was abolished; meanwhile lighthouse reserves and the camping grounds at Lake Eildon were put under private control, while it was foreshadowed that Brambuk and the Buchan caves, among other sites, would go the same way.[46]

In the eyes of gung-ho privateers—as they proceed with their piratisation—national parks are inert and elitist. It has been pointed out that the true ecotourist may spend little or nothing in the wilderness, because in the real wilderness there is nothing on which to spend money. That can seem disdainful, rather than other-directed, and so the Ecotourism Association has been careful to stress, as one of its four goals, that there should be a range of ecotourist opportunities 'available to visitors of all socio-demographic backgrounds'. But minority interests, or those of posterity, are of little account to economic rationalists; as they practise their manipulative populism, democracy becomes for them an aggregate of consumers, expressing itself in the demands of the market.

Conservation bodies have, from time to time, stated that they are only opposed to *some* development, or even that the 'user pays' principle can be admitted so long as it is not seen as a primary source of national park funding, but used instead as a contribution towards the cost of signage, path and road maintenance and other entailments of tourism. The fear is that the primary conservationist purpose of national parks will be forgotten, or eclipsed—with some justice. In 1998 the Victorian Department of Natural Resources and Environment came up with no strategy plan for nature conservation, whereas Tourism Victoria had commissioned thirteen of them, proposing extensive developments in parks for tourism. 'Sound conservation management', wrote Doug Humann of the Victorian National Parks Association, 'has *created* the tourist demand, and so must be given precedence if this demand is to be sustained'.[47]

Too much public asset can be sacrificed for the prospect of short-term private gain. An obtrusively placed 150-bed tourist hotel at Tidal River was part of a Kennett government programme to open up Wilsons Promontory to greater exploitation, but was stopped in its tracks by both green activism and, more tellingly, a surprise result in a local by-election. Still proceeding at the time of writing, amid difficulties, was a scheme based on a recently opened Sea Life Centre at Seal Rocks, Phillip Island, which would run a monorail from the Penguin Parade across the penguin hatchery to the outcrop known as The Nobbies. The developer had also told the government he wanted to privatise the world-famous Parade.[48]

Occasional victories over developmentalism—such as getting the Victorian government to abandon schemes for a large tourist centre and car park at the Twelve Apostles on the Great Ocean Road—remain important. But it is a bit like only being able to muster the resources to demonstrate a building's historic importance the moment it is threatened with demolition. Deep problems remain. One is the tendency of contemporary libertarian governments to discount all forms of capital apart from the financial. Our national parks are also *reserves*; their effective maintenance needs to be considered not only as a public good, but also as a necessary functional cost of tourism. Cutting back on rangers, as has begun to happen, could have dire effects. Already Dr John Wamsley, the creator of a number of highly successful private sanctuaries in South Australia, has reckoned on the day when, owing to insufficient resources to combat feral animals, people will not be going to national parks, but to privately run sanctuaries, to see Australian fauna.

Then there is the voracity of tourism itself, the way it expands, despoils, reaches out further. Business has been slow to support conservation, even when it has been involved in tourism; but tourism becomes ever more businesslike. Russell Blamey, writing for the government Bureau of Tourism Research, notes that idealistic, 'postmaterialist' people have 'the highest propensity' for ecotourism, but constitute only 20 per cent of the potential domestic market. 'This means', he concludes, 'that advertising directed solely at postmaterialists may miss much of the market. The majority of the potential ecotourism market has a materialist disposition'. This is far more sophisticated, of course, but it takes us back to the beginning, to the kind of assumptions underlying the proclamation of the National Park in 1879. But contemporary Australia is not colonial New South Wales. We now have far fewer natural resources.[49]

Packaging Heritage

WHEN THE OUTSPOKEN Melbourne architect Robin Boyd tackled the topic 'The Future of Our Past' at a historic preservation gathering in Canberra in 1967 he noted that every state, even Queensland, could boast a National Trust.[1] He told his listeners that the national trust movement had 'reached a sort of first plateau', and urged them to think 'as broadly as possible about the nature of the work of the Trusts and their role in Australian society'. Boyd regarded the 'protection of our early buildings' as the first task of the Trusts, but also expressed his view that 'we have a strictly limited storehouse of potential national shrines'. Boyd singled out Francis Greenway's St Matthew's Church at Windsor in NSW as such a national shrine. He noted that in the previous four years it had gone from being close to collapse to constituting 'the most elaborate restoration undertaking ever attempted in Australia'.[2]

Since then thousands of buildings, grand and modest, religious and secular, commercial and industrial, have been saved in almost every corner of the nation. Historic houses flourish in every state, regularly opening their doors to the public. Elizabeth Bay House in Sydney and Rippon Lea in Melbourne are two of the best-known examples. Public buildings, including parliament houses and courthouses, have been meticulously restored at the taxpayer's expense. Every state's branch of the National Trust boasts at least a dozen properties open to the public, some many more. The historic areas of some cities—such as The Rocks in Sydney and Salamanca Place in Hobart—have been preserved partially, as have some dozens of country towns. All these places vie for both local and international tourists, as do the historic theme parks, including Sovereign Hill and Old Sydney Town. Packaging Australia's heritage, under various banners, has become big business. Gate receipts, food outlets, merchandising and, increasingly, sound and light shows have become par for the course.

Bluestone and sandstone

That post-1788 Australia had a history and historic structures worthy of preservation was recognised when the Australian Historical Society held its inaugural meeting in Sydney in March 1901. Prompted by federation, the Society also had the recent example of the foundation of the National Trust in England before it. Historical societies were also formed in Victoria and Queensland and later in other states, but it was in Sydney that the consciousness of historic structures was greatest. This was because, once it had overtaken Melbourne in population, development pressures were more extreme in Sydney in the early twentieth century than in the other cities, especially in the city centre and around the harbour. Concerned that the public was losing access to the harbour because of private property-owners claiming foreshore land, a state Labor government resumed some stretches of foreshore in 1910 and 1911, along with 22 acres embracing Vaucluse House and its gardens.

This house, first built in 1803, was acquired by W. C. Wentworth (of Blue Mountains crossing fame) in 1829. A leading figure in the campaign for self-government for the colony of NSW, Wentworth turned the house into a mansion in the Gothic style, with crenellated walls, turrets, huge internal halls and suites of bedrooms. After his death the house fell into other hands. Since Wentworth was the nearest thing to a founding father that NSW could claim, the state government's purchase of the house and grounds in 1910 was soon being described by the Vaucluse House Trust as an acquisition that could give us 'pride in our history'. First opened to the public in 1912, Vaucluse House offered regular opening hours from 1914, along with a visitors book and provision for donations towards upkeep. C. H. Bertie, the Sydney municipal librarian, wrote a souvenir booklet in 1917 that was reprinted many times. In the 1950s the Trust promoted Vaucluse House as a national shrine. It had already taken steps to recover as much of the original furniture as possible in its efforts to display the house as Wentworth had lived in it, from the 'misty landscapes of Conrad Martens' to colonial four-poster beds, 'which remind us that even statesmen have an intimate side to their lives'.[3]

While Sydney's colonial heritage was celebrated in books like Bertie's *Old Colonial Byways* (1928), most of the city's convict structures were demolished, with few voices of regret, by the end of the 1930s. Melbourne did not have convict structures, but it did manage, for its centenary celebrations in 1934, to import Captain Cook's Cottage from Yorkshire and rebuild it in the Fitzroy Gardens. The Melbourne drug manufacturer Sir Russell Grimwade purchased the cottage and paid to have it moved brick by brick and stone by stone to present as a centenary gift to his fellow citizens. Melbourne's many grand nineteenth-century

An early touring party at the remote Macquarie Harbour penal settlement, Tasmania, in 1912

buildings, from the Exhibition Buildings to Parliament House, were simply taken for granted. They remained in poor condition, attracting none of the attention lavished on Cook's Cottage, which featured prominently in tourist guidebooks and brochures. Indeed it was the passably pre-Victorian appearance of Como that secured this mansion's preservation as Melbourne's first historic house.[4]

Tasmania, with a slowly growing population and few pressures for redevelopment, proved to be the only state whose buildings attracted constant admirers. The well-known naturalist Charles Barrett, in his *Heritage of Stone*, spelt out the thoughts of many educated Australians when he wrote in 1945:

> When Victoria and the other younger states were colonised, the style
> of architecture had changed and become ugly. The growth of Sydney was
> so rapid that the early city soon became obliterated. Thus only in Tas-
> mania can there now be found numerous examples of Late Georgian
> architecture.

Barrett found Hobart abounding with 'charming villas, dignified merchants' premises and quaint shops'. He asked why charming villages like Richmond couldn't be protected from decay as had Williamsburg in the United States. His book opened with a frontispiece of the Port Arthur ruins, and he railed against the decay in some of Tasmania's grand but unoccupied houses, particularly the 'lovely, tragic Clarendon'. Barrett argued that the government should create a committee to decide which buildings, both public and private, should be preserved as 'national monuments'. It was some decades before any state government took much interest in becoming the guardian of historic buildings. Until the 1970s that role remained in the hands of the National Trust.[5]

The early enthusiasm shown by the Royal Australian Institute of Architects and the National Trust for Georgian houses, bluestone and sandstone churches and, a little later, for late nineteenth-century terrace houses, soon migrated to the countryside, first in Tasmania, and then in the mainland states. The towns that first attracted attention varied from state to state, depending on the local circumstances, especially

Clarendon, one of Tasmania's grand mansions, dating from 1836. For a long time the house stood empty, its columns gone; after it was acquired by the National Trust in 1962, a restoration programme began. The columns are once more in position.

attitudes to pioneering and notions about what constituted the forma-
tive or most important period of the town's history.[6]

Victoria housed Australia's largest nineteenth-century inland cities,
the gold capitals of Bendigo and Ballarat. Both had retained most of their
grand structures, including cathedrals, hotels, banks and elaborate town
halls. Gold had also enabled them to create elegant botanic gardens.
Beyond these cities were over a hundred small and medium-sized towns
that owed their foundations to gold and its aftermath. Many had almost
ceased to exist, or left only modest reminders of their former glory,
such as the little banking chambers and taverns, now abandoned or used
as residences, that dot the road between Castlemaine and Ballarat.
Towns that by the 1880s had populations of around 3000 acquired many
substantial buildings, including hotels, churches, warehouses, and often
a gaol, a hospital or a market building of considerable dimensions. These
towns were sufficiently important in their region that, while they did not
necessarily prosper for much of the twentieth century, they nonetheless
managed to survive on commercial and government activity—without
being quite prosperous enough to justify demolition and rebuilding.

After the flurry of the early gold rushes, Castlemaine's population
peaked in the 1860s at 10 000. As early as 1880, the Castlemaine District Association of Pioneers and Old Residents kept alive memories of
the gold rush era. A 1939 Victorian Railways brochure on Castlemaine
describes it as rich in historical, scenic and rural features, but the publication concentrates on the 'magnificent panoramas' to be had from the
hills that encircle the town. Only one structure, the Art Gallery and
Historical Museum, then just nine years old, is mentioned. Promotion
of Castlemaine continued in this vein for many years, with the town
presenting itself in the 1950s as 'a wealthy industrial town with a large
iron foundry, woollen mill and brick works', its main tourist attraction
a modern Olympic swimming pool. From 1959 the National Trust took
a close interest in structures under threat in Castlemaine, giving the
Market building an A classification. When it fell into disuse in 1967 and
demolition was contemplated, the Trust undertook to restore it with
state government support. Since the 1970s Castlemaine has been mar-

keting itself as a town rich in history and heritage, with slogans like 'Castlemaine's history can be read in its streets and in its houses'. In 1995 Castlemaine offered the ultimate heritage tourism conversion, its gaol. Dating from the 1850s, the 'Old Castlemaine Gaol' was refurbished to operate as a bed and breakfast establishment, complete with conference facilities. The mess hall became 'The Governors Restaurant'; and the cells 'where prisoners were once incarcerated' now offered 'a level of comfort that has never been known within these granite and sandstone walls'.[7]

Hundreds of country towns around Australia, large and small, have taken up heritage and heritage tourism as a theme, sometimes the dominant theme in their promotional activities. The Victorian gold rushes bequeathed over forty surviving settlements in all, within a few hundred square kilometres. They celebrate their nineteenth-century heritage and their ability to turn those structures, whether courthouses, bakeries, gaols or butcher's shops, into paying propositions for the tourist trade. Sometimes the conversions, and the changes of use, tell us as much about the history of the town as they do about current tourist demand. In Beechworth an old butcher's shop has been turned into a bakery and restaurant, complete with veranda dining.[8] In Maldon butchers, blacksmiths and drapers have given way to antique shops and cafes. In both towns houses have been purchased by the Melbourne middle class as weekend retreats. These owner–tourists often complain about day trippers making parking difficult.

Every other state has seen surviving towns turn their heritage to advantage. Most are nineteenth-century settlements, like Richmond and Stanley in Tasmania, Charters Towers in Queensland, Burra in South Australia, and Albany in Western Australia. A major port town that lost most of its trade to the growth of Fremantle from the early 1900s, Albany's relative decline made possible the survival of many of its commercial and community buildings. Port structures have survived in a number of once-busy ports such as Port Fairy in Victoria and Port Lincoln in South Australia. Eden in NSW, on Twofold Bay, has been less fortunate. There its role as an oil depot and more recently as the site of a Japanese-owned woodchip mill has seen much more demolition. Nearby

Boydtown, with its 1840s Seahorse Inn, managed to escape beachfront developers until the 1980s, by which time its heritage value was finally realised. Murray River port towns like Echuca, Mildura and Swan Hill have seen considerable redevelopment pressures and have had to re-create or rebuild much of their past.

Along with the rise in the popularity of heritage tourism in the last three decades has come the deliberate fashioning of heritage towns. Among the best examples of these are Berrima, in NSW, and Montville, on the Blackall Range in southern Queensland. In Broadbent's 1950 *Guide to the Hume Highway* Berrima, with a population of 200, was listed as consisting of the Surveyor-General Hotel, a Tea Garden, a garage cum general store, and the 'Historic Old Berrima Gaol'. Broadbent's readers learnt that the gaol opened in 1839, 'closed for convicts' in 1908, and was now 'open to inspection by Tourists seven days a week'. Readers of the 1928 *Guide to NSW Leading Towns* were given the added bit of infor-mation that the gaol 'was used as a concentration camp during the Great War'. There wasn't much to Berrima. The gaol, the courthouse and the hotel were thought at the time to be the only structures worthy of note. The 1838 courthouse, threatened with demolition in the late 1920s, sur-vived with the support of architects and the Royal Australian Historical Society. A Berrima Village Trust, created in 1963, aimed to save the town's Georgian character, but was unable to prevent alterations to the Surveyor-General Hotel. Many more buildings were suddenly found worthy of note, including a number of inns and churches. The court-house was restored in the 1970s.[9]

Even before the Hume Freeway bypassed Berrima in the late 1980s, dozens of antique shops, craft shops and cafes had developed at this popular stopping point which, unlike the larger centres of Yass and Goulburn, was not overrun by truck stops. Almost every extant brick and wooden residence on the main street and beyond was converted to heritage-style tourism commerce—everything from day-old antique lavender bags to damper, home-made jams, and not very good cappuc-cinos. Tour buses dropped their passengers off for a bite and a leak, while nearby Canberrans used Berrima as a halfway house to Sydney or as a day-trip destination in itself, as did thousands of Sydneysiders. The historic fabric of Berrima is now almost completely overlaid with the high and low kitsch of heritage tourism. You cannot walk more than a few metres in Berrima without being accosted by commerce dressed up as heritage. Quaintly named cafes service exhausted shoppers who seek refuge in a Devonshire tea.

The Queensland equivalent of Berrima is the once-sleepy settlement of Montville in the Blackall Range, due west of the Sunshine Coast. From around Montville and nearby settlements such as Maleny, magnificent views are to be had of the Glasshouse Mountains. Rich red volcanic soil is home to small stands of residual rainforest, fine dairying country, and the never-ending appetite for hobby farms and suburban ranches for retirees. In the early 1960s, before the rise of the Sunshine Coast, Montville was a rural village with a couple of shops, a school, some tiny timber churches and a bowling club. Within thirty years Montville was to become 'the jewel of the Sunshine Coast hinterland'. It all started with a little local pottery in the mid-1960s, but gradually old structures were converted and new 'colonials' (meaning Queensland wooden houses on stilts) were added to house the Cadman Cottage House of Chimes, the Camphor Cottage, the Dome Galleries, Granny's Macadamia Kitchen, Gumnuts and Lace, the Irish and Scottish Shop, a patisserie, and 'Poppy's Kiosk Fine Fast Foods'. Montville is now, according to the Blackall Range Tourism Association Inc., 'as close to an English Village as you will ever find in Australia'. With its heritage trail it offers a 'walk through history'.

Montville is in fact an incredible mishmash of English village, ethnic heritage commerce and residual laid-back Australian country town. It is the worst of all these worlds, especially when one of its newest structures is an *art-nouveau* cafe—adding a French frisson to this antipodean hill station. Some tourists, desperate for a day in the cool ranges away from the heat and the high-rise living of their beachside apartments, still find Montville preferable to a slightly more antique object of distraction, the purpose-built Bli Bli castle (1973), now surrounded by suburban housing blocks, or the miniature English village at nearby Flaxton.[10]

The Blackall Range, inland from Queensland's Sunshine Coast. The villages of Montville, Flaxton and Mapleton have been spoilt by the process of their reinvention as heritage sites for tourist consumption.

From pioneer village to theme park

Swan Hill, in northern Victoria, began life in the 1860s as a port for Murray River steamers travelling to and from the Darling and Murrumbidgee rivers. It developed as a regional centre with the opening and cultivation of the Mallee; the growth of irrigation enabled dairy farming and the production of grapes, citrus fruits and maize. Like its neighbour Mildura, upstream, it advertised itself as a sunny river settlement.

When the Swan Hill Development Committee produced a marketing brochure in the early 1960s, it showed a fishing rod reaching out to the town, graphically depicted as halfway between Melbourne and Adelaide. As the 'Centre of the Murray Valley' Swan Hill 'lay athwart the pathway of history and the development of inland Australia'. The brochure said little about the township itself but described at length nearby attractions such as the boating at Lake Boga and the merino properties around Balranald, all available within the vast horizons, blue sky and sunshine that is the 'real' Australia.

Swan Hill early realised that a settlement a good day's drive from either Adelaide or Melbourne needed more than blue sky, a river and an agricultural hinterland to attract the thousands of Australians new to car ownership who were looking for places to explore on long weekends, at Easter, or during school holidays. In December 1963 the *Riverlander* praised the 'Folk Museum' to be established in Swan Hill, not least because of the decay, scrapping or deliberate destruction of 'all the horse-drawn and mechanical contrivances used in the opening up of rural Australia'. The *Riverlander* pointed out that there were 'relics in abundance' along the Murray, from agricultural implements to abandoned paddlesteamers. In 1964 Swan Hill opened the nation's first 'Folk and Pioneer Settlement', offering the *Gem*—Australia's largest paddlesteamer —shops, machines and houses. Following Skansen, the world-famous open-air folk museum in Stockholm, and Sturbridge Village in Massachusetts, Swan Hill, 'where past and present meet in the sunshine', enabled children and parents to see blacksmiths and wheelwrights on the job, along with a 'unique aboriginal display'. At the time there were still hundreds of Aborigines living in humpies, tents and huts along the Murray River in Swan Hill and Robinvale. Some had actually moved to the NSW side of the river to escape the Victorian Aboriginal Welfare Board.[11]

Swan Hill Pioneer Village came about through a combination of concern among the local citizenry about the lack of any memorial to their grandparents, 'who opened up this part of the country', and professional advice from Eric Westbrook, Director of the National Gallery of Victoria, who suggested a folk museum. Architect Roy Grounds recommended an outdoor re-creation of the pioneers' way of life. Most of the structures came from elsewhere in Swan Hill or other places in Victoria. The barber shop came from the main street, the printery from near Castlemaine, and the Iron House from South Melbourne.[12] The removal of these properties took place before the existence of the Burra Charter (1978), a heritage manifesto prepared for Australia by the Australian branch of ICOMOS, the International Committee on Monuments and Sites. The notion that historical buildings could be moved to create a new historical village was widely viewed as a genuine form of conservation until the Burra Charter argued the case for in situ preservation of historic buildings.

By the late 1960s, supported by both locals and the Victorian government, Swan Hill attracted over 100 000 visitors per annum; by 1975, 280 000. In that year the Village exported to the United States over one million cans of witchetty grub, yabby bisque, jumbuck broth, mallee chook and pioneer stock pot soups. Mildura thought it had been done in the eye. As the premier Murray River resort town from the 1920s to the 1950s, Mildura feared that its tourism primacy would be usurped by Swan Hill, which even had the hide to appropriate paddlesteamers as its own.[13]

Ballarat, with an energetic historical society, was quick to notice the Pioneer Village arising to its north. In early 1965 the mayor of Ballarat and members of the Historical Society went on a tour of the Swan Hill Village, returning convinced that Ballarat must establish an outdoor museum of its own. The Ballarat Historical Park Association, formed in 1966, listed its aims as erecting on a suitable site 'authentic reproductions' of dwellings, business premises, workshops, churches and mining plants of the early days of 'this great city'. The Victorian Premier, Sir Henry Bolte, offered $300 000 if the Association could raise half that amount, which it did from among both corporate and individual donors.

The first structure at Sovereign Hill, a poppet head erected in 1969, showed the people of Ballarat that the site, a wasteland of mullock heaps, would become a reality. The buildings that followed included both original structures from other sites and re-creations, like the Chinese Joss House, based on nothing more than an illustration on a postcard from Macau. This brick joss house, ready for the opening of Sovereign Hill on 29 November 1970, bore no resemblance to the simple timber Chinese temple that survived in Ballarat until the mid-1950s.[14]

Over the next twenty-five years Sovereign Hill became Australia's most successful historical theme park, attracting 500 000 visitors per annum. It is so successful that it has gone beyond the re-creation of a gold-mining settlement to become a tourist phenomenon in its own right, offering an array of restaurants and shops, and classy accommo- dation on site. A professional staff of 250 work on curatorial, main- tenance, catering and promotional activities. Muskets are fired regularly, school children are introduced to the rigours of primary edu- cation in the 1850s, and horse-drawn coaches ply the unsealed but fre- quently graded streets. New structures and new exhibits are added, while tried and true activities, such as gold panning, particularly popu- lar with school children, remain a basic item on the Sovereign Hill menu. A spectacular light and sound show on the Eureka Rebellion, complete with the burning down of Bentley's Hotel, was added in the early 1990s; and in 1997, to cater for the increasing number of Chinese visitors, a gold pour room was opened with gold sovereigns available for sale. Sovereign Hill and the adjacent Gold Museum are close to the cen- tre of Ballarat, which benefits from the spin-off trade, particularly when visitors, including school parties, stay overnight.

Swan Hill and Sovereign Hill have many imitators, the Lachlan Vintage Village at Forbes (NSW), Coal Creek and Old Gippstown in Gippsland (Victoria), Timbertown at Wauchope (NSW), and the Flag- staff Hill Maritime Village at Warrnambool in Victoria being among them. All of these initiatives grew out of local committees wishing to preserve, resurrect or reinvent their pioneering past. Most, after opening amid much fanfare and local support, have fallen on hard times. Some have closed for good.[15]

Old Sydney Town, while it owes a lot in concept to Swan Hill and Sovereign Hill, was the first historical theme park in Australia to start from scratch in replicating a site in a different locality. The Sydney architect Frank Fox had long been impressed by Disneyland. In the late 1960s he visited Colonial Williamsburg and his thoughts turned to historic re-creations at home. When he found a 250-acre citrus farm for sale at Somersby, near Gosford, he realised that the site bore an uncanny resemblance to prints of early Sydney, complete with a creek over a sandstone bed, not unlike the early Tank Stream. Fox decided to re-create the Sydney of 1810. A small-scale Sydney Cove and Tank Stream were fashioned out of this site, and buildings of both stone and timber were built as scale models, but of sufficient size that they could house the costumed staff who would bring a blend of museum and theatre to implement the two aims of the 'town': education and tourism.

Construction of the town began in 1969, but the early entrepreneurs had underestimated the enormous costs of faithful historical re-creation. By the end of 1974 $3 million had already been spent on the site, much of it from the Westpac Bank and the Whitlam Labor government, which both became one-quarter shareholders in the hope that their investment would become NSW's 'greatest tourist drawcard'.

When Old Sydney Town was opened by Gough Whitlam on Australia Day 1975, it hoped to draw a million visitors in the first year.[30] This figure was never achieved. Despite an array of advertising slogans, from 'More than just history' to 'See Sydney as it was', the theme park never lived up to the hopes of its founders—even with the biggest sandstone windmill in the southern hemisphere and plentiful re-enactments including a magistrate's court, street brawls and pistol fights. In December 1976 the Wran Labor government's Department of Tourism stepped in to take over the commonwealth's government's share (for no fee) and to acquire the Fox family's 49 per cent interest for a mere

A now almost forgotten tourist icon—the Dog on the Tuckerbox, near Gundagai.
Unveiled by Prime Minister Lyons in 1932, this pioneers monument now marks little
more than a refreshment stop.

$80 000. Over $3 million had by then been invested in the site, but the
state government was concerned that its closure would cost seventy
jobs in a marginal electorate. In March 1979 the *Sun Herald* pointed out
that Old Sydney Town was 'recreating history in a way its founders never
intended'. The state government and Westpac lost over $700 000 dol-
lars in 1977/78; unless they kept it going they had no way of ever recov-
ering the money invested in the 'Town' as it was only saleable as a going
concern, with gate fees and food and merchandise sales. In 1987 the site
was let to Warwick Amusements Pty Ltd on an eighty-year lease. The
park attracted only 250 000 visitors that year. With an attendance of less
than half a million in a year it is never likely to be profitable.[16]

Relieved to have extracted itself from a heritage dream gone wrong,
the NSW government already had its hands full with hundreds of heritage properties around the state, from railway stations and courthouses

to the grand and modest dwellings preserved by its own Historic Houses Trust (formed in 1980), whose brief extended from Vaucluse House and Elizabeth Bay House in Sydney to Meroogal, a modest two-storey wooden home in Nowra.

Elsewhere in Australia real historical settlements survived, even if they did not always thrive. Holy Trinity Abbey New Norcia, Western Australia, began as a Benedictine mission to the Aborigines in the 1840s. The Spanish monks had to come to terms with the landscape, the Aboriginal people and the growing numbers of pastoralists. Over the next eighty years they built a monastery, a chapel, a parish church, two large boarding schools (one for boys, one for girls) and undertook agricultural pursuits in wheat, olives, grapes and cattle. A hotel, to cater for the growing tourist trade, opened in 1927. Although the schools closed in the 1980s, New Norcia is still a functioning town, with a police station, a post office, a petrol station/roadhouse, a resident monastic community, a dozen or more nearby farming families, and a strong sense of its place in the history of Western Australia. Even the inexpert eye can see that these buildings and their occupants, in their monastic habits or farming clothes, are real people going about their daily lives. A hundred kilometres north of Perth, New Norcia has catered for a modest trade of pilgrims, travellers and tourists for the past 150 years. It took some weeks to get there in the 1840s, but by the 1990s it was little more than an hour's drive from Perth.[17]

While the state branches of the National Trust, and even sometimes the churches, appreciated the heritage value of such settlements, it was only with the creation of the Australian Heritage Commission in 1975 that the federal government belatedly recognised the wealth of architectural and heritage values to be found in abandoned and working buildings. This realisation coincided with a short-lived enthusiasm by some of the big state museums to re-create heritage structures. Almost all of them, at some time between 1970 and 1990, indulged in re-creating railway stations or cinemas or old shopfronts. Indeed the Powerhouse Museum in Sydney, renamed and revamped to open in 1988, actually participated in the removal of the magnificent Arrivals and Departures

"*Build a new road? Blimey! I hope not—that's the only thing that keeps people in here!*"

When the Sydney cartoonist Mercier visited Cooktown in 1953, its population had slumped to 500. In the 1980s it still took six hours of driving on an unmade road to reach it from Cairns. Cooktown has now been reinvented as an ecological and heritage destination.

board from Central Railway Station in Sydney. Today it is still in the Powerhouse Museum, while railway commuters try to read the print on illegible video monitors. Its removal remains one of Australia's great acts of heritage vandalism, perpetrated in the name of preservation.

Terrace houses and The Rocks

When James Wallace Pty Ltd won the contract to redevelop The Rocks in Sydney in 1963, *Walkabout* magazine described the area as occupied by 'old warehouses and nondescript factory buildings, with a handful of grand sets of terrace houses, reflecting 'the pleasantly solid tastes of 19th century architects'. For the first six decades of the twentieth century The Rocks, even after the big clean-up and wharf-building programme that followed the outbreak of plague in the early 1900s, was regarded as a slum. Most of its residents rented their terrace houses from the Maritime Services Board and other state government authorities. The redevelopment plan required the demolition of most nine-teenth-century buildings, replacing them with a series of residential blocks, offices and a luxury hotel. *Walkabout* concluded its account by observing:

> When this site, which goes back 175 years to the beginning of the first white settlement, finally yields up the last of its old houses so full of charm, Sydney will have lost much of its character, but it will have gained a waterfront gateway equal to any in the world.

The Rocks redevelopment plan was not well received by the National Trust, which, having lobbied successfully to save a number of convict, Georgian and Edwardian structures identified by the architect Morton Herman (including Francis Greenway's Hyde Park Barracks), began to take other convict structures and terrace houses more seriously.[18]

At the same time middle-class professionals in Sydney and Melbourne discovered the charms of some of the substantial terrace houses to be found in suburbs like Paddington and Carlton. When the Sydney photographer Rob Hillier's book *Let's Buy a Terrace House* was published in 1968, it attracted a great deal of attention. Hillier explained that over the past five or six years terrace houses had been taken over by 'authors, artists, architects and actors'. The houses were cheap, often purchased from first-generation migrants, and as the suburbs were transformed there was a spectacular change in both their reputation and in middle-class notions of what made a desirable inner-city location. The generation of young people who purchased these houses in the 1960s included key opinion-makers in attitudes to the presentation, restoration and exploitation of the past. Their views have had an enormous impact on the creation of tourist precincts and the presentation of Australia's historical fabric to domestic and international tourists. Art galleries, book-shops, music stores and cafes suddenly opened in the newly fashionable terrace suburbs, and so these former 'slums' suddenly found themselves popular with tourists.

The Rocks survived a number of later attempts at redevelopment. The Builders Labourers Federation, led by Jack Mundey and aligned with local residents, successfully prevented the NSW government from making another attempt at wholesale demolition in the late 1960s and early 1970s. Meanwhile elegant Georgian mansions were leased to bodies such as the Australian College of General Practitioners, while the Argyle Bond Store was turned into an Arts Centre, 'for handicrafts and artifacts of the sort tourists often prefer to buy and can't'. Cedric Flower, an artist who specialised in nostalgic drawings of Sydney's past, went on to tell readers of *Walkabout* in August 1970 that 'This could be a significant development in an industry where imagination seldom rises above toy koalas and pokerwork boomerangs'.[19]

The Rocks quickly developed as Australia's first self-styled historical precinct. Its Argyle Tavern, its coffee lounges and its Arts Centre catered for local and interstate visitors as well as overseas tourists. Although handily located near the Overseas Terminal, The Rocks developed at the end of the great age of ocean-going tourism: increasingly its visitors came by tour bus or car, attracted by its growing reputation and its proximity to Sydney's two great tourist icons, the Harbour Bridge and the Opera House, then still being built.

Like any major tourist installation, especially one with overall control still vested in a government authority, The Rocks consciously promotes its image. It has a logo made up of the harbour with a backdrop of a bond store. In 1992 the main brochure on The Rocks was subtitled 'Sydney's Original Village'. Two years later this had become 'Sydney's First Place', since dropped because Australia's Aboriginal population had clearly inhabited and created many places well before the first convict structures in The Rocks were erected.

While most of the landscape and buildings of the western part of The Rocks, overlooking Darling Harbour, have remained with only modest alterations and additions, the eastern side, especially where it abuts the central business district, resembles more and more the drastic development plans of the 1960s. A series of high-rise hotels (Regent, 1982; ANA, 1991) and office blocks crowd the landscape. Towards the Harbour Bridge the elegant Hyatt Hotel (1989) was allowed to rise only four floors above the pedestrian boardwalk. It is on the former site of the Sydney water police headquarters, a ramshackle structure quickly forgotten.[20]

271

Cultural tourism

When statisticians study heritage attractions they separate the 'historic' ones (houses, churches, railways, factories that are no longer in production) from others that have been loosely gathered under the term cultural tourism, including museums, art galleries and even wineries. Such activities are difficult to survey because, while some establishments charge an entry fee, many—including churches, town halls, and some museums and art galleries—do not. Accurate figures are collected for people entering Port Arthur, Sovereign Hill, the Swan Hill Pioneer Village, Old Sydney Town, and Warner Brothers Movie World on the Gold Coast. But it is very difficult to estimate the number of people who walk along Collins Street in Melbourne or Macquarie Street in Sydney to admire the nineteenth- and twentieth-century streetscapes. Likewise the Saturday market at Salamanca Place in Hobart is obviously popular, but the numbers attending are only guesstimates.

A survey undertaken in 1986/87 estimated that thirty-six million visitors were going to the major tourist attractions in NSW and Victoria. One-third of these went to zoos, aquariums, botanic gardens and attractions within national parks. The fifty-five theme and entertainment parks, including Sovereign Hill and Old Sydney Town, attracted eight million visitors, while ninety-two historic structures catered for another 2.4 million. Attendance at activities in each state proved to be roughly commensurate with population, except that Victoria's fifty-five historic structures hosted 1 855 000 guests, while the thirty-seven buildings in NSW attracted only 552 000 visitors. A relatively high proportion of Victoria's historic buildings are within easy reach of Melbourne, including all the goldfields towns. Some of the historic structures surveyed in NSW, especially in Broken Hill, are a considerable distance from the Sydney market.

In a nation with relatively few ruins, Port Arthur stands out as the primary site. It is easily accessible by road from Hobart, being less than an hour and a half's drive, and is on the itinerary of most visitors to Tasmania, even if they are there only for the weekend. Since an entry fee

This commercial Convict Exhibition is encountered on the road to Port Arthur, well before the destination.

was imposed, visitors from beyond the state have outnumbered Tasmanians.[21] Australia does house some other spectacular ruins, including the retorts of the abandoned shale oil mine at Glen Davis, near Lithgow, but it is relatively inaccessible, has neither the romance nor the notoriety of Port Arthur, and is virtually unknown as a tourist site.

Industrial structures have not fared well in the preservation stakes. Most historic wharves have been demolished, as have famous industrial buildings, including the Bow Truss warehouse in Geelong and the Bunnerong Power Station on the shores of Botany Bay. Bluestone mill buildings have been preserved in Victoria, and one great iron-roofed 'stick shed', formerly storing wheat, survives at the Mallee town of Murtoa. Once industrial structures have ceased to function as intended, they are rarely preserved unless new uses can be found for them, as is the case with the sandstone warehouses of Salamanca Place in Hobart, or most of Australia's nineteenth-century customs houses, now converted into museums. It remains to be seen what will happen to the steel plants of Newcastle, abandoned in the 1990s.[22]

Museums and art galleries were central to the aspirations of the civic leaders of the Australian colonies. Every capital city opened a government-funded museum and art gallery (sometimes in the same building) by the 1890s. These institutions, invariably housed in imposing structures, displayed both natural history and evidence of the progress of civilisation. By the 1960s and 1970s most of the grander museums had become very run-down. They did not enjoy either the elite patronage or the bequests that kept the state art galleries in better condition. Museums, and even state libraries (usually close by), used the occasion of sesquicentennial and bicentennial celebrations in the 1980s to refurbish themselves, or even to completely rebuild.

Museums no longer play a pivotal role in explaining new scientific and technological advances. That role has been usurped by mass education, television and the Internet. Today the world's most successful museums are either arbiters of taste and repositories of culture—like the great art galleries—or interactive centres of learning, like some children's and science museums. If museums are to remain as key institutions in the next fifty years they will have to become providers of information and images, not remain just repositories. Most galleries and even libraries are now putting their image collections and much of their text-based information on the Internet. But if their collections are available there, why will students, or domestic and international tourists, want to visit the institutions? Even the commodities sold by museums—from art objects to books—can be ordered via the Internet. The only traditional museums to survive as popular attractions will be those where the primacy of the material object—be it a painting, a sculpture or a kitchen setting—is so special that one still wants to see, and in some cases touch, the real thing.[23]

Some museums, faced with a paucity of historic objects, create new ones of their own. The Immigration Museum in Victoria, which opened in the former Melbourne Customs House in 1998, invites people with Victorian forebears to pay $50 and have their forebears' names inscribed in stone. The elegant, made-to-order memorial becomes a museum object in its own right.

The 1988 bicentennial celebrations

European Australians remain uncertain about how to celebrate their history or create their own rituals. Aborigines and Aboriginal iconography have been wheeled out at many earlier national ceremonies in a desperate attempt to display something genuinely Australian. During the sesquicentennial celebrations in Sydney in 1938, and in much larger numbers in 1988 (despite official plans for them) Aborigines demonstrated on their own account.

Australia has relied on the Imperial presence in most of our national ceremonies and grand events. The opening of the Sydney Harbour Bridge is one of the few important twentieth-century rituals where royalty did not officiate. Labor Premier Jack Lang wanted to open it himself. But that was a state, not a national ritual. The opening of the first federal parliament in 1901, Parliament House in Canberra in 1927, the Olympic Games in 1956, the Cook Bicentenary in 1970, the Sydney Opera House in 1973, the Brisbane Expo and the new Parliament House in 1988, have all been undertaken by members of the British

Until the royal tour of 1954, Aboriginal participation in public occasions, including re-enactments, was rare. Here some white country boys take part in the Victorian centenary celebrations at Portland in 1934.

275

royal family. The bicentennial celebrations in Sydney saw the Queen and the Duke of Edinburgh, and also Prince Charles and Princess Diana, presiding over particular functions. The bicentenary should have been the last Imperial hurrah on Australian soil, as the centenary of federation, by definition, ought to be an Australian event.

The Australian Bicentennial Authority could not sustain a year-long ritual. In 1938 the sesquicentenary celebrations lasted only three months, from 26 January to Anzac Day, still our most ritualistic day. Planning a year of celebrations in a country that still has no convincing national day is a risky business. The Authority tried hard to make the 'celebration of a nation' a ritual of national unity. Instead it presided over the greatest one-day spectacle that Australia has ever seen. But it was a one-off display in just one city, Sydney, and did not command the massive international television audience of an Olympic Games. No new national rituals were invented.[24] The heritage package in Australia, no matter how highly orchestrated, continues to lack a day of national celebration, let alone of reflection and reconciliation.

In their attempt to attract tourists, most countries make great play of their national days and their annual festivals. Independence days, republic days, the Venetian regatta, the European *faschnachts* are all part of the tourist calendar. The lacklustre plans for the centenary of federation suggest that, as they approach 2001, Australians are even less sure of themselves, and less able to provide a convincing and relevant celebration, than they were in 1988.

Festivals Incorporated

While Australia has been unable to create a national festival, fairs, folk and arts festivals have a long history, especially in local communities. They usually celebrate crops and other aspects of locality. Kingaroy has a peanut festival, Gatton a potato carnival; the Barossa Valley has a vintage festival, while Bendigo has its Easter Fair.

Capital city festivals, especially since World War II, have often arisen out of the performing arts. Perth established such a festival in 1953, but this was soon eclipsed by the Adelaide Festival of Arts. The other state capitals had been envious of Melbourne's staging of the Olympics in 1956 (the first Olympics to include an arts festival). There was a growing consciousness of the importance of sporting and cultural events in promoting cities. One correspondent to the Adelaide *Advertiser* suggested that Adelaide should abandon its bid for the 1962 Empire Games, not least because they would cost more than £1 million to stage, and concentrate instead on an annual festival of sport and the arts. In December 1958 the Mayor of Adelaide distributed a pamphlet among prospective sponsors and guarantors about a proposal to hold a festival of arts in Adelaide in March 1960.

> It is not expected that the 1960 Festival will result in a profit; on the contrary, it is expected that some cost will have to be borne by the business community, if a Festival worthy of the city is to be presented . . . As the purpose of the Festival is to add to the prestige of Adelaide and to bring visitors to the city, with increased business, most firms will be able to charge any cost to expenses in the ordinary way.[25]

Firms contributing included Elder Smith, the Bank of Adelaide, the *Advertiser,* the retailers John Martin's and Myers, the whitegoods manufacturers Kelvinator and Pope, the Associated Brewers, the Licensed Victuallers and the Adelaide Steamship Co.

Modelled on the Edinburgh Festival, and with the Queen Mother as its patron, the first Adelaide Festival of Arts ran from 12 to 26 March 1960, offering the Sydney and Melbourne symphony orchestras, the Hogarth Puppets from London and Dave Brubeck's jazz group, and staging Australia's first regular 'Writers' Week'. The festival has been held every two years since. The South Australian Tourist Bureau featured it in brochures and posters, as did the airline companies, Ansett and TAA.

The festival put Adelaide on the cultural map. Melbourne had already established a more populist festival, Moomba, which in its own way had also been prompted by the success of the Edinburgh Festival. Maurice Nathan, the proprietor of a furniture company and a city councillor,

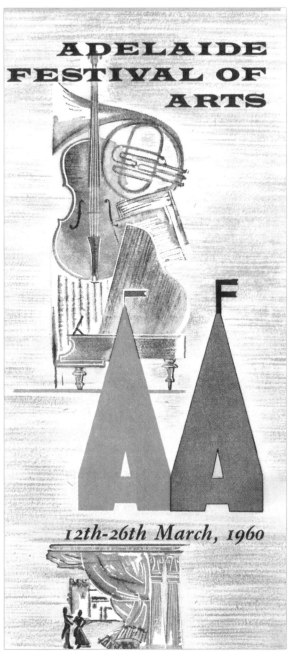

Promotional leaflet for the first Adelaide Festival of the Arts, 1960. The design indicates its high cultural aspirations, which (as the leaflet informs you) did not extend to concert or theatre performances on Sundays.

complained that Melbourne was 'bloody dull' and 'needed livening up'. For their carnival the city fathers seized on the Aboriginal word Moomba, which they were told meant 'let's get together and have fun'. When, more than a decade later, it was revealed that in southern Aboriginal languages 'moom' meant backside, the title was so well established that the organisers could accommodate the fact that their title was a bit of a joke.

Although originally designed to attract interstate visitors as well as Victorians, Moomba remained predominantly a Melbourne event. With the exception of Robert Morley, its most famous kings have been the Melbourne identities Graham Kennedy and Bert Newton. While it has occasionally staged major international acts, including Neil Diamond, the Beach Boys and Boz Scaggs, these have not been high-cultural. Moomba has had its critics. In the early 1970s Don Dunstan, the Premier of South Australia, described it as a 'colossal flop'. In the 1990s it had trouble raising sponsorship dollars, and ran out of iconic personalities to wear the Moomba crown.[26]

The real challenge to Moomba populism has come from the Sydney and Melbourne festivals, cultural events that have managed to garner elite sponsorship and government backing. Sydney's answer to Moomba, the Waratah Festival (named after the state flower), was such a lacklustre event that it was abandoned in 1974, and replaced in January 1977 with the Festival of Sydney. The new Wran Labor government, keen on courting the elite companies that sponsor arts events, invested heavily in both the festival and its promotion, especially on television. By the 1990s the Melbourne and Sydney festivals had become major, professionally organised events, with managers, market researchers and ticket agencies buying acts and measuring their success by ticket sales as well as artistic impact. Their lavish publicity brochures now tell you as much about the sponsors as about the events. It's Esso's Night at the Opera, Westpac's Symphony Under the Stars, the NRMA's Rocks Ride, 2Day FM and Coca Cola's Skyshow 4. Even the State Library of NSW takes a full-page advertisement to announce that it's 'Much more than books'.

The Australian Tourist Commission publishes a directory of festivals. Events organisers, tour wholesalers and travel agents can check dates

Moomba clown face, 1955

and likely visitor numbers online. But Australia's best internationally known event is not a construct of the 1980s and the 1990s, but the Melbourne Cup, first run in 1861. While outside Australia it may be known only in racing circles, it nonetheless features in betting shops around the world, from Britain to Hong Kong. It attracts international entries and foreign tourists, even if they didn't know it was on before they visited. It is literally the only day of the year when Australia, with 24-hour shopping, stops, even if just for the few minutes while the race is on and the workplace sweep earnings are dispersed. While it attracts sponsorship and modern advertising hype, it nonetheless carries with it the force of history and tradition.

Three decades after Robin Boyd postulated a paucity of potential national shrines, the number of heritage sites goes well beyond war memorials, churches and grand houses to embrace remodelled or purpose-built precincts, from The Rocks to Sovereign Hill. These and other heritage sites attract millions of visitors each year. Some are seeking to explain Australia's past; others try, sometimes too hard, to cater for contemporary fashions in cultural tourism. Some ruins and religious sites, including Port Arthur and New Norcia, have resisted overt commodification, whereas the purpose-built heritage sites have turned themselves, as well as the goods and services they sell, into commodities. Such high levels of commodification may undermine any sense of authenticity, but David Lowenthal reminds us that heritage

> has long been vulgarised, faked, and sold: the medieval relic trade out-did any modern scam. What *is* novel is the mistaken notion that such abuses are new and hence intolerable. Critics seem unaware that heritage has always twisted the past for some present purpose.[27]

The difference is that the medieval relic trade sought to establish a material connection between the beholder and the divine. But the present urge to restore, or to recreate in simulacra, is often based on a strong sense of removal from the past, or more particularly, a hubristic sense of advance from it. It can only be an overweening sense of technological superiority that led a Queensland theme park to urge people to come along and 'Laugh at the Past'. Heritage then is seen as being essentially artefactual; there is little sense of past struggles, or past events, or the simple dignity of past lives. Display has become the great equaliser. At the same time, the word 'historic' has come to be applied quite promiscuously. It too has become separated from events: Toorak House, where Victoria's governors resided for twenty years and received the news of Eureka, is hardly thought of at all now, let alone seen as being of historic significance. On the other hand a local newspaper can refer to the 'historic dance floor' of Richmond Town Hall. 'Historic' can simply mean old, or something that everyone can appreciate for its age.

Heritage in Australia is often aligned with Lowenthal's 'present purpose', not least because the history industry here is almost entirely an
outcome of the last fifty years. The advocates of heritage conservation
need to establish a political and sometimes a financial case for preserving sites and structures. Local entrepreneurs and town champions
want their history recognised and marketed, to make them feel proud of
their localities and to attract tourists. Motel chains will back anything
that creates more travellers and more demand for overnight accommodation. And while the various heritage parks may start to resemble
shopping malls, most still have large open-air sections and real streets.
Whatever their faults, they provide welcome respite from the franchised
products of the malls, where constant consumption of standardised brand
names is the only way of life.[28]

Air Travel and the Rise of the Resort

For most of the twentieth century the number of overseas visitors to Australia has exceeded the number of Australians going overseas. Until the 1960s the numbers going in either direction were, by today's standards, modest. Australia did not manage to attract more than 100 000 visitors in any one year until 1962, but by 1992 over 2 500 000 people made their way to the southern continent. From the year 2000, the year of the Olympics, it is estimated that over five million people will visit Australia for business, pleasure or both.

Jet travel made this extraordinary increase possible. The introduction of jet aircraft and the time, fuel and operating economies of the Boeing 707 and 747 made air travel quicker and cheaper and therefore within the reach of more and more people. Even a two-week holiday now allows sufficient time for a major world trip. These changes in transport options, time and cost have been accompanied by a spectacular increase in demand for business and tourist travel to many parts of the world.

In the three decades from 1925 to 1955, Australia didn't ever attract more than 50 000 overseas visitors per annum, nor did more than 50 000 Australians leave these shores. During these decades the great majority of arrivals and departures were by sea; given the length of the journey and the cost, this greatly restricted the numbers that could travel. Only the relatively wealthy, certain categories of professionals, business people and youthful adventurers were able to devote a month to travelling to the other side of the world and, after a sojourn there, spend another month travelling back.

By September 1965, when a New York accounting firm delivered its analysis and recommendations for the Australian 'travel and tourist industry', the aeroplane had supplanted the ship as the main means of international travel and had also shown itself to be an increasingly economical option for longer-haul domestic travel.[1] Nonetheless key decision-makers in Australia were slow to recognise this trend. In the late 1950s the Maritime Services Board, a government authority that controlled Sydney Harbour, decided that Sydney needed a modern wharf on Circular Quay: the new Overseas Terminal opened in 1960. It hosted the new P & O liners, the *Oriana* and (shortly after) the *Canberra*, proud white symbols of Australia's connection to Britain. A year after the terminal opened, Australia's last coastal passenger liner, the *Manoora*, made its final interstate voyage. The heyday of the voyage to the other side of the world was over, but as great liners continued to steam into Sydney Harbour, this was not immediately apparent. By 1964 fewer than 20 000 visitors came to Australia by sea, outnumbered six to one by the 129 000 who arrived by air.

For well over a century Sydney Harbour and Melbourne's Port Phillip Bay had been the great gateways to Australia, with over two-thirds of all arrivals and departures using their wharves. Other ports such as Albany in Western Australia (later supplanted by Fremantle), Port Adelaide and Brisbane also accommodated the great liners. The ports, developed to service both passenger liners and merchant ships, offered an international pot-pourri of sights and sounds. Upmarket hotels jostled with seamen's accommodation. Cafes, bars and a great variety of entertainments catered to the seafaring trade. In Sydney the port area abutted other attractions, such as Luna Park and the Harbour Bridge, so that most Sydneysiders grew up with the realisation that they lived in a port city. In the other capitals the port facilities were more distant. In the case of Melbourne, for instance, the great passenger wharves were just along from St Kilda, so liners were regularly sighted on weekend outings. The main merchant docks, on the other hand, were separated from the city by railway sidings.

The friendly skies

In the island continent the exploits of aviators in the 1920s and 1930s caught the imagination of all Australians, from city-dwellers to outback farmers. Kingsford Smith and Charles Ulm became household names, and their record-breaking trips, along with those of other airmen like Bert Hinkler, were followed on the radio and in the newspapers. Boys grew up with crystal sets, balsa wood model planes and a close knowledge of air routes and even of weather conditions. Girls, while not

By the late 1920s West Australian Airways Limited flew mail and passengers on a coastal route from Perth to Derby, via Port Hedland and Broome.

encouraged to be abreast of the technical details, were introduced to the exploits of the Flying Doctor in *Empire Annual* and school magazines. The drama of aviation was a combination of record-breaking flights and the dangers of the air. Bert Hinkler died in a crash in the Tuscan alps of Italy in January 1933; Charles Ulm and his two companions in *Stella Australis* were lost at sea off Hawaii in December 1934; Kingsford Smith's *Lady Southern Cross* disappeared off the Burma coast in November 1935.

The commonwealth and state governments were well aware of the potential of the new form of transport, not least because of the distances between the capital cities. In 1919 the commonwealth government approached W. Hudson Fysh and P. J. McGinness to survey an air route between Longreach and Darwin. A year later, along with the Queensland pastoralist Fergus McMaster, they formed the Queensland and Northern Territory Aerial Services Ltd (QANTAS), the first airline in eastern Australia. By the late 1930s Qantas had decided to concentrate on international routes, including mail services.[2]

Aeroplane companies, usually with only a handful of aircraft, popped up around the continent, many earning more income through post and freight than from passengers. Charles Ulm and Kingsford Smith formed Australian National Airways in 1929. It ceased operation in 1931 because of the Depression but a firm of the same name, owned primarily by British shipping interests, reappeared in 1936, operating an airmail service across Bass Strait. ANA quickly absorbed other airlines to obtain new routes, including Perth to Adelaide and a series of routes in North Queensland. After the war the company recruited ex-RAAF pilots and purchased planes from the United States.

Other aviators also founded airlines. Reginald Ansett, son of a garage proprietor, obtained his pilot's licence in 1929. Displaying a talent for running transport businesses, he established a rural bus company and set up Ansett Roadways in 1931. In 1936 he began a Hamilton to Melbourne air service, and the following year won the Brisbane to Adelaide air race.[3]

The proliferation of privately owned airlines bothered the Australian Labor Party, but the advent of World War II meant that such domestic matters received little attention. As part of its postwar platform the Chifley Labor government attempted to nationalise the airlines in 1945, but the High Court ruled the legislation invalid. The government then created its own Airlines Commission with Trans-Australia Airlines as its trading name. Both ANA and TAA were soon servicing most of the capital cities. They commissioned colourful posters to promote their services and their destinations. In 1957 Reg Ansett bought out ANA to create Ansett-ANA, which later became Ansett Airlines of Australia. Ansett developed a close relationship with Prime Minister Menzies, and his firm Ansett Transport Industries gained enormous financial benefit from the two-airline agreement, which effectively guaranteed Ansett half of the domestic passenger traffic in Australia. The routes, fares and frequencies of both TAA and Ansett were regulated to ensure the fifty-fifty split of traffic. Although ANA and subsequently Ansett-ANA sometimes made poor commercial decisions, they were protected by the agreement. In the late 1940s ANA replaced its DC3s with Skymaster DC4s. TAA purchased the much superior Convair, which was not only faster but pressurised. In 1954 Ansett-ANA chose the propeller-driven DC6, while TAA purchased the turbo-prop Viscount, enabling TAA to boast that it had brought the Jet Age to Australia. By 1959 both airlines were buying the same aircraft, with the Lockhead Electra going into service that year.[4]

The smaller airlines, such as Airlines WA and Queensland Airlines Limited (QAL), restricted themselves to a state or region. Despite the proliferation of airlines and routes the annual number of air passengers rarely rose above 50 000 per annum. Air travel continued to be a novelty for most Australians. A Queensland Airlines brochure from the mid-1950s explained that passengers were allowed to 'stroll about the cabin' except for take-off and landing, that there was no need to tip the staff, that meals would be served by the hostess, and that the only clothing you should wear was 'whatever you would wear if you were going for a drive in a sedan car'. The airlines guaranteed that you would be free from dust and grit, and that their Douglas Air Liners were insulated from noise. QAL offered twice- or thrice-weekly services between

Brisbane, Kingaroy, Monto, Thangool and Rockhampton, but did not fly on Sundays.[5]

The average aeroplane carried fewer than eight passengers, and fares were expensive, so most travellers were either on business or attending an important family event, such as a wedding or a funeral. In the 1950s families rarely travelled to tourist destinations by air. *Penrod's Guide to South Coast Queensland*, published in 1954, carried advertisements for bus lines operating between Brisbane, Southport, Surfers and Coolangatta and claimed that the resorts 'are all easily accessible by good roads'.[6] It also explained how to get to the region by rail, but nowhere in its 168 pages was there any mention of the tiny Coolangatta airport. Air travel simply did not matter. Fewer than 15 000 people a year used Coolangatta airport, while the local railway station handled many times that number.

Coolangatta got its first airstrip in 1936, on a tract of swampland a few kilometres out of town. The site chosen lay half in NSW and half in Queensland, with the unmarked state border dissecting the airfield. The airstrip, built as an emergency landing ground for craft flying between Sydney and Brisbane on the airmail service, housed a sanitary dump at its northern end. Unlike Brisbane, Townsville or Darwin, this airstrip was not upgraded as a base by US forces during World War II. Regular air services began again in 1947. Two years later a Lockheed Lodestar crashed at the airport, killing all eighteen passengers and three crew. Air crashes, especially at makeshift airstrips, were relatively common and fed understandable public fear of this new mode of transportation. The commonwealth Department of Transport extended the major gravel runway in 1950 and 1951, adding a weatherboard terminal.[7]

With the spectacular growth in car ownership in the 1950s, families began to go well beyond the cities and localities served by rail for their holidays. In every state they headed for the beach, which became the dominant holiday site and symbol of relaxation in the 1950s and 1960s. By 1960 the Queensland Government Tourist Bureau had taken to subtitling its *Guide to Queensland* 'The Sunshine State of Australia: a tourists' paradise'. The book explains that 'thousands of visitors come to

The lure of Queensland. The most lucrative domestic market in Australia remains the winter migration of Victorians to Queensland (Percy Trompf designed this poster for the Queensland Government Tourist Bureau as long ago as 1936).

Queensland each year to avoid the rigour of winter climes, for in this Sunshine State it's playtime all year round'. Queensland offered 'glorious surfing beaches' extending from Coolangatta to Mossman, while the 1250 miles of 'nature's masterpiece', the Great Barrier Reef, provided 'island-studded seaways with irresistible holiday appeal'. Instead of the one-line mention that Coolangatta received in a 1912 guidebook, we are introduced to The Gold Coast, 'the playground of Australia'.

Ansett Airlines, headquartered in Melbourne, promoted Queensland as quickly reached by air, and easy to get around. Ansett-ANA and Avis Rent-a-Car urged potential travellers:

> Speed to Queensland in the luxury of Ansett-ANA's Golden Jet service. You'll receive V.I.P. treatment and enjoy the finest service in the air . . .
> Fourteen airports throughout Queensland are served by Ansett-ANA . . . When you step off your plane, you can have a gleaming Avis car waiting and ready for you to drive as your own . . . Six ride as cheaply as one.

In another advertisement Ansett-ANA promised that their all-new Viscount IIs meant that the sun-drenched northern resorts and Barrier Reef Islands were 'just a few short hours away'.[8]

The aeroplane enabled people from the southern states, particularly Melbourne and Sydney, to head north for a one- or two-week holiday without spending most of that time on the road or in a train. By 1960, 60 000 passengers a year used the Coolangatta airport, but air travel to a beach holiday was still in its infancy. Despite Ansett's advertisements, most interstate travellers, especially from Sydney, still came by road or rail. The Queensland Tourist Bureau was quick to point out that rail links existed to all the other mainland capitals and that the diesel-engined 'Sunlander' took passengers the 1200 miles from Brisbane to Cairns in two days. Two fine coastal liners, the *Kanimbla* and the *Manoora*, still made regular sailings from Melbourne via Sydney and Brisbane to Cairns from May until September. The boats stayed in Cairns, the home port, for two or three days before starting south again. At each major port half-day or day trips could be arranged.

The Western Australian Government Tourist Bureau liked to remind T'othersiders that they could get to their Sunshine State by train, boat or plane (front cover, brochure 1954).

The federal government, the state governments and their tourist bureaus assumed that rail and even interstate sea travel would continue to grow, along with the cars and aeroplanes. In 1956 the Queensland government railways opened a grand new terminal in Cairns, and in the same year the commonwealth parliament agreed on the unification of Australian trunk railways. The following year work started on a standard gauge track from Wodonga to Melbourne to link up with the standard gauge to Sydney. On 3 January 1962 the standard gauge line was opened, and a couple of months later the Southern Aurora offered luxurious overnight transport between Sydney and Melbourne. The railways sought to emphasise their advantages over the airlines, with slogans like 'the railway is the safeway', and interstate rail travel looked set to continue as a major part of the Australian travel landscape. But by the late 1960s businesspeople had switched to the airlines because of both time and convenience, so that by the 1970s the interstate railways were the preserve of the young, students of all ages, poorer families who couldn't afford a car, and men and women who out of choice or necessity declined to drive.[9]

The closure of many rural passenger rail services, begun in the 1930s, proceeded in the 1950s and 1960s. Buses, sometimes run by the railways and sometimes by private companies, replaced trains on most rural routes, and services became less frequent—not least because growing car ownership meant that demand for rail trips fell precipitously. The intercapital rail passenger system survived, along with major freight lines. Suburban passenger lines continued to carry commuters in the mainland capital cities, but in an odd decision the Country Party government in Queensland decided to close the line to Southport in the early 1960s. The closure met with little opposition because most people were besotted with the road and the car. In 1964 the Albert Shire Council, 1300 square kilometres surrounding the city of the Gold Coast, offered its ratepayers a 'dream by-pass to the Pacific Highway' eliminating the 'Surfers Paradise bottlenecks'. The council promised that the by-pass would eventually become a four-lane highway, complete with 'picturesque floral avenues', along with 'Picturesque Motels', 'private enterprise Park and Gardens' and modern service stations.[10]

By 1990 the main passenger lines to survive were the major inter-capital routes. The number of country and interstate rail trips in Australia fell from 46 million in 1965 to just 10 million in 1990, of which six million were in Victoria. Here, rail services to nearby regional centres such as Geelong, Ballarat and Bendigo continued to be popular, not least because some of their inhabitants commuted to work in Melbourne. In Sydney the lines to Newcastle and Wollongong were upgraded, again catering for commuters. Traffic congestion and commuter demand from the spread of Brisbane forced the Queensland government to rebuild its south coast railway, serving the Gold Coast region, three decades after the original route had been torn up.

While rail lines closed and hundreds of country railway stations were abandoned or sold for new uses, the airline industry was busy lobbying for new and improved terminals. The extensive rail system of the inter-war years had comprised thousands of railway stations offering time-table advice and point-of-sale ticketing, but the airline industry and the federal government were quick to realise that only a handful of airports would be really important, including all the state capitals, plus regional airports in Tasmania (at Launceston) and Queensland.

The new terminals

On 30 March 1970 the Queen, Prince Philip, Prince Charles and Princess Anne landed at Sydney's Kingsford Smith Airport at Mascot to attend the Cook Bicentenary celebrations. Despite the red carpet, a run-down, almost makeshift airport greeted them, an old, 'overcrowded shed'. On the trip into the city not even the bunting could disguise the smell of decrepit tanneries and struggling shoe factories. On Sunday, 3 May 1970, the day the Queen concluded her tour, she opened the new Kingsford Smith International Terminal amid statistical hyperbole equal to that of a shopping mall launch.

The new terminal, with 37 000 square metres, was five times larger than the one it replaced. It provided separate levels for incoming and departing passengers, eliminating the congestion in the old shed. Twelve aircraft bays and seven aerobridges ensured that passengers would be under cover at all times. The terminal had been built on what would otherwise have been tarmac space, restricting future runway options. The car park offered 2500 parking places, while the terminal, mechanically ventilated and heated in winter, boasted restaurants, bar and lounges for travellers and friends. To get to the viewing area you had to go through a turnstile and pay five cents, a variant of the 'platform ticket' when seeing off friends or relatives at a 'country trains' terminal.[11]

While rail and road networks remained state responsibilities, the federal government had long had an interest in Australia's domestic and international air connections. It supervised the building of the Sydney terminal and paid for its construction, and the Department of Civil Aviation was responsible for its operation. The fees airlines paid for their planes to use the terminal barely covered operating costs, so in effect it was underwritten by Australian taxpayers in the interests of better national and international links. Both the Liberal/Country Party government and the Labor opposition supported these explicit subsidies to the aviation industry.

Airports not only have to cater for arrivals and departures but, in the case of international terminals, for customs and excise. Until 1962 Australians leaving to travel overseas even had to get a tax clearance. As soon as the terminal opened, the press questioned whether it was big enough to fulfil the requirements of the next decade. At the time the federal government could have purchased adjoining land for a terminal, but chose not to. The *Sydney Morning Herald*'s aeronautical correspondent, Jack Percival, told his readers that

> aviation travel is bursting its seams. With jumbo jets, and airliners even bigger just around the corner, there is in sight the tapping of a great, new potential—the ordinary man in a supersonic transport may soon be able to afford to fly to any part of the world from Sydney within 12 hours.

Percival pointed out that around the world 'there is a mad scramble to build terminals', and that the $31 million spent on Sydney's new terminal was small compared with the $150 million being spent on new ones overseas. He noted that while fifteen foreign airlines had landing rights at Kingsford Smith, twenty-seven served Hong Kong. And he reported the Australian Tourism Commission's prediction that the 380 000 visitors by air in 1969 would almost double to 700 000 by 1975. Percival saw Sydney as a 'natural springboard' for the Pacific and the Americas, and also observed that the potential Asian market 'is just being tapped'.[12]

All the airlines benefited from glamorous new check-in counters, but Sydney's new international terminal had one big disadvantage: it was a couple of kilometres away from Ansett and TAA's domestic terminals. With three separate terminals on the one site, and with limited room for expansion on what would otherwise have been tarmac space, airline congestion continued to worsen. Residents in nearby suburbs had put up with aircraft noise for years, but jets were much noisier than propeller aircraft, and the number of take-offs and landings grew inexorably.

The new Tullamarine terminal in Melbourne had none of these disadvantages, as—at a cost of $50 million—it included within its three-pronged plan domestic terminals for both Ansett and TAA and an international terminal in the middle, all under the one roof. Built on 2150 hectares of open country north-west of central Melbourne, Tullamarine had none of the heavy land reclamation costs associated with Kingsford Smith, which even then amounted to only 650 hectares. Tullamarine had the added benefit of a $30 million freeway, paid for by the state government, linking it with the city 20 kilometres away. The Tullamarine airport superseded the 320-hectare Essendon airport. Sydney, with much more constrained topography, had no obvious alternative to Mascot other than metropolitan fringe sites that seemed remote from the city centre and the business enclaves of the North Shore and the eastern suburbs.[13]

Despite catering for both international and domestic flights, Tullamarine was exactly one-third smaller than the Kingsford Smith terminal, reflecting Sydney's already established dominance in international arrivals and departures. But with such a large site, and without the reclamation constraints at Mascot, Tullamarine proved not only a more efficient airport, but one that could be more readily and more cheaply expanded than Kingsford Smith.

The Minister for Civil Aviation, Senator Cotton, regarded the federal government's $50 million investment in Tullamarine as 'a sound invest-ment in keeping Australia's place high on the list in the air transport world'. The Minister for Works, Senator Wright, said the airport 'will help ensure Australia's position among the world leaders in aviation'. Both men reflected the legacy of Menzies' belief in major government capital investment for the national interest, including the construction of airports in a nation so large and so distant from the rest of the world that airports represented a very special form of national lifeline, as did Qantas, the 'national flag carrier'.[14]

The one big gateway

Kingsford Smith and Tullamarine represented twin gateways to the world. The only other international ports in Australia at that time were Perth and Darwin. Sydney had long been the main international gateway to Australia, even before the new terminal was completed. In 1965/66 Sydney had 424 224 international passengers arriving and departing, whereas Melbourne had 42 447, a mere 10 per cent of Sydney's total. The opening of Tullamarine saw its potential expand dramatically, so that a decade later, in 1975–76, Melbourne's share had risen to slightly more than a third of Sydney's.

On the domestic front the two airports drew closer and closer together, not least because of Tullamarine's greater capacity in terms of take-offs, landings and opening hours. Without Mascot's 11 p.m. to 6 a.m. curfew, Tullamarine could offer overnight services to Western Australia and North Queensland that were simply not available from Mascot.

In both domestic and international travel, the coming of wide-bodied aircraft more than doubled the capacity of the major domestic and inter-national carriers over a very short period of time. It also reduced the number of international airports that mattered. Before the coming of the 747, with its capacity to fly direct from Sydney or Melbourne to Asia, both Perth and Darwin were regular stopping places for jet travel to Asia and Europe.

In 1972 Qantas introduced its first Boeing 747 service from Australia to the USA with one stop. Four years later, in December 1976, Pan Am inaugurated the world's longest non-stop service, from Sydney to San Francisco, with Boeing B747SPs. At last the age of high-capacity air travel had arrived. The 747s, which could carry up to 400 (more than twice as many as the 707), also allowed a range of fares from glamorous first class seating (some of it in the 'big top') to heavily discounted economy tickets. With a wide variety of fares, often requiring advance purchase, the airlines could match demand with supply, creating an optimum payload.

Nevertheless an age of supersonic mass travel did not eventuate. The British–French Concorde made some proving flights to Australia in 1975 but, with its limited seating, high fuel costs and noise, it was never going to be an economic proposition for other than the US–Europe link. The Australian trade simply did not command either the numbers or the wealth of the North Atlantic market, so the Concorde stayed in the northern hemisphere.[15]

The number of people coming to Australia by air had increased from 93 000 in 1960 to 530 000 in 1970, then to two million in 1980 and over four million in 1990. Almost half of these were, of course, Australian residents returning, but the other half were international tourists. Most, with the notable exception of backpackers, came on trips lasting no more than one month. As the majority of international travellers had taken many hours to get here—Europeans and Americans regularly complained about the flights—the prospect of flying even long distances within Australia was not at all offputting, especially as many visitors got reduced internal airfares as part of their package.

The airline resorts

With the development of the two-airline agreement and the growing appetite for travel, both Ansett-ANA and TAA began to court the holiday market, as distinct from business travel and air freight, which had been their mainstay. Ansett was the first Australian airline to follow the

Table 3   International passenger embarkations and disembarkations
            1965–1976

	Sydney	*Melbourne*
1965–66	424 224	42 447
1966–67	483 935	46 606
1967–68	593 046	48 646
1968–69	680 509	51 824
1969–70	824 000	60 475
1970–71	874 575	155 275
1971–72	1 000 639	225 733
1972–73	1 182 273	331 959
1973–74	1 407 374	459 796
1974–75	1 553 528	498 470
1975–76	1 722 596	612 031

Source: ABS, *Rail, Bus & Air Transport*; ABS, *Transport & Communication Bulletin*.

precedent set by the railways and take serious steps to become a provider of resort settings and accommodation as well as of transport. TAA
was hampered, in the first instance, because the Act that established it
prohibited the airline from owning accommodation sites or other forms
of transport.

In September 1947 Reg Ansett wrote to the Queensland Minister for
Health and Home Affairs, Arthur Jones, explaining Ansett's three-stage
tourism programme.

> Initially our attention was necessarily concentrated upon designing and
> providing a fleet of vehicles that would meet the demands not only of
> Australian tourists but of the most exacting of overseas tourists . . . Our
> next step was to obtain an improvement of the standard of accommo-
> dation offered by hotels on the routes on which we operate . . . To this
> end we have secured some twenty freeholds or leases . . . With these
> projects well underway it has been possible to turn our attention to the
> third and highly important phase of our planning—the development of
> certain islands within the Great Barrier Reef. We have, in the past six
> months, both from the air and sea, made a most intensive survey of the
> islands of the Whitsunday group . . .[16]

Table 4   Domestic passenger embarkations and disembarkations
1965–1976

	Sydney	*Melbourne*
1965–66	2 244 218	1 748 478
1966–67	2 435 284	1 880 860
1967–68	2 641 147	2 043 542
1968–69	2 933 795	2 278 032
1969–70	3 390 322	2 603 320
1970–71	3 515 231	2 750 602
1971 72	3 694 498	2 861 896
1972–73	4 162 659	3 226 294
1973–74	4 679 513	3 879 877
1974–75	4 953 051	4 037 585
1975–76	4 788 086	4 125 932

Source: ABS, *Transport and Communication Bulletin*.

Ansett Transport Industries Ltd formed a subsidiary, Barrier Reef
Islands Pty Ltd, to purchase the leases for Daydream and Hayman islands
in the Whitsundays group, while another subsidiary, Pioneer Tourist
Hotels Pty Ltd, took charge of resort operation. Construction began
on the Royal Hayman Hotel, aimed at wealthy Australian and overseas
tourists. Opening in June 1950, it offered thirty luxurious sleeping
lodges, each consisting of two self-contained private suites, along with
'sewered toilets' and a private veranda. The main building housed a
lounge, a dining room, a bar, a cabaret and a cocktail bar, where guests
could dine, dance or chat. The hotel also offered a beauty salon, barber,
shop, sports kit shop, confectionery bar, florist, paper shop and swimming pool—a real novelty on an island surrounded by tropical beaches.

All this was a far cry from the other island 'resorts', including South
Molle, Brampton, Lindeman and Long Island, which had been actively
marketed by the Queensland Government Tourist Bureau from the mid-
1930s. South Molle offered fibro cabins, but the toilets were in an ablu-
tion block just like those in a camping ground. Compared to the Royal
Hayman, South Molle was primitive. The advice on what to take included an electric torch, not least to find your way to the toilet at night.

Tobacco, soft drink, sweets, curios, films and liquor could be purchased at the island store.[17]

The Queensland Government Tourist Bureau welcomed Ansett's £500 000 investment in Hayman Island, among the first of a series of major developments that would alter Queensland's coastal and island landscapes forever. The Proserpine Shire Council partly financed the island's jetty, while the Tourist Bureau reduced its commission on bookings from 10 to 5 per cent because of the size of Ansett's investment and the airline's advertising campaigns. The other Whitsunday islands received no such largesse; indeed the owner of South Molle was unable to secure council support for a badly needed jetty.

Despite government backing, the Royal Hayman lost money in its early years. Reg Ansett told the *Proserpine Guardian* that 'the tourists had not materialised in sufficient numbers, and that even Australians who could well afford to pay for luxuries had been scared lest the "Continental touches" should require "socialite formality" when they wanted to relax'. The tariff was halved and the establishment eventually began to show a profit. Ansett's Daydream Island investment, a more modest resort, ran into even more trouble than the Royal Hayman. Closed in 1952, Daydream remained dormant until rebuilt in 1968. Ansett Transport Industries had no difficulty in absorbing such losses, because the government's two-airline policy virtually guaranteed the profitability of the airline, which could then cross-subsidise the company's more speculative ventures. While nominally committed to private enterprise and market competition, the Menzies government actually presided over a highly regulated airline environment, in much the same way as it handed out television licences to media companies, all of whom had close links to the Liberal Party. Indeed, Ansett Transport Industries itself also had television interests.

Stimulated by the eventual success of the Royal Hayman and a gradual growth in air travel, the other Whitsunday resorts, especially South Molle and Lindeman, began to upgrade their accommodation. Later, in the 1950s, Lindeman's Air Services offered direct flights from Mackay to the island's grass airstrip. Even so, by the late 1950s all the islands

Marketing of the Gold Coast, especially in Victoria, emphasised the ready
availability of women, men, fun and classy hotels, just a few hours away by air
(TAA poster featuring Lennon's Broadbeach Hotel, 1964).

put together were only attracting between 15 000 and 20 000 resident guests per annum. Nonetheless holidaymakers liked the islands, and the importance of air travel to Australia's biggest collection of island resorts was plain for all to see.[18]

The message was not lost on TAA, Ansett's government-owned competitor. TAA had 'developed an image of dependable, friendly efficiency which appealed to business travellers', well captured in its classic hostess poster. Ansett, on the other hand, had developed a progressive holiday outlook, and its posters emphasised exotic island locations. Under pressure from Ansett Airlines and Ansett's Pioneer 'super clipper' coach services, as well as from a revitalised railway industry busily investing in new sleeping cars, TAA called a senior management conference in 1959 to establish a Travel Service Section, to tell customers that the airline offered holiday travel as well as freight and business travel. In developing its own accommodation-based resorts and creating links with other accommodation-providers, TAA had to be careful not to offend the state government tourist bureaus and the travel agents, who by 1960 numbered over 500, compared with TAA's twenty-nine booking offices.

TAA availed itself of the package services already provided by the state tourist bureaus, while also developing its own prestige tours. In 1961 TAA's unique Women's Travel Advisory Section, promoted through talks to women's groups, developed fully escorted tours to North Queensland, Tasmania, Central Australia and Papua New Guinea. The following year TAA offered a tour to the British Empire and Commonwealth Games in Perth, and low-cost package promotions to the Gold Coast, entailing discounts on both the airfares and the accommodation. TAA aimed to break down the belief that air travel was expensive and only for the well-off, launching its 'Fly Away Holiday' campaign in 1963 with a new range of posters, along with display stands and brochure racks.

With the continuing expansion of car ownership, some commentators wondered whether the airlines' traffic would grow sharply or remain relatively static. Road improvements did not keep pace with the proliferation of cars: to drive from Sydney or Melbourne to North Queensland remained a big undertaking. Even to drive from Brisbane could be problematical, as the *Bulletin* informed its readers in August 1964:

> It is a hell of a trip if you don't want to waste time getting there. The chances of reaching Hayman's airport town, Proserpine, with your original windscreen intact are remote if you travel more than 40 mph and like to keep all four wheels on the bitumen. The main Bruce Highway, north of Bundaberg, sports twin broad shoulders of assorted loose gravel, pebbles, stones and small rocks for more than 400 miles . . .[19]

While the Bruce Highway, completed in 1962, allegedly offered an all-bitumen surface from Brisbane to Cairns, road conditions and travel times were such that it was simply not feasible to travel from Melbourne or Sydney to North Queensland for any holiday of less than two weeks duration without spending over half the time on the road. Even by air the trip to the Whitsundays from the southern states remained time-consuming until the introduction of DC9s in the late 1960s. Before then many 'package dealers' came on night flights in Fokkers to Mackay or Proserpine, thence on a rough launch trip from Shute Harbour to arrive at dawn at their destination. At Hayman Island they were greeted by a gaily decorated train, while at some of the other islands they had to walk to their accommodation.

From the mid-1960s to late in the decade most of the islands that did not boast airstrips built helicopter landing pads, but the cost of operating such services saw many of them phased out. Launch and ferry travel, like the regular services between Townsville and Magnetic Island, is again promoted as the carefree start to an island holiday, as it was in the 1930s.

Following on Ansett's renewed marketing of its resorts, TAA took a close interest in the development of a major resort at Brampton Island, being undertaken by the successful owners of the Roylen boating firm. Seventeen miles off the coast of Mackay, Brampton was hard to get to, and until the completion of the jetty in 1966 passengers had to leave their launch and hop into a dinghy to reach the shore. TAA, pursuing its package tour aims, built its own airstrip on the island.

With Brampton and the development of Great Keppel Island off Rockhampton, TAA had armed itself with some glamorous resorts. Destination selling became the core of its marketing campaign. Promotional manuals were produced for travel agents, and in 1968 the commission on package holidays was increased from 5 to 10 per cent. In 1963/64 travel agents wrote only 5 per cent of TAA's holiday travel; by 1968/69 they wrote over 40 per cent.[20]

One of the hallmarks of resort development is that lessees and proprietors are forever having to upgrade their facilities to keep pace with both consumer expectations and changing fashions. In the 1960s all the Whitsunday Island resorts installed swimming pools. A 1966 report on the Queensland islands remarked that pools were becoming an 'essential amenity' even where sea bathing was readily available. Travel brochures increasingly showed that resort accommodation offered both pool and ocean bathing. The pool, surrounded by landscaped tropical gardens, provided a setting for drinking, swimming and socialising, while the beach and the sea were reserved for romantic forays or real oceanic experiences. A 1966 brochure for Hayman Island told visitors that 'exciting lounges, bars, secluded hideaways, the sparkling Hollywood pool and sun terraces are all yours to share with happy holiday makers'.

A choice of waters: purpose-built pools at the Hayman Island resort, self-proclaimed on a 1995 postcard as 'One of The Leading Hotels of the World'.

The trend for resorts to be purchased by other than local operators, who were usually responsible for the initial holiday installation, continued into the 1970s. P & O Australia Ltd purchased Lindeman Island in 1979, the same year that Gold Coast entrepreneur Keith Williams began construction of a new resort on Hamilton Island. With a fondness for white shoes, he became one of the original members of the 'white shoe brigade', a group of 'can-do' Queensland property developers. Many of them went bankrupt in the property crash of the early 1990s.[21]

But in the 1980s, both Ansett and TAA continued to develop their resorts. By the time Qantas purchased Australian Airlines (as TAA had become known) in 1992, the company's resorts on Great Keppel, Brampton, Dunk, Bedarra and Lizard Islands offered 504 rooms, their room sales in 1994/95 representing 20 per cent of the 620 000 room sales by all island resorts off the Queensland coast. The level of facilities, options and cuisine continued to rise. Dunk Island offered sailing, tennis, squash, volleyball, fishing, snorkelling, cricket, badminton, basketball, paddle-skis, golf, horse-riding, water-skiing, skeet shooting and archery, with live music every night and a 'Kid's Korner' for supervised daytime activities. At last resorts were offering even more activities than the grandest ship could ever boast, but if you didn't like the organised activities you could retire to an uncrowded beach where you would not be disturbed. Qantas, which made most of its money from larger-bodied aircraft flights to the major ports of Townsville and Cairns, rather than on flights to resort islands, decided, in 1996, to sell the properties and focus on its core business.[22]

Jet travel not only brought the Queensland island resorts within easy reach of the Sydney and Melbourne markets, but it also made a variety of otherwise inaccessible destinations available to both domestic and international tourists. Apart from Darwin and North Queensland, the most spectacular growth occurred in central Australia (both Alice Springs and Yulara have jet airports) and in the northern WA coastal town of Broome. Before World War II Broome was the centre of a lucrative pearling industry, and at its height had a population of 4000. As it was not connected by rail, travellers had either to sail from Fremantle or, by the 1920s, take a two-day aeroplane trip from Perth, only available on a Saturday. Attacked by the Japanese air force during the war, the town fell on hard times, with the population dropping to well below a thousand.

By the mid-1960s the town population had increased slightly to 1600, but accommodation could only be found in two ageing hotels, the Continental and the Roebuck Bay, or in the local caravan park, which had only one caravan for hire. It took about seven hours in a MacRobertson Miller DC3 Fokker or Fokker Friendship to get from Perth to Broome. The Western Australian Tourist Development Authority's brochure outlined the places of interest as the meatworks, the deep water jetty, the 'oriental and Japanese' section of the cemetery and two local missions to the Aborigines. The Authority also pointed to 'glorious white sandy beaches which are thoroughly cleaned twice daily by the tide—the rise and fall being 28 feet'.[23]

Non-stop jet services to Broome were introduced in the 1970s, by which time travellers from Perth could get there in under three hours. In 1984 Brian Burke, Premier of Western Australia and Minister for Tourism, pointed to the importance of both air travel and sealed all-weather roads in aiding the tourist boom in the north of his state. Modern hotels, motels, self-contained units and caravan parks offering chalet accommodation tempted the visitor. By the late 1980s the population had surpassed its pre-war peak and Lord McAlpine, a British property entrepreneur, embarked on his Cable Beach Resort. Much of it was built in an elegant pastiche of an oriental style. With four restaurants, four bars, two swimming pools, eight tennis courts, a coffee shop, children's playground, outdoor spa and conference centre, Cable Beach Resort, on a beachside setting with 10 hectares of gardens—which originally included a zoo—marketed itself as a destination in its own right. The township of Broome became the exotic backdrop to the resort proper. Both Qantas and Ansett produce brochures devoted to Broome, offering domestic and international tourists three-, five- and seven-day packages. Tourism has replaced the pearl industry as the principal motor of the Broome economy.[24]

But, like the pearl industry, tourism is very sensitive to economic conditions. Broome, together with the Queensland resorts, suffered badly during the 1989 airline pilot strike. And, as with Cairns and the Queensland island resorts, any deterioration in the general economy sees a rapid fall in travel bookings. In a short space of time resorts can go from being crowded and carefree to becoming abandoned-looking, more like film sets than places where people live or holiday.

Terminal destinations

With the inexorable growth in tourist numbers, Sydney International Airport has seen a spate of hotel-building within a couple of kilometres of the tarmac. The airport has started to take on some of the characteristics of traditional shipping ports. Freight forwarders and warehouses have replaced recently abandoned industrial sites. The Sydney Airport Hilton, opened in the 1970s, was an early foray into this territory, as was the Tullamarine Travelodge. The two premises nicely summarise the attitudes of the two cities to their airports. The Sydney Airport Hilton offered spacious grounds surrounded by a golf course; the Melbourne Travelodge was an outsized suburban motel structure surrounded by car parks. By the early 1990s Mascot housed a Sheraton and a Parkroyal, which became conference venues in themselves, as well as handy accommodation for businesspeople landing late or leaving early. These newer hotels, and attendant courier company and freight offices surrounding Mascot, have given Australia's most frequented airport the appearance of a mini-city. All of the other major airports remain as freestanding terminals on ample sites. One of them, Coolangatta, is only a few minutes walk from the beach.

The worsening congestion at Mascot Airport, compounded by the fact that from the 1970s it began to take on the 'hub airport' role so common in the USA, led the federal and state governments to embark on a series of environmental and air traffic studies to augment the take-off and landing capacity of the airport. For the next twenty years the major political parties, at both state and federal elections, attempted to blame each other for the congestion at Mascot and the growing volume of aircraft noise. With only two runways, and uncertain wind conditions, the airport had to offer a number of different flight paths, especially at peak times. More and more households found themselves under one of these flight paths, so that aircraft noise was no longer confined to nearby suburbs.

After eventually building a third runway, followed by a series of rowdy protests that closed the airport, the federal government resumed over 200 houses where the noise levels exceeded World Health Organization standards. Aircraft noise remains a big political issue.[25]

The growing demands on Australia's air terminals continue to test both the capacity of the runways and the efficiency with which they load and unload passengers. All the major terminals embarked on an expansion programme in the 1990s, as ambitious as the building of Mascot and the Tullamarine international terminal in the late 1960s. Brisbane opened a new international terminal in 1995, and both Tullamarine and Mascot underwent vast expansion in 1996 and 1997. Sydney continues to have three major terminals, two domestic (Ansett and Qantas) and one international. Motor traffic congestion at Sydney's domestic terminals proved so bad that in 1998–99 a suspended roadway was built to separate, as at Tullamarine, departing passengers from arrivals. The construction of a railway line to Sydney's domestic and international terminals, opened in time for the Olympics, lessened congestion and made Sydney the only Australian airport with a rapid public transport link with the city centre.

Faced with an ever-increasing demand for more space, and an alleged shortage of government capital funds, the Federal Airports Corporation (FAC) has progressively been privatising its major airports on 99-year leasing terms, with Melbourne, Brisbane and Perth the first to go. There is a striking similarity here with the relationship between the airlines and holiday resorts. The airlines, including the government-owned TAA, built and operated the resorts, but after a couple of decades decided to sell the plant. The FAC, having inherited the airfields and the plant from the old Department of Civil Aviation, is now doing much the same.[26]

Just as air terminals have been disposed of—to insurance companies including AMP, and overseas airport operators—so too have the airlines themselves. News Ltd and Thomas Nationwide Transport purchased Ansett Airlines in 1980, with News Ltd selling its stake to Air New Zealand in the mid-1990s. By the the year 2000 Air New Zealand owned the lot. Of greater symbolic significance, 25 per cent of Qantas was sold, by the Keating Labor government in 1995, to British Airways. The other main bidder, Singapore Airlines, was discouraged from pursuing its bid. It is ironical to contemplate a republican Australia where the British have control of our major international carrier, Qantas.

Until the mid-1960s Australia's major airports were modest affairs— a few hangars, a couple of hundred parking spaces, parking meters within walking distance of the terminals. Today every major airport boasts multi-level parking, bus station facilities, valet parking for the tax-deductible traveller, and an ever-increasing array of goods, services, shops and eateries.

By the 1990s there was a sense in which the air terminals had become resorts/shopping centres/meeting places in their own right. The airline clubs of the 1980s, catering for regular passengers—predominantly business people and senior public servants—had proved so popular that they needed to be expanded and upgraded every few years. They developed extensive food and beverage areas (although alcohol is unavailable until the genteel hour of 3 p.m.) and ever-improved business and meeting facilities, including fax, e-mail, telephone, photocopying and secretarial services. These clubs charge an annual membership fee, but their real role is not to cover costs but to create passenger loyalty in the high-yield business and government market. Children are tolerated but not encouraged. Frequent flyer schemes have also been developed to encourage loyalty both in business travellers and among holidaymakers. As the latter are unable to tax-deduct their fares, the prospect of 'free' reward flights is a real incentive to choose one airline instead of another.

Air travel did not become the dominant mode of international travel until the 1960s, and it will never become the dominant mode of holiday travel in Australia because the car will remain cheaper and more flexible, especially for families. Interstate domestic business travel is another mat-ter. The exclusive 'captains clubs' that cater for elite business people, the upper echelons of the public service and politicians, have already replaced parliamentary lobbies as the site of deal-making.

In the air and in the terminals, business travel and tourist travel have become inextricably linked. Although air travel is still primarily about getting to a destination, the nature and intent of the main airline desti-nations metamorphose over time. Island resorts remain island resorts, but they cater for business conventions as well as holidaymakers. Our giant air terminals have themselves become business and tourist destina-tions, offering better booking services under the one roof than many travel agents can offer. The aeroplane now accounts for almost all travel between Australia and the rest of the world. Many of the airlines may remain national flag-carriers—Qantas still calls Australia home—but their multinational ownership has ruptured almost any sense of locality inherited from our pioneers of aviation.

The Tourism Industry

THE DRAMATIC GROWTH of domestic tourism in the 1950s and early 1960s, when rising car ownership brought more and more destinations within reach of city-dwellers, meant that tourism finally came to be recognised as an 'industry'. Charles Holmes, Managing Director of the Australian National Travel Association (ANTA), had been telling governments and tourist operators that for decades. The state governments, with their railways and their tourist bureaus, had long recognised it. So had the airlines, shipping companies and big city hotels. But for the commonwealth government to take tourism seriously, rather than as a hidden industry, was a new development. On Holmes' retirement in 1957 Basil Atkinson, a former RAAF pilot who had been a journalist in Perth and London, took over as manager of ANTA. Along with his chairman, John Bates, he managed to persuade the commonwealth government to set up an interdepartmental committee in Canberra to determine how tourism should be handled. They obtained the support of Prime Minister Menzies on the condition that all states and territories would work through ANTA as a single national voice.

A new series of advertising campaigns was promptly developed. Using its reopened San Francisco office as a base, ANTA began with 'Come to the Sou'West Pacific', aimed at American servicemen who had served in the Pacific. The campaign flopped. Instead of nostalgic South Seas memories, it got war veterans thinking of mosquitoes and wartime experiences they would rather forget. ANTA adopted other

The necessary adaptability of the souvenir industry. The First & Last Store in Australia operated near the Fremantle wharf.

tactics to woo the American market. Miss USA, a 23-year-old Mormon from Salt Lake City, toured the country for ten days in 1959, pictured with koalas, kangaroos, and the Sydney Harbour Bridge. Apart from her looks, her other claim to fame was that she had never been kissed, making her ideal for promoting Australia as a safe, friendly environment, where Americans already knew the language and the only challenges would be the accent, driving on the other side of the road, and cuddling koalas in the safety of a zoo.[1]

On the other side of the Pacific, the United States Department of Commerce commissioned a report on the future of tourism in the Pacific and the Far East. Published in 1961, it reported that Hawaii, Hong Kong and Japan had over three times the tourist business of the other fifteen main tourist destinations. After Hawaii, Japan and Hong Kong attracted two-thirds of all travellers, Australia drew 12 per cent, New Zealand 5 per cent and Singapore 4 per cent. The report found that Australia received only 60 000 international tourists per annum, of whom 47 000 came from the British Commonwealth and only 6400 from the

USA. Nevertheless, because the Department could 'sense in the Australian economy the kind of dynamic, embryonic situation that existed in the United States only a few years ago', it concluded that Australia had enormous tourist potential and that a modest increase in government spending on tourism could see visitor numbers treble by 1968.[2]

The Department of Commerce estimated that Australia earned $25 million per annum from international tourists, while Australians going overseas spent $62 million. It pointed out that an increase in tourists would be a vital source of foreign exchange in a country that 'suffers from chronic imbalance between imports and exports and is harassed by shifts in wool prices'. Echoing this analysis, ANTA published a booklet in 1962 called *The Case of the Missing £20,* the imbalance between what foreign visitors spent in Australia and what Australians spent overseas. ANTA pointed to irksome visa procedures and the need for foreigners to get an income tax clearance before leaving Australia as just two of the many impediments to an increase in the number of international tourists. Further echoing the US Commerce report, which estimated a multiplier effect of tourists in the general economy at 3.2, ANTA hoped that visitor numbers would double every few years. At the time this seemed like pie in the sky.

ANTA prevailed on Menzies to open the 1964 Pacific Area Travel Association Conference in Sydney. Menzies hailed tourism as a 'smoke-less industry', creating employment and income without being harmful to people's lives. Despite this, the federal government's financial contribution to ANTA remained modest, while extracting contributions from its 352 members—from travel agents to shipping companies—was no easy task. Atkinson realised that a loosely structured body like ANTA would be hard put to promote Australia as a tourist destination against competitors like France and Hawaii, places with well-developed tourist accommodation, huge advertising budgets, and instantly recognisable images such as the Eiffel Tower and Waikiki Beach.

With the federal government's blessing, ANTA commissioned two New York firms, one of chartered accountants and the other a consultancy company dealing in transportation, tourist and recreation development, to survey the state of the tourism industry in Australia and to recommend future directions. Their 250 000-word report, presented to ANTA in 1965 and published in 1966, remains the most substantial stocktake ever undertaken of Australian tourism, from transport and accommodation to taxation, organisation and sources of finance. It also contemplated, albeit briefly, the 'place' of Aborigines in Australia's tourist programme.

The New York consultants recommended the creation of an Australian national travel authority, which would incorporate ANTA's publicity role, providing 'effective promotion' for overseas visitors, but would also co-ordinate the planned development of travel attractions and facilities through its 'Internal Development Division'. This new body would be financed by the Commonwealth, the states, the territories and private industry. The commonwealth government's banking and taxing powers should be used to support this 'development industry', including a company tax concession of up to 50 per cent to encourage investment in 'accommodations and facilities'.[3]

The commonwealth government created the Australian Tourist Commission (ATC) in May 1967. As a statutory authority with an opening budget of $1.5 million, it had more power than ANTA, but its actual brief, to encourage 'visitors to Australia, and travel within Australia, by people from other countries', was narrow, having none of the infrastructure and responsibility for facilities suggested by the New York consultants. These matters remained in the hands of state governments and private industry.

The ATC took over all the staff and assets of ANTA, including the head office in Melbourne and its overseas branches. Many in the travel industry feared that the new body would end up 'over promoting an underdeveloped product', so the previous ANTA board reassembled itself to promote domestic tourism. It continued to publish *Walkabout* magazine, which took on a much more parochial air. ANTA moved its headquarters to Sydney, to distinguish itself from the Melbourne-based ATC.

The ATC moved quickly to capitalise on established markets, including New Zealand, where an advertising campaign pointed out that New

Zealanders could happily survive in Australia on their overseas travel allowance of $14 per day (currency restrictions were still enforced at this time). The Commission also established an office in Tokyo and planned promotions for Japan, Hong Kong and the Philippines, along with targeting the American market, not least because over a quarter of a million American soldiers chose Australia as their R&R (rest and recreation) venue during the Vietnam War.

A review of the ATC conducted by McKinsey and Company in 1969 found too much emphasis on publicity and promotion, along ANTA lines, and not enough on an overall marketing approach. They recommended more staff, an increased budget, and moving the headquarters from Melbourne to Sydney, to forge closer relationships with ANTA, Qantas, and the NSW Government Travel Bureau. By then Mascot was already emerging as Australia's pre-eminent international airport.

The move to Sydney was not to take place till 1987. Forty of the forty-four Melbourne staff then took redundancy packages and a new Sydneycentric organisation emerged with younger staff and close links to PATA, ATIA, and the Australian and Sydney convention bureaus, all of which were located in the same building. The locus of power in Australian tourism had moved irrevocably to Sydney, a power shift confirmed by Sydney's emergence as the pre-eminent financial centre.[4]

The establishment of an office in Japan occurred just four years after the Tokyo Olympics. Government restrictions there on overseas pleasure trips (as distinct from business trips), were finally lifted, coinciding with the meteoric rise of Australian exports to Japan. Australia's early efforts to attract Japanese holidaymakers revealed real difficulties in accommodation and transport. Most Japanese, even honeymooners, usually wanted to travel in groups. They expected guides who could speak Japanese, and fast, modern coaches to pick them up from the airport and take them from place to place. Such facilities were to be found in American destinations like Hawaii and Disneyland, but were hard to come by in Australia in the 1960s. Then new hotels started to sprout in Sydney and Melbourne, and tour operators began to take Japanese wants seriously.

By the late 1970s marketing in Japan concentrated on target groups, such as 'office ladies' (young women working in offices), young single males, honeymooners, and sports fans. Double-page advertisements emphasised scenery, sports, and the Australian way of life. Promotions, which sometimes took place in hotels and department stores, emphasised that Australia as a holiday destination cost about the same as the west coast of the USA and considerably less than travelling to Europe. Australia, in a similar time zone, could be reached in one eight-hour hop. And once Federal Treasurer Keating had allowed the Australian dollar to float in December 1983, the stronger yen meant that Australia became ever cheaper as a holiday destination. Japanese tourism to Australia increased from 5400 in 1967 to 24 100 in 1975, doubling in the five years to 1980, then accelerating to 479 900 in 1990 and 766 600 in 1996.[5]

Japanese tourists ockerising themselves in North Queensland.

The American campaign

The impact of the ATC, and the size of its budget, has varied according to the seniority of the Minister responsible for it, and on the general standing of the tourism industry with the government of the day. The Whitlam Labor government, with its Coombs Task Force on government expenditure (1973) and its subsequent Royal Commission on Australian Government Administration, was not keen on the ATC. Whitlam took a close interest in particular heritage sites and environmental issues, especially in the handover of Ayers Rock to the Central Australian Reserves Board, but had little interest in tourism *per se*. The ATC's budget, at just over $3 million for staff and promotion, did not even keep pace with inflation. General Manager Basil Atkinson left the ATC and headed for the Bahamas, where the government tourist authority had an annual budget of $14 million.[6]

In 1975 visitor arrivals from the USA fell by 16 per cent, a disastrous decline in a market that had been growing steadily for years. Australian travel-sellers were flown to the USA to create personal links with their American counterparts. In 1979/80 $1.3 million was allocated to woo the American consumer market. Colleen McCullough's *The Thorn Birds* had taken the Americans by storm, so print advertisements featured her promoting adventure tourism. Fifty American travel agents and 100 journalists were sponsored to visit Australia, helped by the restoration of a more favourable rate of exchange. These campaigns worked, creating a steady increase in new arrivals.

During the 1983 election campaign both Andrew Peacock, leader of the Liberal Party, and John Brown, ALP shadow minister for tourism, promised more funding for the ATC. With the election of the Hawke Labor government Brown presided over a new Department of Sport, Recreation and Tourism, reflecting not only his own interests but the sport- and image-conscious politics of Hawke. Soon after the election, Paul Hogan, an actor–comedian (formerly a rigger on the Sydney Harbour Bridge) with his own television show, complained to Brown about the lack of knowledge of Australia overseas. Brown, who on a visit to Disneyland in 1977 had found Australia represented by a kangaroo and a koala, concurred. Brown attacked the koala image, complaining about the animals 'piddling'. In 1983/84 the commonwealth government granted the ATC a budget of $19.5 million, the most dramatic increase in federal support ever.

The grant included a special $2 million to exploit *Australia II*'s victory in the America's Cup in September 1983, the first time a non-US boat had won. Hawke, ecstatic at the victory, told a national television audience that any employer who sacked a staff member for not turning up at work the next day was 'a bum'. Hawke was happy to go along with Brown's recommendation of a Hogan TV advertising campaign, aimed at both US and Australian audiences. The local campaign aimed at making Australians take tourism as an industry seriously, and encouraging them to be friendly to visitors. One ad showed Hogan and other well-known Australians on poolside lounge chairs working 'flat out for their country'. Another ad asked Australians to 'Show 'em your pearly whites', taking its cue from the American tradition of 'welcome-wagon' hospitality.

The North American campaign, which built on the success of movies such as *Gallipoli*, showed Hogan throwing another 'shrimp' on the barbie, with the backdrop of Sydney Harbour. While all this was paid advertising, the increasing importance of special events and major events tourism was brought home to Australians during the America's Cup defence on home turf, at Fremantle, in 1987. Bryant Gumbel and Jane Pauley, the hosts of the world's most-watched breakfast TV show, *Today*, broadcast from Fremantle to more than fifteen million viewers in the USA. The cost of equivalent advertising would have been $30 million. The ATC placed advertisements during the five telecasts and got hundreds of thousands of responses.

In 1983 John Brown, as Minister for Sport, Recreation and Tourism, boldly predicted that Australia would attract over two million overseas tourists during the bicentennial year. When, in 1984, Australia attracted one million tourists for the first time, it seemed possible that Brown's prediction might come to fruition. A close look at visitor arrivals in

Table 5   Visitor arrivals 1987/1988

	Number	*Increase since 1984 (%)*
New Zealand	483 400	106
United States	318 300	97
Japan	297 600	239
United Kingdom	245 700	64
Other Asia	292 200	99
Other Europe	237 100	91
Canada	59 600	73

Source: *Australian Government Yearbook*, Canberra, 1989.

1987/88 (total almost two million) tells us a lot about the rapid development of inbound tourism to Australia and the changing importance of particular national markets.

Because of the close British links with the bicentennial celebrations —the starting point being Captain Arthur Phillip's settlement at Sydney Cove on 26 January 1788—the ATC undertook its first television advertisements in Britain. Britons responded to Paul Hogan's deliberately larrikin 'You lot look like you could use a holiday' in the reworked 'shrimp on the barbie' commercial. A much higher proportion of visitors from the UK and Ireland had relatives in Australia than any other source market, apart from New Zealand.

Installations, events and conventions

The increasing popularity and affordability of air travel introduced a new form of tourism to Australia, the business convention. Prior to the 1960s such conventions had been modest affairs, whether they were aimed at domestic or international organisations. Australia, because of the cost and time of getting here, hosted very few international conventions, which is one reason why the 1956 Olympics loomed so large in local thinking. Attracting either national or international domestic and business groups, from Rotarians to psychologists, requires a huge accommodation base and a wide range of conference facilities. In the 1950s and 1960s commentators berated Australia for its lack of such facilities. Even in 1981, when the Commonwealth Heads of Government met in Melbourne, the Exhibition Building was the only venue in the country large enough to hold the function. Big conferences require both work and leisure spaces. In the United States major cities including New York and Chicago dominated the convention market, so smaller cities had to offer extra inducements, such as a casino, to attract delegates.

Australia's first casino opened at Wrest Point in Hobart in 1973. The island state depended so much on the tourist dollar that both the main political parties supported the construction of a casino, not least because the rise of Queensland had further dented Tasmania's importance as a tourist destination in the eyes of mainlanders. Intense opposition to the casino, especially from the north of the state, motivated by both wowserism and jealousy of the south, was placated by a referendum in

When Wrest Point casino opened in 1973, it looked as though Tasmania had stolen a march on the rest of Australia. Sydney and Melbourne did not open their huge casinos until the mid-1990s.

1968, returning a 60–40 yes vote. Successive Labor and Liberal governments assisted Federal Hotels Ltd in every way possible: waterfront
height restrictions were ignored and foreshore land was filled in to provide a 580-car parking lot. The result was a twenty-one-storey casino
and hotel, with 195 bedrooms.[7]

The opening of Australia's first legal casino commanded both national
and international attention. The consortium to finance it had been put
together by Gordon Barton, businessman and leader of the Australia
Party. Some of the finance came from Mr Stanley Ho, a Hong Kong millionaire and casino magnate, who complained that the federal government had limited the level of foreign investment in the scheme. An *Age*
journalist covering the opening found the casino unbelievably luxurious.
At over 60 metres, the fourteen-sided gazebo cost $19 million to build,
with $3 million spent on its interiors, which included roulette wheels,
craps tables, closed-circuit television, sauna baths, squash courts, a
cabaret, a revolving restaurant and an all-night grill. Hobartians were
having difficulty seeing themselves as the Monte Carlo of the south
because the city had only got its first licensed restaurant in 1960, and
even that was in the basement of a hotel.

The Tasmanian Minister for Tourism hailed the casino as vital to the
state's long-term economic salvation. He envisaged planeloads of weekend trippers from the mainland, including honeymooners. He expressed
high hopes of boosting the tourist trade from Japan, America and New
Zealand, with Lloyd Trestino and Flotta Lauro ships now expected to
extend their Tasmanian stopovers to allow for a flutter at the casino. He
also hoped that the American 'millionaire ships' *Monterey* and *Mariposa*
would include Hobart on their Pacific cruises. The Tasmanian government stood to collect 30 per cent of the monthly profits. The casino
management targeted patrons of Sydney's illegal casinos, many of whom
were invited to the opening night. Some Tasmanian parliamentarians
worried about a mainland mafia takeover, especially mainlanders setting
up call-girl establishments. The Tasmanian Minister for Tourism, who
also happened to be the Minister for Police, denied that there was any
prostitution in Tasmania. He aimed to keep it that way.[8]

The next casinos to be established were in the Northern Territory. Any objections were quickly overcome because of the importance of the tourist dollar. The Darwin casino, aimed specifically at the growing Asian market (the Indonesian government forbade casinos), opened in 1979 and another followed at Alice Springs in 1981. Hobart's northern rival, Launceston, got its own casino in 1982.

Just as the NSW Murray River towns—Albury, Moama, Corowa— had benefited enormously from being able to offer poker machines and elaborate club facilities to Victorians starved of both, so the casino states and territories profited from a unique attraction. Neither Queensland nor South Australia could let the competition slip past, so Adelaide opened a casino in its central railway station in 1985, the same year that the giant Jupiters convention centre and hotel complex opened on the Gold Coast, along with the Burswood Island convention centre and casino complex in Perth. Another casino opened in Townsville in 1986. All these establishments offered high glamour for the highrollers, along with vast floors of poker machines and cheaper games. With alcohol at every corner and cigarette smoke heavy in the air, the casinos were a far cry from the sedate bingo halls run by church and charitable groups in working-class suburbs and at the larger seaside resorts. They were family activities, where neither security cameras nor bouncers were required.

Casinos took a lot longer to establish in Sydney and Melbourne, where church-led anti-gambling lobbies capitalised on divisions within the major political parties and emphasised the deleterious impact of gambling on family life. Some of Australia's wealthiest and most power- ful entrepreneurs, including Kerry Packer, were busily eyeing off pro- spective casino sites. Labor Premier Neville Wran had promised NSW a casino, and created the Darling Harbour Authority to resume crown and other land to create the site for one, together with a convention centre, an exhibition centre and a shopping/cafe/trinkets market based on the markets in Boston and Baltimore. A temporary casino did not open in Sydney until 1995, the Star City entertainment complex not till 1997.

Both Sydney and Melbourne were well aware of each other's casino plans. In Melbourne a wealthy entrepreneur with close links with the

Liberal Party, Lloyd Williams, created the world's largest casino, the Crown Entertainment Complex. It opened in temporary premises in 1994 and reopened, amid much glitz and expense, on its Yarra riverside site in 1996. State governments, desperate for both revenue (via a tax on turnover) and tourist/convention attractiveness, vied with each other to embrace the gaming installations. Crown and Star signage appeared, at government expense, throughout the inner areas of Melbourne and Sydney respectively. Both complexes are actively promoted on the road and public transport systems. They are given the status of secular cathedrals, but their impact on tourist numbers is minimal. The profits derive from a small number of highrollers, along with a reliable income stream from working- and lower-middle-class gamblers. Why travel from one capital city to another if you already have a casino at home?[9]

By the 1980s competition for domestic and international tourists had become so intense that state governments plotted against each other for sporting and cultural events. These became known as Hallmark Events, and the costs and benefits of them have been subject to close scrutiny from a variety of sources. These include the promoters (from the Grand Prix circuit to the International Olympic Committee); the state or federal governments that stand to gain prestige, international recognition and possibly income; and critics who query the architectural, environmental and social costs of expos, sporting challenges and such events.

Conventions, exhibitions and hallmark events demand either the refurbishment of existing sites or the creation of new ones. In Sydney Darling Harbour provides the convention centre, while the Royal Easter Show, once the most popular activity on the city's calendar, has been relegated to Homebush, where its grounds are part of the Olympics complex. Its former magnificent eastern suburbs site, abutting the Sydney Cricket Ground, became the home for Rupert Murdoch's Fox studio. In Melbourne the 1880s Exhibition Buildings were given over to the Museum of Victoria for an uncertain future, while the new exhibition centre—colloquially known as Jeff's Shed—arose on the banks of the Yarra.

The immediate economic setting and economic impact of huge purpose-built tourist installations and events is much easier to analyse than longer-term costs and benefits. These always include items well beyond the operational curtilage of a site, such as the impact on real estate prices and rents, longer-term employment prospects (an event can create an employment bubble that cannot be maintained), and traffic and environmental issues. There are also the ethical implications of state and federal governments bowing to the interests of what we might term the event/installation entrepreneurs.[10]

Most of Australia's glamour resorts were built in the capitalist frenzy of the 1980s, when entrepreneurs including Christopher Skase built hotels at a cost of over $250 000 per room. Such developments, like the Mirage resorts at the Gold Coast and Port Douglas, and the ill-fated Floatel of Townsville, simply did not generate sufficient income to justify the capital cost. The seven-storey Floatel, the world's first floating hotel, was moored in the face of the prevailing south-east winds, which made the floating tennis court and the swimming pool pontoon difficult to use. Many guests got seasick. With an occupancy rate of around 20 per cent, it was never going to work. All these resorts and the com-

Magic Mountain, a mini fun park, opened at Mermaid Beach on the Gold Coast in the 1960s. By the early 1990s it could no longer compete with the huge new theme parks such as Warner Brothers Movie World, and was replaced by a town house development.

panies that owned them had to go into liquidation and the resorts had to be recapitalised, at much less than the building cost, before a viable economic entity could emerge. The Floatel ended up being towed to Hanoi.[11]

The same problems of overcapitalisation and uncertain client numbers face the lavish Crown Entertainment Centre in Melbourne. Built at a cost of $2.1 billion, it requires not only high cash flow but high profits to justify the capital outlay. Investors in the publicly listed company that owns Crown demonstrated their nervousness in 1997 and 1998 by selling their shares. Crown abandoned its plans to build a second hotel tower. Australia's richest man, the media magnate Kerry Packer, offered to buy a half-share in the company for $425 million, less than a quarter of what the establishment had cost to build.

EVENTS HAVE BECOME the essence of the tourism calendar. A study of the inaugural Adelaide Grand Prix in 1985, which the state government, as the promoter, proudly proclaimed as the sporting equivalent of the Adelaide Festival, tells us a lot about the real cash costs and income, and the uncertain wider effects, of such events.

At first glance the event looks like a great success. The South Australian government almost covered its direct costs from the income generated, but one needs to know how much of this income went to the international promoters of the event to evaluate the figures accurately.

Table 6   Overview of income, visitor expenditures and costs, Adelaide Grand Prix 1985 ($00 000)

Visitor expenditure		*Income*		*Costs*	
Accommodation	2.3	Admissions	6.6	SA govt	7.5
Food	2.8	Corp. sales	2.3	Comm. govt	5.0
Entertainment	1.0	Sponsorship	1.8		
Transport	1.5	Other	0.9		
Other	2.2				
Totals	9.8		11.6		12.5

The other immediate benefits, the income going to Adelaide's accommodation-providers, food and entertainment outlets, and into public transport fares, rental cars, airline tickets and the like, fall well short of the direct government cost. Such events also raise issues about the tax treatment of profits, and whether the tourism industry should return some of its profits to the principal investor, in this case the South Australian state government.[12]

No one disputes the fact that events like a Grand Prix or the Olympics give a city, and sometimes a nation, a level of prominence in the world media that it would not otherwise have. In the case of a short-lived event, like a Grand Prix, much of the prominence comes from prior tourist promotion as well as the event itself—which is usually televised live around the world. The drivers' helmets and billboards are worth millions of advertising dollars. Dangerous sporting events, such as a car race, offer the macabre possibility that a crash will guarantee even more press coverage, especially on world television news. If the crash has been caused by driver error it will not reflect badly on the venue, but if the crash has been caused by poor road design, the host city may face a public relations disaster.

In an even grimmer context, Tasmania's reputation as a holiday isle will long be marked by the tragic mass killings at Port Arthur on 28 April 1996, when a psychologically disturbed youth gunned down thirty-two people at the historic site. Tasmania certainly gained world-wide attention from this event, but as with an airline or train crash, the attention is more likely to dissuade tourists from visiting rather than encourage them. In the longer term the massacre may blend into the penal history of Port Arthur, adding another unnerving note to a site at once beautiful and chilling.[13]

The competition for events can be intense at both the city and the national level. Melbourne's Kennett-led state government persuaded the promoters of the Formula One Grand Prix to relocate the race from Adelaide to Melbourne. Sydney's Gay Mardi Gras does not depend on international entrepreneurs. Begun in modest circumstances in 1978, it has become a major tourist event. In 1998 it generated $98 million for the Sydney economy, slightly more than the Grand Prix managed to achieve for Melbourne (without taking into account the much higher infrastructure costs of the latter, mostly met by the Victorian government). In the case of the 1996 Olympics, there was not enough local or national backing to make Melbourne's bid credible. Four years later, when Sydney was bidding against Manchester and Beijing for the 2000 Olympics, it was anticipated that the result would be close. All sorts of tactics, concessions and promises—from giving the IOC delegates a good time to creating a sustainable environment in a badly damaged part of Sydney's landscape—were employed. Government and Games officials experienced short-lived embarrassment in 1998 when Sydney's water supply appeared to be contaminated. Longer-lasting was the scandal in 1999 over tactics used by Salt Lake City to secure the Winter Olympics in 2002. Sydney got a bit of residual flak over its own bidding largesse and sponsors got nervous, but the Games had to go on. The Tourism Forecasting Council claims that 1.6 million extra international visitors will come to Australia between 1997 and 2004 because of the Games, generating 150 000 new jobs and $6 billion in extra earnings.[14]

The travel agent

Travel agencies flourished in Australia in the 1960s and 1970s. Most of their work consisted of booking airfares and accommodation, often in package form. Agencies were to be found in almost all prosperous country towns with populations of more than 5000, and in major suburban shopping strips. In the 1980s and 1990s the number of individual travel agents began to contract as big firms and franchise operators like Jetset, Harvey World Travel and STA Travel made their presence felt. In 1987 the fifty-eight firms with more than twenty employees accounted for well over half of all turnover. The larger operators included the motoring organisations, the state government tourist bureaus, the travel agent chains and major transport operators, especially the airlines that continued to run their own holiday booking services.

Table 7   Travel agents Australia 1968–1997

	1968	1979	1987	1997
Retail travel agencies	585	1557	1494	2842
Foreign tourism organisations	27	43	72	n.a.*
Internat. tour oper./wholesalers	40	146	n.a.*	424
Total	652	1746	1566	3266

* Not available

Source: ABS cat. no. 8653.0; Travel Agency Services, Australia.

The increase in travel agency services in Australia reflected the continuing strength of the domestic market and the need to foster the spectacular growth in international tourism, especially from the mid-1980s. In 1997 there were 170 inbound tourism operators, with almost 3000 employees servicing the international market. The 2842 retailers employed 16 000 people primarily selling to Australians for travel within Australia or overseas. Working proprietors and small partnerships owned half of all travel agencies. Australia's eighty tourist bureaus, including branches, employed only 600 people and wrote less than 5 per cent of all travel business, in stark contrast to their dominant position in the inter-war and early postwar years.

But by the 1990s it had become common, with the introduction of credit card booking over the phone, for more and more people to book airfares and even packages directly with the airlines, the railways and the rent-a-car companies. Sophisticated accommodation guides and Internet sites now mean that the role of traditional travel agents is likely to decline, unless their combined buying power enables them to offer better deals than individual consumers can get for themselves.

The domestic and international markets

Understanding the nature of domestic and international markets has become an industry in itself. The Bureau of Tourism Research, through its visitor surveys, and the Australian Bureau of Statistics, via the census and its industry studies, spend millions of dollars each year analysing both domestic and international tourism expenditure and behaviour.

The broad outlines of the two markets are well known. In world terms Australia is a country where people are used to going away for their holidays. Indeed in the OECD group only the French spend more time away from home (twenty-four nights per annum) than Australians (fourteen nights). The Canadians spend nine nights, residents of the UK eight, and the Japanese five nights away from home per annum.[15]

The international market has been growing as a proportion of the total market since the early 1950s, a trend accelerated by quicker and cheaper air travel since the late 1960s. Almost all international travellers arrive by air, and that is also their main mode of travel within Australia. Half of all international travellers visit only one or two destinations, and only 13 per cent use a car as their main form of transportation. International tourists stay on average for twenty-four nights, but that masks enormous differences: between Japanese visitors, who stay an average of eight nights, usually in hotels; visitors from the UK, who are here for an average of forty-five nights and are likely to stay with friends and relatives; and Scandinavians, many of whom are younger back-packers, staying an average of forty-nine nights, usually in backpacker establishments or hotels. Japanese tourists pay most per night ($197), spend most in the shops ($1022) and have the shortest average stay. Visitors from the USA and Canada spend less on shopping than any other nationalities, but Americans pay much more for their hotel accommodation than Canadians. These statistics are pored over by tourist analysts, especially when creating new resort environments aimed at specific markets.

Domestic tourist patterns are much more complicated to study than is international behaviour. Domestic tourists are more likely to combine a business trip with visiting friends and relatives, not least because they obviously have many more friends and relatives to visit. With the increasing job and geographical mobility of the Australian labour market, most Australians have friends and relatives in at least one other state, and many in two or more other states. Almost half of all accommodation for domestic tourism in Australia is with friends or relatives, with one-fifth staying in hotels and motels, 14 per cent in camping grounds and caravan parks, and almost 10 per cent in self-contained accommodation.

Table 8   International arrivals 1986–1996 (000s)

	1986	*1996*
North America	292	378
UK & Ireland	183	388
Other Europe	164	411
New Zealand	337	672
Japan	146	813
Singapore	45	223
South Korea	5	228
Taiwan	8	159
Other Asia	142	701
All others	107	192
Total	1429	4165

Source: *Forecast*, vol. 3, no. 2, Tourism Forecasting Council, June 1997.

Table 9   Top twenty regions and attractions for international visitors 1995–1996

Regions (% visitation)		*Attractions (ranked in descending order)*
Sydney	60.8	Sydney shopping
Gold Coast	25.6	Sydney Opera House
Melbourne	23.6	Darling Harbour, NSW
Brisbane	19.3	The Rocks, NSW
Far North Qld	18.1	Sydney Harbour cruise
Perth, WA	12.3	Sydney Tower
Uluru	6.9	Sydney beaches
Adelaide, SA	6.9	Kings Cross, NSW
Canberra ACT	5.8	Chinatown, NSW
Alice Springs NT	5.8	Zoos, aquariums, NSW
Sunshine Coast, Qld	4.0	Melbourne shopping
Darwin, NT	3.9	Blue Mountains
Gympie/Maryborough Qld	3.2	Sea World, Qld
Northern Qld	3.2	Kuranda/Atherton, Qld
Upper North Coast, NSW	3	Great Barrier Reef
Fitzroy, Qld	2.4	Botanical Gardens, NSW
Great Ocean Road, Vic	2.3	Movieworld, Qld
Great Barrier Reef	2.3	Taronga Zoo, NSW
Whitsunday Islands, Qld	2.3	Jupiters Casino, Qld
Kakadu, NT	2.0	Queen Victoria Markets, Vic

Source: *International Visitor Survey*, 1996, Bureau of Tourism Research, Canberra, December 1997.
The survey is a sample of the 3 404 100 international visitors in 1995–96.

A disproportionate apartment block hovers over a residual fibro dwelling on the Gold Coast, 1982 (left). *Real estate developers lure gullible southern investors, 1998* (right). *Many of these apartments are fully occupied only during the school holidays.*

Just over 10 per cent of domestic tourists use planes as their main mode of getting to their primary destination, but the car remains the dominant means of domestic travel in Australia, accounting for 78 per cent of all primary trips. While the average length of stay for domestic trips is seven nights, many are obviously much shorter (overnight or weekend trips) or much longer, especially over the Christmas/New Year school holiday period.[16]

The Bureau of Tourism Research defines domestic tourism as a stay away from home of one or more nights and requiring a journey of at least 40 kilometres from home. Three-quarters of all such travel in Australia is within the home state. Most of those travellers, as the following table shows, are either on holiday or visiting friends and relatives, while 11.2 per cent are on business trips or attending conferences. The main

capital cities, which contain almost two-thirds of the country's population, have extensive hinterlands offering coastal and rural holiday and
travel options. Four major cities, namely Sydney, Canberra, Wollongong
and Melbourne, are also within easy reach of snowfields during winter.
Interstate travel follows a rather similar pattern to intra-state travel in
terms of the primary purpose of the trip, but airlines are much more
likely to be used as the main mode of travel in this case. The airlines
hardly figure at all for intra-state travel, with the exception of long-distance travel within Queensland and Western Australia.

One-third of domestic trips were made by people aged twenty-five to
thirty-nine, a little higher than their proportion of the population, while
teenagers and people over fifty-five travelled less than other age groups.
Almost half of all travel in Australia was undertaken by people on much
lower than average incomes, under $10 000 per head, or on higher than
average incomes, over $40 000 per head. The lower-income group in-
cludes children, teenagers, retirees and the unemployed, who may have
fewer time or travel constraints than the middle-income group, or be
looking for work. The highest income bracket accounted for almost
one-third of interstate trips, and people in this category were much
more likely to use planes as their mode of travel than any other group.
Even so, only 30 per cent of business travellers go by air, with 60 per

Table 10   Primary purpose of trip, domestic travel 1995–1996 (%)

	Interstate	Intra-state
Holiday	8.5	27.0
Visiting friends, relatives; personal reasons	8.4	29.7
Business/conference	5.9	11.2
Other	2.2	7.0
Percentage total	25	75
Total travellers	15 750 000	47 230 000

Source: Calculated from *Domestic Tourism Monitor 1995–96*, Bureau of Tourism Research,
Canberra, December 1997.

cent using their own or hired vehicles. As business travel is tax-deductible, such travel is in effect being cross-subsidised by other travellers who have to bear their own costs.

New South Wales, and especially Sydney, is the most popular destination for interstate travellers, with over 38 per cent visiting that state in 1995–96, followed by Queensland, 22 per cent, Victoria 20 per cent, South Australia 9 per cent, Western Australia and Tasmania 4 per cent each; figures for the Northern Territory were 3 per cent and the ACT 12 per cent. The relatively high figure for the ACT is explained by a combination of school visits, public service and business travel. Moreover, as the ACT is now only three hours drive from Sydney, like the Gold Coast and the Sunshine Coast it is within very easy reach of a capital city.[17]

By 1996–97 domestic tourism expenditure in Australia reached $39 billion, with a little over one-third spent on day trips and almost two-thirds on stays of one night or more. The average number of nights per trip peaked in 1986–87 at 4.7, and has fallen slightly to four nights since then, reflecting the importance of Easter, long weekends and short breaks, along with cheap Saturday-night-stay airline packages.

The tourism workforce is difficult to define and therefore hard to study, as are claims about the economic size and impact of tourism. The core workforce—in hotels, restaurants, sporting activities, car rental agencies—is much easier to examine than its contextual workforce, people in the wider accommodation, transport, food and retailing industries. The multiplier effect of tourism activities on the wider economy is obvious, but hard to quantify. While some employees deal only with tourists, for instance everyone working on a resort island, many other workers encounter tourists as just part of their clientele.

Tourism-dependent industries, from publishers of guidebooks to duty-free shops, have flourished over the past two decades. Lonely Planet, which began as a tiny operation in Melbourne in the 1980s, is now one of the world's major guidebook publishers, and it has a massive web site to back this up. Such guides are now supplanting travel agents as the main information (as distinct from booking) source for tourists.

Meanwhile duty-free shops have proliferated beyond the airports to the capital cities. Other major retailers also now cater specifically for inter-state and international tourists, with products as varied as wine, high-cost craft goods, art works and designer clothing.[18]

PEOPLE WORKING IN tourism have traditionally been characterised by rapid turnover and seasonality in employment. Over two-thirds of the workers are unskilled or semi-skilled, with the proportion in more highly skilled occupations such as chef or manager very small. In 1989 an Industries Assistance Commission inquiry characterised the workers as 'poorly paid, lowly unionised and highly mobile'. The Commission found shortages of managers, chefs and staff with foreign-language skills, and that only 4 per cent of hospitality establishments spent money on staff training.

Until the 1980s most tourism training in Australia took place in TAFE colleges—in cooking, front-of-house work, bookkeeping, ticketing and other applied subjects. It was usually referred to as hospitality or travel. Only a handful of Australian tertiary institutions, all of them in the tech-nical and CAE area, took tourism as a subject seriously. The main pro-viders were the Footscray Institute of Technology and the Ku-ring-gai Chase CAE. All the CAEs teaching tourism were converted into or sub-sumed by universities, and a number of longer-established universities also took up teaching and research in tourism. The subject is still treated with suspicion by established disciplines, including history, economics and geography—not least because it employs a variety of method-ologies and is usually taught within a business faculty.

Nonetheless the number of students studying tourism in Australian universities has increased from a couple of thousand in 1980 to 20 000 in 1997. Even more are studying in TAFE, from airline ticketing to becoming a registered travel agent. A number of registered private pro-viders have also appeared in recent years, including the Australian Inter-national Hotel School in Canberra, the Blue Mountains International Hotel Management School, and the Australian College of Travel and Hospitality in Melbourne. Tourism has also been taken up as a topic in some state high school systems.[19]

Canberra: a government tourist destination

Despite global transport companies and accommodation chains, tourism remains a site-specific business. One of the most intriguing and most expensive examples of site creation in Australia is Canberra. A new national capital, located because of Sydney–Melbourne rivalry at the time of federation, at least 100 miles from Sydney but within the state of NSW, had to establish both its political presence and its image from scratch. The whole venture needed the ratification of tourists. The Australian National Travel Association, keen to please the federal government, in the early 1930s commissioned a series of posters of Canberra with the slogan Visit Your National Capital. Most early publicity for Canberra described it as 'the garden city' or 'a city of flowers'. Shortly afterwards the federal Department of the Interior helped underwrite the cost of a lavish *Official Tourist Guide to Australia's National Capital (1937)*. In the foreword the departmental wordsmith remarked:

> To some, Canberra is a wonderful garden. To others, it is a Sportsman's Paradise, with swimming, golfing, tennis, bowling, shooting and trout-fishing, all within easy reach of the city's palatial hotels. Still others find in the quaint and ancient aboriginal relics and prehistoric drawings in time-worn caves on the mountain-side, a never-ending source of interest, and for tourists generally there is the magnetic attraction of Federal Parliament House.

Federal Parliament House certainly had magnetic qualities, judging from the number of posters, souvenir cup and saucer sets and postcards produced for the visiting public. But to call a place with a population of 9000, and most of them public servants, a 'city' with 'palatial hotels' stretched credulity. The hotels and guest-houses were all built by the government; some were leased to managers. While all had hot and cold water in the bedrooms, they were freezing. Guests had to seek out log fires in the lounges and the dining room. The cheapest establishment, the Acton Guest House, didn't promise log fires but it did grow its own vegetables and had its own cows.

These cards show the gradual crystallisation of Canberra. It was a tourist site even before it existed. Note how in the late 1890s Bathurst, in its bid to become the capital, had inserted the word 'Federal' above the lettering on an existing postcard.

Canberra, which did not get its first rail passenger service until 1923, consisted of a number of grand and modest public buildings, shops, hotels, guest-houses and suburban houses, all built by the government on leasehold land. Loosely based around Walter Burley Griffin's axial plan, the proposed lake did not eventuate until the mid-1960s. Canberra was a government town, on a grander scale than the State Electricity Commission of Victoria's garden settlement at Yallourn, but a government town nonetheless. With a smaller population than Goulburn, its compact nineteenth-century neighbour to the north, Canberra sat on a number of sheep stations—a nice twist in a nation that thought of itself as riding on the sheep's back.

For the amusement of public servants, the government provided two up-to-date picture theatres. The Capital Theatre, seating 1100, and the Civic Theatre, seating 800, at least offered central heating, while the Albert Hall was described, somewhat extravagantly, as 'Canberra's Opera House'. The Federal Capital Development Commission developed 'eminences' at the Mount Stromlo observatory as 'vantage points from which tourists may view the fine panoramas in the territory'. The Commission regretted that the formation of a number of 'circular shaped lakes' had been deferred for the moment. Nonetheless kiosks, bandstands, shelter sheds and bathing sheds were erected on the banks of the Murrumbidgee and Cotter rivers.[20]

Aware of the continuing need to justify the new capital to the nation, the Department of Home Affairs announced in 1931 a publicity campaign to boost Canberra. This included offering journalists all-expenses-paid trips to the city, even though the nation was in the midst of the Depression. The *Canberra Times* told its readers that 'every Australian taxpayer' would have 'cause for satisfaction' at this overdue publicity campaign, presumably on seeing their taxes at work. The newspaper went on to point out that when government departments started moving from Melbourne this would 'not so much involve the expenditure of money on Canberra as the saving of money', not least because many government-built houses were empty.[21]

Intending tourists had to wait quite a while for any attractions other than Parliament House. In its first full year of opening, 1943, the Australian War Memorial had over 50 000 visitors. From 1957 it attracted more than 250 000 a year, many of them school children on overnight excursions to the national capital from Sydney or Melbourne. It became, along with Parliament House, one of Australia's great tourist attractions. Since 1982 it has had well over a million visitors a year (the Aquarium at Darling Harbour attracts a similar number).

Canberra grew slowly in the war and early postwar years, and was described by *Holiday and Travel* magazine in March 1950 as a 'well conducted country town', with a population of 16 000. Intending travellers were warned to book 'well in advance' with the government tourist office, otherwise they might not be able to 'get in'. Its spectacular growth came after 1958, when the Menzies government created a National Capital Development Commission (NCDC) to plan, construct and develop 'the City of Canberra as the National Capital'. The NCDC planned a grand, circular road system, mapped out sites for national institutions, and started plans for putting water into Lake Burley Griffin, over which two imposing road bridges were constructed across the usually dry Molonglo river bed. The waters of Lake Burley Griffin started to flow in September 1963 and tourist boats took to the lake soon after.

There followed an extraordinary succession of buildings within the parliamentary triangle, including the National Library, the High Court (nicknamed the Gar Mahal, after the then Chief Justice, Garfield Barwick) and the National Gallery of Australia. Telecom erected a communications tower, with viewing platforms, on Black Mountain, much to the disgust of environmentalists. In its insatiable encouragement of tourists the NCDC allowed two drive-ins, new hotels and motels, and Billabong Park, a horse era museum celebrating Australia's early settlers. After years of debate about its location, the National Museum of Australia will now be located on the lakeside site of an imploded hospital.

Federal government spending on all aspects of Canberra's infrastructure, from roads to cultural attractions, has fallen since the coming of

This James Northfield poster depicts Canberra in the late 1920s. The provisional
Parliament House is accompanied by one public service office block.

self-government to the Australian Capital Territory in 1989. Nonetheless, a succession of ACT governments have continued to try pump-priming exercises to attract tourists, including a casino and a convention centre. An enormous advance was made to cover acquisition of the decrepit Hotel Kurrajong, which was duly refurbished for training in the hospitality industry. In conjunction with Cornell University, the Australian International Hotel School offers an extraordinarily expensive Bachelor of Hotel Management, which has failed to compete with degrees from better-located institutions. The most notable of these is the International College of Tourism and Management at Manly, situated in the old St Patrick's seminary overlooking the Pacific Ocean.[22]

Most of Canberra's original monuments—the 1927 Parliament House, the Prime Minister's Lodge, the Australian–American War Memorial and the domed Academy of Science—have been eclipsed by the new Parliament House, even though it is built into a hill. Nearby is the Chinese Embassy, a huge Asian compound in one of Australia's most European cities. Canberra may indeed be a 'capital landscape', but it still fails to capture the Australian imagination. Prime Minister John Howard was able to get away with living at Kirribilli House in Sydney, relegating the Lodge to a place for staying overnight. Similarly, Canberra does not attract any more overseas tourists per annum than Alice Springs (200 000 each), while Far North Queensland has 600 000 international visitors per annum. The schools still do the rounds of Parliament House and the War Memorial, and the latter remains an object of intrigue to Japanese tourists, but Canberra simply does not attract the number of tourists to justify the massive government investment in its tourist infrastructure.[23]

The coast of enterprise: Cairns

Outside the mainland state capitals and the Gold Coast, Cairns, like Canberra, has more four- and five-star hotels than anywhere else in Australia. One city is almost entirely the construct of government, whereas the other, which has gone from a sleepy provincial town to a major international tourist destination in the space of three decades, is testament to the innovation and the avarice of private enterprise.

When the New York consultants came to survey the Australian tourist industry in 1964 they found Cairns to be 'an attractive, tropical city' handicapped by extensive mud flats and mangroves at low tide. They suggested dredging the foreshore to eliminate this 'unsightliness', to improve navigation and to provide areas for marinas. Cairns' thirty-seven accommodation establishments provided 701 rooms, of which 488 did not have private facilities.

Described by the Queensland Government Tourist Bureau in 1960 as 'Australia's most remote city', Cairns was not a destination in itself, other than for government officials, school teachers, railway staff and bankers who came on business, or people visiting friends and relatives. A pictorial survey of Cairns in 1966 highlighted St Monica's War Memorial Cathedral, the bowling and RSL clubs, municipal buildings, late nineteenth-century and 1930s hotels and a handful of motels. The town was promoted as a gateway to Port Douglas, Green Island and the verdant Atherton Tableland.

Palm Cove, a few kilometres north of Cairns, has seen massive development over the last 25 years. Australian and international tourists play tennis in the tropics.

Cairns exploded onto the Australian tourism landscape in the 1980s and 1990s. In the early 1980s its room numbers were little more than double the 700 rooms of the early 1960s. A few classy motels and some apartment blocks had been built. Its 1700 rooms of 1984 had by June 1986 become 4900 rooms and a year later 6500 rooms, one of the biggest annual increases in the history of Australian tourism. In 1986/87 the 73 per cent occupancy rate was higher than anywhere else in Queensland. Its airport, upgraded to take international flights in 1984, had by 1987 become the eighth biggest in Australia. By 1993 it was busier than Adelaide and approaching the traffic levels of Brisbane and Perth. A large marina, an ocean cruise liner terminal and a vast shopping centre over the unsightly mangroves were all completed between the late 1980s and the early 1990s.[24]

Such a rapidly growing tourist destination runs particular risks, because it is posited on continued growth and very high levels of occupancy. In recent years Cairns has suffered two dramatic downturns in its tourist trade, first with the airline pilots' dispute and then with the Asian economic crisis of the late 1990s. The first setback was straightforward and, as it transpired, relatively short-lived. The great majority of all travellers to North Queensland get there by air, whether from interstate, overseas, or even from southern Queensland. Without regular air services the tourist trade simply dried up, not just for the duration of the dispute (August 1989 to March 1990, when 1649 pilots resigned) but well into the peak winter months of 1990 as well.

In 1997 the Cairns convention centre, backed by the Queensland government, could promote the place as 'one of the world's most convenient cities'. In an obvious comparison with Asian competitors, Cairns was claimed to be 'pollution and traffic jam free' and 'one of the most dynamic and accessible cities' in the Asia–Pacific. An accompanying map showed Cairns as a centre of Asia–Pacific travel, with direct air links to most major Asian countries: 'Its relatively short flight time from Asia places it in close proximity to the economic powerhouses and major international hubbing centres of the world'.[25]

As one of Australia's biggest industries, now worth more in export dollars than minerals or agricultural produce, tourism in this island continent is vital to the economic future of the nation. Australians spend almost as much money travelling overseas as overseas visitors spend here. Without these visitors Australia would have a balance-of-trade deficit of such proportions that it would soon become a Third World economy. What many people thought of as a 'smokeless industry' in the 1960s has often become one of the most intrusive features of the Australian landscape. Tower blocks overshadow beachside resorts, airports have to be continually expanded, and tourist entrepreneurs are forever looking at new ways to make a dollar, whether with 'environmentally sensitive' tree canopy chair lifts or inground poolside bars abutting the beach.

12

Postscript: Tourism Über Alles

TRADITIONALLY TOURISM HAS often been regarded as a trivial pursuit—concerned only with leisure, divorced from people's real lives, and dowsed in popular culture. It has therefore not been seen by many people —whether academics on the one side or those in the industry eager to advance their current concerns on the other—as having had a history. The very idea has seemed contradictory.

Yet tourism history not only reveals another strand of the past, but also throws into relief, by virtue of its hyper-real quality, certain assumptions of a given period perhaps more clearly than most social activities. The anglophile assumptions of Edwardian Australia are brought into focus by the revelation that Tasmania, just before World War I, received almost as many visitors as there were people in Hobart: visitors drawn by the cool summers, the lush greens, the passably 'English' landscape. It was then Australia's number one long-range tourist destination. It is well down the list now; by contrast Ayers Rock – Uluru has risen from drawing a mere couple of hundred visitors in 1957 to some 350 000 per annum forty years later. At work here has been a reversal, or more correctly a long, slow subversion, of the very values exhibited in the Tasmanian tourism of almost a century ago. The travelling class is broader; a sense of engagement with nature is sought, right up to the limits to which it can be confidently handled, so that ecotourism is the desirable thing now, rather than plush accommodation fuelled by enor-

344

mous meals. Moreover the English connection has become enfeebled, with white Australians almost daily seeming to seek greater spiritual meaning in the land they live in, their eyes having only recently become accustomed to its subtler beauties. So prime destinations change.

Even where the same places continue to draw significant numbers, shifts in social preoccupations will influence the hierarchy of attractions at any particular destination. Crowds continue to go to Glenelg, although not in droves on South Australia's Proclamation Day; and the Proclamation Tree, once a symbol for the state, is now relatively unvisited and unrepresented on the range of postcards available. Different periods, different priorities; the Tree was too closely connected with a formal statement about the colonial past. But it is important to realise that some of these shifts are not so readily explicable—which means that the tourist industry, rather than falling victim to its own hype, needs to monitor visitor response rather than assume that the vectors will climb ever upwards. A good example of a somewhat inexplicable decline in touristic interest is afforded by caves. Until the 1950s they were still relatively popular, but began to lose appeal long before a more factually based education system loosened its grip on schools. Today the Buchan caves—Victoria's largest—do not draw sufficient numbers to rank among the state's top twenty tourist attractions.

Fashion also has a way of curling back on itself, of recycling what a previous period has discarded. The Victorian resort of Lorne never dropped entirely out of favour, although the rise of air travel meant that for a while it lost the romance it possessed in the 1930s. The demolition of a large hotel in the mid-1980s to build the sprawling Cumberland Resort—despite much opposition to its obtrusive contemporary style—announced the town's recycling as a modern resort with convention facilities. Lorne's thirteen guest-houses are now two, but in their place are motels, bed and breakfast establishments, A-frame cottages for backpackers, and self-contained flats. Meanwhile, closer to Melbourne, Queenscliff was coming out of the doldrums: having no surfing beach had at once becalmed and preserved it from the worst of

In the 1930s, enough people still believed in fairies for Percy Trompf to make them an enticement to visit the popular caves resort of Buchan.

1960s development, so that its Victorian building stock—however run-down—was remarkably complete. No fewer than three of its grand hotels have now been restored, and in a heritage-conscious age are able to pay their way.

New anxieties can also reanimate old forms: the threat to health posed by the thinning of the ozone layer has led to some experimentation with neck-to-knee swimming costumes again, while the mountains have been advanced as an alternative to the beach. 'The only resort with outside air conditioning', ran a panel on a Melbourne tram a few years ago. 'Thredbo summer. Rise above it all.' The ski resort, in its off-season, was marketing itself as if it had been Mt Buffalo a century ago.

Amenities have always been part of the appeal of tourist destinations. Perhaps it was only dedicated travellers—particularly upper-class ones, armed with their Baedekers (which would think nothing of, for example, listing all the Pharaohs of Egypt complete with their hieroglyphics from inscriptions)—who were capable of being intrigued by places for their own sake. For tourists, as the nature writer Donald Macdonald recognised as early as 1925, it was very different.

> One of the fictions of holiday making is to assume that scenery means much, so in publicity they still dwell upon it. With the spread of home games and recreations such as golf, bowls, tennis and dancing, the scenery has nowadays very little influence in attracting tourists anywhere. It is something to talk about, but not anything that really counts. Old age may find it agreeable; youth has no time for it.[1]

With the growth of tourism, and the proliferation of amenities, there has been a further flattening out of a sense of place in what has become an increasingly homogenised world. Tourist destinations have come to promote what they consider to be the main product they have to offer: in their emphasis on sun and sand, leaflets advertising resorts in Mauritius and North Queensland are virtually interchangeable. It is not surprising, then, that events have come to eclipse places, particularly in First World cities. This can be seen most clearly in Jeff Kennett's programme to radicalise Melbourne's attractions, in a way that often ran counter to the traditional temper of the city. And the increasing primacy of events can also be seen by comparing the relative scale of the promotion of the 1956 Olympics in Melbourne with Sydney 2000.

The Olympics—1956 and 2000

The Melbourne Olympics were all event, seemingly bestowed from on high. Although Australia was one of only four countries to have participated in all the Olympics to that time, the news of Melbourne's selection was greeted in Australia with disbelief. It would be the first city in the southern hemisphere to host the Games, indeed the first outside Europe and the USA. So unused was Australia to being the focus of international attention that for a long time there seemed an air of unreality about the Games—heightened, rather than lessened, by the popular British film *Geordie*, the story of an athlete who would compete in them. Complete with a substantial predictive episode in Melbourne, the film appeared in Australia almost a year before the event.

The importance of the occasion was underlined by W. S. Kent-Hughes, a Liberal politician who had himself competed in the 1920 Olympiad in Antwerp. A sense of the world being on parade was as strong in him as the realisation that 'a new city and a new land will be the setting for the most glorious festival of sport known to ancient and modern man'. The Olympics, for Kent-Hughes as for many others, were 'a truly international institution', whose spirit 'rises above differences of race, creed and politics'.[2] In fact, given the recent Suez War and the Hungarian uprising, international politics were to prove unusually intrusive, particularly in the bloody water polo match where the Hungarians nobbled the Russians.

Austral innocence, as Barry Humphries would term it, or a simple homespun quality, probably helped save the day. The grand plans for a stadium to rival Berlin's built for the 1936 Olympics had to be shelved, the familiar (though slightly revamped) Melbourne Cricket Ground being substituted. A velodrome and an ultra-modern swimming pool were constructed, while a purpose-built village to house the athletes went up in outer-suburban Heidelberg. The 6000 athletes, trainers and officials from seventy nations, along with some friends and family, in themselves stretched Melbourne's limited accommodation resources. There were appeals to people to take visitors into their homes. But the traditional Australian emphasis on informality perhaps reached its apotheosis in the closing ceremony: for the first time national teams were abandoned as the athletes marched behind the Olympic banner in a worldwide phalanx of friends and associates.

There was much speculation as to how many international visitors would come; interstate visitors were not much discussed. One Melbourne paper predicted 40 000 Americans, but Charles Holmes of ANTA thought 2000 'nearer the mark', with 8000 overseas tourists in all. 'It is well to remember', he wrote, 'that Australia is an "outpost" country on the travel map, and that the majority of people with the time and money to travel half way around the world are matured folk; they want comfort and are not much concerned with sporting events'. Nevertheless ANTA circulated booklets and posters to 3500 travel agencies around the world. Bulletins were sent to major newspapers, and Radio Australia was used to spread the message through much of Asia. But since there were no more than 50 000 domestic and international visitors, Holmes was largely correct in seeing the Games as an 'honour' rather than a tourist bonanza.[3]

Forty years on, the most striking contrast afforded by Sydney 2000 is that the Olympics have been transformed from an international sporting event, where the impact is most obvious within the host city, to a multi-billion-dollar media event, where advertising agencies and media firms are just as important to the success of the Games as the sporting administrators who used to call most of the shots. When Melbourne was threatened in 1953 with losing the Olympics because of the tardiness of its preparations, the International Olympic Committee could have carried out its threat. Because of the billions of dollars now tied up in the Olympics, the IOC can no longer put such pressure on a city; too many media contracts and sponsorship deals would be brought undone if the event were moved elsewhere.

Neither the NSW government nor the federal government could afford to finance the infrastructure required for a modern Olympics without sponsorship and media income. Nonetheless the host city has to provide a secure environment, prevent outrageous profit-taking (hence attempts to contain the cost of hotel rooms), ensure that the transport system can cope with the pressure, and make at least one event seem affordable to most people—if they could buy a ticket. The Olympics have been marketed in close collaboration with major transport firms, banks and media companies. Ansett, United Airlines, the Westpac Bank and Channel 7 have all claimed the Olympics and offered their clients front-row seats.

The Sydney Organising Committee for the Olympic Games, a semi-privatised group with both government and commercial representatives, proudly proclaimed its mission: 'At the dawn of a new millennium . . . to deliver to the athletes of the world and to the Olympic movement, on behalf of all Australians, the most harmonious, athlete-oriented, technically excellent and culturally enhancing Olympic Games of the modern era'. Efficiency, rather than idealism. SOCOG anticipated 250 000 interstate and international spectators visiting Sydney during the Games, housed in about 40 000 hotel, motel, college and backpacker rooms augmented by a vast accommodation homestay programme.

In terms of national and international presentation, the games posed intriguing issues. When Cathy Freeman won the 400 metres race at the Commonwealth Games in Canada in 1994 she ran her lap of honour with both the Aboriginal and the Australian flag. SOCOG hoped 'to observe Aboriginal and Torres Strait islander protocol in the Olympic Ceremonies'. The 'torch relay', begun in Australia from the prime indigenous site of Uluru-Ayers Rock, would set the tone; but few would have anticipated the strong Aboriginal presence in the opening ceremony, culminating in Freeman's lighting of the Olympic flame.

There was a net fall in tourist revenue during both the Los Angeles and Atlanta Olympics, as many intending travellers postponed their visits till after the games. The real tourism benefits of the Olympics are much more likely to come well after the event, when its image value, via the world media, can be tested. Sydney is already the best-known Australian city. The Olympics may mean that it becomes the only Australian city with widespread international recognition.

Coping with the influx

Even major world cities now feel obliged to create a tourist identity for themselves. Elegant boulevards, art galleries and cathedrals are not enough. New attractions have to be added all the time. Paris has Euro-Disney, London its Millennium Dome, Melbourne a truncated Federation Square and a new stadium at Docklands, while Sydney continues to pour money into refurbishing the Opera House and making the surrounding waterfront a haven for middle-class tourists. Most of this activity is still concentrated in or near the city centres. Only airports, fun parks and sporting facilities—huge consumers of land—tend to be away from the city centres. Many fun parks, including Australia's Wonderland in western Sydney, Old Sydney Town, and Warner Brothers Movie World on the Gold Coast, rely on visitors coming by car. But bigger facilities, including Sydney's Homebush Bay Olympic site and Euro-Disney, have rail connections, as does Hong Kong's new airport, with a planned capacity of 89 million passengers per annum.

All these developments are predicated on a vast expansion of international tourism. By 2030, on current trends, Australia can anticipate about twenty million international visitors a year, more than its present population. Paris is already in that position. Many visitors stay for only a night or two, but parts of the city are already dominated by tourists. Queuing to go to the Louvre, to the Tower of London, to the Uffizi Gallery in Florence, or to St Peter's Cathedral in Rome can take hours. Some of these sites, indeed some entire cities, are at the limit of their tourist-carrying capacity already. Their accommodation is frequently booked out and their primary attractions hopelessly overcrowded. This is not simply a case of cultural domination—*Frühstück* on the Costa Brava, McDonald's in Venice—it is more a case of facilities stretched beyond belief.

Sydney, Australia's greatest tourist site, still attracts only two million visitors a year, but most stay for more than a few nights, so the figure is probably comparable with about six million in a European city. Parts of Sydney, especially Darling Harbour, Circular Quay, the Opera House and The Rocks, are already overrun with domestic and international tourists. Melbourne and Brisbane are less swamped, but smaller settlements, including the Gold Coast and Cairns, are also near their optimum carrying capacity.

It is hard to overestimate the impact tourism has already had on particular Australian landscapes and societies. In the last three decades Cairns has been transformed from a sleepy country town with a productive hinterland to a major site of domestic and international tourism. The tallest building in town is no longer the government hospital, but a five-star resort. Over half of the central area of Cairns has been rebuilt. Schools, convents, community halls, shops, pubs, even the mangrove swamp, have given way to vast shopping centres, a casino, entertainment piers and open-air markets. Nearby cane farms have been turned into 18-hole golf courses, and the rainforest now hosts canopy chair lifts. An international airport beckons the honeymoon, golfing and convention trade, along with tourists who come to consume the reef and the rainforest.

In Surfers Paradise tourist development is so intense that many sites have seen three different structures since the 1950s; some have even gone to five. Generations of building, demolition and rebuilding have seen fibro flats and shacks give way to single-storey motels, which in turn have been demolished for three-storey blocks or high-rise apartments. Surfers Paradise is such a mature tourist landscape that the Magic Mountain infotainment complex, built in the 1960s, was demolished in the late 1980s to make way for expensive apartments. Huge shopping centres built in the 1960s were replaced, in the 1990s, by even larger cathedrals of retailing. Only a handful of the more successful Australian resorts—including Byron Bay and Lorne—have managed to keep their hotels and apartment blocks under four storeys. In stark contrast, Cairns, the Sunshine Coast, the Gold Coast and much of the NSW north coast now boast blocks of ten or more storeys, towering above the beaches they overlook and often overshadow. Advertising agencies and photographers go to great lengths to show these blocks at their best, surrounded by greenery and open-air cafes, apparently at one with their environment.

One of the major problems of cities in the latter half of the twentieth century—coping with the congestion of the journey to work by car to central city areas—is likely to be overshadowed, in the twenty-first century, by the difficulties of handling huge surges of tourists. Even so, every Australian capital city hopes for a boost in numbers on the scale of Sydney. The Docklands development in Melbourne, with its new football stadium and residential tower blocks, is an attempt to compete with Sydney and other world cities in the icon and tourist precinct stakes. In this battle the other capital cities, especially Canberra, Adelaide and Perth, are likely to be left behind.

Some societies have already asked questions about the types of tourists they wish to attract, but few governments or tourist organisations,

Frank Lucas, an enthusiastic general provider at Pretty Beach, out from Gosford, NSW. Makeshift and elaborate tourist signage is still characteristic of the district today.

other than those administering natural sites, have contemplated restricting the sheer number of them. The Thai government has actively campaigned to reduce sex tourism to Thailand, but in every other way is desperately attempting to increase the number of tourists. There may come a time when Australia no longer wishes to attract package tourists, particularly from Japan, the main source of such travellers at the moment. Most of the Japanese package tour visitors stay only seven days, but their sheer numbers (450 000 per annum) create severe accommodation shortages in the most popular centres, Sydney and the Gold Coast. In contrast backpackers, at 250 000 per annum, stay for an average of forty-five nights and take up accommodation throughout the continent, providing much-needed income for quite obscure coastal and inland locations.

There will never be an attempt to ban tourists, because such bans can easily be interpreted as racist or class-based. But a switch in marketing can achieve a similar result. Australia is now attempting to attract the international study tourism market, especially university students who come for a semester. Each such student attracts an average of 1.3 extra visitors, usually friends and relatives. Managing tourist flows, to maximise income, to minimise environmental damage and to retain the attractiveness of a place, will be one of the key roles that both governments and private interests play in the twenty-first century.

Overtaking life—and what comes after

A good deal of tourism is licensed stickybeaking. There have long been famous tours such as those of the sewers of Paris, but in recent years there has also grown up the notion of workplace tours. These have existed on a small scale in Australia for a long time—for example through the Cadbury chocolate factory at Claremont in Tasmania, where a spectacular natural setting was combined with advanced working conditions and a dream product. But now there would be takers for a tour of legal Melbourne. An early indicator of this trend was to be seen in the 1980s in the French town of Nancy, where the local newspaper had made its entire front wall of glass, so that at night-time the passing reader could see the next morning's paper being put together. Transparent journalism perhaps, but more likely a flow-on from the open floor plan.

While the host would think in terms of the openness of a site, for the tourist there is the idea of exclusivity, of privileged access. This applies, too, to destinations: Russia was a highly desirable goal in the early 1960s, then became commonplace; increasing danger is making it a tourist trophy once again. Tourist entrepreneurs therefore seek to create this sense of thrill, and in ever more surprising contexts. In England, tourists are being offered the chance to spend their holidays as armed bounty-hunters, tracking down criminals in America. Closer to home, tourists can now visit the gallows in Kuala Lumpur where the convicted drug-dealers Barlow and Chambers were hanged, and hear a tape recording of a prisoner's thumping heartbeat trail away to death. Then there is Pentridge prison in Melbourne, 'unlocked after 150 years', when—after it had been closed down—organised tours of the place were arranged. It is not impossible that the old jokes about being a guest of Her Majesty will attain an oblique realisation, since part of the

Humorous postcard, packaging the then Pentridge Prison as a hotel. Closed in the mid-1980s, the prison has since gone halfway to realising this fantasy by being redeveloped as middle-class apartments.

complex could be redeveloped as a hotel. In an age of transgressive chic, such a facility is bound to be popular. Meanwhile a working gaol such as the new Darwin one has also been presented as a resort, with manicured lawns and palm trees, attractive photographs being put on display by the Northern Territory Department of Corrective Services at the Alice Springs Show. It was almost as though they were enticing custom.[4]

There was once a time, stretching into the 1960s, when high culture was thought of by most Australians as being English, or essentially imported. The idea that Australians would find sufficient spiritual nourishment directly from this country would then have seemed laughable. But, along with transgressive chic (and the recuperation of convict ancestry), and along with the frenetic gambling in casinos and elsewhere, there has nonetheless been an increasing search for the sacred, particularly over the past decade. A sign of a maturing culture is its ability to sustain such differentiation; the tourism equivalent is market segmentation, a real phenomenon even if some individuals figure in all three segments.

As Mary McKillop advances towards sainthood, the tourist industry —including the Catholic church itself—has not been far behind. The signage on the roads around Penola now indicates a pilgrims' way, and in the South Australian town there is an impressive new shrine to Mother Mary. Meanwhile the convent in Sydney where she died has been opened up, full throttle. A promotional leaflet speaks of her as 'the battler who became our first Aussie saint'. Visitors are encouraged to watch videos of four bishops denouncing her, re-enacting McKillop's excommunication. 'Saints alive!', exclaims the leaflet, 'Meet some famous saints . . . in person!' But as if realising that Catholicism unvarnished might not quite do the trick, there is reference to 'the spirit of the Dreamtime', and an actual ceiling in Western Desert style, modestly likened to the Sistine Chapel.

As Christianity weakens, and as identification with the famous European sites of pilgrimage disappears, there has been a compensatory appropriation of Aboriginal sites by white Australians. Some years ago a book appeared entitled *Sacred Places of Australia*: all were Aboriginal. In one sense this is an extension of environmentalism, an eagerness to come to terms with the place, to connect with its psychic past and feel spiritually rooted here. 'Whether this ancient land is sacred presence', writes David Tacey, 'or simply great scenery, depends almost entirely on the condition of the ego-personality that meets it'. But he urges an almost voluptuous renunciation, writing that a recognition of the 'sacredness of the centre' will become evident 'only when we achieve the courage to leave the psychological edge'. Evident here perhaps is a feeling that, as others have written, 'whiteness is a state of incompleteness'; in a multicultural Australia it is 'not ethnic *enough*'.

Whatever the case, it has led to some extraordinary manifestations at Ayers Rock – Uluru in particular. Early in the 1990s the Crystal People, a cult with peculiar rites based in America, decided to send 6000 people to Uluru to join hands around its base: permission to do so was refused by the traditional owners. The Rock has had an iconic significance for white Australians since the early 1970s; many tourists go there with a willingness to acknowledge its spiritual force. An added twist was given to this recently when a book appeared entitled *Uluru Journey: An Exploration into Narrative Theology*. Uluru had become the focus of a Christian pilgrimage, with an account modelled on *The Canterbury Tales*.[5]

The tourism vector

Meanwhile tourism rampages onwards. Fifty per cent of Florida is now said to be covered by tourist developments; perhaps this kind of thing effectively complements the reports we increasingly hear of yet more species disappearing from the face of the earth every hour. What is not in dispute is the scale of contemporary tourism. So self-evident has this become that John Urry draws a comparison between the automobile industry, with its emphasis on manufacture—which could be said to epitomise 'organised' capitalism—and tourism, which he sees as epitomising the dominance of non-material forms of production. 'Disorganised' capitalism, as he styles the contemporary form, involves a greater role for culture and for globalism, and practises post-materiality even as it stresses consumption. Tourism, then, as its own specificity is dissolving, is also tending to take over and even organise much contemporary social and cultural experience. We are all tourists now.[6]

Urry writes as though all of this is a good thing, as though the consumption tourism promotes is equally available to everyone. The word 'exclusive' (connected with a variety of attractions) has always sounded glamorous, so it was useful to have the developer Mike Gore come along and remind us, by his referring to ordinary tourists as 'cockroaches', that exclusive also means excluding. But it is not only the market that is being segmented; so too is the workforce. Tourism industry jobs cost less than most to establish, but they also tend to pay less. Unionism is poorly developed, mobility high—partly because many people rationalise their poor working conditions by persuading themselves that they are constantly moving in a social ambience. Then a move like the Kennett government's inclusion of training at McDonald's in the Victorian Certificate of Education clearly demonstrates how tourism imperatives can work to accelerate proletarianisation.

Tourism is undoubtedly central to the contemporary experience. As Urry writes, 'In postmodernity many spheres of social and cultural life are de-differentiated. Tourism is nowhere and yet everywhere'. People 'surf' the Net; they 'visit' sites. Increasingly presentations—even lectures—aspire to the condition of infotainment; it becomes harder to differentiate a real situation from a staged one. When the Port Arthur gunman opened fire, some people thought it was just a re-enactment. Similarly, when a disturbed man brandished a sword recently in a crowded Melbourne street, elements in the crowd seemed oblivious of any danger, and urged action by shouting, 'We're getting bored!' Evident here was a disjunctive individualism, dissociating itself from any consequences as it insisted on the right to be entertained.[7]

The cost of producing the movie *Titanic*, which fortunately for its backers became the highest-grossing movie of the twentieth century, was slightly more than the cost, inflation adjusted, of building the original ship itself. That an infotainment product can cost more than the real thing is testament to a world where makebelieve or virtual experience seems to be valued more.

Abbreviations

A&R	Angus & Robertson (publishers, Sydney)
ABS	Australian Bureau of Statistics (Canberra)
ADB	*Australian Dictionary of Biography*
AE	*Australian Encyclopaedia* (various editions)
AGPS	Australian Government Publishing Service (publishers, Canberra)
ANPWS	Australian National Parks & Wildlife Service
ANTA	Australian National Travel Association
ANU	Australian National University
ATIA	Australian Travel Industry Association
CLC	Central Land Council
FSW	Fairfax, Syme and Weldon (publishers, Sydney)
ML	Mitchell Library (Sydney)
MUP	Melbourne University Press (publishers, Melbourne)
NMM	National Maritime Museum (Greenwich, UK)
NSWGTB	New South Wales Government Tourist Bureau
NSWYB	*New South Wales Yearbook*
NTRS	Northern Territory Records Service
NTTC	Northern Territory Tourist Commission
OSN	Orient Line archives (held at National Maritime Museum)
OUP	Oxford University Press (publishers, Melbourne)
P & O	Pacific and Orient archives (held at National Maritime Museum)
PATA	Pacific Area Travel Association
QGTB	Queensland Government Tourist Bureau
RAASA	Royal Automobile Association of South Australia

RACQ	Royal Automobile Club of Queensland
RACV	Royal Automobile Club of Victoria
SMH	*Sydney Morning Herald*
TA	Tasmanian Archives
TCA	Thomas Cook archives (London)
TGTB	Tasmanian Government Tourist Bureau
TTA	Tasmanian Tourist Association
UNSWP	University of NSW Press (publishers, Sydney)
UWAP	University of Western Australia Press (publishers, Perth)

Currency

On 14 February 1966 Australian currency changed from pounds, shillings and pence (£ s d) to dollars and cents at the rate of £1=$2. Twelve pence made up one shilling; twenty shillings made up one pound; and twenty-one shillings made up one guinea.

Weights and Measures

1 inch	2.54	centimetres
1 foot (12 inches)	30.5	centimetres
1 mile	1.61	kilometres
1 acre	0.4	hectare

Notes

Introduction: Tourism, Postmodernism and Australia

1   Contemporary tourism: 'Dream Factories: A Survey of Travel and Tourism', *Economist*, 10 Jan 1998, p. 3.
2   Tourism precursors: Clayton and Price, *The Seven Wonders of the Ancient World*, p. 12; Michael Pearson, 'The meanings of journeys', *Australian Cultural History*, no. 10 (1991), p. 129.
3   Mark Twain, *The Innocents Abroad*, pp. 995, 515.
4   Un-tourists: Barthes, 'The Blue Guide', *Mythologies*, p. 74. Luzern: Bernard, *Rush to the Alps*, p. 7. 'Pooles': Ousby, *The Englishman's England*, p. 130.
5   Broadening of the Grand Tour: Brendon, *Thomas Cook*, pp. 10, 11, 182.
6   Thomas Cook & Son: Brendon, *Thomas Cook*, esp. pp. 3, 32, 60, 80, 120, 136–8, 182, 183, 190–1, 200–1; Boorstin, *The Image*, pp. 86, 88; God's earth: Turner and Ash, *The Golden Hordes*, p. 53.
7   Leed, *The Mind of the Traveler*, pp. 286–7.
8   Australian tourism: figures from *Forecast*, vol. 3, no. 2, Tourism Forecasting Council, June 1997; Morris, 'Life as a Tourist Object in Australia', in Lanfant, Allcock and Bruner, *International Tourism*, p. 182; John Edwards, 'Crash and Learn', *Australian's Review of Books*, vol. 3, no. 7 (Oct 1998), p. 12.
9   Introduction, Lanfant, Allcock and Bruner, *International Tourism*, p. 3.
10 Tourist as postmodernist: MacCannell, *The Tourist*, p. x; Baudrillard, *America*, p. 31; Jameson, 'Postmodernism', p. 64.
11 Tourist and consumption: hypnosis, Fussell, *Abroad*, p. 42. Fijian: Bosselman, *In the Wake of the Tourist*, p. 110. Guides: Ousby, *Englishman's England*, p. 5; Fussell, *Abroad*, p. 43.
12 MacCannell, *The Tourist*, pp. 44–5; Joe Rollo, 'Monumental pull at the heartstrings', *Age*, 29 Apr 1998.
13 Simulacra: for an anthology of Australian 'bigs', see Amdur, *It Really Is a Big Country*. Eco, title essay, *Travels in Hyperreality*, p. 19; Baudrillard, *America*, pp. 41, 86, 104; Urry, *Consuming Places*, p.149.
14 Baudrillard, *America*, p. 76.
15 Australians and 'Home': McInnes, *The Road to Gundagai*, pp. 115–18; White, 'Bluebells and Fogtown', p. 44.
16 V. Smith (ed.), *Hosts and Guests*, p. 1.
17 Lévi-Strauss, quoted in Leed, *The Mind of the Traveler*, p. 285.

1 Origins

[1] The abortive Cook's tour: *Cook's Excursionist*, vol. 31, no. 1 (1 Feb 1881), p. 31; American line: Withey, *Grand Tours and Cook's Tours*, p. 272; low ebb: T. R. Reese, *History of the Royal Commonwealth Society* (London: OUP, 1968), pp. 10–11; Joyce and Edwards (eds), *Trollope's Australia*, p. 63; advertisement in *Walch's Tasmanian Guide Book*.

[2] Explorers: see Carter, 'Invisible Journeys'.

[3] Bradshaw: Brendon, *Thomas Cook*, p. 12; *Bradshaw's Guide to Victoria*, preface.

[4] Early guides: *The Stranger's Guide to Sydney*; *The Handbook to Sydney and Suburbs*, p. vii; Thomas, *Guide for Excursionists from Melbourne*. See also Directories, Guidebooks and Publicity Materials section of Select Bibliography.

[5] Nature of guides: Edwin Burton, *Visitors' Guide to Sydney* (1874 edn), preface; *Handbook to Sydney*, p. 5; Meredith: Vivienne Rae-Ellis, *Louisa Ann Meredith, A Tigress in Exile* (Hobart: St David's Park, 1990), p. 251.

[6] Selecting attractions: Burton, *Visitors' Guide*, preface; *Walch's Tasmanian Guide Book*, p. 4; Thomas, *Guide for Excursionists from Melbourne*, p. 198, raw amusements, pp. 78, 98, 37–8; Heywood, *A Vacation Tour at the Antipodes*, pp. 44–5.

[7] Joyce and Edwards (eds), *Trollope's Australia*, pp. 43–6. For other guidebooks, see Jenkins, 'Sydney Harbour Panorama', pp. 280–6.

[8] Caves: Joyce and Edwards (eds), *Trollope's Australia*, pp. 526–8; Robert Whitworth, *Official Handbook & Guide to Melbourne*, p. 12; Jenolan description: *Guide to Sydney*, p. 85; geological: Cook, *The Jenolan Caves*, preface.

[9] Jenolan: Burke, Images of Popular Leisure in the Blue Mountains, pp. 40, 55, 57; Foster, *The Jenolan Caves*, p. 14; *Railway Guide of NSW*, 1879, 1889; *Trickett's Guide to the Jenolan Caves*, 1899.

[10] Western Australian caves: Keenan: *West Australian*, 22 Apr 1904; Robinson, clippings in Western Australia Archives, PR5241/1; funding cuts, 1909: Moore, 'Tourists, Scientists and Wilderness Enthusiasts', pp. 114–19.

[11] Mountains: Garran (ed.), *Australia: The First Hundred Years*, pp. 52–3; Dilke, *Greater Britain*, p. 304; Katoomba, 1889 account quoted in Burke, Images, p. 113.

[12] 'Hill stations': Macedon, Milbourne, *Mt Macedon*, pp. 138–9, 104, 63; Kuranda, Humston, *Welcome to Kuranda*, pp. 34–5.

[13] Blue Mountains: Speirs, *Landscape Art and the Blue Mountains*, pp. 60, 62.

[14] Katoomba: 1889 account quoted in Burke, Images, pp. 112–13; *Railway Guide*, 1884, pp. 43–4; Burke, Images of Popular Leisure in the Blue Mountains, p. 21; Smith, *From Katoomba to Jenolan Caves*, pp. 9–11.

[15] Women: Julia Horne, Favourite Resorts, pp. 77–92, 151, 152, 158.

[16] Railways: largest, Gunn, *Along Parallel Lines*, p. 197; fares, *NSW Government Gazette*, 1874–1898; facilities, Belbin and Burke, *Full Steam Across the Mountains*, pp. 98–101; numbers, *Official Yearbook of New South Wales*, 1904–5, p. 134; Burke, Images, pp. 15, 28–30, 50.

[17] Glenelg: Perry, *The Place of Waters*, pp. 140–1, 32, 143; Brown, *Glenelg: An Urban Village, 1836–1972*, pp. 27, 45–7; *Glenelg Visitor Guide and Holiday Planner, 1992*, p. 11; see also Davidson, 'The Rise and Fall of Proclamation Day'.

[18] Bendigo: Cronin, *Colonial Casualties*, p. 161; *AE*, 1963 edn, vol. 2, p. 352; *1972 Bendigo Easter Fair Souvenir Program*, pp. 9, 11, 35; *Bendigo Advertiser*, 20 April 1897.

[19] Exhibitions: Davison, 'Exhibitions', p. 17; Parris and Shaw, 'The Melbourne International Exhibition 1880–1881', p. 250; Buck-Morss, *The Dialectics of Seeing*, pp. 85, 399.

[20] Melbourne 1880: Davison, *Marvellous Melbourne*, p. 2; *Age*, 5 Oct 1880; rail fares: *Argus*, 24 Sep,

but *Age* not till 18 Oct 1880; *Excursionist*, vol. 31, no. 1 (Feb. 1881), p. 31; John Lee, *Glenelg Historical Guide & Directory 1883*, p. 15.

21 Melbourne 1888: Davison, *Australians 1888*, pp. 23, 26; Parris and Shaw, p. 243; Maya V. Tucker, 'Centennial Celebrations, 1888', pp. 19–21; A. Higgins to Thos Cook, 10 Apr 1888, TCA.

22 Hotels: Freeland, *The Australian Pub*, pp. 147–9, Magee, *The French Second Empire Influence*, p. 133; Allom, Lovell & Associates, *The Hotel Windsor*, pp. 133, 10, 23, 15–16, 24; Spicer, *Duchess*, p. 43; Morris, *Pax Britannica*, p. 285.

23 Tasmanian cruise: E. T. Luke and J. G. Ballard, *A Southern Breeze: the Record of an Easter Trip* (Ballarat, privately printed, 1893).

24 Fares and tariffs: Burke, *Images*, p. 46; *NSW Government Gazette*, 1883.

25 Holidays: Echo, Burke, *Images*, opp. p. 47; Edwin Burton, *Visitors' Guide to Sydney* (1874), p. 44; 'Holidays', *AE*, 1962 edn, vol. 4, p. 518; Craik, *Resorting to Tourism*, p. 46; Steinke, 'The Long-term Decline in the Standard Working Year', p. 417.

2 Messing About in Boats

1 Henley: Dodd, *Henley Royal Regatta*, pp. 10, 106, 110; Suffolk et al., *The Encyclopaedia of Sport*, vol. II, p. 294; Rickards, *Rowing in Victoria*, p. 8; 'Rowing', *Australia Today*, 8 Dec 1906, p. 139; *Argus* quoted in Colin Jones, 'Henley on Yarra: The Lost Festival', *This Australia*, vol. 2, no. 4 (1983); Lang, *The Victorian Oarsman*, pp. 9, 23, 27, 33.

2 Proudfoot's: Kellaway, *'A most complete establishment.'*

3 Melbourne ferries: Jones, *Ferries on the Yarra*, esp. pp. 86, 15, 29, 67, 57, 74.

4 Port Phillip Bay steamers: The Vagabond, 'Queenscliff', *Leader*, 2 Dec 1893, p. 52; W. K. Fitchett, *Down the Bay*, esp. pp. 14, 17, 28–9, 30–1, 90–1; C. Dickson Gregory, *The Romance of the Edina* (Melbourne: Robertson & Mullens, 1935), pp. 59–66; Nepean Historical Society, *The Peninsula Story: Sorrento and Portsea*, p. 55; Loney, *Bay Steamers and Coastal Ferries*, p. 32; *Centennial Almanac 1889/Guide to Sorrento*, p. 9.

5 Queenscliff: Dunn, *Borough of Queenscliffe*; Allom, Lovell & Associates, *Queenscliffe Urban Conservation Study*, pp. 5–7, 9, 37; *Queenscliff Sentinel*, e.g. 8 Jan 1887; *Illustrated Australian News*, 25 Feb 1874, p. 26; Vagabond, 'Queenscliff,' *Leader*, 2 Dec 1893, p. 52; Whitfield, *Geelong and District Directory 1906–07*, pp. 138–42.

6 Sorrento: Bagot, *Coppin the Great*, p. 331; *A Guide to Sorrento*, pp. 3, 31; *Centennial Almanac 1889/Guide to Sorrento*, p. 14; *Australasian*, 31 Dec 1892, p. 1299; Winzenried, *Tram to Sorrento*, p. 22; Poynter, *Doubts and Certainties*, p. 371; Nicholson, 'Tourism on the Mornington Peninsula', p. 87.

7 Coastal shipping: Pemberton, *Australian Coastal Shipping*, pp. 12, 83, 141, 146, 153–4; Bach, *A Maritime History of Australia*, pp. 196, 249; advertisement in *Cook's Traveller's Gazette*, vol. LX, no. 11 (Nov 1910), p. 32.

8 Tasmania—shipping and numbers: North-West Tourist Assoc., Devonport: *Tasmania's North-West Coast: The Switzerland of Australia* (1908), p. 3; Cox, *Bass Strait Crossing*, pp. 113, 115–16; Morris, *In Pursuit of the Travelling Man*, pp. vi–vii, and 1895–1905 section, p. iii.

9 Tasmania—sanitorium: Robson, *History of Tasmania*, vol. II, pp. 243, 283; Thomas, *Guide to Excursionists between Australia and Tasmania* (1883), epigraph on title page; Tasmanian Government Railways, *Guide to Tasmania, Premier Health Resort of the Commonwealth* (1906); Pierce, *The Oxford Literary Guide to Australia*, pp. 193–4.

10 Hobart Regatta: Morris, *Travelling Man*, p. vi; Young, *Profiting from the Past*, p. 48; Cowling, 'The Royal Hobart Regatta', esp. pp. 2, 4, 73, 79.

[11] Tasmanian Tourist Association: Robson, *History*, pp. 284–5; Morris, Travelling Man, pp. 18–25, 47, 38, 145; Tasmanian Government Railways, *Illustrated Guide to Tasmania* [*c.* 1903], p. 34; TTA, 'Warramunga', *Trip to Hartz Mountains* [n.d.]; TTA, *Hobart Carnival 1910, Official Programme*; TTA, *Official Souvenir of the Hobart Historical Pageant 1910*.

[12] Mt Wellington: Morris, Travelling Man, p. 31; Robson, *History*, pp. 284, 286.

[13] North-West Coast: Haywood, *Colonists' Advertiser & Visitors' Guide to Tasmania via the North West Coast* (1888); North-West Tourist Assoc., *Tasmania's North-West Coast: The Switzerland of Australia* (1908) and *Tasmania's NWC: The Riviera of Australia* [*c.* 1906]; Humphrey McQueen, *Tom Roberts* (Sydney: Macmillan, 1996), p. 420; *Tourist and Visitors' Guide to Burnie, Wynyard, Penguin and Waratah* (*c.* 1915); Morris, Travelling Man, pp. 44–5.

[14] Port Arthur: this account draws heavily on Young, Profiting from the Past, esp. pp. 39, 72, 62, 123, 39, 53–5, 27, 38, 140, 138, 147; see also Davidson, 'Port Arthur: A Tourist History', esp. p. 664. Guidebooks referred to here are the *Tasmanian Tourist Association Guide Book and Gazetteer* [*c.* 1905], p. 29; Thomas, *Guide For Excursionists from the Mainland to Tasmania* (1869), p. 159; J. W. Beattie, *Port Arthur, The British Penal Settlement in Tasmania*, a guidebook on sale until relatively recent times; flyer for *S.S. Nubeena*, Tasmaniana Library, State Library, Hobart; Anna T. Brennan, *Peace at Port Arthur*, p. 1; Tasmanian Tourist Association, *Beautiful Tasmania*, p. 70.

[15] Fishing: William Senior, *Travel and Trout in the Antipodes* (Melbourne: George Robertson, 1880), pp. 121, 158; Gilmore, in Rolls (ed.), *An Anthology of Australian Fishing*, p. 127; Harvey J. Taylor, *Shannon Rise Revisited* (Huonville, Tasmania: 1993), pp. 3, 11, 56, 9, 44; R. Slater, *Rod and Line in Tasmania* (Launceston: 1904), p. 23; Tasmanian Government Railways, *Illustrated Guide to Tasmania* [1903], p. 30; TTA, *Accommodation Directory, Season 1915–1916*, p. 6; Don Gilmour, *The Tasmanian Trout* (Launceston: 1973), pp. 149, 46–7, 268.

[16] Shipping lines other than P & O and Orient Line: Pemberton, *Australian Coastal Shipping*, p. 25; Australian Shipping News, *Victoria of To-day*, inside front cover, pp. 41–3; *Australasian Handbook*, 1906, pp. 28, 34, vi; *Cook's Australasian Sailing List*, 1911, p. 2; Maber, *North Star to Southern Cross*, pp. 189, 221.

[17] P & O and mail contracts: Radson and O'Donoghue, *P & O: A Fleet History*, p. 13; Bach, *Maritime History*, p. 150, 136; *P & O Pocket Book*, 1888, p. 42; Cable, *A Hundred Year History of the P & O*, p. 120.

[18] P & O as imperial line: *Australasian Handbook*, 1906, p. iv; 'P & O Steamship Company', *Fortune*, vol. XXXIV, no. 3, p. 122; gun platform: *Aberdeen Free Press*, 9 Mar 1888, Press Cuttings P & O Archives 98/20; Maber, *North Star to Southern Cross*, p. 17.

[19] P & O basic statistics: *P & O Pocket Book*, 1900, p. 24; Maber, *North Star to Southern Cross*, p. 105; passenger numbers, Orient Lines Services to Australia, Booking Figures 1880–1926, OSN/22/6; fares, *Leader Annual*, 1913, encl. TA PD1 38/24/14; profits, Reports to Shareholders, P & O Archives 6/13, 1883–1897.

[20] P & O and shipping disasters: Cable, *Hundred Year History*, p. 206.

[21] 'Home': McInnes, *The Road to Gundagai*, pp. 115–18; passengers: *Illustrated London News*, 21 Sep 1895; *P & O Pocket Book*, 1900, pp. 36–8, 1888, p. 73; Australia: Hume Nesbit in *P & O Pocket Book*, 1888, pp. 234–7 and *Pocket Book*, 1900, pp. 168–75; Beatrice Grimshaw, in *P & O Pocket Book*, 1908, pp. 137, 139; comforts: *Harrowgate Herald*, 12 Dec 1888; Lord Inchcape, P & O Archives 6/23, pp. 3–4, 1927; P & O *Regulations*, 1952, p. 57; Lind, *Sea Jargon*, p. 144; 'at home' and athletics: Diary of a Passenger on the Orient Line OSN /31/5, 10 and 11 Apr 1896; Orient Royal Mail Line, *Post Card Souvenir No 1*.

[22] Orient Line: Maber, *North Star to Southern Cross*, p. 104; Gordon, *From Chusan to Sea Princess*, pp. 26, 45; stowaways: Lilley, Bound for Australia, 1885, typescript in OSN/22/4, p. 2; route: 'The P & O Steamship Company', p. 166; 1928 British tourists: 'Memo. Tourist traffic to Australia', OSN/22/4, 26 July 1928.

[23] Modernisation: Gordon, *From Chusan to Sea Princess*, pp. 53–4, 60; Padfield, *Beneath the House Flag*, pp. 123–7.

[24] Final phase: optimism about planes, 'The P & O Steamship Company', p. 174; Currie, Launch of *Canberra*, 16 Mar 1960, P & O 97/11; 1970s: Gordon, *From Chusan to Sea Princess*, p. 95.

3 The Rise and Fall of the Tourist Bureau

[1] The early interest of Cook's: *Cook's Excursionist*, vol. 31, no. 1 (1 Feb 1881), p. 31; quotations from John Cook to Frank Cook, 4 August 1887, TCA; Brendon, *Thomas Cook*, p. 213; Memo of Instructions for Mr Hatch, 26 Aug 1890, Setting Up Business in Australasia, TCA.

[2] Cook's network: offices and agencies, *Cook's Australasian Traveller's Gazette and Tourist Advertiser*, 11 Jan 1890, p. 5; *Cook's Excursionist*, vol. 43, no. 11 (18 Nov 1893); *Cook's Australasian Trav. Gaz.*, 1 Mar 1892, p. 1, 2 May 1892, p. 3, 11 Jan 1890, p. 5, 1 Aug 1892, p. 3, 5 Jan 1894, p. 3.

[3] Cook's facilities: Brendon, *Thomas Cook*, p. 213; *Cook's Australasian Trav. Gaz.*, 1 Oct 1898, p. 3, 14 Mar 1893, p. 3, 1 Apr 1892, p. 3, 1 Oct 1900, p. 3.

[4] Cook's rail excursions etc: Brendon, *Thomas Cook*, pp. 237, 213; *Cook's Australasian Trav. Gaz.*, 2 Nov 1894, p. 17, 1 Sep 1893, p. 3, 1 Dec 1891, p. 3.

[5] Cook's package tours: *Cook's Australasian Trav. Gaz.*, 5 Jan 1894, p. 4; 1 Mar 1892, p. 9.

[6] Cook's in Tasmania: *Cook's Australasian Trav. Gaz.*, 2 Nov 1893, p. 5, 2 July 1894, p. 9, 2 Dec 1896, p. 4, 2 Oct 1899, p. 5, 1 Nov 1895, p. 6, 2 Nov 1894, p. 7, 1 Nov 1895, p. 6. See also John Ferguson, *Bibliography of Australia*, vol. V (Sydney: A&R), pp. 697–8; *Cook's Australasian Trav. Gaz.*, 1 Nov 1895, p. 6.

[7] Foundation of TTA: *Constitution . . . and Annual Report for 1899;* Harris, Selling Tasmania, p. 19; Morris, In Pursuit of the Travelling Man, pp. 23, 25.

[8] TTA and the wilderness: *Annual Report for 1899*; Morris, Travelling Man, pp. 28–9, 40, 46, 50.

[9] TTA and Cook's: Young, Profiting from the Past, pp. 126–8; Morris, Travelling Man, p. 48; *Annual Report for Year 1910–11*, p. 4.

[10] TTA difficulties: Harris, Selling Tasmania, pp. 23, 15–20.

[11] Railways: 1913 guidebook, *Complete Guide to Tasmania*; E. T. Emmett, History of Tasmania's Tourist Bureau, part 1; Harris, Selling Tasmania, p. 29.

[12] Foundation of TGTB: potential, American consul's statement, *TTA Annual Report for the Financial Year 1912–13*, p. 2; 'national', G. W. Smith to E. T. Emmett, memo, 13 Oct 1916, TA 35 PD1/38/84/16; Harris, Selling Tasmania, pp. 35, 47, 45, 40. Emmett's resourcefulness extended to convening a meeting in 1929 to found the Hobart Walking Club. Bardwell, National Parks in Victoria, p. 143.

[13] Foundation of NSW Intelligence Dept: NSW Premier's Department, *The Establishment of an Intelligence Department in NSW*, n.d., pp. 13, 2, 9, 3–4, 16, 14, 10, 6.

[14] Intelligence Dept, office and priorities: TTA *Annual Report*, 1908–09, p. 10; [NSW] *Intelligence Dept Bulletin*, no. 21, pp. 6, 22, 31, 27–8, 32.

[15] NSW tourist programme: [NSW] *Intelligence Dept Bulletin*, no. 21, pp. 33–5, 39; *Annual Report*, 1910.

[16] Mt Kosciuszko: 'The Scot we know, C. D. Paterson', in *Scottish Australasian*, June 1918, p. 6320; [NSW] *Intelligence Dept Bulletin*, no. 21, p. 37; Tourist & Immigration Department Report, *NSWYB*, 1910, *Hansard*, 13 Nov 1919, p. 2639.

[17] Tourism in Intelligence Dept: immigration statistics, *NSWYB* 1909–10; *The Establishment of an Intelligence Department in NSW*, pp. 11, 14.

[18] Tourism and immigration: TTA *Annual Report*, 1908–09, p. 5; Tas ad., *Australia Today*, 1 Nov 1913, p. 80; *Cook's Australasian Trav. Gaz.*, vol. 8, no. 12 (1896), p. 4; settler following tourist: Connolly,

WA Colonial Secretary, *West Australian*, 8 Feb 1910; Northern Rivers: [NSW] *Intelligence Dept Bulletin*, no. 21, p. 35; Emmett, quoted in Harris, *Selling Tasmania*, p. 46.

[19] Personal links, NSW Immigration & Tourist Bureau: *Assisted Passages to NSW/How to Nominate A Friend for an Assisted Passage* (1910); 'Back to', e.g. Beechworth, see Griffiths, *Beechworth*, p. 49.

[20] Railways influence: C. E. Norman, Commissioner VR, to Acting Premier, Tas., 23 Apr 1913, TA 35 PD1/38/11/14.

[21] Intelligence Departments etc.: Correll, 'The History of South Australia's Department of Tourism', p. 2; Tourist Committee: Bardwell, National Parks, p. 15; WA ad., *Australia Today*, 1 Nov 1913, p. 31.

[22] Budgets: Periodical Reports on Touring Matters, TA 35 PD1/38/2/14.

[23] Postwar changes: Soley, Tourist Development in Victoria 1919–1939, pp. 43, 52, 58, 10, 28.

[24] Railways and other initiatives: Soley, Tourist Development, pp. 39, 42, 45–8, 11; *Herald*, 2 Jan 1926, pp. 53, 62. The Tourists' Resorts Committee was a later version (1922) of the Interdepartmental Tourist Committee of 1911.

[25] Proposal to develop the Tourist Business of the Commonwealth and to stimulate greater travel amongst Australians, confidential printed report, n.p. 1927 and 1928 appendix (Melbourne: Development and Migration Commission, 1928).

[26] *Walkabout* March 1938, p. 62.

[27] *NSW Parliamentary Debates* 14 Sept 1928, p. 135.

[28] P. Spearritt 'Sites and sights: Australian Travel Posters 1909–1990', *Trading Places*, Monash University Gallery, 1991; Entries on Trompf and Northfield in *ADB*, vol. 12, vol. 15.

[29] First edition Hutchinson, London, 1933, pp. 233, 148–9.

[30] *Walkabout*, December 1934, p. 7.

[31] *Walkabout* advertising flyer, n.d., *c.* 1938, Spearritt collection.

[32] South Australian Centenary: Series GRC 7/29 (1935–1937). SAA is the main source here, in particular files 316 (1935), Correspondence with the Agent-General, and 21 (1937), Report of the State Organizing Director. Quotations come from Agent-General to Director, 3 Jan 1936, and Crawford Vaughan to Director, 1 Nov 1935, File 323 (1935). Other information from the Notes/Description in the Index to the Tourism holdings in SAA and Correll, *The History of South Australia's Department of Tourism*, p. 6.

[33] G. Souter, 'Skeleton at the feast', in Gammage & Spearritt (eds.), *Australia 1938*.

[34] Evans 1930: NSWTB brochures and correspondence, Spearritt collection.

[35] See *The Tourist*, a short-lived monthly magazine issued by the NSWGTB 1920 (ML).

[36] Leo J. Harrigan, *Victorian Railways to '62*, Victorian Railways, 1963. State Development Committee, 'Tourist Facilities Government Tourist Bureaux', *Victorian Parliamentary Papers*, 1950–51.

[37] Harris et al. 1965, p. 74, p. 73, pp. 82–3.

[38] See Loker, Taking Australia to the World: a history of the Australian Tourist Commission.

[39] See entries on railways in successive editions of the *Australian Encyclopaedia* (1925–1996).

[40] *RACV Accommodation Guide*, 1st edn, 1959, 102 pages; 2nd edn, 1965, 184 pages.

4 Rooms at the Inn

[1] Hotels as precursors: McGuire, *Inns of Australia*, pp. 180, 166; on Frankston: McGuire, p. 250, Jones, *Frankston*, p. 51.

[2] Early hotels and Chisholm: Austin, *A Pictorial History of Cobb & Co*, pp. 117–18; Gilgandra: Dormer, *The Bushman's Arms*, pp. 4, 47; Cady, 'Inns, Hotels and Temperance Hotels', pp. 13–28.

[3] Coaching inns: Freeland, *The Australian Pub*, pp. 100, 96, 123; Austin, *Cobb & Co*, pp. 107, 113.

[4] Impact of railways: Beechworth, *Bradshaw's Guide to Victoria*, May 1856, p. 35, cf. Jan 1875, pp. 14,

82; 1924: Austin, *Cobb & Co*, p. 188; stables: *Cobb & Co's Guide*, 1883–84, p. 44; expense: Freeland, *The Australian Pub*, p. 146; Grand Pacific: Cecil, *Lorne. The Founding Years*, p. 54, also McGuire, p. 210; Euroa, *Traveller*, vol. III, no. 8 (1892), p. 8.

5   Commercial travellers: Grainger, 23 Oct 1908, in Dreyfus, *Farthest North of Humanness*, p. 237; *Traveller*, vol. I, no. 10 (1891), pp. 6–7; Horne, 'The Ambassadors of Commerce', pp. 40, 42.

6   The beer revolution: Freeland, *The Australian Pub*, pp. 141, 152, 143.

7   Women and hotels: de Mori, '*Time, Gentlemen*', p. 112; Higgs, 'But I Wouldn't Want My Wife to Work There!', esp. pp. 69, 71, 74, 78.

8   WA State Hotels: J. R. Campbell, Gen. Manager, State Hotels and Inspection of Liquors Dept, to Acting Under Secretary, 25 Oct 1920, WA Archives 981–AN 15/1 file 91/1921, item 22; same series, file 79/25; 'legitimately restrict', same series, file 112/17, item 193; hotel licence ratios and rates exemptions, de Mori, '*Time, Gentlemen!*', pp. 63, 67; refused service, de Mori, p. 62; sold off, de Mori p. 67.

9   Renmark: Grosvenor, *Red Mud to Green Oasis*, p. 118; McGuire, *Inns of Australia*, p. 162.

10 Rough conditions: Travers, *Ninety-Four Declared* (London: Elm Tree Books, 1991), p. 39; marginal note, p. 2 of OSN/22/4, Tourist Traffic to Australia, memo 26 July 1928, NMM; Alice Springs, Blakeley, *Hard Liberty*, p. 154; 1950s to present, Shute, *A Town Like Alice*, p. 229, Donovan, *Alice Springs*, pp. 324–5, Davie, *Age*, 5 Sep 1992, Extra 5. For a somewhat theatrical description of the dreadfulness of old-style country pubs, see Barry Humphries, *More, Please*, pp. 144–5.

11 Dunstan, *Flag: the First Thirty Years*.

12 For a fictional account of running a large Australian country hotel see Debra Adelaide's novel *Hotel Albatross* (Sydney: Random House, 1995). Greenacres motel opened December 1964, *RACV Accommodation Guide*, 1964.

13 Humphries, p. 39.

14 Quotes are from postcards are in Davidson's possession, as is the Erskine House brochure and a similar one from Kalimna. The unusual advertisement on the Carinya card may have originated in its having appeared in another series, the Southern Cross; image, message and number were all transferred to become Rose P. 2128. For moral standards at Carinya, see Soley, Tourist Development in Victoria, p. 26.

15 *Wentworth Magazine*, February 1930, pp. 1, 56; E. R. Gribble, 'Forty years with the Aborigines', *Wentworth Magazine*, October 1930, p. 19; depression: *Wentworth Magazine*, October 1930, p. 56.

16 For an analysis of dividends paid by Australia's five largest brewing companies between 1933 and 1935 see Welborn, *Swan: the history of a brewery*, pp. 156–7; Hotel Manly: *Building Magazine*, February 1935.

17 The Canberra pamphlet, Brisbane 1935; *Hotel Australia* booklet, Melbourne 1938.

18 Kirkby, *Barmaids*, pp. 177–9, p. 183.

19 *RACV Accommodation Guide*, 1st edn 1959, 1965; *Hotel Metropole: services and information*, brochure, 1966.

20 Susan Priestley, *Making their Mark* (Sydney: FSW, 1984), p. 249.

21 *RACV Accommodation Guide*, 1960, p. 16; *Chevron: Australia's leading private hotel*, brochure, c. 1960, Spearritt collection.

22 Chevron Qld Ltd, *Annual Reports*, 1957–60; Chevron Sydney Ltd, *Prospectus*, 1959.

23 *The Regent, Sydney* (Sydney: The Regent Hotel, 1983), p. 6.

24 M. McVey and Brian King, 'Hotels/accommodation' Economist Intelligence Unit, *Travel and Tourism Analyst*, no. 4, 1989.

25 See the ABS annuals, *Tourism Accommodation Australia* and *The Australian Hotel Industry Survey of Operations*, 1984 to present.

26 B&B establishments are not listed in the *Australian National Tourguide*, 1989, published jointly by

the RACV and the RAASA, nor in the RACQ's *Queensland Accommodation Guide* 1989–90; the RACT's *Accommodation and Touring Guide*, 1993; J. & J. Thomas, *The Australian Bed and Breakfast Book*, 1994; *Homes, Farms, Guesthouses* (Dee Why: Moonshine Press, 1993), p. 10.

27 James Halliday, *Wine Atlas of Australia and New Zealand* (North Ryde: A&R, 1991); *Australian National Tourguide*, RACV, 1989; *RACV Accommodation Guide 1998/99*.

28 Australian Bureau of Statistics census itemises dwellings of four or more storeys by locality.

29 Robert Longhurst, *Gold Coast: our heritage in focus* (Brisbane: State Library of Queensland Foundation, 1995).

30 *Western Australian Tourist Guide and Accommodation Directory, 1938–39, Principal Cities, towns and holiday resorts* (Perth: Government Tourist and Publicity Bureau, 1938); Ferguson, *Rottnest Island.*

5 Beside the Seaside

1 Beginnings: Courbin, *The Lure of the Sea*, pp. 62–7, 70, 78, 149, 230.

2 Brighton: Courbin, *Sea*, pp. 76, 254–5, 268, 276; Bainton-Williams, *Town and City Maps of the British Isles 1800–1855*, p. 100; Hern, *The Seaside Holiday*, p. 166; Bainbridge, *Pavilions on the Sea*, pp. 74–6, 135, 190.

3 Australian piers: Wells, *Sunny Memories*, p. 61; Spearritt, *Sydney's Century*, pp. 223–8; Brown, *Glenelg*, pp. 79, 84.

4 St Kilda: Cooper, *History of St Kilda*, vol. I, pp. 173, 175, 178, vol. II, pp. 149–50, 208, 292, 315; Longmire, *St Kilda: The Show Goes On*, pp. xi–xii, 1–2, 7–9; Marshall, *Luna Park*, p. 41; Blackpool: Pimlott, *The Englishman's Holiday*, pp. 176–7; *Wimpole's Visitor's Guide*, pp. xviii, 21; camping, quote from legend on Tuck's postcard of Brighton, *c.* 1910; Davison and Dunstan, 'St Kilda', p. 136.

5 The rising sun: Robertson, *The Early Buildings of Southern Tasmania*, vol. 2, pp. 310, 314–16; Fussell, *Abroad*, p. 138; Howarth, *When the Riviera was Ours*, p. 138.

6 Manly: Maxwell, *Surf*, p. 17.

7 Early swimming: Pearson, *Surfing Subcultures*, p. 35; Wells, *Sunny Memories*, p. 77; Cooper, *St Kilda*, vol. II, p. 188.

8 Problems with regulations: Wells, *Sunny Memories*, pp. 22, 25–35, 77, 89, 100–1, 140; Maxwell, *Surf*, p. 6; Cooper, *St Kilda*, vol. II, pp. 194–5; Longmire, *St Kilda*, pp. 55, 68.

9 Polynesia: Maxwell, *Surf*, pp. 10, 235.

10 Early lifesaving: Pearson, *Surfing Subcultures*, p. 37; Maxwell, *Surf*, pp. 16, 17, 89, 202–3; Wells, *Sunny Memories*, pp. 170, 171, 177.

11 Quoted in Booth, 'War off water' p. 142.

12 Early club history: Galton, *The Gladiators*, chapter 1; *History of Bondi Surf Bathers' Life Saving Club 1906–1956* (Sydney: the Club, 1956.) Appendix includes list of all Australian clubs at February 1956; Galton, *Gladiators*, p. 14; J. R. Winders, *Surf Life Saving in Queensland* (Brisbane: Surf Life Saving Association of Australia [Qld], 1970).

13 Wells, p. 122; Galton, *Gladiators*, p. 16.

14 Jean Curlewis *Beach Beyond* (Melbourne: Ward Lock, 1923); on sesquicentennial celebrations: Gammage and Spearritt (eds), *Australians 1938*, p. 376.

15 Galton, *Gladiators*, chapter 4.

16 McRobbie, *The Surfers Paradise Story*, pp. 33–57. Note that this has an index, unlike the same author's *The Real Surfers Paradise!* Pan News, 1988.

17 *Blue Coast Caravan*, p. 104.

18 Eve Keane, *Gold Coast* (Sydney: Oswald Ziegler, 1959); McRobbie, pp. 108–9; 116–17, 183–5.

19 *Penrod's Guide to the South Coast*, 1954, pp. 16 and 39; 'It's the gold coast', *Courier Mail Annual*, 1954, pp. 19–22, includes modernist paintings by Elaine Haxton that capture the 'air of slick

sophisticated' Surfers Paradise.

20 *Maroochydore–Mooloolaba on the Sunshine Coast*, Murray Studios, Gympie, 1958, View Folder; Real Estate Institute: *Courier Mail*, 10 March 1960.

21 Advertisement in *Guide to Queensland*, QGTB, *c.* 1959, p. 89.

22 Despite the claims made for Sydney beach imagery, it remains parochial. See J. Kent (ed.), *Bondi* (Sydney: James Fraser, 1984). See also Dutton, *Sun, Sea, Surf and Sand*. Sydney can claim iconographical domination in harbour imagery—in high art courtesy of Lloyd Rees, Brett Whiteley and others, and in popular art via Ken Done. Done's beachside imagery draws as much on North Queensland as it does on NSW.

23 *The Seaside Calls Victoria Australia*, brochure, Victorian Railways, 1940. *Seaside Calling*, brochure, Victorian Railways, 1947.

24 *The Golden Thousand: Victoria's Beaches*, VGTB, *c.* 1961.

25 See Jones, *A Sunny Place for Shady People*, on Gold Coast real estate.

26 See the TV documentary 'The Battle for Byron', 1997, and the articles on the redevelopment of St Kilda and Port Phillip Bay that appeared in the *Age* between 26 and 31 December 1997.

27 Young, *The History of Surfing*, p. 92.

28 Carter, 'The board riding scene', in *Surf Beaches of Australia's East Coast*, pp. 38–59.

29 Young, *The History of Surfing*, p. 93.

30 This account is based on personal experience of beaches in NSW, Queensland and Victoria in the 1960s. See also Neilma Sidney, *Beaches, Life in Australia Series* (Melbourne: OUP, 1964) and Helen Townsend, 'Getting wet', in *Baby Boomers: Growing up in Australia in the 1940s, 50s and 60s* (Brookvale, NSW: Simon & Schuster, 1988).

31 *The Oxford Companion to Australian Sport*, 2nd edn, OUP, 1997, pp. 408–9.

32 See McRobbie, 'The Erosion Battle and Civic War 1967–1973', in *The Surfers Paradise Story*.

33 Script of Albie Thoms, 'From Neck to Knee to Nude: the strange history of the Aussie Cossie', *c.* 1985, documentary made for the Seven network. Australian Nudist Federation, *Australia and New Zealand Nudist Club Guide incorporating free beach guide* (Canberra: the Federation, 1981); interviews with students from North Sydney Boys High School and Stella Maris Convent, Manly, re the period 1970–80.

34 Robert Drewe (ed.), *The Picador Book of the Beach* (Sydney: Pan Macmillan, 1993), pp. 6–7.

35 *Walkabout*, January 1963; Spearritt, 'The Commercialisation of Public Space'.

6 Mobility and Its Consequences

1 Jim Fitzpatrick, *The Bicycle and the Bush*, pp. 33, 128–9, 185–90, 220–1.

2 See *Hostel Travel*, Summer 1992/93, Youth Hostels Association of NSW.

3 Dorney, *The First Motor Honeymoon Around Australia* (Brisbane: Read Press, 1927), part 2, pp. 51, 66–7.

4 *The Herald Road Guide*, (Melbourne: Herald & Weekly Times, 1936). The date of the first edition appears to be 1929.

5 Davison, *Blue Coast Caravan*, pp. 61, 80–1.

6 *Gregory's Guide to NSW*, 1954; Davison, *Blue Coast Caravan*, p. 103; *Herald Road Guide*, 1936, p. 205. See Keith Winser (ed.), *Highways of Australia, Royal Tour Edition* (Melbourne: Motor Manual, 1954) and *Melbourne Brisbane Sydney: Highway Guide* (Melbourne: RACV, *c.* 1960).

7 For Broadbent see *ADB*, vol. 7.

8 Anderson, *Roads for the People*, pp. 230–3. See also R. Hyett, *The Great Ocean Road: a traveller's guide* (Port Campbell: Great Ocean Publications, 1995); for Gregory, see *ADB*, vol. 14.

9 *Redex Reliability Trial Annual*, 1954, pp. 1–2 and *passim*.

[10] This account is based on Keith Winser's *Highways of Australia*; D. H. Day, *The Herald Road Guide*, 26th edn, 1956; Carroll, *The Hume*, 1983, and the BP *Explore Australia* guides of the 1990s.

[11] Quoted in Broomham, *On the Road*, p. 108.

[12] See for instance Peter and Kim Wherrett's *Explore Australia by Four-Wheel Drive* (Ringwood: Penguin, 1993), a 600-page hardcover book that weighs well over 1 kilogram.

[13] *Radiator*, December 1936, p. 9.

[14] Dale Collins, *Victoria's My Home Ground* (Melbourne: Cheshire, 1951), p. 200.

[15] *Caravanning at Victoria's Peninsula Paradise*, brochure, *c.* 1959.

[16] See *Penrod's Guides* to the North Coast and South Coast (Qld), 1954, and *Penrod's 150 Miles Around Brisbane*, 1956.

[17] *Radiator*, 15 July 1936, p. 10; see also Whiteman, *The History of the Caravan*.

[18] *Caravan-eer and Air Traveller*, 1 Jan 1938, pp. 72–3, iv.

[19] Keith Winser, *On the Trail: Motoring Holidays in Australia* (Melbourne: Motor Manual, 1956). See also Belasco, *Americans on the Road*, 1979.

[20] *Caravan Park and Outdoor World*, March 1992, pp. 28–9.

[21] The 5 June 1950 issue of the *Current Affairs Bulletin* on 'Holidays' advocated Butlin-style holiday camps for Australia, but other than for trade union and religious camps and units, the idea did not take hold. See Belasco, *Americans on the Road*. Figures from October 1960 motel supplement to *RACV Accommodation Guide*, 1960.

[22] *Hotel and Café News*, September 1955, November 1955; McRobbie, *The Surfers Paradise Story*, claims that by 1956 there were three motels in Australia (p. 96), but he does not name the third motel; *Hotel and Café News*, May 1956, June 1956.

[23] *RACV Accommodation Guide*, 1964.

[24] Spearritt, 'What's Wrong with Australia's Motels'.

[25] Listed in *MFA Directory*, September 1961. Description of Black Dolphin motel from *c.* 1965 advertising brochure; see also G. Serle, *Robin Boyd: a life* (Melbourne: MUP, 1995), pp. 193–4.

[26] For travel destinations of international tourists by birthplace, see the *International Visitor Survey*, 1988– . On cars, see Spearritt, 'Cars for the People', pp. 118–29 and *Travel by Australians 1998* (Canberra: Bureau of Tourism Research, 1999).

7 The Rediscovery of the Centre and Aboriginal Tourism

[1] Alice Springs up to WWII: Donovan, *Alice Springs*, pp. 136, 219; Madigan, *Central Australia*, p. 69; *Alice Springs and the Centre*, p. 7; Clune, *The Red Heart*, p. 2; Groom, *I Saw A Strange Land*, p. 5.

[2] 'A Town Like Alice': McKenzie, *No Town Like Alice*, p. 35; Harney, *To Ayer's Rock and Beyond*, p. 18; Pearl Tuit interview, NTRS 226/24/TS 406 and cutting [*c.* 1963] in NTRS 348 114/2/6; Shute, *A Town Like Alice*, pp. 81, 86; Moorehead, *Rum Jungle*, p. 39.

[3] Early tour operators: Kurt Johannsen Life, NTRS 1329 114/3/4; Victor de Fontenoy interview, NTRS 226/35/TS 510; Donovan, *Alice Springs*, p. 230; Pearl Tuit interview, and 1957 cutting from *People* in Len Tuit file, both listed in n. 2.

[4] Tourism in the 1950s: Roy D. Charlton, 'Riding the New Ghan', *Walkabout*, vol. 25, no. 5 (May 1959), p. 26; Donovan, *Alice Springs*, pp. 236, 233, 235; Gorey, *The Alice*, p. 85; cutting re TAA, Len Tuit file; Pearl Tuit interview; Harney, *To Ayer's Rock and Beyond*, p. 22; McKenzie, *No Town Like Alice*, p. 35; Reg Rechner interview, NTRS 226/19/TS 309-1-2.

[5] Growth: *Alice Springs and the Centre*, p. 8; Donovan, *Alice Springs*, pp. 222, 277, 309, 286. In 1996 the town's population was 22 488.

[6] Suburbanism: Dept of NT, Alice Springs, *The Alice*; Alice Springs Tourist Promotion Committee, *Alice Springs*, pp. 7, 12, 15.

[7] Early Ayers Rock: Clune, *The Red Heart*, p. 2; Johannsen, NTRS 1329/TS 114/3/4; Berzins, 'New Territory', p. 79; Groom, *I Saw A Strange Land*, pp. 166–7; Layton, *Uluru*, pp. 78, 75; Donovan, *Alice Springs*, pp. 231, 232, 234, 288; Len Tuit, NTRS 348/TS 114/2/6; Peter Severin, NTRS 226/TS 528; Harney, *To Ayer's Rock and Beyond*, pp. 52, 62, 58.

[8] Harney and Aboriginal presence: H. C. Giese, in Harney, *Significance of Ayers Rock*, p. 3; Harney, *To Ayer's Rock and Beyond*, pp. 10, 96, 124, 114, 62, and 'The Dome of Uluru', *Walkabout*, vol. 23, no. 10 (Oct 1957), p. 34; for a telling critique of Harney's views, see Barry Hill, *The Rock*, pp. 108–12; Joyce Batty, 'The Allure of Ayers Rock', *Walkabout*, vol. 26, no. 3 (Mar 1960), p. 20; Groom, *I Saw A Strange Land*, p. 4; Donovan, *Alice Springs*, pp. 231, 351; Layton, *Uluru*, p. 53; Mountford, *Ayers Rock: Its People, Their Beliefs and Their Art*, pp. 179, xiv.

[9] Impact of tourism: Groom, *I Saw A Strange Land*, pp. 167–8; Ovington et al., *A Study of the Impact of Tourism at Ayers Rock-Mt Olga National Park*, pp. 15, 106, 41–67, 129, 105, 16, 125, 20, 128, 135; climb figures, Hill, *The Rock*, p. 94; Kinnaird Hill, de Rohan & Young, *Ayers Rock – Mt Olga National Park Economic Evaluation*, pp. 46–8, 1, 44, 17–27, 6–10; Donovan, *Alice Springs*, p. 325.

[10] Yulara: Cox, *Yulara*, pp. 12, 63, 60, 6–7; *Northern Territory News*, 4 Nov 1997.

[11] Aborigines, to Handback: Cox, *Yulara*, pp. 59, 63; Ovington et al., *A Study*, p. 129; Harney, *To Ayer's Rock and Beyond*, pp. 52, 37–8; Tim Rowse, 'The Centre: A Limited Colonisation', pp. 162–5; Layton, *Uluru*, p. 82; Kinnaird Hill et al., *Ayers Rock*, pp. 40, 71; Altman, *Aborigines, Tourism and Development*, pp. 62, 169; ANPWS, *Sharing the Park*, pp. 34, 140.

[12] Uluru since Handback: ANPWS, *Sharing the Park*, pp. 56, 92, 57, 63, 58, 4, 65, 103, 12, 83, 85, 140: ANPWS, *Uluru . . . National Park: Plan of Management* (1991), p. 2; Altman, *Aborigines, Tourism and Development*, pp. 75, 64, 145, 147, 118; Diane James, 'Desert Tracks', in Commonwealth Dept of Tourism, *A Talent for Tourism*, pp. 10–12; international craft sales: Stephen Fox, 16 Feb 1998; Anangu involvement: Brad Nesbitt, interview 10 July 1992; Hill, *The Rock*, p. 280; Sydney, A. A. T. King's, Alice Springs, communication 12 Jan 1998; visitor numbers, NTTC, *Selected Statistics, 1997–8*, p. 23; Burgess, 'Towards an Ecology of Culture', p. 107, and interview, Sep 1991.

[13] Range of Aboriginal tourism: Altman, *Aborigines, Tourism and Development*, pp. 58–9, and Altman, *Indigenous Australians in the National Tourism Strategy*, p. 2; Diane James, interview 7 July 1992; Kennedy, *Northern Territory Tourism*, p. 67; attitudes to tourism, Chris Burchett, interview 22 July 1992.

[14] Scale of Aboriginal tourism: Chris Burchett, interview 22 July 1992; Brokensha and Guldberg, *Cultural Tourism*, p. 202; NTTC, *Tourism Development Masterplan* (1994), p. 53; artefact production: NTTC, *Aboriginal Tourism Discussion Paper* (1994), pp. 13–14; cultural centres: *Aboriginal Tourism Strategy* (1996), p. 23, and NTTC *Masterplan* (1994), p. 57. *Tiwi Islands Region Economic Development Strategy* (Darwin: Tiwi Land Council, 1996), pp. 36–40.

[15] Problems: PATA Task Force report, Central Australia, p. 11; Altman and Finlayson, pp. 5, 9; Tony Press, interview 17 July 1992; Altman, *Aborigines, Tourism and Development*, p. 153; inalienable: Alan Clements and Toly Sawenko, interview at Central Land Council, Alice Springs, 6 July 1992; Altman, 'Tourism Dilemmas', pp. 471–2.

[16] Training: Crough, Howitt and Pritchard, *Aboriginal Economic Development*, p. 49; NTTC Annual Report 1996–97, p. 52; *Review of Aboriginal Tourism Training*, 1996, p. 3; NTTC, *Masterplan* (1994), p. 58; 1999: *Tourism & Hospitality Industry Training Plan*, pp. 15, 25–6, App. I.

[17] Cultural tourism and its limitations: Altman, 'Tourism Dilemmas', p. 472; Brokensha and Guldberg, p. 111; Altman and Finlayson, *Aborigines, Tourism and Sustainable Development*, p. 18; Altman, *Indigenous Australians*, p. 6; Diane James, 'Desert Tracks', p. 12.

[18] Mounting pressures: 'non-presence', PATA Task Force Report, *Central Australia*, p. 30, also Kennedy, p. 41; Brokensha and Guldberg, p. 113; international visitors: figures supplied by NTTC, 12 Mar 1998; case-size: Altman and Finlayson, p. 14; Greg Crough, interview 13 July

1992; Mereenie: CLC 1998 *Mereenie Tour Pass*; Graeme Lightbody, interview 8 July 1992; Watarrka: NTTC, *Selected Statistics, 1997–8*, p. 23; Uluru and Ayers Rock: McKercher and du Cros, 'I Climbed', pp. 377, 380; internationals: Table 5.1, NT Parks, *Master Plan* (1993), p. 6, cf. Altman, *Indigenous Australians*, p. 6. Indifference in 1991–92 was even higher, with 86 per cent of Territorians expressing no interest in Aboriginal culture, together with 54 per cent of interstate visitors.

8 National Parks, Zoos and the Green Revolution

[1] Health: Bonwick, *Climate and Health in Australasia*, Vic section, p. 62; Bruck, *Guide to the Health Resorts*, pp. 22, 65, 57, 56.

[2] Hydrotherapy: Wishart, *The Spa Country*, p. 10; Groutier, *Taking the Waters*, pp. 109, 111, 123, 148.

[3] Clifton Springs: Wynd, *Balla-wein*, pp. 111–13; Huddart Parker, *Guide to Geelong and District*, p. 32; *Tourists' Guide to Geelong & Southern Watering Places*, pp. 57–8; Wishart, *The Spa Country*, p. 179; Brownhill, *History of Geelong*, pp. 577–8.

[4] Daylesford-Hepburn: *Illustrated Handbook & Guide to Daylesford*, 1885, p. 20; Brady, *The Mineral Springs of Daylesford and Hepburn*, pp. 3, 4, 23, 29–30, 50–2, 68, 100.

[5] Moree: NSWGTB, *Moree Bore Hot Water Baths* [1906]; *Moree Artesian Bore Baths: Nature's Gift to Suffering Humanity* [c. 1925].

[6] Medlow Bath: Low, *Pictorial Memories: Blue Mountains*, pp. 40–1; Shaw, 'The Hydro Majestic', pp. 156–9.

[7] Perceptions of landscape: George Seddon, 'The Evolution of Perceptual Attitudes', in Seddon and Davis, *Man and Landscape in Australia*, pp. 10–11; Sutherland, 'A Camp in the Mountains', p. 41; Ritchie, *Seeing the Rainforests in Nineteenth Century Australia*, pp. 78–9.

[8] Ferntree Gully and beyond: *Australasian Sketcher*, vol. IX, no. 122 (23 April 1881), p. 135; *Town and Country Journal*, 16 Oct 1875, p. 621; Bardwell, National Parks in Victoria, p. 391; Pickersgill, *Victorian Railways Tourist's Guide*, p. 225; [N. J. Caire and J. W. Lindt], *Companion Guide to Healesville, Blacks' Spur, Narbethong & Marysville*; Griffiths, *Secrets of the Forest*, pp. 78–9; Jones, *J. W. Lindt*, p. 17.

[9] The 'National Park': Myers, *Coastal Scenery, Harbours, Mountains and Rivers of NSW*, p. 37; [Erwell], *Official Guide to the National Park of NSW* (1894 edition), p. 7; Martin, *Henry Parkes*, pp. 368–9.

[10] The National Park: Turner, National Parks in NSW, 1879–1979, pp. 184, 195, 202, 200; military: *Official Guide*, 1894, p. 21; deer: Mullins and Martin, *Royal National Park*, p. 9; Marcus Clarke, preface to Adam Lindsay Gordon, *Poems*, p. v.

[11] Anti-environmentalism: Black and Breckwoldt, 'Evolution of systems of National Park Policy-making in Australia', p. 192; King's Park: Bolton, *Spoils and Spoilers*, p. 105; Murray River and wildflowers: Hall, *Wasteland to World Heritage*, pp. 93–4, 111.

[12] Park administration: Queensland, Bardwell, National Parks in Victoria, p. 223; Castles, Handcuffed Volunteers: A History of the Scenery Preservation Board in Tasmania; Wingan Inlet in Victoria in the late 1940s had no board of management whatsoever, Bardwell, p. 533; Wilson's Promontory: Bardwell, p. 387, Barrett, *National Parks of Victoria*, p. 2; liaison: Bardwell, p. 500.

[13] Field Naturalists and Barrett: for Barrett, see Roe, *Nine Australian Progressives*, pp. 57–88; degrees: Bardwell, National Parks in Victoria, p. 353; Griffiths, *Hunters and Collectors*, pp. 142, 130.

[14] Wyperfeld: Mattingley, 'National Parks', *Argus*, 31 Aug 1908, and 'The Wyperfield [*sic*] National Park', *Victorian Naturalist*, vol. XLVII (1931), p. 216.

[15] Early walking: off-season, Priestley, *Making Their Mark*, p. 222, and Miles Dunphy ed. Thompson, *Selected Writings*, p. 117; *Tramways Guide Melbourne & Suburbs* (1895); Hamlet: Dunphy, p. 3; Brereton, *Landlopers*, pp. 32, 126; H. J. Tompkins, *With Swag and Billy* (1907, reprinted 1913, 1914).

[16] Mountain Trails Club: Dunphy, *Selected Writings*, pp. 6, 16, 12, 4, 7–8, 25, 12, 11; women in Field Naturalists: Griffiths, *Hunters and Collectors*, p. 141.

[17] Bushwalkers and tourism: Garrawarra, Dunphy, *Selected Writings*, pp. 20, 64–9.

[18] Walkers' gear: rambler, Griffiths, *Secrets of the Forest*, p. 76; nineteenth-century guidebook, Pickersgill, *Victorian Railway Tourist's Guide* (1885), pp. 255–7; Germany: Croll, *I Recall*, p. 82; Dunphy, *SelectedWritings*, pp. 4, 11; Pallin, *Never Truly Lost*, p. 221.

[19] The hiking craze: Croll also published a sequel in 1930, *Along the Track*; Griffiths, *Secrets*, p. 79; *The Hiking Guide* (1932), pp. 22, 38; Harper, 'The Battle for the Bush', esp. pp. 42–6.

[20] Bushwalkers and conservation: Blue Gum campaign advertisement, *The Hiking Guide*, p. 2; dances and socials: Gilbert, 'The State and Nature', p. 21; Melbourne: Bardwell, *National Parks in Victoria*, p. 198; NPPAC influence: Bardwell p. 202; Kosciuszko: Bardwell, pp. 198–201, and Hall, *Wasteland to World Heritage*, pp. 113–16.

[21] *Terra nullius* attitudes: Seddon, *Landprints*, p. 73; 'English' birds, *Guide to Sir Colin MacKenzie Sanctuary* [1962], p. 4; protection: Bolton, *Spoils and Spoilers*, p. 98; Gilbert, 'The State and Nature', p. 14; skins: Ritchie, *Seeing the Rainforests*, p. 139.

[22] Old-style zoos: de Courcy, *The Zoo*, pp. 15, 18–19, 224, 245, 236–7, 208; *Official Illustrated Guide to Taronga Zoological Park*, 1930, p. 21.

[23] New-style zoos and sanctuaries: de Courcy, *The Zoo*, pp. 71–2; Healesville: Symonds, *Healesville: History in the Hills*, pp. 113–24; *Guide to the Sir Colin MacKenzie Sanctuary* [1962], p. 32.

[24] The contemporary zoo: de Courcy, pp. 100, 151, 260.

[25] Early skiing: Hunter, *Australian Ski Year Book*, *1928*, pp. 6, 43, 131, 13, 192.

[26] Mt Buffalo and Victoria: Webb and Adams, *Mount Buffalo Story*, pp. 44, 50, 70, 71, 81, 121, 102, 107; Plociennik, *Australia's Snowfields*, p. 12; *The Mt Buffalo National Park*, booklet, 1927, pp. 19, 34.

[27] Postwar skiing: 'Snow for Sale', *Holiday & Travel* (July 1949), pp. 10, 17; Humphries, 'Snow Complications', in *A Nice Night's Entertainment*, pp. 76, 78–80; McGregor, *Profile of Australia*, p. 142; Plociennik, *Snowfields*, p. 12; *Australian Ski Year Book 1928*, p. 3.

[28] National parks, 1945–56: Bardwell, *National Parks in Victoria*, pp. 492–4, 537, 547, 217, 196, 513–14; Robin, 'The Little Desert Case', p. 28.

[29] National Parks reforms: Bardwell, '100 Years', p. 4; Bardwell, *National Parks*, p. 584; for details of the 1967 NSW Act and its emulation elsewhere, see Hall, *Wasteland to World Heritage*, pp. 124–33; 'compelling grandeur': Heathcote, 'The Visions of Australia', p. 88.

[30] Surge of interest: slogan, Turner, *National Parks in NSW*, p. 63, Kinchega, p. 250; ACF: Robin, 'Nature Conservation as a National Concern', p. 8; NP visitors: Priestley, *Making Their Mark*, p. 332; Wyperfeld: Bardwell, *National Parks*, p. 615.

[31] Scientific interest: Robin, 'Nature Conservation as a National Concern', pp. 1–3, 9, 'The Little Desert Case' and, on 'gap analysis', her thesis, *The rise of ecological consciousness*, pp. 247–8; Bardwell, '100 Years', p. 5; Doug Humann, 'Going, Going, Gone', *Park Watch*, 189 (June 1997), p. 4.

[32] Radicalism: *Report of the Committee of Inquiry into the National Estate*, p. 20, but see Bonyhady, 'The Stuff of Heritage', pp. 144–62; greenies: Robin, 'Of desert and watershed', p. 143; 'ditch', quoted Dunphy, *SelectedWritings*, p. 25; Pallin, *Never Truly Lost*, p. 221.

[33] Kakadu environment: Palm Springs, buffalo leases, Rose and Hare, 'The Reserves of the Northern Territory', p. 40; 1991 wilderness definition: *Kakadu NP Draft Plan of Management 1996*, p. 94; Sen. Gareth Evans quoted in Lloyd, 'The Politics of Kakadu', p. 111.

[34] Kakadu tourists: *Kakadu NP Plan of Management* (1991), pp. 10, 93; *Draft Plan 1996*, p. 88; Northern Territory Tourist Commission, *Selected Statistics 1996/7*, p. 21.

[35] Ecotourism: Durham, 'Some Thoughts on Ecotourism', *Park Watch*, no. 186 (Sep 1996), p. 12; for examples of environmental abuse by ecotourist guides, see letter from Denise Goodfellow, *Age*, 8 Sep 1992; for definitions, see Commonwealth Department of Tourism, *National Ecotourism Strategy* (1994), p. 3; Blamey, *The Nature of Ecotourism*, pp. 1–2, Figgis, 'Eco-tourism', p. 8; Richardson, *Ecotourism & Nature-based Holidays*, p. vi.

[36] International perspective: Dutch comparison, Caswell, 'ACF Towards 2000', p. 6; *National Economic Strategy*, p. 1.

[37] Australian attractions: Ciaot Day, interview with Richard Warren, London, 11 Apr 1991; Figgis, 'Eco-tourism', pp. 8–9.

[38] Statistics: McKercher, *The Business of Nature-based Tourism*, p. 4; Blamey, *The Nature of Ecotourism*, pp. 70, 3.

[39] Domestic ecotourism: Blamey, *The Nature of Ecotourism*, pp. 37, 5, 144.

[40] Ecotourism ventures: Australia, Richardson, *Eco-tourism & Nature-based Holidays*, pp. 32–3; Harris and Leiper (eds), *Sustainable Tourism*, pp. 117, 141, 143–4.

[41] Ecotourism resorts: Harris and Leiper (eds), *Sustainable Tourism*, pp. 109–116; Susan Kurosawa, 'Proudly Eco-centric', Review p. 27, *Weekend Australian*, 8–9 Aug 1998, and 'How green was my chalet', *Australian*, 9 Oct 1998.

[42] Wilderness difficulties: Hall, *Wasteland to World Heritage*, pp. 229–51; one-third: *Guardian Weekly*, 11 Oct 1998, p. 29; policy devolution: Rodney Waterman, 'For Better or Worse?', *Park Watch*, no. 193 (June 1998), p. 5; for the human dimension see Griffiths, *Hunters and Collectors*, pp. 255–77 and his *Secrets From the Forest*, p. 84.

[43] Aboriginal Kakadu: *Kakadu National Park Plan of Management* (1980), p. v; KNP *Draft Plan of Management*, 1996, pp. 4, 1.

[44] Aborigines and the environment: de Lacy and Lawson, 'The Uluru-Kakadu Model', pp. 186–7; Langton, 'Art, wilderness and *terra nullius*', pp. 17, 24; Rowse, *After Mabo*, pp. 113–14, 106, and see also the useful discussion of the very different Aboriginal landscape aesthetic on pp. 125–7.

[45] Adventure tourists: Blamey, *The Nature of Ecotourism*, pp. 39, 10.

[46] Kennett government policies: 'locked up', Doug Humann, 'Parks or Profit?', *Park Watch*, no. 187 (Dec 1996), p. 3; Alpine excision: Jenny Barnett, 'Selling Off our National Parks', *Park Watch*, no. 193 (June 1998), p. 4; Geoff Durham, 'The First 12 Months of Parks Victoria', *Park Watch*, no. 192 (Mar 1998), pp. 21–2; 'Money, Money, Money', *Park Watch*, no. 193 (June 1998), p. 3.

[47] Privatisations versus environmentalists: no spending, Richard Butler, 'Alternative Tourism: the Thin Edge of the Wedge', in Smith and Eadington (eds), *Tourism Alternatives*, p. 42; Ecotourism Association, *Australian Ecotourism Guide*, 1997/8, p. 9; some development (and later quote), Humann, 'Parks or Profit?', p. 3; signage: ACF in Harris and Leiper (eds), *Sustainable Tourism*, p. 55; plans: Debra Farrell, 'Just Another Tourism Asset?', *Park Watch*, no. 192 (March 1998), p. 14.

[48] Humann, 'Parks or Profit?', pp. 3–5, and Humann, 'Parks in crisis and people in action', *Park Watch*, no. 188 (Mar 1997), p. 3; Nobbies: *Age*, 6 Jul 1998.

[49] Conclusion: Port Campbell, *Age*, 1 Oct 1998; internality: Emanuel de Kadt, 'Making the Alternative Sustainable', in Smith and Eadington (eds), *Tourism Alternatives*, p. 62; rangers: Durham, 'The first 12 Months of Parks Victoria', p. 21; Wamsley in Harris and Leiper (eds), *Sustainable Tourism*, p. 8; Blamey, *The Nature of Ecotourism*, p. 121.

9 Packaging Heritage

[1] National Trust foundation dates: NSW 1945; Vic 1956; SA 1955; WA 1959; Tas 1960; Qld 1963.

[2] Robin Boyd 'The Future of Our Past' in *Historic Preservation in Australia* (Canberra: Dept of Adult Education, ANU, 1967), pp. 1–9.

[3] C. H. Bertie, *The Story of Vaucluse House*, 1917 and subsequent editions. *Vaucluse House, Sydney NSW*, brochure published by NSW Department of Tourist Activities & Immigration and the Nielsen-Vaucluse House Park Trust, 1960.

[4] On Sydney: Spearritt, 'Demolishing Sydney: property owners versus public rights', *Heritage Aus-*

tralia, Winter 1985, pp. 2–5; on Grimwade see *ADB*, vol. 9; see also *Cook's Cottage*, National Trust of Australia and the Melbourne City Council, 1957; the provenance of the cottage remains uncertain but by the 1980s the Council acknowledged that it was more accurately described as housing Cook's parents; see also Dunstan, *Victorian Icon*.

5 Charles Barrett, *Heritage of Stone* (Melbourne: 1945), pp. 7–8 and *passim*. See *Australia's National Estate: the role of the Commonwealth*, AGPS, Canberra, 1985.

6 See 'The National Trusts of Australia', *Walkabout*, October 1958. For Tasmania see Sharland, *Stones of a Century*, (Hobart: Oldham, Beddome and Meredith, 1952), *Oddity and Elegance* (Hobart: Fullers Bookshop, 1966), Tasmanian Georgianism is discussed in Davidson, 'Tasmanian Gothic', p. 308. The Architects Institutes in each state made fewer aesthetic and historical judgements in their attempts to analyse buildings than the National Trusts. See *Buildings of Queensland* (Brisbane: Jacaranda, 1959), which documented a motel and a drive-in bank (both 1958) as well as grand Victorian, Edwardian and art deco structures.

7 Griffiths, *Beechworth*, p. 61; Herald Touring Club, Castlemaine Touring Club, *c.* 1955; *Castlemaine and the Market* (National Trust of Victoria, 1974); *Castlemaine and Vaughan Springs* (Victorian Railways, 1939, 1945); *Sightseeing Castlemaine* (Promote Castlemaine Inc., 1966); *The Great Escape: Old Castlemaine Gaol*, 1996.

8 On the fate of the veranda in Australia, and the penchant for replacing verandas even where they didn't exist, see Griffiths, *Hunters and Collectors*, pp. 239–42.

9 See Griffiths, *Hunters and Collectors*, pp. 243–4, and R. Roxburgh, *Berrima Courthouse*, brochure (Berrima Court House Trust, 1981), and S. O. Wrightson, *Notes on Early History of Berrima Village*, booklet (Berrima Village Trust, January 1968). See also Mary Quick, *Stone Walls: Engravings of Old Buildings at Berrima, N.S.W.* (Burradoo: Juniper Press, 1952). For a local history attempt to reclaim a sense of heritage in the face of development pressures see Maurice Ryan, *The Days and Ways of Old Time Nimbin* (Nimbin Chamber of Commerce, 1999).

10 *The Blackall Range: Sunshine Coast Hinterland*, brochure, 1997.

11 *Swan Hill: The Centre of the Murray Valley*, brochure (Swan Hill Development Committee, *c.* 1961); *Riverlander*, December 1963; *Swan Hill*, brochure (Swan Hill Development Committee, *c.* 1964); Aborigines, see *Age*, 16 June 1967.

12 *Sunraysia Daily*, 17 November 1961; *Riverina Herald*, 12 Dec 1960; Colin Simpson, *The New Australia* (Sydney: A&R, 1971), pp. 248–53. See also Portanier, Sequestering the Past . . . The Swan Hill Pioneer Village.

13 *Sun*, Melbourne, 18 June 1975; see also Sinclair, The Murray: A History of a River, its People and Ecology 1945–1999.

14 M. Evans, 'Historical Interpretation at Sovereign Hill', in Rickard and Spearritt (eds), *Packaging the Past*.

15 See Jan Penney, 'Pioneer Settlements', in *Oxford Companion to Australian History* (Melbourne, OUP, 1998). On real and reproduced sites see Jeans and Spearritt, *The Open Air Museum*.

16 *Australian Women's Weekly*, 15 May 1974, pp. 8–9; see also 'Old Sydney Town', *History Teachers Association of NSW Newsletter*, 1976; *Old Sydney Town Heritage Park Somersby*, brochure, *c.* 1977; *SMH*, 23 November 1974, p. 4; *SMH*, 1 December 1976; *Sun Herald*, 4 March 1979; 'Old Sydney Town gets a facelift', *SMH*, 26 Feb 1988.

17 David Hutchison (ed.), *A Town Like no Other: the living tradition of New Norcia* (Fremantle Arts Centre Press, 1995); Spearritt, 'New Norcia for Pilgrims, Travellers and Tourists', pp. 67–75.

18 M. Herman, *The Early Australian Architects and Their Work* (Sydney: A&R, 1954); *The Architecture of Victorian Sydney* (Sydney: A&R, 1956).

19 Rob Hillier, *Let's Buy a Terrace House* (Sydney: Ure Smith, 1968), p. 7; M. & V. Burgmann, *Green Bans: Red Unions. Environmental activism and the NSW Builders Labourers' Federation* (Sydney: UNSWP,

1998), pp. 257–9; 'Old Sydney Lives on at the Rocks', *Walkabout*, August 1970, pp. 2–8.

[20] *Sydney since the Opera House: An Architectural Walking Guide* (Sydney: Institute of Architects, 1990).

[21] Young, *Making Crime Pay*; Davidson, 'Port Arthur'.

[22] Spearritt, 'Money, taste and industrial heritage', in Rickard and Spearritt (eds), *Packaging the Past*.

[23] See 'Museums', in *AE*, 1956, vol. 6; for a discussion of the role of museums see Horne, *The Great Museum*.

[24] Spearritt, 'Celebration of a Nation'.

[25] Quoted in Whitelock, *Festival: the story of the Adelaide Arts Festival*, pp. 30–2.

[26] K. Dunstan, *Moomba*, pp. 3–5, 56.

[27] Lowenthal, *The Heritage Crusade*, p. 101.

[28] For international trends see Urry, *The Tourist Gaze*, pp. 104–5, and *Consuming Places*. For Australia see Davison and McConville (eds), *A Heritage Handbook*. See also *The Heritage of Australia: The Illustrated Register of the National Estate*.

10 Air Travel and the Rise of the Resort

[1] Harris, Kerr, Foster & Co, Stanton Robbins & Co, *Australia's Travel and Tourist Industry*, 1965.

[2] *AE*, 1956, vol. 1.

[3] See Fysh, *Qantas Rising*; John Gunn, *The Defeat of Distance—Qantas 1919–1939* (Brisbane: UQP, 1985).

[4] John Ulm, interview 1997; *Macquarie Book of Events* (Sydney: Macquarie Library, 1997), entries on aviation.

[5] *Things you'll want to know—By Q.A.L.*, brochure, *c.* 1955.

[6] *Penrod's Guide to South Coast Queensland*, Brisbane, 1954, p. 5.

[7] Federal Airports Corporation, Coolangatta Airport: Significant Events (unpublished, 44 pages, 1994).

[8] *The Pocket Queensland* (Brisbane: QGTB, 1912); *Guide to Queensland: the sunshine state of Australia* (Brisbane: QGTB, 1960).

[9] On the NSW system see Belbin and Burke, *Changing Trains*, and Gunn, *Along Parallel Lines*. NSW is the only state to have a thorough rail history to date.

[10] *The Albert Shire: South Coast, Queensland, The Shire with the Greatest Potential for Future Development*, n.d., 28 pages, *c.* 1964.

[11] *SMH* supplement, 1 May 1970, p. 1; John Ulm, interview 1997; see Gall, *From Bullocks to Boeings*.

[12] *SMH* supplement, 1 May 1970.

[13] See Fitzgerald, *The Sydney Airport Fiasco*.

[14] *SMH* supplement, 1 May 1970.

[15] See Hudson and Pettifer, *Diamonds in the Sky*; Fysh, *Qantas Rising*.

[16] Quoted in Barr, *No Swank Here?*, p. 37.

[17] *Tropic Luxury on Hayman Island*, Ansett brochure, *c.* 1951; *South Molle Island, Whitsunday Passage Queensland*, brochure, *c.* 1938.

[18] Barr, pp. 38–43. See also Blackwood, *The Whitsunday Islands: An Historical Dictionary*.

[19] 'TAA's Australia: the holiday story of the sixties' in R. A. Layton (ed.), *Australian Marketing Projects*, Hoover Awards for Marketing, 1969; *Bulletin*, 1 August 1964.

[20] Hugh Curnow, 'Islands in the Sun', *Bulletin*, 1 August 1964, pp. 32–5; Barr, p. 51; Layton, *Australian Marketing Projects*.

[21] Barr, pp. 56–9; Gold Coast property prices often come under press scrutiny. In February 1999 analysis of property prices showed that while local investors paid fair prices for units, southern-

ers and purchasers from rural Queensland often paid inflated prices. *Australian*, property supplements, February 1999.

22 *Australia's Great Barrier Reef Islands*, Australian Airlines brochure, 1991; Qantas press release, 20 May 1996; *Weekend Australian*, 7–8 Dec 1996.

23 *WA Tourist Guide & Accommodation Directory 1929; Northwest Australia Travel Guide*, c. 1966; *West Kimberley Region WA Broome-Derby*, brochure, 1967.

24 *Your Guide to the Amazing North*, 3rd edn, 1985; *Qantas Australian Holidays: Broome*, 1997.

25 See Fitzgerald, *Sydney Airport Fiasco*.

26 *Age*, 11 May 1997.

11 The Tourism Industry

1 Loker, Taking Australia to the World, pp. 1–18.

2 H. G. Clement, *The Future of Tourism in the Pacific and the Far East* (Washington DC: US Department of Commerce, 1961), pp. 191–7 and *passim*.

3 Loker, pp. 19–20; Harris and Leiper (eds), pp. 4–5.

4 Loker, pp. 28, 31–6, 143–5. On Sydney's pre-eminence see Spearritt, *Sydney's Century*, chapter 12.

5 Loker, pp. 89, 94, 119. For an analysis of successive marketing campaigns see Spearritt, 'Holiday continent: symbols of Australia', *Journal of Australian Studies*, vol. 9, Australian Studies Association of Japan, December 1997, pp. 52–7.

6 This account is based on Loker, pp. 52–65, 68–9, 88, 114, 146.

7 'Staid old Hobart is all set to play the casino game', *Age*, 3 February 1973, p. 12.

8 *Age*, 3 Feb 1973; *SMH*, 12 Feb 1973; *Age*, 3 Feb 1973.

9 See M. Walker, *Gambling Government: the economic and social impacts* (Sydney: UNSWP, 1998), and Cathcart and Darian-Smith (eds), *Place Your Bet: Gambling in Victoria*; ABS cat. no. 8683, *Casinos* (Canberra: ABS, 1997–98).

10 See Roche, 'Mega events and micro-modernisation: on the sociology of the new urban tourism', *British Journal of Sociology*, vol. 43, no. 4, 1992, pp. 563–600.

11 See Jane Cadzow's article 'Hotel du flak' in Good Weekend magazine, *SMH*, 29 October 1998, pp. 14–23.

12 J. P. A. Burns and T. J. Mules, 'An economic evaluation of the Adelaide Grand Prix', in G. J. Syme et al. (eds), *The Planning and Evaluation of Hallmark Events* (Aldershot: Avebury, 1969), pp. 172–85.

13 Young, *Making Crime Pay*.

14 See the account by McGeoch with Korporaal, *Bid: How Australia won the 2000 Games;* estimates from *The Olympic Effect*, Tourism Forecasting Council, Canberra, 1998.

15 IBIS report to Tourism Council of Australia, *Domestic Tourism Growth Challenge* 1998–2002, (Melbourne: IBIS Business Information, 1998), p. 31.

16 Stimson et al., *Tourism in Australia*, pp. 53, 49.

17 *Domestic Tourism Monitor*, 1995–96 (Canberra: BTR, 1997), pp. 8–10, 28.

18 For an early assessment see *Tourism Shopping in Australia* (Canberra: AGPS, 1988).

19 Industries Assistance Commission, *Travel and Tourism*, Report no. 423, September 1989, pp. 140–4. See *Tourism Managers of the Future: An employers guide to Australian tourism, hospitality, travel and leisure courses*, Council of Australian Tourism Students, Tourist Council of Australia 1997, for a list of the major courses and specialities. For the school textbook market see Janet Baker, *Travelling to the Future: Tourism and its Effect on Society* (Port Melbourne: Reed, 1996).

20 Federal Capital Development Commission memorandum, 9 Dec 1927 (Australian Archives 1/1:27/6508).

²¹ *Canberra Times*, 30 September 1931. Information on journalists' airfares from AA1/1:31/3680.

²² Auditor General's Report: *Australian International Hotel School*, report no. 8, ACT, 1996.

²³ See Freeland, *Canberra Cosmos*; *This Week in Canberra*, no. 260, 8 January 1970. For a contrary, positive view on Canberra's attractions see M. K. Stell, 'Monuments of a new era', in Davison (ed.), *Journeys into History*, pp. 277–89.

²⁴ Harris et al., pp. 214–15; *Cairns and Hinterland*, brochure, 16 pages, QGTB, 1960; *North Queensland Annual*, no. 4, 1966, no pagination. For a photographic survey of Cairns and its attractions see M. Hamilton-Wilkes, *What to See Around Cairns* (Sydney: A&R, 1969); *Queensland Yearbook*, 1988, p. 119; G. Aplin, 'Cairns' in *AE*, 1996, vol. 2.

²⁵ *Cairns Convention Centre*, publicity booklet, 12 pages, Cairns, 1997.

12 Postscript: Tourism Über Alles

¹ Resorts and cycles of tourism: Melbourne tram, Jan 1991; Baedeker, *Upper Egypt* (Leipzig, 1878), pp. 116–22; Macdonald, quoted in Soley, Tourist Development in Victoria, p. 6.

² W. S. Kent-Hughes, in ANTA large format booklet, *Melbourne Olympic Games* (Melbourne: ANTA, 1956).

³ C. H. Holmes, on Olympic Games, *Walkabout*, September 1955, pp. 37–8.

⁴ Transgressive chic: bounty hunters, *Age*, 4 Feb 1998; Barlow and Chambers, *Herald-Sun*, letter, 15 May 1997, p. 20; Pentridge, *Melbourne/Yarra Leader*, 26 Jan 1998; Alice Springs Show, July 1992.

⁵ Religion and tourism: folder, 1998, Mary McKillop Place, North Sydney; Cowan and Beard, *Sacred Places in Australia*; Tacey, *Edge of the Sacred*, p. 32; Gelder & Jacobs, *Uncanny Australia*, p. 99; Crystal People: Chris Burchett interview, 22 Jul 1992; Christian pilgrimage: Grierson, *Uluru Journey*.

⁶ Tourism and consumption: Florida, Dr David Weston, ABC Radio National, 30 Dec 1997; Urry, *Consuming Places*, p. 148.

⁷ Tourism's centrality: Urry, *Consuming Places*, p. 154; swordsman, *Age*, 8 Sep 1998.

Select Bibliography

Sources for a history of tourism in Australia are to be found at all levels of government and in the records of transport operators, accommodation providers and small businesses—from kiosk proprietors to commercial sanctuaries.

In the nineteenth and early twentieth century promotional material was often designed to attract new settlement and investment, but since the 1930s more and more government instrumentalities have been encouraging tourism as an activity in its own right, with every local council in Australia attempting to promote its shire or municipality. Records of such activities, drawn upon for this study, are commonly found in state government and council archives, and in local history collections. We have drawn heavily on brochures and booklets produced by state government promotional agencies, especially their tourist bureaus and their railways.

Key sources for the study of tourism vary over time, reflecting changes in technology, markets and tourist preferences. Shipping company records provide a large amount of information on Australian destinations up to the 1950s, as do the railways—the major providers of long-distance travel in Australia from the 1860s to the 1950s. Advertising campaigns conducted by airlines, travel agencies, car manufacturers and motoring organisations tell us much about modern tourist aspirations and behaviour. Since the 1980s guidebooks, especially the Lonely Planet series, have re-emerged as major sources of information for intending tourists. In the twenty-first century websites must become the dominant supplier of both travel information and booking facilities.

With the privatisation of airlines, and even some railway systems, more and more of the decision-making about tourism hides behind the rubric, 'commercial in confidence'. Since even the annual reports of some big travel operators—from Qantas to Jetset Travel—are not very informative, we have resorted to commentary on these matters, particularly in the press (as documented in the notes to each chapter).

A handful of major travel companies have excellent archives that are open to the public. Of these, the most useful to our study have been the Thomas Cook archives in London, and the P & O archives now in the National Maritime Museum, Greenwich. Given the paucity of equivalent company archives in Australia, we have relied heavily on the Australiana collections in each state, including the Mitchell Library (Sydney), the La Trobe Library (Melbourne), the Battye Library (Western Australia) and the Allport Collection (Hobart).

The development of tourist routes, sites and accommodation in Australia has been charted by mapping companies (Gregory's, Broadbent's) and by motoring clubs. From the late 1950s the motoring organisations in each state became the main providers of such information. Their periodicals and other publications have been a vital resource for this study.

Statistical information about tourism in Australia can be gleaned from state and federal government publications. State yearbooks, published annually, remain a useful source of state and regional information. The *International Visitor Survey* dates back to 1969; since the 1980s it has been notably augmented by the Bureau of Tourism Research, which published the *Domestic Tourism Monitor* and has now replaced it with the *National Visitor Survey*. The Australian Bureau of Statistics also publishes data on accommodation; natural, cultural and purpose-built attractions; travel agencies; retailing; and the tourism workforce and tourism economy. These series are summarised in the Bureau's *Directory of Tourism Statistics*.

The principal books and articles consulted for this study are listed in the Select Bibliography. We have drawn on a growing international literature about tourism as both an experience and a commodity. Direct quotations and other data or interpretation not widely available are sourced in the notes, which include some ephemeral items not listed here. Among these are postcards, tourist pamphlets, information sheets, timetables and accommodation directories.

The promotion of travel and tourism goes well beyond specific travel magazines such as *Walkabout* (1934–74) to find a place in daily newspapers, weekly periodicals and travel supplements. All have been drawn on here, but an exhaustive bibliography would have run to hundreds of pages.

Newspapers, periodicals and trade magazines

A wide array of newspapers and periodicals were used for this study, including metropolitan newspapers, and particular articles are cited in the notes. The

National Library of Australia, Melbourne University Archives and the Mitchell Library also provided access to a number of short-lived consumer and trade journals. The following serial publications are particularly useful for the study of tourism in Australia.

Argus, 1880–1935 (Monday to Saturday, indexed for most of this period).

Australia Today (Melbourne: United Commercial Travellers' Association of Australasia, 1904–1973, annual).

Cook's Australian Traveller's Gazette and Tourist Advertiser, 1890–1900.

Cook's Excursionist, 1851–1939 (This periodical went through a number of name changes and subsidiary versions for particular countries, including Australia. The best collection of the *Excursionist* and its offshoots is to be found in the Thomas Cook archives in London.)

Courier Mail Annual, 1954–1968.

Melbourne Walker, 1929–1984 (annual).

News Bulletin (Melbourne: ANTA, 1962–1966).

Open Road (NRMA), 1927– (monthly).

Park Watch, 1992– (quarterly).

Royal Auto (RACV), 1927– (monthly).

Sydney Mail, 1901–1938 (weekly).

Transair (TAA), 1947–1986 (monthly).

Traveller, 1890–1892.

Walkabout, 1934–1974 (monthly).

Directories, guidebooks and publicity materials

The following is an indication of the range of material drawn on in the book, including items of use to readers interested in a particular period and/or region.

Alice Springs and the Centre (Blackburn, Vic: Regional Information Series, vol. 3, chapter 3 [1980]).

The Alice . . . Centre of the Outback (Alice Springs: Dept of the Northern Territory [1973]).

Alice Springs: Heart of Australia's Secret Wonderland (Adelaide: Tourist Promotion Committee [1968]).

Australasian Handbook: Shippers, Importers & Professional Directory & Business Guide (London and Melbourne: Gordon & Gotch, 1906).

Ballantyne, James, *Our Colony in 1880* (Melbourne: M. L. Hutchinson).

Blair's Guide to Victoria (title varies; Melbourne: Blair's Guide, 1983–).

Bradshaw's Guide to Victoria, 1856, 1875.

Burton, Edwin, *Visitors' Guide to Sydney . . .* (Sydney: William Maddock, 1874; also, without Burton's name, 1879 and 1889 edns).

[Caire, N. J. and Lindt, J. W.], *Companion Guide to Healesville, Blacks' Spur, Narbethong and Marysville* (Melbourne: Atlas Press, 1904).

Camping and Caravan Directory (Sydney: NRMA, 1935–).

Caravan and Camping Guide (Melbourne: RACV, 1959– : title changes later to *Tourist Park Accommodation Guide*).

Centennial Almanac 1889/Guide to Sorrento (Melbourne: Bay Excursion Co., 1887).

Cobb & Co's Guide, 1883–84, Oct 1887.

Cook's Australasian Sailing List (Mar and Apr 1911).

The Country Hotel and Boarding House Guide and Tourists' Handbook (title varies; Melbourne: Victorian Railways, 1911–12 to 1958–59). The 1958–59 edition is entitled *Where to Go in Victoria: Hotels, Motels and Guest Houses*.

Daily Australian Shipping News, Victoria of To-Day, 1851 to 1901 (Melbourne: DASN, 1902).

DeMarco, C., Riera, B. and Spearritt, P., *Aird's Guide to Sydney* (Melbourne: Aird Books, 1991).

Explore Australia: The Complete Touring Companion, 18th edn (Ringwood: Penguin, 1999).

Explore Australia by Four-wheel Drive (Peter and Kim Wherrett; Ringwood: Penguin, 1993 and subsequent edns).

Fuller's Sydney Handbook . . . (Sydney, 1879).

Guide to the Sir Colin MacKenzie Sanctuary Badger Creek Healesville [1955, 1962].

A Guide to Sorrento (Melbourne: Stillwell & Knight, 1876).

Guide to Sydney comprising Description of the City and its Institutions with which is incorporated The Tourists' Handbook (Sydney: Maddock, 7th edn, *c.* 1889).

The Handbook to Sydney and Suburbs, With a Plan of the City (Sydney: S. T. Leigh [1867]).

The Herald Road Guide [national road guide with Victorian bias] (Melbourne: Herald & Weekly Times, various editions, *c.* 1929–1970).

Huddart, Parker & Co's Guide to Geelong and District (Ballarat, 1890).

Lee, John, *Glenelg Historical Guide & Directory* (1883; reprinted Adelaide: Pioneer Books, 1981).

Maclehose, J., *Picture of Sydney; and Strangers' Guide in New South Wales in 1839* (Sydney: reprinted John Ferguson, 1977).

Moree Artesian Bore Bath: Nature's Gift to Suffering Humanity (Moree: Champion Print, *c.* 1925).

Myers, Francis, *The Coastal Scenery, Harbours, Mountains and Rivers of New South Wales* (Sydney: Government Printer, 1886).

New South Wales Government Tourist Bureau, *Moree Bore. Hot Water Baths. NSW* [1906].

North West Tourist Association, *Tasmania's North-West Coast: The Switzerland of Australia* (Devonport, 1908).

An Official Guide to the National Park of New South Wales (Sydney: Government Printer, 1894, 1902).

Official Illustrated Guide to Taronga Zoological Park Sydney (Sydney: Government Printer, 1930).

Orient Line Post Card Souvenir [bound booklet with text] (London, *c.* 1908).

Pallin, Paddy, *Bushwalking and Camping* (Sydney: Envirobook, 1993).

Peninsular & Oriental Steam Navigation Co., *Regulations, Instructions & Advice for Officers in the Service of . . .* (1952).

Penrod's Guide . . . to South Coast Queensland . . . to North Coast . . . to Brisbane (title varies; Brisbane: Penrod's Guide Book Co., *c.* 1954–1965).

P&O Pocket Book, 1888, 1900, 1908.

Queenscliffe! How to See It (1876–77; republished Queenscliffe Historical Society, 1984).

RACV Accommodation Guide (title varies; Melbourne: RACV, 1959, 1960, 1964, 1965–).

The Railway Guide of New South Wales (For the use of Tourists, Excursionists, & Others) (Sydney: Government Printer, 1879; 2nd edn, 1884).

The Stranger's Guide to Sydney (Sydney: James William Waugh, 1861).

Tasmanian Government Railways, *A Guide to Tasmania, the Premier Health Resort of the Commonwealth* (Hobart: TGR, 1906).

—— *Complete Guide to Tasmania* (Hobart: Government Printer, 1913).

Thomas, H., *Guide to Excursionists Between Australia and Tasmania* (Melbourne: Thomas, 1884).

—— *Guide for Excursionists from Melbourne* (Melbourne: Thomas, 1868).

—— *Guide to Melbourne and Suburbs* (Melbourne: Thomas, 1880).

—— *Handbook of Victoria: Historical, Social and Descriptive; . . . Road Guide* (Melbourne: Thomas [1881]).

Through Tasmania: Howard Haywood's Illustrated Guide for Visitors and Colonists 1885–6 (Launceston: *Examiner*, 1886).

Tompkins, H. J., *With Swag and Billy* (Sydney: Government Tourist Bureau, 1914).

Tourists' Guide to Geelong and Southern Watering Places (Melbourne: M. L. Hutchinson, *c.* 1892).

The Tourists' Paradise: Daylesford-Hepburn and the Mineral Springs (Daylesford: Advocate, *c.* 1910).

Tramway Guide, Melbourne & Suburbs (Melbourne: Tramway & Omnibus Co. Ltd [1895]).

Trickett, O., *Guide to the Jenolan Caves* (Sydney: Government Printer [1905]).

Victorian Government Tourist Bureau: *Trips Round Melbourne: A Guide for the Visitor* [1912].

Victorian Railways, *The Mt Buffalo National Park* (Melbourne: 1927).

—— *Victorian Railways Tourist's Guide*, ed. Jos. Pickersgill (Melbourne: Sands & McDougall, 1885).

The Victorian Tourist's Railway Guide, ed. 'Telemachus' (Melbourne: Ferguson & Mitchell, 1892).

Walch's Tasmanian Guidebook (Hobart, 1871).

'Wanderer, A', *Illustrated Handbook and Guide to Daylesford & Surrounding Districts* (Daylesford: Borough Council, 1885).

Western Australian Tourist Guide and Accommodation Directory (title varies; publisher's name has slight variations; Perth: WAGTB, 1928–29, 1938–39).

Whitfield, John (compiler), *Geelong & District Directory 1906–07* (Geelong: Deller & Whitfield, 1905).

Whitworth, Robert P., *Massina's Popular Guide to the Melbourne International Exhibition of 1880–1* (Melbourne: A. H. Massina).

—— *The Official Handbook & Guide to Melbourne* (Melbourne: Bailliere, 1880).

Wimpole's Visitors Guide to Melbourne, Its Suburbs & Interesting Places of Resort (St Kilda: George Hotel, 1881).

Winser, Keith (ed.), *Highways of Australia Road Atlas: Motor Manual's Tourist Guide to All Towns in All States* (edns 1–9, *c.* 1949–1966, various publishers).

Industry reports, statistics and papers

ACF-ACTU Green Jobs in Industry Project, *Green Jobs in Industry* (Fitzroy: Australian Conservation Foundation, 1994).

Allom, Lovell & Associates, The Hotel Windsor . . . An Assessment of Cultural Significance (Melbourne, 1991).

—— 'Queenscliffe Urban Conservation Study' (Melbourne, 1984).

Altman, J. C., *Indigenous Australians in the National Tourism Strategy: impact, sustainability and policy issues* (Canberra: Centre for Aboriginal Economic Policy Research, ANU, 1993).

Altman, J. C. and Finlayson, J., *Aborigines, Tourism and Sustainable Development* (Canberra: Centre for Aboriginal Policy Research, ANU, 1992).

Australian Outback Tourism Developments Pty Ltd, *A Review of Aboriginal Tourism Training in the Northern Territory* (Darwin: NTTC, 1996).

Australian Tourism Commission, *Annual Report*, 1967/68– .

Blamey, Russell K., *The Nature of Ecotourism* (Canberra: Bureau of Tourism Research, Occasional Paper no. 21, 1995).

Burchett, Chris, A New Direction in Travel. Aboriginal Tourism in Australia's Northern Territory (typescript; Darwin: NTTC, 1992).

Burgess, Gregory and Associates, *Uluru National Park Cultural Centre. Project brief and Concept design* (Hawthorn, 1990).

Clements, H. G., *The Future of Tourism in the Pacific and the Far East* (Washington: US Department of Commerce, 1961).

Crough, Greg, Howitt, Richie and Pritchard, Bill, *Aboriginal Economic Development in Central Australia* (Report for the combined Aboriginal organisations of Alice Springs, 1989).

Cultural Tourism in Australia (Canberra: Bureau of Tourism Research, 1998).

Domestic Tourism Monitor (Title varies; published intermittently since 1985; publisher varies. Final edition 1998 replaced by the *National Visitor Survey*, published by the Bureau of Tourism Research from 2000.)

Harris, Kerr, Foster and Co., Stanton Robbins and Co., *Australia's Travel and Tourist Industry* (Melbourne: Australian National Travel Association, 1965).

International Visitor Survey, published intermittently by the Australian Tourism Commission from 1969, annually from 1981; published by the Bureau of Tourism Research since 1988.

Kakadu National Park. Plan[s] of Managment, 1980, 1991, 1996.

Kennedy, J. J., *Northern Territory Tourism. The Way Ahead (Review of NTTC)* (Darwin: Government Printer [1992]).

Northern Territory Tourist Commission (Darwin), *Aboriginal Tourism in the NT. Discussion Paper* (1994).

—— *Aboriginal Tourism Strategy* (1996).

—— *NT Tourism Development Masterplan: 'A Commitment to Growth'* (1994).

—— *Top End Regional Tourism Development Plan* (1996).

—— *Annual Report, 1996–7*.

—— *Selected Statistics, 1997–8*.

Ovington, J. D., Groves, K. W., Stevens, P. R. and Tanton, M. T., *A Study of the Impact of Tourism at Ayers Rock – Mt Olga National Park* (Canberra: Dept of Forestry, ANU, 1972).

Pacific Asia Travel Association, *Central Australia. Tourism Planning, Development and Marketing* ([Alice Springs] 1991).

Parks and Wildlife Commission of the Northern Territory, *NT Parks Master Plan, 'Towards a Future Secured'. Draft for Discussion* (Darwin: NTPWC, 1996).

Report of the Commission of Inquiry into the National Estate (Canberra: AGPS, 1974).

Stimson, R. J. et al., *Tourism in Australia: An Overview of Trends, Issues and Prospects* (Canberra: Bureau of Tourism Research, 1996).

Tasmanian Tourist Association, *Constitution . . . and Annual Report for 1899; Annual Reports* [exact title varies] for 1908–09, 1910–11, 1912–13.

Tiwi Land Council, *Tiwi Islands Region Economic Development Strategy* (Darwin: NT Government Printing Office, 1996).

Tourism, Australia's Passport to Growth: A National Tourism Strategy (Canberra: Department of Tourism, 1992).

Tourism Shopping in Australia (Canberra: AGPS, 1988).

Tourism Training NT, *1999. Tourism & Hospitality Industry Training Plan* (Darwin, 1998).

Books, articles, and chapters in books

Adelaide, Debra, *Hotel Albatross* (Sydney: Random House, 1995).

Altman, J. C., *Aborigines, Tourism, and Development: the Northern Territory Experience* (Darwin: ANU North Australia Research Unit, 1988).

——— 'Tourism Dilemmas for Aboriginal Australians', *Annals of Tourism Research*, vol. 16 (1989), pp. 456–76.

Amdur, Mark, *It Really is a Big Country* (Sydney: A&R, 1991).

Anderson, Janice & Swinglehurst, Edmund, *The Victorian and Edwardian Seaside* (London: Country Life, 1978).

Anderson, W. K. *Roads for the People: A History of Victoria's Roads* (Melbourne: Hyland House, 1994).

Aslin, H. J., Clay, R. E. and Hingston, R. E. K., *National Parks: Perceptions and Expectations—a South Australian Study* (Adelaide: Centre for Environmental Studies, University of Adelaide, 1988).

Austin, K. A., *A Pictorial History of Cobb & Co: The Coaching Age in Australia, 1854–1924* (Adelaide: Rigby, 1977).

Australian Cultural History, no. 10 (1991): Travellers, Journeys, Tourists.

Australian National Parks and Wildlife Service, *Sharing the Park: Anangu Initiatives in Ayers Rock Tourism* (Alice Springs: Institute for Aboriginal Development, 1991).

——— *Uluru (Ayers Rock-Mt Olga) National Park, Plan of Management* (Canberra, 1991).

Australia's National Estate: the role of the Commonwealth (Canberra: AGPS, 1985).

Bach, John, *A Maritime History of Australia* (Melbourne: Nelson, 1966).

Bagot, Alex, *Coppin the Great* (Melbourne: MUP, 1965).

Bainbridge, Cyril, *Pavilions on the Sea* (London: Robert Hale, 1986).

Bainton-Williams, Ashley, *Town and City Maps of the British Isles 1800–1855* (London: Studio Editions, 1992).

Barr, Todd, *No Swank Here? The development of the Whitsundays as a Tourist Destination till the early 1970s* (Townsville: James Cook University of North Queensland, 1990).

Barrett, Charles, *Around Australia* (Melbourne: Cassell, 1942).

—— *Australian Caves, Cliffs and Waterfalls* (Melbourne: Georgian House, 1944).

Barrett, Sir James, *National Parks of Victoria: Summary of an Address . . .* (Melbourne: privately printed, 1920).

—— *The Twin Ideals: An Educated Commonwealth* (2 vols, London: Lewis & Co., 1918).

Barthes, Roland, *The Eiffel Tower and Other Mythologies* (New York: Hill and Wang, 1979).

—— *Mythologies* (London: Jonathan Cape, 1972).

Bates, Geoff, *Centenary of Carrington Hotel 1880–1980* [Katoomba: Carrington Hotel, 1980].

Baudrillard, Jean, *America* (London: Verso, 1989).

Baume, F. E., *Tragedy Track: The Story of the Granites* (Sydney: Frank C. Johnson, 1933).

Belasco, W. J., *Americans on the Road: From Autocamp to Motel 1910–1945* (Cambridge, MIT Press, 1979).

Belbin, Phil and Burke, David, *Changing Trains: A Century of Travel on the Sydney–Melbourne Railway* (Sydney: Methuen, 1982).

—— *Full Steam Across the Mountains* (Sydney: Methuen, 1981).

Bernard, Paul B., *Rush to the Alps. The Evolution of Vacationing in Switzerland* (Boulder, USA: East European Quarterly, 1979).

Berzins, Baiba, 'New Territory: Tourism and the Northern Territory from the 1920s', *Oral History Association of Australia Journal*, no. 19, 1997, pp. 78–81.

Black, Alan and Breckwoldt, Roland, 'Evolution of Systems of National Park Policy-making in Australia', in David Mercer (ed.), *Leisure and Recreation in Australia* (Malvern: Sorrett, 1977).

Blackwood, Ray, *The Whitsunday Islands: an historical dictionary* (Rockhampton: Central Queensland University Press, 1997).

Blakeley, Fred, ed. Muriel V. Morley, *Hard Liberty: A Record of Experience* (London: Harrop, 1938).

Bolton, Geoffrey, *Spoils and Spoilers* (North Sydney: Allen & Unwin, 1992).

Bonwick, James, *Climate and Health in Australasia* (London: Street & Co., 1886).

Bonyhady, Tim, *Images in Opposition. Australian Landscape Painting 1801–1890* (Melbourne: OUP, 1985).

—— *Places Worth Keeping: Conservationists, Politics and Law* (Sydney: Allen & Unwin, 1993).

—— 'The Stuff of Heritage', in Tim Bonyhady and Tom Griffiths (eds), *Prehistory to Politics. The Humanities and the Public Intellectual* (Melbourne: MUP, 1996), pp. 144–62.

Boorstin, Daniel J., *The Image, or What Happened to the American Dream* (London: Weidenfeld and Nicolson, 1961).

Booth, D., 'Surfing 60's: A Case Study in the History of Pleasure and Discipline', *Australian Historical Studies*, no. 103 (October 1994), pp. 262–79.

—— 'War off water: the Australian Surf Life Saving Association and the Beach', *Sporting Traditions*, vol. 7, no. 2 (May 1991).

Bosselman, Fred P., *In the Wake of the Tourist: Managing Special Places in Eight Countries* (Washington: Conservation Foundation, 1979).

Braden, D. R. and Endelman, J. E., *Americans on Vacation* (Dearborn, Mich.: Henry Ford Musem, 1990).

Brady, E. J., *The Overlander: The Prince's Highway* (Melbourne: Ramsay, 1926).

Brendon, Piers, *Thomas Cook. 150 Years of Popular Tourism* (London: Secker & Warburg, 1991).

Brereton, J. Le Gay, *Landlopers* (Sydney: William Brooks & Co. [1896]).

Broeze, Frank, *Island Nation: A History of Australians and the Sea* (Sydney: Allen & Unwin, 1998).

Brogden, Stanley, *Australia's Two-Airline Policy* (Melbourne: MUP, 1968).

Brokensha, Peter and Guldberg, Hans, *Cultural Tourism in Australia* (Canberra: AGPS, 1992).

Broomham, Rosemary, *On the Road: the NRMA's first 75 years* (Sydney: Allen & Unwin, 1996).

Brown, Tom, *Glenelg: An Urban Village, 1836–1972* (Adelaide: Strehlow, 1973).

Brownhill, W. R., *The History of Geelong and Corio Bay* (Geelong: Advertiser, 1990).

Bruck, Ludwig, *Guide to the Health Resorts of Australia, Tasmania and New Zealand* (Sydney: Australian Medical Gazette, 1888).

Bryson, John, *Evil Angels* (Ringwood: Penguin, 1985).

Buck-Morss, Susan, *The Dialectics of Seeing: Walter Benjamin and the Arcades Project* (Boston: MIT Press, 1989).

Burgess, Gregory, 'Towards an Ecology of Culture', *Architecture and Urbanism*, no. 320 (May 1997), pp. 102–7.

Butler, R. W., 'The Concept of a Tourist Area Cycle of Evolution: Implications for Management of Resources', *Canadian Geographer*, vol. 14, no. 1 (1980), pp. 5–13.

Butler, Richard and Pearce, Douglas (eds), *Change in Tourism: People, Places, Processes* (London: Routledge, 1995).

Cable, Boyd, *A Hundred Year History of the P & O . . . 1837–1937* (London: Weidenfeld & Nicolson, 1937).

Cady, Bruce, 'Inns, Hotels and Temperance Hotels in the Armidale District', *Armidale and District Historical Journal*, no. 35 (May 1992), pp. 13–28.

Carroll, Brian, *The Hume: Australia's Highway of History* (Kenthurst: Kangaroo Press, 1983).

Carroll, Peter et al. (eds), *Tourism in Australia* (Sydney: Harcourt, Brace, Jovanovich, 1991).

Carter, Jeff, *Surf Beaches of Australia's East Coast* (Sydney: A&R, 1968).

Carter, Paul, 'Invisible Journeys: Exploration and Photography in Australia, 1839–1889', in Paul Foss (ed.), *Island in the Stream: Myths of Place in Australian Culture* (Leichhardt: Pluto Press, 1988).

—— *The Road to Botany Bay* (London: Faber, 1977).

Cater, Erlet and Lowman, Gwen, *Ecotourism: A Sustainable Option?* (Chichester: John Wiley, 1994).

Cathcart, Michael and Darian-Smith, Kate (eds), *Place Your Bet: Gambling in Victoria* (Australian Centre, University of Melbourne, 1996).

Cecil, Keith L., *Lorne—The Founding Years* [to 1888] (Lorne: Historical Society, 1989).

Clayton, Peter and Price, Martin, *The Seven Wonders of the Ancient World* (New York: Dorset Press, 1988).

Clune, Frank, *The Red Heart: Sagas of Centralia* (Melbourne: Hawthorn Press, 1944).

Collins, Jock and Castillo, Antonio, *Cosmopolitan Sydney: explore the world in one city* (Sydney: Pluto Press, 1998).

Commonwealth Department of Tourism, *A Talent for Tourism: Stories About Indigenous People in Tourism* (Canberra: CDT, 1994).

Cook, Samuel, *The Jenolan Caves: An Excursion in Australian Wonderland* (London: Eyre & Spottiswoode, 1889).

Cooper, John, *The History of St Kilda . . . from 1840 to 1930* (Melbourne, Printers Proprietary, 2 vols, 1931).

Correll, Ted, *The History of South Australia's Department of Tourism* (Adelaide: Department of Tourism, 1986).

Courbin, Alain, *The Lure of the Sea* (Harmondsworth: Penguin, 1995).

Coutts, James, *Vacation Tours in New Zealand and Tasmania* (Melbourne: George Robertson, 1880).

Cowan, James and Beard, Colin, *Sacred Places in Australia* (East Roseville: Simon & Schuster, 1991).

Cox, Philip, *Yulara* (McMahons Point: Panda Books, 1986).

Craik, Jennifer, *Resorting to Tourism: Cultural Policies for Tourist Development in Australia* (Sydney: Allen & Unwin, 1991).

Croll, R. H., *Along the Track* (Melbourne: Robertson and Mullens [1930]).

—— *I Recall* (Melbourne: Robertson and Mullens, 1939).

—— *The Open Road in Victoria* (Melbourne: Robertson and Mullens, 1928).

Cronin, Kathryn, *Colonial Casualties: Chinese in Early Victoria* (MUP, 1982).

Cusack, Frank, *The Shamrock Story* (Bendigo: Shamrock Hotel, 1981).

Davidson, Jim, 'Brambuk, Capital of Garriwerd', *Australian Society*, vol. 10, no. 12 (Dec 1991), pp. 32–5.

—— 'Port Arthur: a tourist history', *Australian Historical Studies*, vol. 26, no. 105, pp. 653–65, 1995.

—— 'The Rise and Fall of Proclamation Day', *Meanjin*, vol. 51, no. 4 (Summer 1992), pp. 795–807.

—— 'Tasmanian Gothic', *Meanjin*, vol. 48, no. 2 (Winter 1989), pp. 307–24.

Davison, Frank Dalby, *Blue Coast Caravan* (Sydney: A&R, 1935).

Davison, Graeme, 'Exhibitions', *Australian Cultural History*, no. 2 (1982/83), pp. 5–21.

—— *The Rise and Fall of Marvellous Melbourne* (Melbourne: MUP, 1978).

Davison, Graeme (ed.), *Journeys into History* (Sydney: Weldon Russell, 1990).

Davison, Graeme and Dunstan, David, 'St Kilda', in Graeme Davison (ed.), *Melbourne on Foot* (Adelaide: Rigby, 1980).

Davison, Graeme, McCarty, J. W. and McLeary, Ailsa (eds), *Australians 1888* (Sydney: FSW, 1987).

Davison, Graeme and McConville, Chris (eds), *A Heritage Handbook* (Sydney: Allen & Unwin, 1991).

de Courcy, Catherine, *The Zoo Story* (Ringwood: Penguin, 1995).

De Lacy, Terry and Lawson, Bruce, 'The Uluru-Kakadu Model: Joint Management of Aboriginal-owned National Parks in Australia', in Stan Stevens (ed.), *Conservation Through Cultural Survival. Indigenous Peoples and Protected Areas* (Washington DC: Island Press, 1997), pp. 155–87.

de Mori, Caroline, *'Time, Gentlemen': A History of the Hotel Industry in Western Australia* (Perth: WA Hotels Association [1989]).

Dilke, Charles, *Greater Britain* (London: Macmillan & Co., 1872).

Dod, H. C., 'The Growth of Queenscliff', *Victorian Historical Magazine*, vol. XIII, no. 1 (1928–29), pp. 1–14.

Dodd, Christopher, *Henley Royal Regatta* (London: Stanley Paul, 1989).

Donovan, Peter, *Alice Springs: Its History & the People Who Made It* (Alice Springs: Town Council, 1988).

Dormer, Marion, *The Bushman's Arms: Bush Inns and Hotels of Gilgandra and the Castlereagh* (Gilgandra: Museum and Historical Society, 1983).

Dreyfus, Kay (ed.), *The Farthest North of Humanness: Letters of Percy Grainger 1901–14* (South Melbourne: Macmillan, 1985).

Dunstan, David (ed.), *Victorian Icon: The Royal Exhibition Building Melbourne* (Melbourne: Australian Scholarly Publishing, 1993).

Dunstan, Keith, *Flag, The First Thirty Years: the growth and experiences of the hospitality industry in Australia* (Melbourne: Flag International, 1991).

—— *Moomba: the first 25 years* (Melbourne: Sun News-Pictorial, 1979).

Dutton, G., *Sun, Sea, Surf and Sand: the myth of the beach* (Melbourne: OUP, 1985).

Eco, Umberto, *Travels in Hyperreality* (San Diego: Harcourt, Brace, Jovanovich, 1986).

Emmett, E. T., *Tasmania by Road and Track* (Melbourne: MUP, 1952).

Farwell, George, *The Outside Track* (Melbourne: MUP, 1951).

Ferguson, R. J., *Rottnest Island: history and architecture* (Perth: UWAP, 1968).

Fitchett, K., *Down the Bay: The Story of the Excursion Boats of Port Phillip* (Adelaide: Rigby, 1973).

Fitzgerald, P., *The Sydney Airport Fiasco* (Sydney: Hale & Iremonger, 1998).

Fitzpatrick, Jim, *The Bicycle and the Bush: man and machine in rural Australia* (Melbourne: OUP, 1980).

Foster, J. J., *The Jenolan Caves* (Sydney: Government Printer, 1890).

Freeland, Guy, *Canberra Cosmos: the pilgrim's guidebook to sacred sites and symbols of Australia's capital* (Canberra: Primavera, 1995).

Freeland, J. M., *The Australian Pub* (Melbourne: MUP, 1966).

Fussell, Paul, *Abroad: British Literary Travelling Between the Wars* (New York: OUP, 1980).

Fysh, Hudson, *Qantas Rising* (Sydney: A&R, 1965).

Gall, J., *From Bullocks to Boeings: an illustrated history of Sydney Airport* (Canberra: AGPS, 1986).

Galton, Barry, *The Gladiators: The Australian surf life saving championships—a history* (Frenchs Forest: Reed, 1984).

Gammage, B. and Spearritt, P. (eds), *Australians 1938* (Sydney: FSW, 1987).

Garran, Andrew (ed.), *Australia: The First Hundred Years* [facsimile of *Picturesque Atlas of Australasia*, 1888] (Sydney: Ure Smith, 1974).

Gelder, Ken and Jacobs, Jane M., *Uncanny Australia. Sacredness and Identity in a Postcolonial Nation* (Melbourne: MUP, 1998).

Gibson-Wilde, Dorothy and Bruce, *A Pattern of Pubs: Hotels of Townsville 1864–1914* (Townsville: James Cook University, 1988).

Gilbert, Alan, 'The State and Nature', *Australian Cultural History*, vol. 1 (1982), pp. 9–28.

Goding, Alison, *This Bold Venture: Lake Tyers House, Place and People* (Kew, Victoria: A. Goding, 1990).

Gordon, Adam Lindsay, *Poems* (preface by Marcus Clarke; Melbourne: Massina [1882]).

Gordon, Malcolm R., *From Chusan to Sea Princess: The Australian Services of the P & O and Orient Lines* (Sydney: Allen & Unwin, 1985).

Gorey, Nathalie (compiler), *'The Alice'* (Alice Springs: CWA, 1960).

Grierson, Denham, *Uluru Journey: An exploration into narrative theology* (Melbourne: Joint Board of Christian Education, 1976).

Griffiths, Tom, *Beechworth: An Australian Country Town and its Past* (Richmond, Vic: Greenhouse, 1987).

—— *Hunters and Collectors. The Antiquarian Imagination in Australia* (Melbourne: Cambridge University Press, 1996).

Griffiths, Tom (ed.), *Secrets of the Forest. Discovering history in Melbourne's Ash Range* (North Sydney: Allen & Unwin, 1992).

Groom, Arthur, *I Saw A Strange Land* (Sydney: A&R, 1950).

Grosvenor, G. Arch, *Red Mud to Green Oasis* (Renmark: Town Corporation, 1979).

Groutier, Alev Lytle, *Taking the Waters* (New York: Abbeville Press, 1992).

Gunn, John, *Along Parallel Lines: A History of the Railways of NSW* (Melbourne: MUP, 1989).

Hall, Colin Michael, *Tourism in the Pacific Rim* (Melbourne: Longman, 2nd edn, 1997).

—— *Wasteland to World Heritage: Preserving Australia's Wilderness* (Melbourne: MUP, 1992).

Hall, Colin Michael and McArthur, Simon (eds), *Heritage Management in New Zealand and Australia* (Melbourne: OUP, 1993).

Hall, C. Michael and Shultis, John, 'Railways, Tourism and Worthless Lands: The Establishment of National Parks in Australia, Canada, New Zealand and the United States', *Australian Canadian Studies*, vol. 8, no. 2 (1991), pp. 57–74.

Harney, Bill, *To Ayer's Rock and Beyond* (London: Robert Hale, 1963).

Harney, W. E. [Bill], *The Significance of Ayers Rock for Aborigines* [Darwin: NT Reserves Board, 1968].

Harper, Melissa, 'The Battle for the Bush: Bushwalking vs Hiking Between the Wars', *Journal of Australian Studies*, no. 45 (June 1995), pp. 41–52.

Harris, Rob and Leiper, Neil (eds), *Sustainable Tourism: An Australian Perspective* (Chatswood: Butterworth-Heinemann, 1995).

Heathcote, R. L., 'The Visions of Australia', in Amos Rapoport (ed.), *Australia as Human Setting* (Sydney: A&R, 1972), pp. 77–96.

Henderson, John, *Excursions and Adventures in New South Wales* (London, W. Shoberl, 2 vols, 1851).

The Heritage of Australia: The Illustrated Register of the National Estate (Melbourne: Macmillan, 1981).

Hern, Anthony, *The Seaside Holiday: The History of the English Seaside Resort* (London: Cresset Press, 1967).

Hewison, Robert, *The Heritage Industry: Britain in a Climate of Decline* (London: Methuen, 1987).

Heywood, B. A., *A Vacation Tour at the Antipodes . . . in 1861–62* (London: Longman, 1863).

Higgs, Bronwyn, ' "But, I Wouldn't Want My Wife To Work There!" A History of Discrimination Against Women in the Hotel Industry', *Australian Feminist Studies*, no. 14 (Summer 1991), pp. 69–81.

Hill, Barry, *The Rock. Travelling to Uluru* (St Leonards: Allen & Unwin, 1994).

Hoad, J. L., *Hotels and Publicans in South Australia* (Adelaide: AHA, SA branch, 1986).

'Holidays', *Current Affairs Bulletin*, vol. 6, no. 6, June 1950 (Sydney: Commonwealth Office of Education).

Horne, Donald, *The Great Museum: the re-presentation of history* (Sydney: Pluto Press, 1984).

—— *The Intelligent Tourist* (Sydney: Margaret Gee, 1992).

Horne, Mary Lou, ' "The Ambassadors of Commerce": Victorian Commercial Travellers in the 1880s', *Australia 1888 Bulletin*, no. 8 (Sep 1981), pp. 40–50.

Howarth, David and Stephen, *The Story of P & O: The Peninsular & Orient Steam Navigation Company* (London: Weidenfeld & Nicolson, 1986).

Howarth, Patrick, *When the Riviera Was Ours* (London: Century, 1988).

Hudson, Kenneth and Pettifer, Julian, *Diamonds in the sky: a social history of air travel* (London: Bodley Head, 1979).

Humphries, Barry, *More Please: An Autobiography* (London: Viking, 1992).

——— *A Nice Night's Entertainment: Sketches and Monologues 1965–1981* (Sydney: Currency, 1981).

Humphries, Barry and Garland, Nicholas, *The Complete Barry McKenzie* (Sydney: Allen & Unwin, 1988).

Humston, Shep, *Welcome to Kuranda: The village in the rainforest, 1888–1988* (Kuranda: S. Humston, 1988).

Hunter, Percy (ed.), *The Australian Ski Yearbook 1928* (Sydney: Kosciusko Alpine Club, Ski Club of Australia & Associated Clubs).

Hurley, Frank, *Australia: a Camera Study* (Sydney: A&R, 1955).

Inglis, Andrea, *Beside the Seaside: Victorian Resorts in the Nineteenth Century* (Melbourne: MUP, 1999).

Jakle, John A., *The Tourist: Travel in Twentieth Century North America* (Lincoln: University of Nebraska Press, 1985).

Jameson, Fredric, 'Postmodernism, or the Cultural Logic of Late Capitalism', *New Left Review*, vol. 146 (July–Aug 1984), pp. 53–93.

Jeanes, W. H. (compiler), *Glenelg: Birthplace of South Australia* (Glenelg: City Council [1955]).

Jeans, Denis and Spearritt, Peter, *The Open Air Museum: The Cultural Landscape of NSW* (Sydney: Allen & Unwin, 1980).

Jenkins, Sascha, 'Sydney Harbour Panorama. The Redefinition of Sydney Harbour as Tourist Landscape', in Lynette French and Chris McConville (eds), *Images of the Urban. Conference Proceedings* (University College of the Sunshine Coast, 1997), pp. 279–87.

Jones, Colin, *Ferries on the Yarra* (Collingwood, Vic.: Greenhouse, 1981).

——— 'Henley on Yarra. The Lost Festival', *This Australia*, vol. 2, no. 4 (Spring 1983), pp. 7–11.

Jones, Michael, *Frankston. Resort to City* (Sydney: Allen & Unwin, 1989).

——— *A Sunny Place for Shady People* (Sydney: Allen & Unwin, 1986).

Jones, Rebecca, 'An Ideal Holiday Experience: Guesthouses of the Gippsland Lakes', *Gippsland Heritage Journal*, no. 17 (Dec 1994), pp. 25–30.

Joyce, R. B. and Edwards, P. D. (eds), *Trollope's Australia* (St Lucia: UQP, 1967).

Kellaway, Carlotta, *'A most complete establishment.' Proudfoot's Boathouse Hopkins River, Warrnambool* (Melbourne: Historic Buildings Council, n.d.).

King, Brian, *Creating Island Resorts* (London: Routledge, 1997).

Kinnaird Hill, de Rohan & Young Pty Ltd, *Ayers Rock – Mt Olga National Park Economic Evaluation* (Canberra: Dept of the Interior, 1972).

Kirkby, Diane, *Barmaids: A History of Women's Work in Pubs* (Melbourne: CUP, 1997).

Lanfant, Marie-Françoise, Allcock, John B. & Brunner, Edward M., *International Tourism: Identity & Change* (London: Sage, 1995).

Lang, John, *The Victorian Oarsman, with a Rowing Register 1857 to 1919* (Melbourne: Massina & Co., 1919).

Langton, Marcia, 'Art, wilderness and *terra nullius*', *Ecopolitics IX: Perspectives on Indigenous Peoples Management of Environmental Resources. Conference papers and resolutions* (Darwin: NLC, 1995), pp. 11–24.

LaPlanche, Shirley, *Stepping Lightly on Australia: A Traveller's Guide to Ecotourism* (Sydney: A&R, 1995).

Lay, M. G., *History of Australian Roads* (Vermont, Vic: Australian Roads Research Board, 1984).

Layton, Robert, *Uluru. An Aboriginal History of Ayers Rock* (Canberra: Aboriginal Studies Press, 1989).

Leed, Eric J., *The Mind of the Traveler from Gilgamesh to Mass Tourism* (New York: Basic Books, 1991).

Lind, Lew, *Sea Jargon* (Kenshurst: Kangaroo Press, 1982).

Lloyd, Clem, 'The Politics of Kakadu', in Peter Hay, Robyn Eckersley and Geoff Holloway (eds), *Environmental Politics in Australia and New Zealand* (Hobart: Centre for Environmental Studies, University of Tasmania, 1989), pp. 103–18.

Lloyd, Janis M., *Skiing into History, 1924–1984* (Ski Club of Victoria, 1986).

Lofgren, Ovar, *On Holiday: a History of Vacationing* (Berkeley: University of California Press, 1999).

Longmire, Anne, *St Kilda: The Show Goes On. The history of St Kilda, vol. 3, 1930–1983* (Hawthorn: Hudson Publishing, 1989).

Low, John, *Pictorial Memories: Blue Mountains* (Crows Nest: Atrand, 1991).

Lowenthal, David, *The Heritage Crusade and the Spoils of History* (Harmondsworth: Viking, 1997, 1988).

Luke, E. T. and Ballard, J. G., *A Southern Breeze: The Record of an Easter Trip* (Ballarat: privately printed, 1897).

Maber, John N., *North Star to Southern Cross* (Preston, Lancs: T. Stephenson & Sons, 1967).

MacCannell, Dean, *The Tourist: a new theory of the leisure class* (New York: Shocken Books, 1976).

McGeoch, R. and Korporaal, G., *Bid: How Australia Won the 2000 Games* (Melbourne: Heinemann, 1994).

McGregor, Craig, *Profile of Australia* (Ringwood: Penguin, 1968).

McGuire, Paul, *Inns of Australia* (Melbourne: Heinemann, 1952).

McInnes, Graham, *The Road to Gundagai* (London: Hamish Hamilton, 1965).

McKenzie, Maisie, *No Town Like Alice* (Adelaide: Rigby, 1977).

McKercher, Bob, *The Business of Nature-based Tourism* (Elsternwick: Hospitality Press, 1998).

McKercher, Bob and du Cros, Hilary, 'I Climbed to the Top of Ayers Rock but Still Couldn't See Uluru': The challenge of reinventing a tourist destination', *Australian Tourism and Hospitality Research Conference [papers]* (Gold Coast: Griffith University, 1998), pp. 376–85.

McRobbie, Alexander, *The Surfers Paradise Story* (Surfers Paradise: Pan News, 1982).

Madigan, C. T., *Central Australia* (Melbourne: OUP, 1944).

Marshall, Sam, *Luna Park: Just for Fun* (Sydney: Luna Park Reserve Trust, 1995).

Martin, Allan, *Henry Parkes* (Melbourne: MUP, 1980).

Mattingley, A. H. E., 'The Wyperfield [*sic*] National Park', *Victorian Naturalist*, vol. XLVII (1931), p. 216.

Maxwell, C. Bede, *Surf: Australians Against the Sea* (Sydney: Halstead Press, 1949).

[Menzies Hotel], *One Hundred Years of Hospitality 1853–1953* (Melbourne: Menzies Hotel, 1953).

Milbourne, Jean, *Mt Macedon: Its History and Its Grandeur* ([Melbourne]: Cambridge Press, 1981).

Moore, Bryce, 'Tourists, Scientists and Wilderness Enthusiasts: early Conservationists of the South-West', in Brian de Garis, *Portraits of the South West* (Nedlands: UWAP, 1993), pp. 110–35.

Moorehead, Alan, *Rum Jungle* (London: Hamish Hamilton, 1953).

Morris, James, *Pax Britannica: The Climax of an Empire* (London: Faber & Faber, 1968).

Mountford, C. P., *Ayers Rock: Its People, Their Beliefs and Their Art* (Sydney: A&R, 1965).

Mullins, Barbara & Martin, Margaret, *Royal National Park* (Sydney: Reed, 1979).

Murphy, P. E., *Tourism: A Community Approach* (New York: Methuen, 1985).

Murphy, P. E. (ed.), *Quality Management in Urban Tourism* (Chichester: Wiley, 1997).

Nepean Historical Society, *The Peninsula Story: Sorrento & Portsea—Yesterday* (Sorrento, 1966).

O'Donnell, Mietta, *Eating and Drinking in Australia* (Melbourne: Bookman, 2000).

Ogilvie, F. W., *The Tourist Movement* (London: King, 1933).

O'Hara, John, *A Mug's Game: A History of Gaming and Betting in Australia* (Sydney: UNSWP, 1988).

Ousby, Ian, *The Englishman's England: Taste, travel and the rise of tourism* (Cambridge: CUP, 1990).

Padfield, Peter, *Beneath the House Flag of P & O* (London: Hutchinson, 1981).

Pallin, Paddy, *Never Truly Lost—The Recollections of Paddy Pallin* (Sydney: UNSWP, 1987).

Parris, John and Shaw, A. G. L., 'The Melbourne International Exhibition 1880–1881', *Victorian Historical Journal*, no. 202, vol. 51, no. 4 (November 1980), pp. 237–54.

Pearce, Douglas, *Tourist Development* (London: Longmans 1981).

Pearce, P. L., *The Social Psychology of Tourist Behaviour* (Oxford: Pergamon, 1982).

Pearson, Kent, *Surfing Subcultures in Australia and New Zealand* (St Lucia: UQP, 1979).

Pemberton, Barry, *Australian Coastal Shipping* (Melbourne: MUP, 1979).

Pemble, John, *The Mediterranean Passion: Victorians and Edwardians in the South* (Oxford: OUP, 1988).

'The Peninsular & Oriental Steamship Company', *Fortune*, vol. XXXIV, no. 3 (Sep 1946), pp. 122, 168–74.

Perry, Dulcie, *The Place of Waters: A Story of Glenelg's First Fifty Years* (Glenelg: City of Glenelg, with National Trust of South Australia, 1985).

Pesman, Ros, Walker, David and White, Richard (eds), *The Oxford Book of Australian Travel Writing* (Melbourne: OUP, 1996).

Pierce, Peter, *The Oxford Literary Guide to Australia* (Melbourne: OUP, 2nd edn, 1993).

Pimlott, J. A. R., *The Englishman's Holiday: A Social History* (London: Faber, 1947).

Plociennik, Henry, *Australia's Snowfields* (Dee Why West: Paul Hamlyn, 1976).

Powell, J. M., *Environmental Management in Australia 1788–1914* (Melbourne: OUP, 1976).

Poynter, J. R., *Doubts and Certainties. A Life of Alexander Leeper* (Melbourne: MUP, 1997).

Priestley, Susan, *The Crown of the Road: The Story of the RACV* (South Melbourne: Macmillan, 1983).

Radson, Stephen & O'Donoghue, Kevin, *P & O: A Fleet History* (Kendal: World Ship Society, 1988).

Read, Peter, *Returning to Nothing: the Meaning of Lost Places* (Melbourne: CUP, 1996).

Richardson, J. I., *A History of Australian Travel and Tourism* (Melbourne: Hospitality Press, 1999).

—— *Marketing Australian Travel and Tourism* (Melbourne: Hospitality Press, 1996).

—— *Travel and Tourism in Australia: The Economic Perspective* (Melbourne: Hospitality Press, 1995).

Rickard, John, *Australia: A Cultural History* (London: Longmans, 2nd edn, 1996).

Rickard, John and Spearritt, Peter (eds), *Packaging the Past: Public Histories* (Melbourne: MUP, 1991).

Rickards, Fred G., *Rowing in Victoria: the First Hundred Years of the Victorian Rowing Association 1876–1976* (Melbourne: VRA, 1976).

Ritchie, Rod, *Seeing the Rainforests in Nineteenth Century Australia* (Sydney: Rainforest Publishing, 1989).

Robertson, E. Graeme, *The Early Buildings of Southern Tasmania* (Melbourne: Georgian House, 2 vols, 1970).

Robin, Libby, *Defending the Little Desert: the Rise of Ecological Consciousness in Australia* (Melbourne: MUP, 1998).

—— 'The Little Desert Case', *Eureka Street*, vol. 8, no. 8 (Oct 1998), pp. 28–31.

—— 'Nature Conservation as a National Concern: The Role of the Australian Academy of Science', *Historical Records of Australian Science*, vol. 10, no. 1 (June 1994), pp. 1–24.

—— 'Of desert and watershed: The rise of ecological consciousness in Victoria, Australia', in Michael Shortland (ed.), *Science and nature: essays in the history of the environmental sciences* (Oxford: British Society for the History of Science, 1993).

Robson, L. L., *A History of Tasmania*, vol. 2 (Melbourne: OUP, 1991).

Roe, Michael, 'Sir James Barrett', in *Nine Australian Progressives: Vitalism in Bourgeois Social Thought 1890–1960* (St Lucia: UQP, 1984), pp. 57–88.

Rolls, Eric (ed.), *An Anthology of Australian Fishing* (Ringwood: McPhee Gribble, 1991).

Rose, A. L. and Hare, W. T., 'The Reserves of the Northern Territory', in D. A. Whitelock and S. Cavenor (eds), *Practical problems of National Parks* (Armidale: University of New England, 1966).

Rowse, Tim, *After Mabo* (Melbourne: MUP, 1993).

—— 'The Centre: A Limited Colonisation', A. Curthoys et al. (eds), *Australians From 1939* (Sydney: FSW, 1987).

—— 'Hosts and Guests at Uluru', *Meanjin*, vol. 51, no. 2 (1992), pp. 247–258.

Russell, J. T., *The First 25 Years: A History of the Australian Federation of Travel Agents Ltd* (Sydney: AFTA, 1982).

Seddon, George and Davis, Mark (eds), *Man and Landscape in Australia: Towards an Ecological Vision* (Canberra: AGPS, 1976).

Sellick, Douglas (compiler), *First Impressions: Albany Travellers' Tales 1791–1901* (Perth: WA Museum, 1997).

Sharpe, Alan, *Pictorial Memories: Manly to Palm Beach* (Crows Nest: Atrand, 1983).

Shaw, M., 'The Hydro Majestic', in Rotary Club of Blackheath, *Historic Blackheath* (Katoomba: J. Bennett & Son [1976]).

Shute, Neville, *A Town Like Alice* (London: Heinemann, 1950).

Sillitoe, A., *Leading the Blind: A Century of Guide Book Travel 1815–1914* (London: Macmillan, 1995).

Smith, Jim, *From Katoomba to Jenolan Caves. The Six Foot Track 1884–1984* (Katoomba: Second Back Row Press, 1984).

Smith, Valene (ed.), *Hosts & Guests: The Anthropology of Tourism* (Philadelphia: University of Pennsylvania Press, 1989).

Smith, Valene L. and Eadington, William R., *Tourism Alternatives: Potentials and Problems in the Development of Tourism* (Philadelphia: University of Pennsylvania Press, 1992).

Sorkin, Michael (ed.), *Variations on a theme park: the new American city and the end of public space* (New York: Noonday Press, 1992).

Souter, Gavin, *Mosman: a history* (Melbourne, MUP, 1994).

Spearritt, Peter, 'Cars for the People', in A. Curthoys et al. (eds), *Australians From 1939* (Sydney: FSW, 1987).

—— 'Celebration of a Nation: The Triumph of Spectacle' in S. Janson and S. Macintyre (eds), *Making the Bicentenary* (Melbourne: Australian Historical Studies, 1988), pp. 3–20.

—— 'The Commercialisation of Public Space', in P. N. Troy (ed.), *Environment, Equity, Efficiency* (Melbourne: MUP, 2000).

—— 'New Norcia for Pilgrims, Travellers and Tourists', *New Norcia Studies*, no. 3 (July 1995), pp. 67–75.

—— 'Sites and sights: Australian Travel Posters 1909–1990', *Trading Places* (Clayton: Monash University Gallery, 1991).

—— *Sydney's Century: a History* (Sydney: UNSW Press, 1999).

—— 'What's Wrong with Australia's Motels', *Australian Society*, no. 10 (1991), pp. 1–2, 56.

Speirs, Hugh, *Landscape Art and the Blue Mountains* (Sydney: Alternative Publishing Co-operative, 1981).

Spicer, Chrystopher J., *Duchess. The Story of the Windsor Hotel* (Main Ridge, Loch Haven, 1993).

Stapleton, Austin, *Ayers Rock, The Olgas and Yulara* (Hawthorndene, SA: Investigator Press, 1991).

Steinke, John, 'The Long-term Decline in the Standard Working Year', *Journal of Industrial Relations*, vol. 25, no. 4 (Dec 1983), pp. 416–30.

Suffolk and Berkshire, Earl of, with Hedley Peek and F. G. Aflalo, *The Encyclopedia of Sport* (London: Lawrence & Bullen, 2 vols, 1897).

Sutherland, Alexander, 'A Camp in the Mountains', *Melbourne Review*, vol. 7, no. 25 (1882), pp. 41–54.

Syme, G. J. et al. (eds), *The Planning and Evolution of Hallmark Events* (Aldershot: Avebury, 1969).

Symonds, Michael, *One Continuous Picnic: A History of Eating in Australia* (Adelaide: Duck Press, 1982).

Symonds, Sally, *Healesville. History in the Hills* (Lilydale: Pioneer Design Studio, 1982).

Tacey, David, *Edge of the Sacred: Transformation in Australia* (Melbourne: HarperCollins, 1995).

'Tempe', *A Summer Holiday in Victoria and New Zealand, or Leaves from a Tourist's Notebook* (Singleton: Argus Printing Works, 1882).

Towner, J., 'Approaches to Tourism History', *Annals of Tourism Research*, vol. 15, 1988, pp. 47–62.

Trollope, Anthony, *Travelling Sketches* (London: Chapman & Hall, 1866).

Tucker, Maya V., 'Centennial Celebrations, 1888', *Australia 1888 Bulletin* no. 7 (Apr 1981).

Turner, Louis and Ash, John, *The Golden Hordes—International Tourism and the Pleasure Periphery* (London: Constable, 1975).

Twain, Mark, *The Innocents Abroad, or, The New Pilgrims' Progress* (New York: Library of America, 1981).

Urry, John, *Consuming Places* (London: Routledge, 1995).

——— *The Tourist Gaze* (London: Sage, 1991).

Van den Abeele, Georges, 'Sightseers: the Tourist as Theorist', *Diacritics* (Winter 1980), vol. 10, no. 4, pp. 3–14.

Waterhouse, Richard, *Private Pleasures, Public Leisure: A History of Australian Popular Culture Since 1788* (Melbourne: Longman, 1995).

Webb, Dan and Adams, Bob, *The Mount Buffalo Story 1898–1998* (Melbourne: MUP, 1998).

Weiler, Betty (ed.), *Ecotourism, incorporating the Global Classroom. 1991 International Conference papers.* (Canberra: Bureau of Tourism Research, 1992).

Welborn, Suzanne, *Swan: the history of a brewery* (Nedlands: UWAP, 1987).

Wells, Lana, *Sunny Memories: Australians at the Seaside* (Richmond, Vic.: Greenhouse, 1982).

Whelan, Tenslie (ed.), *Nature Tourism: Managing for the Environment* (Washington: Island Press, 1991).

White, Richard, 'Bluebells and Fogtown: Australians' First Impressions of England, 1860–1940', *Australian Cultural History*, no. 5 (1986), pp. 44–59.

Whitelock, Derek, *Festival: the story of the Adelaide Arts Festival* (Adelaide: the author, 1980).

Whiteman, W. M., *The History of the Caravan* (London: Blandford, 1973).

Whitham, Charles, *Western Tasmania: a Land of Riches and Beauty* (Queenstown: Mt Lyell Tourist Association, 1924).

Wilde, William H., Hooton, Joy and Andrews, Barry (eds), *The Oxford Companion to Australian Literature* (Melbourne: OUP, 1985).

Winzenried, A. P., *Tram to Sorrento* (Melbourne: APW Publications, 1984).

Wishart, Edward and Moira, *The Spa Country* (Daylesford: Spa Publishing, 1990).

Withey, Lynne, *Grand Tours and Cook's Tours. A History of Leisure Travel 1750 to 1915* (London: Aurum Press, 1997).

Wood, Katie and House, Syd, *The Good Tourist: A Worldwide Guide for the Green Traveller* (London: Mandarin, 1992).

Wynd, Ian, *Balla-wein: A History of the Shire of Bellarine* (Drysdale: Shire of Bellarine, 1988).

Yorke, D. A., J. Margolies and E. Baker, *Hitting the Road: The Art of the American Road Map* (San Franciso: Chronicle Books, 1996).

Young, David, *Making Crime Pay: the evolution of convict tourism in Tasmania* (Hobart: Tasmanian Historical Research Association, 1996).

Young, Nat (with Craig McGregor), *The History of Surfing* (Sydney: Palm Beach Press, 1983).

Theses and typescripts

Bardwell, Sandra, National Parks in Victoria: 1866–1956, PhD, Monash University, 1974.

Brady, Anita, The Mineral Springs of Daylesford and Hepburn: An Introductory History and Guide to Sources, MA, Monash University, 1990.

Burke, Anne, Images of Popular Leisure in the Blue Mountains, BA Hons, University of Sydney, 1981.

Castles, G., Handcuffed Volunteers: A history of the Scenery Preservation Board in Tasmania, 1915–1971, BA Hons, University of Tasmania, 1986.

Emmett, E. T., History of Tasmania's Tourist Bureau, typescript made available by Ed Patterson, Department of Tourism, Sport and Recreation, Hobart.

Harris, Simon, Selling Tasmania: Boosterism and the Creation of the Tourist State 1912–1928, PhD, University of Tasmania, 1993.

Horne, Julia, Favourite resorts: Aspects of Tourist Travel in Nineteenth Century New South Wales, PhD, University of NSW, 1995.

Loker, Laurie, Taking Australia to the World: a history of the Australian Tourist Commission, *c.* 1992, 250-page typescript made available by the author, James Cook University of North Queensland.

Magee, Ros, The Second Empire Influence in Victorian Architecture, Humanities Research Report, School of Architecture, University of Melbourne, 1980.

Morris, C. A., In Pursuit of the Travelling Man: A Study of Tasmanian Tourism to 1905, BA Hons, University of Tasmania, 1974.

Mosley, J. G., Aspects of the Geography of Recreation in Tasmania, PhD, Australian National University, 1963.

Nicholson, Vivienne, As good and as agreeable as could well be desired: Tourism on the Mornington Peninsula, MA, Monash University, 1995.

Portanier, S., Sequestering the Past: the commemoration of pioneering life at Australia's first outdoor museum: Swan Hill Pioneer Settlement 1961–1998, MA, Monash University, 1999.

Robin, Libby, The rise of ecological consciousness in Victoria: the Little Desert dispute, its context and consequences, PhD, Monash University, 1993.

Sinclair, Paul, The Murray: A History of a River, its People and Ecology, PhD, Monash University, 1999.

Soley, Stuart J., Tourist Development in Victoria 1919–1939, BA Hons, Monash University, 1983.

Turner, Andrew, National Parks in NSW, 1879–1979: Participation, Pressure Groups and Policy, PhD, Australian National University, 1979.

Young, F. D., 'Profiting from the Past: The Relationship between History and the Tourist Industry in Tasmania 1856–1972', PhD, University of Tasmania, 1995.

Index

compiled by Alan Walker

Bathurst Island

DARWIN

Kakadu
NP

• Katherine

Wyndham •

+ Palm Springs

NT

Broome •

• Alice Springs
+ Stanley Chasm
+ King's Canyon

+ Uluru

Carnarvon •

WA

SA

• Gwalia

• Kalgoorlie

Port
Augusta •

• New Norcia

Rottnest Island •
PERTH
Fremantle

Great Australian
Bight

Port Lincoln •

Glenelg

Albany •

Mour

0   500 km